Explainable and Responsible Artificial Intelligence in Healthcare

Scrivener Publishing
100 Cummings Center, Suite 541J
Beverly, MA 01915-6106

Publishers at Scrivener
Martin Scrivener (martin@scrivenerpublishing.com)
Phillip Carmical (pcarmical@scrivenerpublishing.com)

Explainable and Responsible Artificial Intelligence in Healthcare

Edited by

Rishabha Malviya

Department of Pharmacy School of Medical and Allied Sciences, Galgotias University

and

Sonali Sundram

Department of Pharmacy School of Medical and Allied Sciences, Galgotias University

Scrivener Publishing

WILEY

This edition first published 2025 by John Wiley & Sons, Inc., 111 River Street, Hoboken, NJ 07030, USA and Scrivener Publishing LLC, 100 Cummings Center, Suite 541J, Beverly, MA 01915, USA

For more information about Scrivener publications please visit www.scrivenerpublishing.com.

Wiley Global Headquarters
111 River Street, Hoboken, NJ 07030, USA

For details of our global editorial offices, customer services, and more information about Wiley products visit us at www.wiley.com.

Library of Congress Cataloging-in-Publication Data

ISBN 978-1-394-30241-3

Cover image: Adobe Firefly
Cover design by Russell Richardson

Set in size of 11pt and Minion Pro by Manila Typesetting Company, Makati, Philippines

Printed in the USA

10 9 8 7 6 5 4 3 2 1

Contents

Foreword

The application of artificial intelligence (AI) in healthcare has enormous potential for shaping patient care, enhancing diagnosis precision, and advancing medical research. However, it remains essential that AI technologies are effective, reliable, transparent, and ethical. This book is a thorough assessment of these critical themes, covering topics such as XAI-based reinforcement learning in smart healthcare systems, diagnostic and surgical applications of explainable AI, biomedical data analysis, and chronic wound classification.

One of the most impressive elements of this book is its unwavering commitment to promoting transparency and accountability in AI-powered healthcare solutions. By suggesting explainable and responsible AI applications, the authors not only increase trust in these technologies but also establish the framework for their ethical and long-term inclusion into clinical practice. To promote applications of AI, I believe this book will be an inspiration that will guide the ethical progress of AI in healthcare.

Dr. Rishabha Malviya meticulously compiled this volume and explored the AI applications in various medical disciplines, providing insightful case studies and scholarly analysis, highlighting the transformative potential of AI while also addressing ethical considerations. Each chapter offers a nuanced exploration of AI applications in various medical disciplines, from neurology to dentistry, and diagnostic imaging to telehealth.

Best wishes and happy reading.

Dr. Dhruv Galgotia
CEO
Galgotias University,
Greater Noida

Preface

The application of artificial intelligence (AI) in healthcare has the potential to transform patient care, diagnosis, and treatment. However, such systems must be efficient, transparent, responsible, and ethically sound. This book is an in-depth study of the relationship between AI approaches and the complicated fields of contemporary healthcare.

The book explores the significance of explainable and responsible AI applications in various medical fields, beginning with an in-depth analysis of XAI-based reinforcement learning and natural language processing in smart healthcare systems. It then proceeds to explore XAI and RAI uses in neuroscience, diagnostic imaging, surgical planning, and other fields. Each chapter provides a distinct viewpoint on how XAI and RAI approaches can help healthcare practitioners increase diagnosis accuracy, optimize treatment plans, and improve patient outcomes. The editors and writers are enthusiastic about AI's potential to drive positive change in healthcare, but they also acknowledge the ethical, legal, and societal ramifications of AI integration. The book builds upon diverse perspectives while also providing readers with the knowledge and skills they need to appropriately navigate the complicated field of healthcare-based AI.

We believe that this book will be a significant resource for healthcare practitioners, scientists, administrators, and every individual interested in using AI to improve human health. We are grateful to the contributors who contributed, as well as the readers who joined us on this journey. Finally, the editors thank Martin Scrivener and Scrivener Publishing for their assistance and publication of this book.

The Editors
December 2024

1

Uncapping Explainable Artificial Intelligence–Centered Reinforcement Learning and Natural Language Processing in Smart Healthcare System

Bhupinder Singh[1]*, Rishabha Malviya[2], Christian Kaunert[3,4] and Sathvik Belagodu Sridhar[5]

[1]*School of Law, Sharda University, Greater Noida, India*
[2]*Department of Pharmacy, School of Medical and Allied Sciences, Galgotias University, Greater Noida, India*
[3]*School of Law and Government, Dublin City University, Dublin, Ireland*
[4]*Director of the International Centre for Policing and Security at the University of South Wales, Cardiff, UK*
[5]*Department of Clinical Pharmacy and Pharmacology, RAK College of Pharmacy, RAK Medical and Health Sciences University, Ras Al Khaimah, United Arab Emirates*

Abstract

Smart healthcare involves utilizing technologies like cloud computing, Internet of Things (IoT), and artificial intelligence (AI) to establish an effective, convenient, and tailored healthcare system. Health data gathered at a user level can be shared with healthcare professionals for further evaluation. AI, combined with this data, aids in health screening, early disease detection, and treatment planning. Explainable AI (XAI) is a key component of the responsible AI approach and is a prerequisite for the responsible application of AI. The goal of XAI's approach is to investigate several approaches in order to provide a variety of strategies that will provide future developers with a range of design options that address the trade-off between explainability and performance. Natural language processing (NLP) techniques are revolutionizing electronic health record (EHR) management within the healthcare sector. Utilizing recurrent neural network models, NLP methods are

**Corresponding author*: bhupindersinghlaw19@gmail.com

Rishabha Malviya and Sonali Sundram (eds.) Explainable and Responsible Artificial Intelligence in Healthcare, (1–26)

employed to analyze unstructured EHR notes, extracting clinical information such as signs and symptoms represented by named entities. This chapter comprehensively explores the diverse arena of XAI-based reinforcement learning in smart healthcare sector with NLP.

***Keywords*:** Explainable artificial intelligence (XAI), healthcare, natural language processing techniques, patient engagement, clinical practices

1.1 Introduction

The term "smart healthcare" refers to a framework for the delivery of healthcare that makes use of cutting-edge technologies such as big data, blockchain, artificial intelligence (AI), cloud/edge computing, and the Internet of Things (IoT) to create a variety of intelligent systems that connect healthcare stakeholders and improve the standard of care [1, 2]. These applications include medical picture analysis, cancer-related sickness analysis, patient health data recording, and relevant economic data [3]. Historically, cloud-based AI learning and data analytics capabilities have been the main focus of smart healthcare systems [4, 5]. However, because raw data transfer results in inefficient communication delay, this centralized strategy is unable to attain significant network scalability [6, 7]. Regulations like the US Health Insurance Portability and Accountability Act apply to personal data in e-healthcare. Also, a dispersed AI system over a broad Internet-of-Medical-Things (IoMT) network may be required if a centralized AI system is not found to be feasible in future healthcare systems [8]. As such, moving to distributed AI techniques at the network edge is essential for intelligent healthcare systems that are both scalable and privacy-preserving [9].

Smart healthcare involves utilizing technologies like cloud computing, IoT, and AI to establish an effective, convenient, and tailored healthcare system [10]. These technologies enable real-time health monitoring through healthcare apps on smartphones or wearables, empowering individuals to manage their well-being [11]. Health data gathered at a user level can be shared with healthcare professionals for further evaluation. AI, combined with this data, aids in health screening, early disease detection, and treatment planning [12]. However, in healthcare, the ethical dilemma of transparency concerning AI and the skepticism surrounding the opaque nature of AI systems necessitates the development of AI models that can be elucidated [13]. These AI methods, geared toward explaining AI models and their predictions, are referred to as explainable AI (XAI) techniques [14].

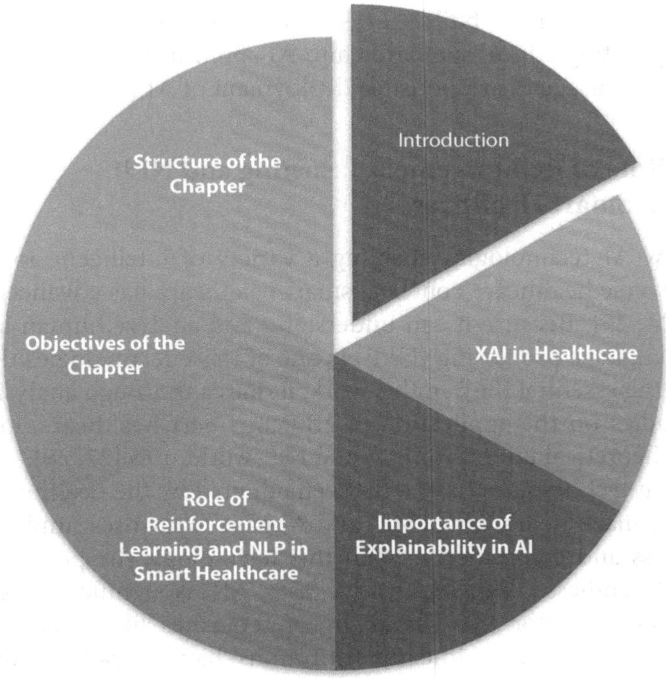

Figure 1.1 Landscapes of introduction split section.

1.1.1 XAI in Healthcare: Relevance and Overview

The emergence of the IoMT has led to notable changes in the way healthcare institutions operate, improving the quality of care that they offer [14, 15]. The IoMT devices are frequently used to gather healthcare data because they are capable of sensing and transmitting updates on an individual's health [15, 16]. Artificial intelligence is then employed to process this data, leading to a variety of healthcare applications, such as illness prognosis and remote patient monitoring [17].

1.1.2 Importance of Explainability in AI

Explainable AI is a key component of the responsible AI approach and is a prerequisite for the responsible application of AI [18, 19]. This method emphasizes justice, model explainability, and accountability while promoting the broad use of AI approaches in actual corporate contexts [20, 21].

The organizations must build AI systems based on trust and transparency by incorporating ethical standards into AI applications and procedures in order to encourage the responsible deployment of AI [22, 23].

1.1.3 Role of Reinforcement Learning and NLP in Smart Healthcare

With new AI technologies enabling a variety of intelligent applications across diverse healthcare contexts, smart healthcare has advanced significantly [24, 25]. Because it can understand and analyze human language, natural language processing (NLP) is one of these technologies that stand out as being essential [26]. In this work, it does a thorough analysis of previous studies on the application of NLP in smart healthcare, looking at both its theoretical underpinnings and real-world uses [27, 28].

Modern technologies have long been adopted by the healthcare industry, where machine learning (ML) and AI have many uses similar to those in business and e-commerce. With this technology, the possibilities are practically endless. With its creative uses, ML is significantly changing the healthcare sector [8]. Driven by prerequisites like electronic medical records (EMR), healthcare institutions have already incorporated next-generation data analytics using big data techniques. With ML technologies, this process may be further improved, leading to higher-quality automation and more intelligent decision-making in public healthcare systems and primary/tertiary patient care [29]. This has the potential to significantly enhance the standard of living for billions of people around the globe. Personalized medicine, treatment planning, scheduling surgeries and appointments, and other complex medical decision-making problems have found a strong advocate in reinforcement learning (RL) [30]. Within the field of NLP, RL has attracted a lot of attention due to its ability to learn the best possible methods for tasks such as question answering, machine translation, and conversation systems [31].

1.1.4 Objectives of the Chapter

This chapter has the following objectives:

- to provide a contemporary overview of federated learning (FL)–based AI in healthcare, starting with fundamental concepts of FL and key AI principles, alongside features of

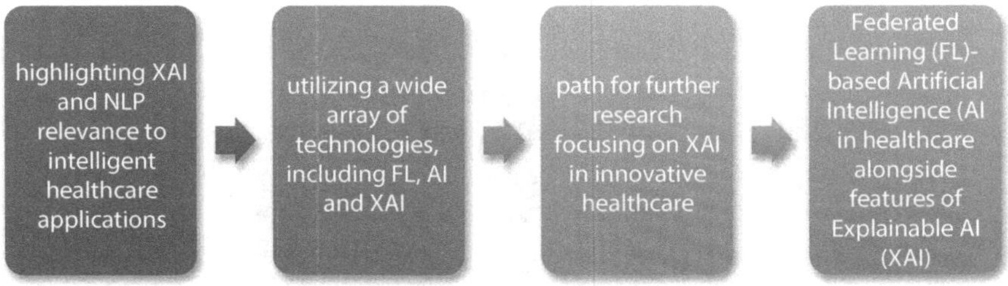

Figure 1.2 The objectives of the chapter.

XAI, followed by an in-depth exploration of the efficiency of smart healthcare;
- to introduce recent advancements in FL-XAI taxonomies and emerging integrations of AI-FL, highlighting their relevance to intelligent healthcare applications;
- to tackle technical challenges existing within current systems and propose solutions utilizing a wide array of technologies, including FL, AI, and XAI, within healthcare applications; and
- to scrutinize the challenges posed by various applications and chart a path for further research focusing on XAI in innovative healthcare domains.

1.1.5 Structure of the Chapter

This chapter comprehensively explores the XAI-based RL and NLP in smart healthcare system. Section 1.2 expresses the XAI-based RL in smart healthcare systems. Section 1.3 discusses the NLP in smart healthcare systems. Section 1.4 specifies the incorporation of XAI-based RL and NLP. Section 1.5 highlights the synergies between XAI, RL, and NLP in healthcare. Section 1.6 elaborates the patient engagement and care management in health sector: XAI and NLP methods. Finally, Section 1.7 concludes the chapter, as well as the future scope and implications for healthcare practice.

1.2 XAI-Based Reinforcement Learning in Smart Healthcare Systems

Reinforcement learning (RL) has become a potent method for addressing intricate medical decision-making challenges, including treatment

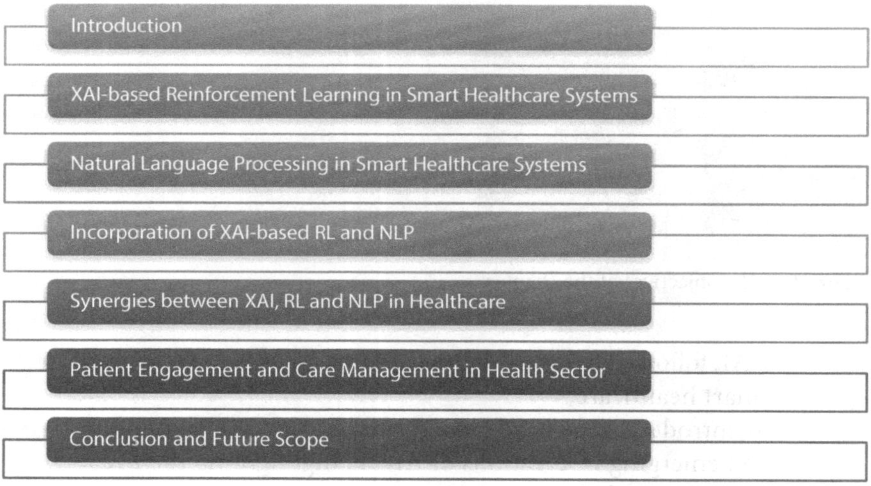

Figure 1.3 The flow of this chapter.

planning, personalized medicine, and optimizing surgery and appointment schedules [32]. However, the opaque nature of AI based on deep learning algorithms makes physicians unsure about the results of their diagnoses [33, 34]. Providing strong proof of these results is difficult because AI models and human understanding differ, a phenomenon known as "black-box" transparency [35, 36]. A lot of research efforts are focused on making AI models more understandable so that physicians may feel more confident about using them. For example, XAI was first proposed by the US Defense Advanced Research Projects Agency in 2015. The utility of XAI in multidisciplinary fields like computer science, statistics, and psychology was subsequently shown by a trust AI project in 2021, indicating that the explanations offered by XAI may improve user trust [37, 38].

Techniques such as XAI can explain their own behavior, pointing out its advantages and disadvantages as well as offering predictions about how it will behave in the future [39, 40]. The goal of XAI's approach is to investigate several approaches in order to provide a variety of strategies that will provide future developers with a range of design options that address the trade-off between explainability and performance [8, 41]. Expert system explanations go beyond summarizing the behaviors of the system to explain the reasons behind them, which requires knowledge of the system's design and building process [42, 43].

The architecture of explainable expert systems (EES) was developed to capture the design components required to produce thorough explanations [44]. EES represents both the underlying ideas that guided the creation of the system and the execution of those concepts with a focus on capturing how a general principle was implemented inside a particular domain or scenario [45]. In order to provide useful explanations, a system has to learn more and provide its explanations in a responsive and adaptable way [46]. It must understand how its justifications were constructed in order to offer further detail or clarity as necessary. Users find it difficult to understand the activities of computer-controlled entities in military simulations due to the growing complexity of AI systems and behavioral models [47]. In order to explain the behavior of simulated entities, a number of research have suggested new modular and domain-independent designs that include elements like the ability to explain the reasoning behind entity behaviors and modularity to make interaction with other components easier [48].

1.3 Natural Language Processing in Smart Healthcare Systems

The goal of the computer science and AI field of NLP is to automatically analyze, represent, and interpret human language [49, 50]. In recent years, NLP has become a vibrant field of study, receiving substantial interest from a range of research communities. Natural language processing (NLP) is essential to smart healthcare because it allows robots to comprehend and communicate with humans through the use of human language, which is the fundamental mode of communication for intelligent systems. Text and speech are the two main ways that human language is expressed. Text records, articles, dialogues, and more may all be examples of this [51].

Since its first development in AI in the 1950s, NLP has been evolving for several decades. Three primary categories may be used to classify approaches to NLP: rule-based, statistical, and deep learning–based techniques [52]. In the early years of NLP, from the 1950s to the 1980s, most research was done using rule-based methods, in which linguists and computer scientists created rules that took into account human language. But even well-crafted rules have coverage gaps because of human language's flexibility and complexity [53]. Statistical NLP systems have been more and more popular since the 1980s. These systems use statistical and ML techniques to extract features from big datasets, or corpora. Their better performance and durability led to their eventual replacement of rule-based NLP systems [54]. Neural NLP has gained prominence from the early days of neural probabilistic language models and the subsequent fast progress in deep learning after 2013. Neural network NLP has become the dominating method in current research, achieving state-of-the-art performance in many NLP tasks by utilizing neural networks and large corpora for automated feature learning [55].

Propelled by growing AI technologies that enable numerous intelligent applications across multiple healthcare contexts, smart healthcare has achieved considerable progress [56, 57]. Because it can understand and analyze human language, NLP is one of these technologies that stand out as being extremely important [60]. This work performs a thorough analysis of previous research on NLP in smart healthcare, looking at both theoretical approaches and real-world implementations [58]. From a technical standpoint, the evaluation mostly focuses on feature extraction and modeling for a variety of NLP tasks found in smart healthcare [59]. The conversation around NLP-based smart healthcare applications mostly focuses on standard cases including clinical practice, hospital administration, individual care, public health campaigns, and medication research [61].

1.3.1 Applications of NLP in Healthcare Industry

1.3.1.1 Deidentification of Clinical Records

Natural language processing (NLP) techniques are revolutionizing electronic health record (EHR) management within the healthcare sector [62]. Utilizing recurrent neural network models, NLP methods are employed to analyze unstructured EHR notes, extracting clinical information such as signs and symptoms represented by named entities [63]. Besides, NLP systems are utilized to extract data from EMRs containing clinical free text, with the objective of integrating top-notch annotators [64]. The rule-based learning is effectively employed for the deidentification of clinical records, representing a typical application in medical informatics. Also, assistive diagnostic systems have been developed, enabling simultaneous disease diagnosis and generation of corresponding syndromes [65].

1.3.1.2 Medical Text Mining

The next important use of NLP in the healthcare industry is health text mining [66]. Notably, models based on deep learning have been created to replicate the distinction of lung cancer syndrome [67, 68]. These models use data gathered from actual treatment cases by lung cancer specialists from unstructured medical records as input [69]. End-to-end models are being developed to improve medical record output and enable lung cancer therapy [70]. Hiring the right target population is crucial for accurately classifying documents that describe clinical trial eligibility requirements [71]. These attempts are being made to develop ensemble learning techniques that combine deep learning models, like BERT, ERNIE, XLNet, and RoBERT using the advantages of several models to provide results that are more accurate and consistent [72].

1.3.1.3 *Extraction of Medical Information*

In biomedical text mining, automated connection extraction between substances and illnesses is essential [73, 74]. Narratives that describe the course of a condition, prescriptions, treatments, surgical operations or discharge summaries frequently contain temporal information [75]. Clinical research and practice may be advanced by the extraction and standardization of temporal expressions, which can greatly improve narrative clinical text analysis and understanding [76]. Also, current research investigates the use of NLP approaches to extract family history information from synthetic clinical narratives [77, 78].

1.3.1.4 *Text Data Management*

Textual data, encompassing diagnosis records, operation records, discharge summaries, eligibility criteria of clinical trials, social media comments, online health discussions, and medical publications, is abundant within the medical domain in an unstructured format [79]. NLP techniques offer valuable assistance in addressing this information overload by aggregating and summarizing patient notes, analyzing treatment data, extracting and retrieving information from extensive discharge summaries, and comprehending the semantic nuances of patient inquiries [80, 81]. NLP can aid in medical decision-making by automatically analyzing patterns within large volumes of textual data, identifying commonalities and differences, and suggesting appropriate actions on behalf of domain experts [82, 83].

1.3.1.5 *Health Information Graph*

Health insurance is another big obstacle in the field of medicine, especially when it comes to making sure that prescription drugs are clinically suitable for the patient's ailment [84]. This is a critical step in the detection of fraud, waste, and abuse [85]. Techniques for deep learning provide an answer to this problem [86, 87]. A multilevel similarity-matching approach has been devised for entity linking, extracting entities and connections from

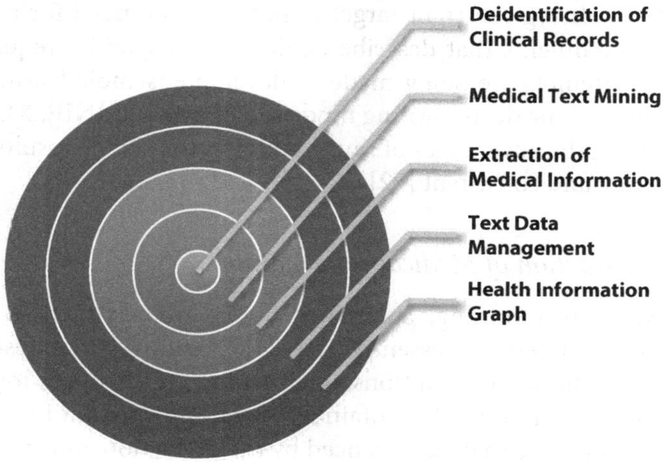

Figure 1.4 The applications of NLP in healthcare industry.

information sources using health knowledge graph [88]. The issues with text representation, extraction speed, and knowledge graph size limitations still exist. It is expected that these issues will be resolved as ML methods advance over time [89].

1.4 Incorporation of XAI-Based RL and NLP

The wide ranges of applications for ML technology are available to improve clinical trial research [90, 91]. Medical practitioners may evaluate a wider range of data and cut down on the expense and duration of examinations by using advanced predictive analytics on clinical trial candidates [92]. Clinical trial efficiency may be further improved by a variety of ML applications [93, 94]. ML can help determine the best sample sizes for increased efficacy and reduce data inaccuracies by utilizing EHRs [95]. This tackles a major issue in the healthcare sector because there are less and fewer highly qualified radiologists in the world [96]. The ability to provide more dynamic and effective tailored medicines by fusing personal health data with predictive analytics is another benefit of ML in the healthcare industry. There is a lot of promise for ML research and clinical trials [97]. Predictive research powered by ML may help identify latent clinical trial volunteers from a variety of data sources, such as past medical visits and social media activity [98]. While ML algorithms can scan electronically recorded medical imaging data and find abnormalities and patterns equivalent to highly competent radiologists, ML technologies may also be used to monitor trial participants in real-time and expedite trial administration operations [99, 100]. As a result, it is expected that the use of these platforms to assist radiologists will increase [101].

Real-time trial participant observation can further enhance trial management, and ML-based predictive analytics can help researchers quickly discover possible clinical trial volunteers from a variety of data sources [102]. In this case, ML can help researchers figure out the best sample size to test and reduce database inaccuracies using electronic records. This paper's main goal is to investigate ML's enormous potential in the medical field [103]. Although ML model developments remain a major driver of NLP's success, the field has great potential for the changing healthcare sector [104]. Data availability is one of the main issues because it might be challenging to get a fair sample of objective health data because of worries about data privacy and preservation. The issue is further compounded by the variability of the few data that is currently accessible [105, 106]. The dialects, linguistic variances, and specialist terminology provide difficulties for NLP algorithms in correctly comprehending the information that is currently accessible. In light of this, it may be said that NLP is still a developing field with a lot of unrealized promise [107].

1.5 Synergies Between XAI, RL, and NLP in Healthcare

Artificial intelligence is revolutionizing the healthcare industry in a number of ways [98]. In order to successfully handle the physical and emotional issues that the population faces, this discipline is subjected to considerable study with the goal of enhancing overall healthcare development [99]. Such method in AI that offers a variety of skills in areas like data management, clinical trials, and well-informed medical decision-making is NLP, a deep learning technology [100]. A multitude of models have been created, exhibiting encouraging results concerning improving data administration and fostering mental and physical health [101].

The term "explainable AI" (XAI) refers to a collection of approaches designed to make AI systems comprehensible and visible and the typical methods include some of the following.

1.5.1 Rule-Based Systems

These systems base their choices on a predetermined set of clear guidelines or rational presumptions. It is not too difficult to grasp how the system makes decisions because the rules are clear and easy to interpret [102].

1.5.2 Bayesian Networks

These systems depict links between several variables by using probabilistic models [103]. They aid in clarifying the reasoning behind certain actions by assessing the likelihood of possible outcomes [104].

1.5.3 Decision Trees

These systems show various decision routes with a structure like a tree. Every node in the tree represents a choice, and the branches stand in for possible results [105]. This hierarchical structure makes the decision-making process easier to understand [106].

1.5.4 Deep Learning Models

Although they are the most complex kind of AI system, methods like layer-wise relevance propagation and attention processes can make deep learning models easier to understand [107, 108].

Depending on the type of AI system and the issue that it aims to solve, a particular XAI strategy may be chosen [109]. The following are several benefits of using XAI in healthcare.

1.5.5 Enhanced Trust

Patients and healthcare practitioners can cultivate a higher level of confidence in AI systems by providing comprehensible and transparent explanations for AI judgments [110].

1.5.6 Improved Understanding

XAI helps medical professionals understand how to use AI to make decisions about patient care, which raises the standard of care as a whole [111].

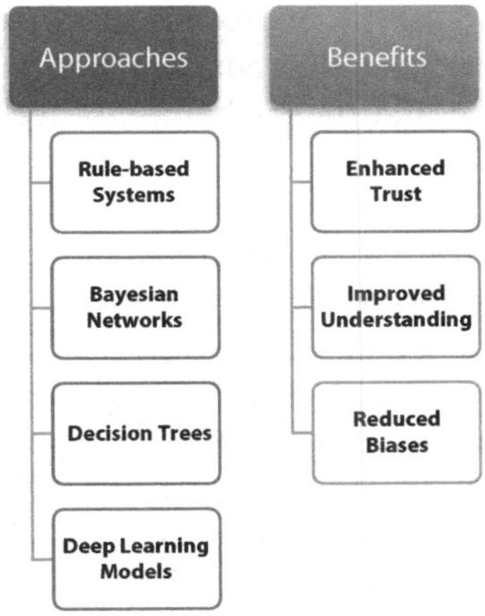

Figure 1.5 A collection of approaches and benefits of XAI in smart healthcare.

1.5.7 Reduced Biases

XAI makes it easier to identify and correct biases in AI systems, guaranteeing that patients receive fair and unbiased treatment [112].

1.5.8 Enhanced Adherence to Regulatory Standards

XAI could be necessary to comply with legal requirements, as those outlined in the General Data Protection Regulation of the European Union [113].

1.6 Patient Engagement and Care Management in Health Sector: XAI and NLP Methods

The patient engagement of XAI has completely changed the healthcare industry [114, 115]. In order to investigate the role of AI in healthcare, this thoroughly reviews the literature, concentrating on a number of important areas, including virtual patient care, medical research and drug discovery, patient engagement and compliance, rehabilitation, and other administrative applications [116]. The effects of AI can be seen in many domains such as the early diagnosis of clinical conditions using medical imaging, the management of EHRs, the discovery of new drugs and vaccines, the identification of medical prescription errors, the provision of virtual patient care using AI-driven tools, the improvement of patient engagement and adherence to treatment plans, the reduction of administrative burden on healthcare professionals, and the facilitation of technology-assisted rehabilitation [117, 118].

While medical coding uses NLP to give appropriate codes to medical procedures and diagnoses, clinical documentation uses NLP to automate the writing of patient information [119]. NLP is used in clinical decision support to evaluate patient data and deliver treatment suggestions to medical professionals; it is also used in patient engagement to enhance patient engagement and communication [120]. The application of NLP in the medical field dates back to the 1970s. At first, NLP was mostly used to automate transcription of medical records. Clinical trials, disease surveillance, and sentiment analysis are examples of NLP's public health applications in healthcare [121, 122]. Sentiment analysis uses NLP to examine social media and other internet sources in order to understand public attitudes and viewpoints on health-related topics. NLP is used in clinical trials to find eligible people and examine trial information [123]. NLP is used in disease surveillance to keep an eye on and track disease trends and outbreaks [124]. But as NLP has developed so too have its usefulness

Figure 1.6 The patient engagement and care management in health sector.

in healthcare, now including a wider range of complex applications [125]. This explores the many uses of NLP in the medical field, dividing them into two primary areas: public health applications and clinical applications [126]. The goal of clinical NLP applications in healthcare is to improve patient care by providing medical professionals with the knowledge and resources that they need to make well-informed decisions about patient treatment [127]. Clinical documentation, medical coding, clinical decision support, and patient engagement are some of these uses [128].

Numerous technological, moral, and social issues arise when AI is integrated into healthcare [129]. These issues include privacy concerns, safety concerns, the freedom to experiment and make decisions, financial implications, information transparency and consent, availability of AI-driven healthcare solutions, and the efficacy of AI interventions [130, 131]. In order to guarantee patient safety, accountability, and confidence among healthcare professionals, effective governance of AI applications is crucial [132]. This will increase adoption and provide notable health effects. Precise governance structures are required to support the adoption and application of AI in healthcare while addressing challenges relating to trust, ethics, and regulations [133]. Following the pandemic, AI has emerged, bringing about a revolutionary change in the healthcare industry and perhaps leading the way in meeting future healthcare demands [134].

1.7 Conclusion and Future Scope—Implications for Healthcare Practice

The term "smart healthcare" refers to a framework for the delivery of healthcare that makes use of cutting-edge technologies such as big data, blockchain, AI, cloud/edge computing, and the IoT to create a variety of intelligent systems that connect healthcare stakeholders and improve the standard of care. The public at large, healthcare service providers, and third-party healthcare companies are the three main groups of stakeholders in smart healthcare. These parties are engaged in a range of smart healthcare scenarios, such as smart hospitals and homes, health management, public health campaigns, advanced life sciences research and development, and rehabilitation therapy, among other things. Within the smart healthcare framework, Figure 1.1 shows the key players, new technology, and illustrative situations. As AI in healthcare continues to progress explainability and openness in AI decision-making become increasingly crucial.

References

1. Sasaki, N., Rosenberg, M., Shin, J.H., Kunisawa, S., Imanaka, Y., Hidden Populations for Healthcare Financial Protection in the Super-Aging Society: Closing the Gap Between Policy and Practice. *Clin. Soc. Work J.*, 1, 1–12, 2024.
2. Singh, B., Kaunert, C., Vig, K., Reinventing Influence of Artificial Intelligence (AI) on Digital Consumer Lensing Transforming Consumer Recommendation Model: Exploring Stimulus Artificial Intelligence on Consumer Shopping Decisions, in: *AI Impacts in Digital Consumer Behavior*, T. Musiolik, R. Rodriguez, H. Kannan (Eds.), pp. 141–169, IGI Global, USA, 2024, https://doi.org/10.4018/979-8-3693-1918-5.ch006.
3. Singh, B., Featuring Consumer Choices of Consumable Products for Health Benefits: Evolving Issues from Tort and Product Liabilities. *J. Law Torts Consum. Prot. Law*, *7*, 1, 15, 2024.
4. Gostin, L.O., A framework convention on global health: health for all, justice for all. *JAMA*, *307*, 19, 2087–2092, 2024.
5. Tulenko, K., Mgedal, S., Afzal, M.M., Frymus, D., Oshin, A., Pate, M., Zodpey, S., Community health workers for universal health-care coverage: from fragmentation to synergy. *Bull. World Health Organ.*, *91*, 847–852, 2023.
6. World Health Organization, *Delivering global health security through sustainable financing: 26-27 July 2017, Seoul, Republic of Korea* (No. WHO/WHE/CPI/2018.38), World Health Organization, 2018.
7. Hill, P.S., Understanding global health governance as a complex adaptive system. *Global Public Health*, *6*, 6, 593–605, 2021.
8. Singh, B., Blockchain Technology in Renovating Healthcare: Legal and Future Perspectives, in: *Revolutionizing Healthcare Through Artificial Intelligence and Internet of Things Applications*, pp. 177–186, IGI Global, USA, 2023.
9. World Health Organization, Everybody's business–strengthening health systems to improve health outcomes: WHO's framework for action, 2007.
10. Singh, B., Unleashing Alternative Dispute Resolution (ADR) in Resolving Complex Legal-Technical Issues Arising in Cyberspace Lensing E-Commerce and Intellectual Property: Proliferation of E-Commerce Digital Economy. *Rev. Bras. Altern. Dispute Resolut.-Braz. J. Altern. Dispute Resolut.-RBADR*, *5*, 10, 81–105, 2023.
11. Singh, B. and Kaunert, C., Integration of Cutting-Edge Technologies such as Internet of Things (IoT) and 5G in Health Monitoring Systems: A Comprehensive Legal Analysis and Futuristic Outcomes. *GLS Law J.*, *6*, 1, 13–20, 2024.
12. Kickbusch, I., Hein, W., Silberschmidt, G., Addressing global health governance challenges through a new mechanism: the proposal for a Committee C of the World Health Assembly. *J. Law Med. Ethics*, *38*, 3, 550–563, 2024.
13. World Health Organization, Decade of healthy ageing: baseline report, WHO, Japan, 2020.

14. Gostin, L.O., Habibi, R., Meier, B.M., Has global health law risen to meet the COVID-19 challenge? Revisiting the International Health Regulations to prepare for future threats. *J. Law Med. Ethics*, *48*, 2, 376–381, 2020.
15. Bodeker, G. and Kronenberg, F., A public health agenda for traditional, complementary, and alternative medicine. *Am. J. Public Health*, *92*, 10, 1582–1591, 2022.
16. Bodeker, G., *WHO global atlas of traditional, complementary, and alternative medicine*, vol. 1, World Health Organization, Japan, 2023.
17. Magnusson, R.S., Rethinking global health challenges: towards a 'global compact' for reducing the burden of chronic disease. *Public Health*, *123*, 3, 265–274, 2019.
18. Singh, B., Green Infrastructure in Real Estate Landscapes: Pillars of Sustainable Development and Vision for Tomorrow. *Natl. J. Real Estate Law*, *7*, 1, 4–8, 2024.
19. Singh, B., Tele-Health Monitoring Lensing Deep Neural Learning Structure: Ambient Patient Wellness via Wearable Devices for Real-Time Alerts and Interventions. *Indian J. Health Med. Law*, *6*, 2, 12–16, 2023.
20. World Health Organization, Global strategy on human resources for health: workforce 2030, 2016.
21. Gostin, L.O., Sridhar, D., Hougendobler, D., The normative authority of the World Health Organization. *Public Health*, *129*, 7, 854–863, 2024.
22. World Health Organization, *Global action plan for the prevention and control of noncommunicable diseases 2013-2020*, World Health Organization, 2013.
23. World Health Organization, *Promoting mental health: Concepts, emerging evidence, practice: Summary report*, World Health Organization, 2004.
24. Singh, B., Cherish Growth, Advancement and Tax Structure: Addressing Social and Economic Prospects. *J. Taxation Regul. Framework*, *7*, 1, 7–10, 2024.
25. Singh, B., Legal Dynamics Lensing Metaverse Crafted for Videogame Industry and E-Sports: Phenomenological Exploration Catalyst Complexity and Future. *J. Intellect. Prop. Rights Law*, *7*, 1, 8–14, 2024.
26. Fortanier, F., Kolk, A., Pinkse, J., Harmonization in CSR reporting: MNEs and global CSR standards. *Manage. Int. Rev.*, *51*, 665–696, 2021.
27. Meier, B.M., Cinà, M.M., Gostin, L.O., Advancing human rights through global health governance, in: *Foundations of global health and human rights*, 2020.
28. Van Lerberghe, W., *The world health report 2008: primary health care: now more than ever*, World Health Organization, Japan, 2018.
29. Singh, B., Federated Learning for Envision Future Trajectory Smart Transport System for Climate Preservation and Smart Green Planet: Insights into Global Governance and SDG-9 (Industry, Innovation and Infrastructure). *Natl. J. Environ. Law*, *6*, 2, 6–17, 2023.
30. Sharma, A. and Singh, B., Measuring Impact of E-commerce on Small Scale Business: A Systematic Review. *J. Corp. Gov. Int. Bus. Law*, *5*, 1, 45, 2022.

31. Lachat, C., Van Camp, J., De Henauw, S., Matthys, C., Larondelle, Y., Remaut–De Winter, A.M., Kolsteren, P., A concise overview of national nutrition action plans in the European Union Member States. *Public Health Nutr.*, *8*, 3, 266–274, 2023.
32. Gostin, L.O. and Sridhar, D., Global health and the law. *N. Engl. J. Med.*, *370*, 18, 1732–1740, 2024.
33. Marcus, M., Yasamy, M.T., van Ommeren, M.V., Chisholm, D., Saxena, S., Depression: A global public health concern, 2012.
34. Al-Shaar, L., Vercammen, K., Lu, C., Richardson, S., Tamez, M., Mattei, J., Health effects and public health concerns of energy drink consumption in the United States: a mini-review. *Front. Public Health*, *5*, 286776, 2017.
35. Gostin, L.O., A framework convention on global health: Health for all, justice for all. *JAMA*, *307*, 19, 2087–2092, 2022.
36. Singh, B., Relevance of Agriculture-Nutrition Linkage for Human Healthcare: A Conceptual Legal Framework of Implication and Pathways. *Justice Law Bull.*, *1*, 1, 44–49, 2022.
37. Singh, B., COVID-19 Pandemic and Public Healthcare: Endless Downward Spiral or Solution via Rapid Legal and Health Services Implementation with Patient Monitoring Program. *Justice Law Bull.*, *1*, 1, 1–7, 2022.
38. Singh, B., Global science and jurisprudential approach concerning healthcare and illness. *Indian J. Health Med. Law*, *3*, 1, 7–13, 2020.
39. Singh, B., Profiling Public Healthcare: A Comparative Analysis Based on the Multidimensional Healthcare Management and Legal Approach. *Indian J. Health Med. Law*, *2*, 2, 1–5, 2019.
40. Kickbusch, I., Brindley, C., World Health Organization, Health in the post-2015 development agenda: an analysis of the UN-led thematic consultations, High-Level Panel report and sustainable development debate in the context of health. World Health Organization, 2023.
41. Jebril, N., World Health Organization declared a pandemic public health menace: a systematic review of the coronavirus disease 2019 "COVID-19". *Int. J. Psychosoc. Rehabil.*, 24, 9, 2020, Available at SSRN 3566298.
42. Singh, B., Blockchain Technology in Renovating Healthcare: Legal and Future Perspectives, in: *Revolutionizing Healthcare Through Artificial Intelligence and Internet of Things Applications*, pp. 177–186, IGI Global, USA, 2023.
43. Callaway, M.V., Connor, S.R., Foley, K.M., World Health Organization public health model: a roadmap for palliative care development. *J. Pain Symptom Manage.*, *55*, 2, S6–S13, 2018.
44. Drager, N. and Sunderland, L., Public health in a globalising world: The perspective from the World Health Organization, in: *Governing Global Health*, pp. 67–78, Routledge, USA, 2024.

45. World Health Organization, *A global brief on hypertension: Silent killer, global public health crisis: World Health Day 2013* (No. WHO/DCO/WHD/2013.2), World Health Organization, 2013.
46. Cueto, M., Brown, T.M., Fee, E., *The world health organization: A history*, Cambridge University Press, USA, 2019.
47. World Health Organization, Essential public health functions, health systems and health security: developing conceptual clarity and a WHO roadmap for action, 2018.
48. Buliva, E., Elhakim, M., Tran Minh, N.N., Elkholy, A., Mala, P., Abubakar, A., Malik, S.M.M.R., Emerging and reemerging diseases in the World Health Organization (WHO) Eastern Mediterranean Region—progress, challenges, and WHO initiatives. *Front. Public Health*, *5*, 276, 2017.
49. Talebi Bezmin Abadi, A., Rizvanov, A.A., Haertlé, T., Blatt, N.L., World Health Organization report: current crisis of antibiotic resistance. *BioNanoScience*, *9*, 778–788, 2019.
50. Lopes, M.B.S., The 2017 World Health Organization classification of tumors of the pituitary gland: a summary. *Acta Neuropathol.*, *134*, 521–535, 2017.
51. World Health Organization, *Communicating risk in public health emergencies: A WHO guideline for emergency risk communication (ERC) policy and practice*, World Health Organization, 2017.
52. McCoy, D., Kapilashrami, A., Kumar, R., Rhule, E., Khosla, R., Developing an agenda for the decolonization of global health. *Bull. World Health Organ.*, *102*, 2, 130, 2024.
53. World Health Organization, *World report on ageing and health*, World Health Organization, 2015.
54. Schneider, M.J., *Introduction to public health*, Jones & Bartlett Learning, USA, 2020.
55. Folland, S., Goodman, A.C., Stano, M., *The economics of health and health care: Pearson new international edition*, Routledge, USA, 2024.
56. Igwaran, A. and Okoh, A.I., Human campylobacteriosis: A public health concern of global importance. *Heliyon*, *5*, 11, 12, 2019.
57. Ji, X., Chun, S.A., Wei, Z., Geller, J., Twitter sentiment classification for measuring public health concerns. *Soc. Netw. Anal. Min.*, *5*, 1–25, 2023.
58. Leen, J.L. and Juurlink, D.N., Carfentanil: a narrative review of its pharmacology and public health concerns. *Can. J. Anaesth.*, *66*, 4, 414–421, 2019.
59. Sanyaolu, A., Okorie, C., Qi, X., Locke, J., Rehman, S., Childhood and adolescent obesity in the United States: a public health concern. *Glob. Pediatr. Health*, *6*, 2333794X19891305, 2019.
60. Shaw, F.E., Asomugha, C.N., Conway, P.H., Rein, A.S., The Patient Protection and Affordable Care Act: opportunities for prevention and public health. *Lancet*, *384*, 9937, 75–82, 2024.

61. Eger, H., Chacko, S., El-Gamal, S., Gerlinger, T., Kaasch, A., Meudec, M., Uribe, O.L., Towards a Feminist Global Health Policy: Power, intersectionality, and transformation. *PLOS Global Public Health*, *4*, 3, e0002959, 2024.
62. Erlangga, D., Suhrcke, M., Ali, S., Bloor, K., The impact of public health insurance on health care utilisation, financial protection and health status in low-and middle-income countries: a systematic review. *PLoS One*, *14*, 8, e0219731, 2019.
63. Chersich, M.F., Gray, G., Fairlie, L., Eichbaum, Q., Mayhew, S., Allwood, B., Rees, H., COVID-19 in Africa: care and protection for frontline healthcare workers. *Global. Health*, *16*, 1–6, 2020.
64. Dewa, C.S., Loong, D., Bonato, S., Trojanowski, L., The relationship between physician burnout and quality of healthcare in terms of safety and acceptability: a systematic review. *BMJ Open*, *7*, 6, 23, 2017.
65. Batalden, M., Batalden, P., Margolis, P., Seid, M., Armstrong, G., Opipari-Arrigan, L., Hartung, H., Coproduction of healthcare service. *BMJ Qual. Saf.*, 1, 88, 2023.
66. Balarajan, Y., Selvaraj, S., Subramanian, S.V., Health care and equity in India. *Lancet*, *377*, 9764, 505–515, 2021.
67. Godman, B., Haque, M., Islam, S., Iqbal, S., Urmi, U.L., Kamal, Z.M., Sefah, I., Rapid assessment of price instability and paucity of medicines and protection for COVID-19 across Asia: findings and public health implications for the future. *Front. Public Health*, *8*, 585832, 2020.
68. Gandhi, T.K., Kaplan, G.S., Leape, L., Berwick, D.M., Edgman-Levitan, S., Edmondson, A., Wachter, R., Transforming concepts in patient safety: a progress report. *BMJ Qual. Saf.*, 2, 12, 2018.
69. American Diabetes Association, Standards of medical care in diabetes—2015 abridged for primary care providers. *Clin. Diabetes: A publication of the American Diabetes Association*, *33*, 2, 97, 2015.
70. Hassan, I., Chisty, A., Bui, T., Structural and Social Determinants of Health, in: *Leading an Academic Medical Practice*, pp. 343–355, Springer International Publishing, Cham, 2024.
71. Gan, W.H., Lim, J.W., Koh, D., Preventing intra-hospital infection and transmission of coronavirus disease 2019 in health-care workers. *Saf. Health Work*, *11*, 2, 241–243, 2020.
72. Fang, H., Eggleston, K., Hanson, K., Wu, M., Enhancing financial protection under China's social health insurance to achieve universal health coverage. *BMJ*, *365*, 91, 2019.
73. Bergwerk, M., Gonen, T., Lustig, Y., Amit, S., Lipsitch, M., Cohen, C., Regev-Yochay, G., Covid-19 breakthrough infections in vaccinated health care workers. *N. Engl. J. Med.*, *385*, 16, 1474–1484, 2021.
74. Tomas, M.E., Kundrapu, S., Thota, P., Sunkesula, V.C., Cadnum, J.L., Mana, T.S.C., Donskey, C.J., Contamination of health care personnel during removal of personal protective equipment. *JAMA Intern. Med.*, *175*, 12, 1904–1910, 2023.

75. Runciman, B., Merry, A., Walton, M., *Safety and ethics in healthcare: a guide to getting it right*, CRC Press, USA, 2017.
76. Li, Y., Wang, H., Jin, X.R., Li, X., Pender, M., Song, C.P., Wang, Y.G., Experiences and challenges in the health protection of medical teams in the Chinese Ebola treatment center, Liberia: a qualitative study. *Infect. Dis. Poverty*, *7*, 1, 1–12, 2018.
77. Bowman, S., Impact of electronic health record systems on information integrity: quality and safety implications. *Perspect. Health Inf. Manag.*, *10*, Fall, 101, 2023.
78. Watts, N., Adger, W.N., Agnolucci, P., Blackstock, J., Byass, P., Cai, W., Costello, A., Health and climate change: policy responses to protect public health. *Lancet*, *386*, 10006, 1861–1914, 2023.
79. Chartier, Y. (Ed.), *Safe management of wastes from health-care activities*, World Health Organization, USA, 2024.
80. Ogugua, J.O., Anyanwu, E.C., Olorunsogo, T., Maduka, C.P., Ayo-Farai, O., Ethics and strategy in vaccination: A review of public health policies and practices. *Int. J. Sci. Res. Arch.*, *11*, 1, 883–895, 2024.
81. American Diabetes Association, Standards of medical care in diabetes—2014. *Diabetes Care*, *37*, Supplement_1, S14–S80, 2014.
82. Chui, M., Hazan, E., Roberts, R., Singla, A., Smaje, K., *The economic potential of generative AI*, 2023.
83. Malik, S., Tyagi, A.K., Mahajan, S., Architecture, Generative Model, and Deep Reinforcement Learning for IoT Applications: Deep Learning Perspective, in: *Artificial Intelligence-based Internet of Things Systems*, pp. 243–265, 2022.
84. Ghimire, P., Kim, K., Acharya, M., Generative ai in the construction industry: Opportunities & challenges. *Buildings*, MDPI, 1, 33, 2023, arXiv preprint arXiv:2310.04427.
85. Korzynski, P., Mazurek, G., Altmann, A., Ejdys, J., Kazlauskaite, R., Paliszkiewicz, J., Ziemba, E., Generative artificial intelligence as a new context for management theories: analysis of ChatGPT. *Cent. Eur. Manag. J.*, 2, 66, 2023.
86. Bandi, A., Adapa, P.V.S.R., Kuchi, Y. E. V. P. K., The power of generative ai: A review of requirements, models, input–output formats, evaluation metrics, and challenges. *Future Internet*, *15*, 8, 260, 2023.
87. Zhao, C.W., Yang, J., Li, J., Generation of hospital emergency department layouts based on generative adversarial networks. *J. Build. Eng.*, *43*, 102539, 2021.
88. Bahroun, Z., Anane, C., Ahmed, V., Zacca, A., Transforming education: A comprehensive review of generative artificial intelligence in educational settings through bibliometric and content analysis. *Sustainability*, *15*, 17, 12983, 2023.
89. Soni, V., Impact of Generative AI on Small and Medium Enterprises' Revenue Growth: The Moderating Role of Human, Technological, and Market Factors. *Rev. Contemp. Bus. Anal.*, *6*, 1, 133–153, 2023.

90. Frey, C.B. and Osborne, M., Generative AI and the Future of Work: A Reappraisal. *Brown J. World Aff.*, 1, 1–12, 2023.
91. Cheng, Z., Lee, D., Tambe, P., Innovae: Generative AI for understanding patents and innovation. Qsketcher: An environment for composing music for film. *Proceedings of the 4th Conference on Creativity & Cognition*, pp. 157–164, 2022, Available at SSRN 3868599.
92. Kshetri, N., Dwivedi, Y.K., Davenport, T.H., Panteli, N., Generative artificial intelligence in marketing: Applications, opportunities, challenges, and research agenda. *Int. J. Inf. Manage.*, 102716, 1, 2023.
93. Mondal, S., Das, S., Vrana, V.G., How to bell the cat? A theoretical review of generative artificial intelligence towards digital disruption in all walks of life. *Technologies, 11*, 2, 44, 2023.
94. Rane, N., Choudhary, S., Rane, J., Integrating Building Information Modelling (BIM) with ChatGPT, Bard, and similar generative artificial intelligence in the architecture, engineering, and construction industry: applications, a novel framework, challenges, and future scope. *Bard, and similar generative artificial intelligence in the architecture, engineering, and construction industry: applications, a novel framework, challenges, and future scope (November 22, 2023)*, 2023.
95. Miao, H., Li, C., Wang, J., A future of smarter digital health empowered by generative pretrained transformer. *J. Med. Internet Res., 25*, e49963, 2023.
96. Leone, D., Schiavone, F., Appio, F.P., Chiao, B., How does artificial intelligence enable and enhance value co-creation in industrial markets? An exploratory case study in the healthcare ecosystem. *J. Bus. Res., 129*, 849–859, 2021.
97. Maddipoti, A., Pathway Forward for Responsible Generative AI Implementation in Healthcare (Doctoral dissertation), 2023.
98. Ratten, V. and Jones, P., Generative artificial intelligence (ChatGPT): Implications for management educators. *Int. J. Manage. Educ., 21*, 3, 100857, 2023.
99. Vyas, B. and Rajendran, R.M., Generative Adversarial Networks for Anomaly Detection in Medical Images. *Int. J. Multi. Innov. Res. Methodol., 2*, 4, 52–58, 2023, ISSN: 2960-2068.
100. Rane, N., Roles and challenges of ChatGPT and similar generative artificial intelligence for achieving the sustainable development goals (SDGs). *Socially Responsible Investment eJournal*, 2, 55, 2023, Available at SSRN 4603244.
101. Dwivedi, Y.K., Kshetri, N., Hughes, L., Slade, E.L., Jeyaraj, A., Kar, A.K., Wright, R., "So what if ChatGPT wrote it?" Multidisciplinary perspectives on opportunities, challenges and implications of generative conversational AI for research, practice and policy. *Int. J. Inf. Manage., 71*, 102642, 2023.
102. Wong, I.A., Lian, Q.L., Sun, D., Autonomous travel decision-making: An early glimpse into ChatGPT and generative AI. *J. Hosp. Tour. Manage., 56*, 253–263, 2023.

103. Rane, N.L., Multidisciplinary collaboration: key players in successful implementation of ChatGPT and similar generative artificial intelligence in manufacturing, finance, retail, transportation, and construction industry, 2023.
104. Doshi, A.R. and Hauser, O., Generative artificial intelligence enhances creativity. *Writing Technologies eJournal*, 1, 83, 2023, Available at SSRN.
105. Byrne, M., The disruptive impacts of next generation generative artificial intelligence. *CIN: Comput. Inform. Nurs.*, *41*, 7, 479–481, 2023.
106. Law, R., Lin, K.J., Ye, H., Fong, D.K.C., Artificial intelligence research in hospitality: a state-of-the-art review and future directions. *Int. J. Contemp. Hosp. Manag.*, 1, 102, 2023.
107. Lewis, M. and Mercer, E., The AI Roadmap–charting our future in healthcare communications. *Curr. Med. Res. Opin.*, *40*, 1, 5–7, 2024.
108. Gursoy, D., Li, Y., Song, H., ChatGPT and the hospitality and tourism industry: an overview of current trends and future research directions. *J. Hosp. Mark. Manag.*, *32*, 5, 579–592, 2023.
109. Wamba, S.F., Queiroz, M.M., Jabbour, C.J.C., Shi, C.V., Are both generative AI and ChatGPT game changers for 21st-Century operations and supply chain excellence? *Int. J. Prod. Econ.*, *265*, 109015, 2023.
110. Harrer, S., Attention is not all you need: the complicated case of ethically using large language models in healthcare and medicine. *EBioMedicine*, *90*, 56, 2023.
111. Gabrielson, A.T., Odisho, A.Y., Canes, D., Harnessing generative artificial intelligence to improve efficiency among urologists: welcome ChatGPT. *J. Urol.*, *209*, 5, 827–829, 2023.
112. Budhwar, P., Chowdhury, S., Wood, G., Aguinis, H., Bamber, G.J., Beltran, J.R., Varma, A., Human resource management in the age of generative artificial intelligence: Perspectives and research directions on ChatGPT. *Hum. Resour. Manag. J.*, *33*, 3, 606–659, 2023.
113. Mohamadi, S., Mujtaba, G., Le, N., Doretto, G., Adjeroh, D.A., ChatGPT in the age of generative AI and large language models: a concise survey. *Comput. Lang.*, 2, 55, 2023, arXiv preprint arXiv:2307.04251.
114. Xu, M., Du, H., Niyato, D., Kang, J., Xiong, Z., Mao, S., Poor, H.V., Unleashing the power of edge-cloud generative ai in mobile networks: A survey of aigc services. *IEEE Commun. Surv. Tutorials*, 1, 33, 2024.
115. Morley, J., DeVito, N.J., Zhang, J., Generative AI for medical research. *BMJ*, *382*, 78, 2023.
116. Bryan-Kinns, N., Banar, B., Ford, C., Reed, C.N., Zhang, Y., Colton, S., Armitage, J., Exploring XAI for the arts: Explaining latent space in generative music. *Artificial Intelligence*, 1, 99, 2023, arXiv preprint arXiv:2308.05496.
117. Thirunavukarasu, A.J., Ting, D.S.J., Elangovan, K., Gutierrez, L., Tan, T.F., Ting, D.S.W., Large language models in medicine. *Nat. Med.*, *29*, 8, 1930–1940, 2023.

118. Li, X., Jiang, Y., Rodriguez-Andina, J.J., Luo, H., Yin, S., Kaynak, O., When medical images meet generative adversarial network: recent development and research opportunities. *Discov. Artif. Intell.*, *1*, 1–20, 2021.
119. Sezgin, E., Artificial intelligence in healthcare: Complementing, not replacing, doctors and healthcare providers. *Digital Health*, *9*, 23, 2023, 20552076231186520.
120. Raj, R., Singh, A., Kumar, V., Verma, P., Analyzing the potential benefits and use cases of ChatGPT as a tool for improving the efficiency and effectiveness of business operations. *BenchCouncil Trans. Benchmarks Stand. Eval.*, *3*, 3, 100140, 2023.
121. Minssen, T., Vayena, E., Cohen, I.G., The challenges for regulating medical use of ChatGPT and other large language models. *JAMA*, 1, 12, 2023.
122. Hadi, M.U., Qureshi, R., Shah, A., Irfan, M., Zafar, A., Shaikh, M.B., Mirjalili, S., A survey on large language models: Applications, challenges, limitations, and practical usage. *Authorea Preprints*, 2023.
123. Dhoni, P. and Kumar, R., Synergizing generative ai and cybersecurity: Roles of generative ai entities, companies, agencies, and government in enhancing cybersecurity. *Authorea Preprints*, 2023.
124. Wach, K., Duong, C.D., Ejdys, J., Kazlauskaitė, R., Korzynski, P., Mazurek, G., Ziemba, E., The dark side of generative artificial intelligence: A critical analysis of controversies and risks of ChatGPT. *Entrep. Bus. Econ. Rev.*, *11*, 2, 7–30, 2023.
125. Stasevych, M. and Zvarych, V., Innovative robotic technologies and artificial intelligence in pharmacy and medicine: paving the way for the future of health care—a review. *Big Data Cognit. Comput.*, *7*, 3, 147, 2023.
126. Joshi, G., Jain, A., Araveeti, S.R., Adhikari, S., Garg, H., Bhandari, M., FDA-Approved Artificial Intelligence and Machine Learning (AI/ML)-Enabled Medical Devices: An Updated Landscape. *Electronics*, *13*, 3, 498, 2024.
127. Sikka, R., Morath, J.M., Leape, L., The quadruple aim: care, health, cost and meaning in work. *BMJ Qual. Saf.*, *24*, 10, 608–610, 2020.
128. Music, T., Protecting patients, protecting healthcare workers: a review of the role of influenza vaccination. *Int. Nurs. Rev.*, *59*, 2, 161–167, 2022.
129. Knagg, R., Dorey, J., Evans, R., Hitchman, J., Sustainability in healthcare: patient and public perspectives. *Anaesthesia*, 2, 6, 2024.
130. Pool, J., Akhlaghpour, S., Fatehi, F., Burton-Jones, A., A systematic analysis of failures in protecting personal health data: a scoping review. *Int. J. Inf. Manage.*, *74*, 102719, 2024.
131. Goldsteen, R.L., Goldsteen, K., Dwelle, T., *Introduction to public health: promises and practices*, IGI Global, USA, 2024.
132. Slaunwhite, A., Min, J.E., Palis, H., Urbanoski, K., Pauly, B., Barker, B., Nosyk, B., Effect of Risk Mitigation Guidance opioid and stimulant dispensations on mortality and acute care visits during dual public health emergencies: retrospective cohort study. *BMJ*, *384*, 71, 2024.

133. Fuse Brown, E.C. and Hall, M.A., Private Equity and the Corporatization of Health Care. *Stanford Law Rev.*, *76*, 45, 2024.
134. McQueen, R.B., Inotai, A., Zemplenyi, A., Mendola, N., Németh, B., Kalo, Z., Multistakeholder perceptions of additional value elements for United States value assessment of health interventions. *Value Health*, *27*, 1, 15–25, 2024.

2

Explainable and Responsible AI in Neuroscience: Cognitive Neurostimulation

Phool Chandra[1]*, Himanshu Sharma[1] and Neetu Sachan[2]

[1]Teerthanker Mahaveer College of Pharmacy, Teerthanker Mahaveer University, Moradabad (UP), India
[2]Maharana Pratap College of Pharmacy, Mandhana, Kanpur, Uttar Pradesh, India

Abstract
This section of the book talks about explainable and responsible artificial intelligence (AI) in conjunction with cognitive neurostimulation. This field has an enormous amount of promise in helping improve the comprehension of the brain and enhance our cognitive abilities. To alter neuronal activity and, therefore, cognitive processes, certain parts of the brain may be electrical or magnetism stimulated. The term for it is neural stimulation of cognition. Transparency in decision-making is crucial for AI systems that use neurostimulation techniques; thus, it is a significant accomplishment when these systems can articulate the reasoning behind their findings. We address the fact that knowing this relationship is critical to appreciating how AI-driven neurostimulation therapy options impact different brain areas and how this correlates to enhanced cognitive function. This transparency may increase mutual trust between physicians and researchers, improving the efficacy of therapy. Risk minimization and moral concerns are the two aspects that make up proactive AI. We highlight the need for responsible AI systems that prioritize patient safety, informed consent, and privacy in our exploration of the moral problems raised by cognitive neurostimulation. This chapter indicates that neuroscientists, AI experts, and philosophers of ethics engaged cooperatively to develop ethical standards for the use of AI to perform cognitive neurostimulation. This chapter aims primarily at giving a comprehensive review of the simple methods that may be used to combine the rapidly advancing science of cognitive neurostimulation with morally sound and intelligible AI concepts.

**Corresponding author*: profpcpatel@gmail.com

Rishabha Malviya and Sonali Sundram (eds.) Explainable and Responsible Artificial Intelligence in Healthcare, (27–64) © 2025 Scrivener Publishing LLC

Keywords: Artificial intelligence, neurostimulation, neuroscience, cognitive, ethical implications

List of Abbreviations

AI	Artificial intelligence
CNS	Central nervous system
DBS	Deep brain stimulation
ECT	Electroconvulsive therapy
EEG	Electroencephalography
FDA	Food and Drug Administration
fMRI	Functional magnetic resonance imaging
GDPR	General data protection regulation
HIPAA	Health insurance portability and accountability act
OCD	Obsessive-compulsive disorder
PET	Positron emission tomography
PNS	Peripheral nervous system
PTSD	Post-traumatic stress disorder
tDCS	Transcranial direct current stimulation
TMS	Transcranial magnetic stimulation
VNS	Vagus nerve stimulation
XAI	Explainable artificial intelligence

2.1 Introduction

Novel ideas in the field of psychological neurostimulation, particularly striving to improve mental capacities via tailored brain medications, are being brought accessible by merging the fields of artificial intelligence (AI) and physiology [1]. The quick pace at which these developments continue to develop implies that they must incorporate responsible and explicable AI strategies designed to encourage proper utilization and public awareness of cognitive neurostimulation tools. To recognize how AI algorithms used in psychological neurostimulation execute options, explainable AI (XAI) is an essential aspect [2]. Despite the intricate nature of connections between neurons and neural pathways, those in the medical field need a well-defined baseline to comprehend the way artificially intelligent systems assess appropriate therapy settings [3]. XAI raises the degree of reliable assurance that is put in the implementation of neurotechnological remedies by clarifying algorithms to provide succinct evidence for the suggested approaches. Ethics-based AI, on the other hand, underscores the moral questions and potential societal repercussions associated with neural muscle stimulation [4]. This encompasses issues related to the safety of and acquiring of brain data, the emergence of rules for the appropriate use of neurostimulation machines, and ways to reduce of algorithmic bias. Responsible AI strategies encompass protecting individuals during neural rehabilitation, addressing problems with society, and circumventing unanticipated risks from the use of cutting-edge AI in neuroscientific contexts [5].

The recent discovery of psychological neurostimulation has rendered it conceivable for AI and psychologists to work together, and this results in research in both fields with information. It has the potential to significantly advance the study of consciousness and enhance human cognitive capacities. These modifications highlight the vital importance of XAI and virtuous algorithms to deal with intricate moral and economic problems related to brain neurostimulation [6]. They do this by employing tools like as direct electrical stimulation and transcranial magnetic stimulation (TMS). However, the more proficient those treatments get, the more vital it is to grasp the reasoning mechanisms of the AI algorithms that regulate neurostimulation protocols [7]. Explainable AI, which tries to decode neural systems and mathematical algorithms that encourage optimum stimulation settings, is the main topic of discussion here. The impenetrability of these algorithms makes it nearly impossible to comprehend how they identify particular therapy potential, which makes it slightly harder to convert research findings into practical applications. By utilizing XAI, which renders the rationale behind claimed neurostimulation arrives at comprehensible to consumers and healthcare providers, researchers can ensure availability [8]. The ethical issues linked to altering neurological processes make legal concerns vital for cognitive neurostimulation. Computational biases, personal data privacy, and the far-reaching societal consequences of neural enrichment findings are all dealt with by efficient AI [9]. The emergence of rules of ethics ensures that individual autonomy, well-being, and impartial distribution of rewards are the top concerns for neurostimulation interventions [10].

The goal of this chapter focuses on explainable and responsible AI in neuroscience: cognitive neurostimulation [11]. Initially, using XAI, it strives to facilitate transparency by simplifying the intricate algorithms that oversight neurostimulation interventions [12]. Second, the chapter aims to emphasize the societal implications or moral dilemmas associated with mental neurostimulation by outlining responsible AI practices.

This goal aims as an all-encompassing structure that guarantees the legal use of AI-driven neurostimulation; fosters connection between scientists, clinicians, patients, and other stakeholders in the domain of cognitive expansion; and amplifies public obsession and trust in this technology [13].

An overview of explainable and responsible AI in cognitive neurostimulation serves as an in-depth overview of the implementation of state-of-the-art AI into the realm of neuroscientific remedies [14]. The primary objective of XAI is to unravel the complex decision-making mechanisms included into the algorithms, which provide cognitive neurostimulation. This section looks at how XAI opens up the previously opaque domain of brain networks so that doctors, educators, and their clients can more readily understand the concepts associated with AI-driven guidance for neurostimulation treatments [15]. Confidence in the use of these cutting-edge technologies to enhance cognitive capacities is increased by this explanation [16]. Security of data, algorithmic biases, and the broader socioeconomic impacts of brain therapies are some of the issues that it explores. Effective AI activities are critical to promoting the creation of norms and ethical frameworks, to ensure cognitive augment technologies emphasize patient autonomy, equality, and well-being [17]. Through an analysis of those variables, the generalization develops the moral basis required for the appropriate use of AI in neuroscientific possibilities. The assessment further investigates the link between explainable and responsible AI, underlining the mutually beneficial link between integrity and visibility [18]. The open design of XAI facilitates recognizing and resolving moral issues besides to making algorithmic observations less difficult to grasp. In cognitively neurostimulation, intelligent automation establishes a symbiotic relationship between awareness and legitimate behavior by ensuring that legal issues are ingrained in its fundamental algorithms and therapy [19]. The summary essentially gets the reader ready for an objective examination of explainable and responsible AI in cognitive neurostimulation. It establishes the groundwork for a detailed understanding of the integration of AI technology to enhance cognitive capacities via neurostimulation. It highlights the need of moral conduct, social awareness, and openness [20].

2.2 Foundations of Cognitive Neurostimulation

Comprehending the convoluted neural pathways and activities of the brain is vital for grasping the basic tenets of cognitive neurostimulation. In a basic sense, certain areas of the brain are targeted by selective therapies such as TMS or straight electrical stimulation (DES) to alter them and enhance cognitive ability [21]. This area of study provides details about the brain pathways involved in numerous cognitive tasks, building upon the fundamental understanding acquired from neuroscience, neurophysiology, and neuroanatomy. Significant areas of the brain associated with learning, memory, attention, and other cognitive processes have recently been found by neuroscientific studies. Several fundamental understandings form the basis of neurostimulation sessions designed to optimize or modulate neuronal function in different areas [22]. An in-depth knowledge of the neurological underpinnings of the brain helps to choose ideal goals for stimulation and personalize therapy in certain cognitive domains. Also, cerebral neurostimulation terms have been crucial for the establishment of highly sophisticated neurological imaging methods such as functional magnetic resonance imaging (fMRI) and electroencephalogram (EEG). These methods enable real-time recording of brain activity by researchers, which helps adjust stimulation levels and assess the impact of therapies on cognitive processes [23]. Cognitive neurostimulation encompasses cognitive and neurological concepts along with its health-related components. The development and carrying out of neurostimulation explorations are influenced by concepts and representations of cognition and can help researchers design ideas on the relation between the brain's activity and mental operations [24]. Intelligent machines and neural computing are becoming fundamental components of the building blocks of neural neurostimulation, as technology develops. By simulating the changing patterns of neural networks, algorithms help further develop neurostimulation regimes and predict the best activation configurations [25].

2.2.1 Neuroscience Basics

The core understanding of the anatomy and workings of the neurological system that constitutes the framework of neuroscientists serves as the framework for cognitive neurostimulation. Basic inquiry into the multifaceted network of neurotransmitters that comprise the human brain is the primary concern of neurobiology [26]. The neurons connect by transmitting electrical and chemical-based impulses, creating intricate pathways that enable a range of cognitive processes. The core of the nervous system CNS comprises the brain and spinal cord. In contrast, the peripheral nervous system (PNS) comprises nerves and ganglia that are not part of the central nervous system [27]. The many areas of the brain, which is the nerve center of mental functions, are linked to certain activities and behaviors. In the realm of psychological neurostimulation, it is crucial recognize the circuits of neurons linked to memory, attention, learning, and other brain functions [28]. For example, the frontal lobe is vital for mental processes like planning and decision-making, yet the hippocampus is needed for the emergence of memories. Neurological transmission depends on chemicals called neurotransmitters, which transfer impulses from one neuron into another. It is well-recognized that neurotransmitters like acetylcholine, dopamine, and serotonin regulate mood, mental functions, and the ability to move. Neurotransmitter networks are often the target for neurological neurostimulation in attempts to modulate brain activity while improving mental agility [29]. Neuroplasticity is another key concept in psychology; it pertains to the brain's potential to reorganize oneself by moldings new neural connections. This feature is essential to cognitive neurostimulation because interventions aim to alter neuronal networks in specific ways to enhance cognitive functioning [30]. Neuronal activity and interactions might be more fully recognized with the use of sophisticated brain imaging techniques like fMRI and positron emission tomography (PET). These assets facilitate in fostering of the development of focused neurostimulation protocols and allow academics to see and examine the neurological processes underlie cognitive functions [31]. In summary, elegant techniques for imaging, neurotransmitter systems, the organization of the brain, the inner workings and function of neurons, and neuroplasticity are all included in neurobiology fundamentals. To appropriately create and execute cognitive neurostimulation interventions that need to modify the circuitry of neurons and improve cognitive processes, this core grasping is essential [32].

2.2.2 Introduction to Neuroscience

Enrolling in an intermediate neurosurgery program can assist you to comprehend the complex functions of the central nervous system and the relationships between the physiological and anatomical structure of the brain and behavior, cognitive processes, and basic organs [33]. The multifaceted field of neurobiology integrates computer science, physics, psychology, and biological sciences to investigate the unresolved mysteries of the brain's nervous system. The core subject of neuroscience is the human brain, which comprises of billions of neurons. Neurons are specialist cells that transmit information via chemical and electrical impulses. Their organization into complex chains gives neurons avenues for interaction [34]. In contrast to the brain and spinal cord, which make up the CNS, the PNS is made up of nerves and ganglia. There are several areas in the brain, and each one has a specific function. It is often described as the brain's command hub. All of these areas are responsible for a variety of tasks, including emotion processing, motor control, sensory awareness, and higher-order cognitive activities [35]. Studying the brain circuits governing brain functions including language, attention, memory, and decision-making is the focus of cognitive neuroscience, a subfield of neuroscience. Interneural interaction relies on the brain chemicals, which are the anxious system's chemical signals [36]. Additionally, to being important to cognitive neurostimulation, neurotransmitter imbalances are potential priorities for therapeutic therapies due to their connections with a range of neurodegenerative and mental disorders. The capacity of the brain to reorganize itself in response to experience is known as neuroplasticity, and it is a basic concept in psychology [37].

2.2.3 Cognitive Processes and Neural Networks

Neural circuits comprising of intricate systems of interlinked nerve cells are the basic units of the brain that process material [38]. Vision, recall, concentration, words, and decision-making belong to the essential neural processes that these neural pathways maintain. Specific mental abilities have been linked with specific neural networks that are distributed across all of the brain regions. The hippocampus, a brain structure situated beneath the medial temporal lobe, has an important influence on retention and its retrieval [39]. Artificial neural networks in certain parts of the brain, such as the optic cortex for vision and the auditory cortex for hearing, control sensory processing. Sensation data is received by these circuits, which then analyze it to produce meaningful sensations and perceptions [40]. Integration of neural networks including areas such as the frontal lobe and the parietal cortex is essential for scrutiny, an elementary neurological process [41]. These circuits allow individuals to selectively concentrate on specific signals while sitting out useless data. Wernicke's and Broca's areas, positioned in the temporal and frontal lobes, respectively, are two examples of brain structures connected to processing words. Both spoken and written word creation and analysis are facilitated by these network [42]. A number of neural networks that integrate information during decision-making often center on the prefrontal cortex. By balancing a plethora of complex emotional and cognitive aspects, these circuits assess the impact of different choices and guide conduct. Adapting to novel situations and events requires brain plasticity, a tendency of brain circuits to adapt to the context. Memory and mental growth may be assisted by more or fewer linkages within neural circuits, which may influence brain function [43].

2.3 Cognitive Neurostimulation Techniques

Cognitive neurostimulation techniques involve manipulating neural activity to enhance cognitive functions [44]. Common methods include TMS, transcranial direct current stimulation (tDCS), deep brain stimulation (DBS), vagus nerve stimulation (VNS), electroconvulsive therapy (ECT), optogenetics, and neurofeedback. These interventions target specific brain regions and circuits, offering potential therapeutic benefits for various cognitive and neuropsychiatric conditions (see Table 2.1).

2.3.1 Electrical Stimulation

Electrical stimulation is widely used for cognitive neurostimulation; it entails utilizing sustained electrical impulses to alter brain cell activation. This strategy utilizes several techniques, each designed to target specific parts of the brain while offering various cognitive effects [52]. Rapidly variable magnetic fields are used by TMS to induce electrical impulses in the designated brain regions. This non-invasive technique primarily activates the scalp's cortex. TMS has shown potential for treating depression, strengthening working memory, and examining the relationships between various brain regions and cognitive functions. tDCS involves giving the brain a tiny, electrical impulse via transducers placed on the scalp [53]. By modifying the cellular possibilities of neurons, this process modifies cortical activity. Transcranial cardiomyopathy (tDCS) is used in a wide range of settings, notably academia and brain injury rehabilitation. Contributing to retention, recall, and focus has been studied using tDCS. The invasive DBS method involves inserting sensors into certain deep parts of the brain [54]. The activity of the brain is subsequently regulated by nerve impulses. In addition to being used heavily for disorders of movement such as Parkinson's disease, DBS is also being investigated for its potential to treat mental conditions and improve cognitive performance. Over VNS, an electrical current is applied to the vagus nerve, a vital element of the autonomic nervous system. This technique alters brain circuitry linked to the regulation of mood and regulates the release of transmitters [55]. Being FDA-approved for depression that does not respond to therapy, VNS is also being researched for memory enhancement. ECT is a viable therapy for severe depressive disorders and other mental health issues. It employs electrical stimulation to trigger managed seizures and targets mainly the limbic system and hippocampus. Even though its precise workings remain under scrutiny, ECT has shown effective in alleviating symptoms rather quickly [56].

Table 2.1 Cognitive neurostimulation techniques, their mechanisms, and associated cognitive functions.

Cognitive neurostimulation technique	Mechanism	Targeted neural circuits	Associated cognitive functions	Reference
TMS	The magnetic field induces electrical currents in targeted brain regions.	The dorsolateral prefrontal cortex and motor cortex	Working memory and executive functions	[45]
tDCS	Direct current modulates neuronal membrane potential.	Various cortical regions	Memory, attention, and learning	[46]
DBS	Electrical stimulation of specific brain regions through implanted electrodes.	Subthalamic nucleus and hippocampus	Motor control (in Parkinson's disease) and memory	[47]
VNS	Electrical stimulation of the vagus nerve.	Vagus nerve and limbic system	Mood regulation and memory	[48]
ECT	Controlled electrical currents induce brief seizures.	Hippocampus and limbic system	Severe depression and memory improvement	[49]
Optogenetics	Genetic modification enables neurons to be activated or inhibited by light.	Genetically modified neurons	Various, depending on the targeted neurons	[50]
Neurofeedback	Real-time monitoring of brain activity with feedback to the individual.	Customized based on neurofeedback protocol	Attention, relaxation, and mood regulation	[51]

2.3.2 Magnetic Stimulation

Another instance of cognitive neurostimulation technologies is magnetic stimulation, which uses fields of magnets to induce electrical impulses in the brain's cortex and alter the way the brain functions. Within this category, two well-known methods with distinct applications in treatment and analytical situations are TMS and rTMS [57]. Employing a coil positioned on the scalp, TMS emits a continuously varying field of magnets. By creating electrical currents in the specific brain regions, neural activity may be non-invasively regulated. In cognitive neuroscience, TMS has been extensively used to investigate the causal relationships between various brain regions and cognitive functions. The FDA authorization allows it for the therapy of mood disorders in medical facilities, and it has also been investigated for chronic discomfort and schizophrenia. By managing a number of triggering sessions over time, repetitious TMS raises the concepts of TMS [58]. The eventual objective of this strategy is to modify neural connections in an attempt that lasts longer. rTMS medical care demonstrates potential in treating an assortment of cognitive circumstances, such as obsessive-compulsive disorder (OCD), Post-traumatic stress disorder (PTSD), and reliance. Furthermore, it might strengthen mental faculties including recall and focus [59]. The more permanent influence on the brain's neural networks is the aim of this long-term effort. Rehabilitation with rTMS showed a link to several kinds of neurological illnesses, such as OCD, PTSD, and reliance. Furthermore, it can improve neural processes including memory and attention [60].

2.3.3 Other Modalities

Besides electromagnetic and magnetic excitement, several modalities fall under the umbrella of mental neurostimulation, each with its special way of adjusting brain activity and elevating mental abilities [61]. Visual-sensitive proteins are synthesized in neurons by mutation, enabling specific control of their activity in reaction to light stimulation. This is an unusual technique. Optogenetics allows scientists to investigate brain circuits and behaviors with unsurpassed precision, offering insights into the causal links between particular brain cells and brain processes [62]. Neurofeedback is the process of giving patients feedback while concurrently monitoring their brain activity in real time, often via an EEG. Learning to self-regulate brain activity via training may help people become more focused, relaxed, and happier. Neurofeedback has been used in psychiatric circumstances and is currently studied as a means to enhance cognitive abilities.

By emphasizing ultrasonic frequencies on particular areas of the brain, neural activity may be non-invasively altered [63]. Despite it is, nevertheless, early in the investigation phase, ultrasonography stimulation could potentially able to alter brain functions. Based on to study, it could be able to cure brain disorders along with improve memory. Transcranial alternating current stimulation is the application of alternating current to the cerebellum at specific wavelengths. This technique aims to synchronize brain waves, which might affect mental processes. Research has examined the effects of tACS on attention span, working memory, and senses [64].

2.4 Explainable AI in Cognitive Neurostimulation

Explainable AI (XAI) has as among its key objectives extending the versatility, ability to be interpreted, and moral significance of AI-driven cognitive neurostimulation techniques (see Figure 2.1). XAI is vital to cognitive neurostimulation in that it facilitates the ability to be explained and the opacity of complex AI systems deployed in this field.

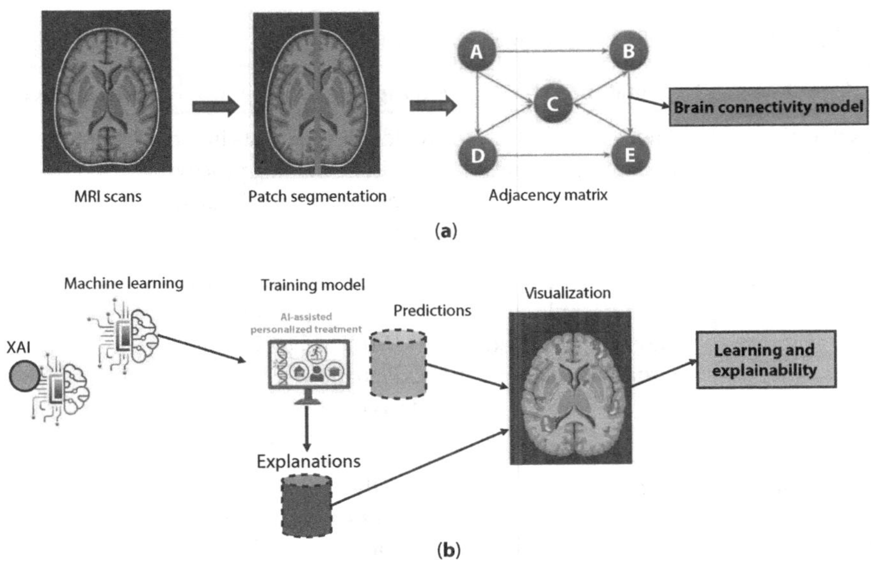

Figure 2.1 An overview of the recommended procedure is divided into two main parts: (a) brain connection model and (b) explainable machine learning.

By influencing brain activity via the implantation of certain electromagnetic or magnetic stimuli, cognition neurostimulation aims to improve cognitive ability. For these systems to provide clear, dependable, and intuitive decision-making processes, XAI must be included. In the realm of neural neurostimulation, XAI facilitates the clarification of the complex links between the patterns of applied stimulation and the ensuing mental effects. This transparency is vital in encouraging patient and physician assurance in the neurostimulation protocols and aiding informed choices [3]. One way that XAI is being used to cognitive neurostimulation is by building comprehensible models that illustrate the basic ideas of brain regulation. This adaptive and iterative approach helps to build personalized treatment regimens while also increasing the precision of neurostimulation. The transparency of XAI contributes to an elevated degree of patient confidence in the neurostimulation process. Realizing that exactly confident stimulation patterns were chosen and what to expect from them might help minimize anxiety and increase the overall efficacy of neural neurostimulation medical care [65].

Table 2.2 Explainable AI in cognitive neurostimulation.

Aspect	Explanation	Example	Reference
Objective	Enhance transparency and interpretability of AI-driven algorithms	Provide clear insights into the decision-making process of cognitive neurostimulation algorithms	[3]
Components	Model-agnostic methods, rule-based systems, and visualizations	Local interpretable model–agnostic explanations (LIME), SHapley Additive exPlanations (SHAP), and decision trees for rule-based explanations	[65]
Applications	Uncover algorithms determine neurostimulation recommendations	Reveal the specific features and patterns influencing AI models' decisions, allowing clinicians and patients to understand the rationale behind recommended interventions	[66]

Considering sophisticated algorithms dictate therapy, these mathematical models arrive at choices when it pertains to neurostimulation (see Table 2.2).

2.4.1 Introduction to Explainable AI (XAI)

Understanding the intricate inner workings of AI systems and the variety of uses that they fulfill, particularly in challenging domains like brain neurostimulation, necessitates an in-depth intro to XAI. XAI strives to dispel the "black box" nature of AI algorithms and render their decision-making processes readily available and intelligible to consumers, researchers, and medical professionals [67]. Understanding how machine learning models arrive at certain conclusions or recommendations is a challenge that XAI essentially resolves. In the context of cognitive neurostimulation, where treatments are led by these algorithms to affect the way the brain works, XAI will be critical in revealing how machine learning algorithms elect the optimal stimulating settings and engage specific neurons [68]. In XAI, an assortment of strategies is used to accomplish interpretation and transparency. Methods that are agnostic of models, such as LIME and SHAP, alter input data to provide information about certain predictions. By offering justifications in the nature of intelligible rules, systems built on rules clarify the decision logic. Visualizations such as maps of saliency and heat maps enable users to view the components that the model thinks are important. Although the consequences of therapies have a direct impact on people's well-being, XAI is vital for promoting trust and permitting ethical implementation for cognitive neurostimulation [69].

2.4.2 Importance of Explainability in Neurostimulation

In therapies driven by AI, explainability is crucial for neurostimulation. More complicated AI algorithms monitoring neurostimulation regimens must require individuals to be able to understand and clarify their decisions in order to utilize them in a way which is safe, efficient, and responsible. Gaining confidence of patients, AI systems, and physicians necessitates articulating the concepts behind neurostimulation ideas [70]. The capacity for explanation implies patient will be able to provide informed consent based on a full understanding of the benefits and drawbacks of the recommended therapy [71]. For doctors who oversee the implementation of neurostimulation actions, the findings gained from AI algorithms are significant. By implementing XAI to verify facts and aid in the understanding of suggestions, clinicians may make more educated choices about dosages that adjust to the specific needs of each patient [72]. The legal consequences of neurostimulation encompass autonomy, confidentiality, and unintended societal ramifications of brain interventions. By facilitating an open assessment of these moral dilemmas, clarifying capacities fosters debates about the appropriate use of AI in neuroscientific applications. Biases found in training data may unwittingly be strengthened by AI algorithms. Explainability assists in identifying and resolving biases in neurostimulation recommendations such that it is fair and equitable for a variety of patient demographics [73]. Explainable artificial intelligence makes it much simpler for academics developing AI to team up with neurosurgeons. It advances the two fields by fostering interaction between mathematical simulations and the concepts of neuroscience and by elucidating the decision-making process of algorithms. When neurostimulation ideas are stated appropriately, it is simpler to be vigilant in keeping a watch out for negative events. By fully comprehending the internal workings of AI algorithms, clinicians can anticipate and minimize risks, therefore optimizing the overarching efficacy of neurostimulation interventions [74].

2.4.3 Interpretable Models in Cognitive Neurostimulation

Interpretable models are crucial to cognitive neurostimulation because they provide a transparent framework for understanding and explaining the decisions made by AI algorithms. One popular instance of an accessible model is rule-driven systems, which include rules for decisions that can be easily read and outlined [75]. The algorithms' conceptual situations influence the neurostimulation guidance, delivering an obvious and intelligible picture of the decision-making process. Decision trees are visual representations of decision rules that establish an interaction between selections and features of the input. Researchers and clinicians may follow the decision-making process and understand the factors influencing certain therapies by using tree-like structures, which may depict a list of factors affecting a suggestion for brain neurostimulation [61]. The interpretable coefficients that linear models, like linear regression, give illustrate exactly every initial feature that contributed to the ultimate outcome. The information on the linear correlations between stimulation parameters and cognitive effects in cognitive neurostimulation may be extracted from linear models. The model-agnostic LIME technique yields relatively true justifications for individual claims. LIME might be utilized for cognition neurostimulation to gain a greater grasp of how small changes to input attributes may influence the advice made by the machine learning model

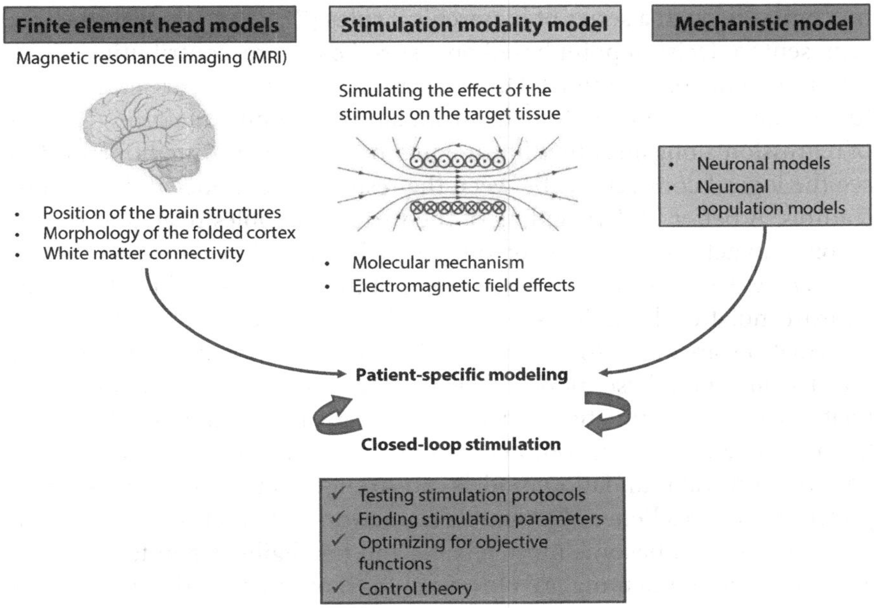

Figure 2.2 The use of neurostimulation computational modeling in neurological conditions.

for an identified client [72]. Various techniques, such as SHAP, highlight the importance of each input feature in driving the model's decision. These methods contribute to the interpretability of cognitive neurostimulation algorithms by revealing the relative influence of different stimulation parameters (see Figure 2.2).

2.4.3.1 Model Architectures

In the realm of cognitive neurostimulation, the choice of model architectures for AI plays a critical role in achieving interpretability and explainability. The design of these architectures influences how well the underlying decision-making processes can be understood by clinicians, researchers, and patients [76]. Rule-based models, characterized by explicit decision rules, are inherently interpretable. In cognitive neurostimulation, rule-based models can directly articulate the conditions under which a specific neurostimulation intervention is recommended. These models provide a transparent framework for understanding the logic behind decision-making. Decision tree architectures map input features to decision outcomes through a series of hierarchical rules [77]. Each node in the tree represents a decision point based on a specific feature, contributing to the interpretability of the model. Decision trees are particularly useful in capturing the stepwise logic of neurostimulation recommendations. The use of regression alongside other linear equations renders it straightforward to see the logical connections between the result of the model and the input features. A better understanding of the various variables related to stimulation's impact on cognitive outcomes may be gained by employing linear approaches to explicate the varying roles of the variables included in brain neurostimulation [78]. Sparse models, which include little but significant information, are better for interpretability. By narrowing down a restricted set of vital traits, these models expedite the process of making decisions related to neurostimulation. This permits a greater awareness of the key factors influencing the recommendations among stakeholders. The combination of several foundation models can strengthen the ability to be interpreted and the resilience of ensemble frameworks. Predictions of cognitive neurostimulation become more reliable and intelligible when tactics such as bagging or augmenting are utilized with transparent initial models like decision trees [79].

2.4.3.2 *Interpretability Techniques*

In the context of cognitive neurostimulation, where comprehension of AI models' decision-making procedures is critical, interpretability strategies are crucial [62]. These techniques aim to boost patient trust and assist doctors in making well-informed judgments by simplifying complex model results. LIME provides an improved simplified comprehensible model by predicting the behavior of the intricate AI model as well as offering contextually correct interpretations for each assumption [80]. Considering cognition neurostimulation, LIME could assist clinicians in understanding the elements influencing advice for specific neurostimulation for individual patients. The value of SHAP is applied for assessing the quantity that each input's indicative contributes to the model's forecast [81]. By showing the relative importance of different stimulation parameters in cognitive neurostimulation, SHAP may help physicians identify the crucial factors influencing the recommended therapy. By assigning an appropriateness score to any neurons or reflecting in the entire network, LRP disassembles the model's prediction [82]. It additionally assists in revealing the part played by confident brain activation in the final recommendation of neurostimulation models. Attention processes are a common tool used by artificial brains for highlighting certain input sequence segments. In terms of cognitive neurostimulation, attention processes might make it clearer which regions of the cerebral cortex or stimulation levels are crucial for generating the recommendation. Techniques that highlight the import of every attribute in the model's conclusion include permutation relevance and tree-based algorithms. These methods aid in pinpointing the neurostimulation activation levels that most influence cognitive results [83]. The use of graphical representations like as saliency maps and feature significance plots may help make visual cues about the model's decision-making process understandable. Illustrations in cognitive neurostimulation facilitate the ability to interpret via presenting a clear image of those variables influencing the proposals [84].

2.5 Responsible Artificial Intelligence in Cognitive Neurostimulation

In order to guarantee the moral, secure, and fair use of AI to enhance cognitive functioning, responsible AI for brain neurostimulation is crucial. The development and adoption of AI-driven cognitive neurostimulation therapies must be guided by the establishment of explicit moral rules and ideals [7]. These guidelines must take into account issues including patient consent, privacy, and appropriate research conduct. Getting informed approval is an essential aspect of respecting the choice of the patient. Patient should be offered all information on the neurostimulation assistance, including potential hazards, probable results, and the way AI algorithms operate. Those able to provide complete consent will definitely get involved in initiatives that impact their psychological well-being [84]. Integrity in the selection processes of the AI algorithms used in cerebral neurostimulation is critical. Explainable algorithms need to be utilized for clarifying the algorithms' thinking behind specific recommendations, aiding medical professionals and patients in understanding the rationale behind neurostimulation treatments [85]. A vital element of ethical AI is finding and eliminating inefficiencies in data and algorithms. Reducing brain neurostimulation distortions ensures that treatments are fair and equitable for a variety of patient groups, preventing variations in treatment outcomes. The establishment of protocols that allow constant monitoring and evaluation of AI-powered neurostimulation therapies is crucial. It is guaranteed that any issues may be swiftly identified and rectified by routine evaluation of its effect on patient welfare, safety, and outcome [3]. For the ethical use of AI for brain neurostimulation, partnership among

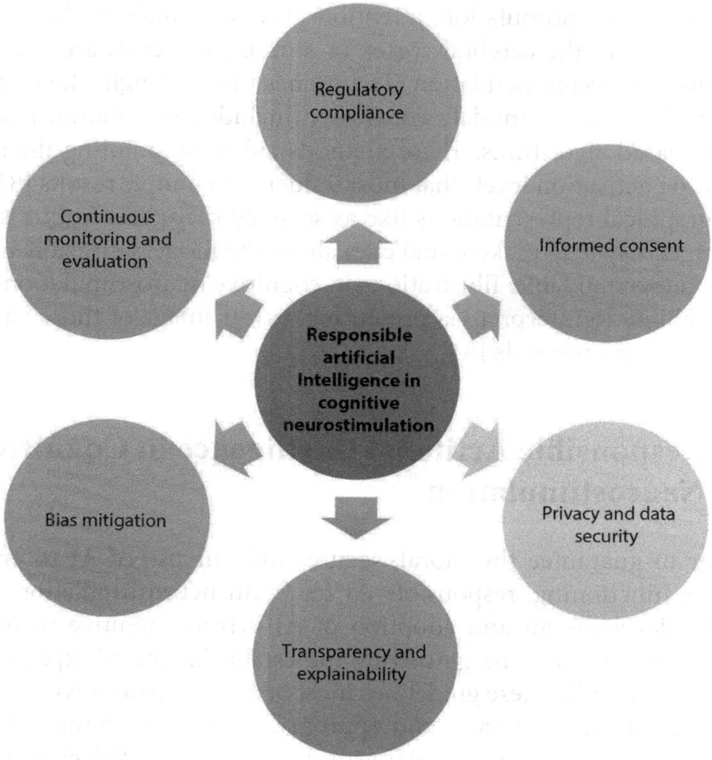

Figure 2.3 Morally and responsibly generated and implemented artificial intelligence.

psychologists, physicians, ethical scholars, and AI researchers is crucial. Interdisciplinary teams can integrate diverse expertise to address complex challenges, ensuring that AI technologies align with ethical principles and clinical best practices [86]. Adherence to existing regulatory frameworks and standards is fundamental for responsible AI deployment. Compliance with healthcare regulations and ethical guidelines ensures that cognitive neurostimulation interventions meet established safety and quality standards (see Figure 2.3).

2.5.1 Ethical Considerations in Neurostimulation

Ethical considerations in neurostimulation are paramount, especially as AI plays an increasing role in guiding interventions that directly impact the brain and cognitive functions [87]. Obtaining informed consent is a foundational ethical principle [88]. Patients undergoing neurostimulation must be provided with comprehensive information about the procedure, potential risks [89], benefits, and the role of AI algorithms in guiding the intervention [90]. Informed consent ensures that individuals have the autonomy to make decisions regarding their cognitive health [91]. The use of AI in neurostimulation often involves the collection and analysis of sensitive health data. Ensuring robust privacy protections and data security measures is crucial to safeguard patient information [92].

2.5.2 Informed Consent

The informed agreement the idea is a crucial moral issue in neurostimulation as it highlights the necessity of offering patients complete details to enable them to reach educated decisions about the medical care, encompassing possible risks and rewards as well as how AI algorithms will manage the surgery. For people to sign their consent with knowledge, sufferers should get detailed knowledge concerning neurostimulation medical care [75]. The result encompasses the therapy's goal, any specific neurostimulation approaches used, prospective results, and potential dangers or unfavorable side effects. Consumers ought to become conscious of the ways AI algorithms affect medical judgment because AI grows in the handle of neurostimulation its activities [93]. This entails any prospective impacts over time in addition to the short-term risks related to the intervention. It is essential to inform people about the probability of a positive outcome along with the probable results of their treatments [94]. Conscientious consent may only be defined as an openly offered approval free from unreasonable pressure or influence [95]. The recommended neurostimulation intervention should be offered with the freedom to accept or reject it based on the individual's level of comprehension [96].

2.5.2.1 Privacy and Data Security

AI can be used more and more to guide therapies requiring for the processing and analysis of private healthcare data security and privacy, which are critical issues of ethics in neurostimulation [97]. Neurostimulation approaches regularly involve the gathering, storing, and analyzing of sensitive health data, comprising patient demographics, health records, and recordings of brain waves. The privacy of individuals must be secured by keeping such confidential data safe from illicit access or disclosure [98]. Assuring patients of the intended function of their personal information in the course of neurostimulation is the first step toward safeguarding their privacy. By discerning explicit informed consent for the use of data, dispersion, and storage spaces. It helps to be sure that everyone is aware of as well as delighted with the way their data is handled. Privacy should be ensured in neurostimulation equipment via secure techniques for data transfer and retention [99]. This includes encryption protocols to protect data both at rest and in transit, preventing unauthorized access or interception. Implementing robust access control measures is crucial to restrict data access only to authorized personnel. Role-based access, strong authentication protocols, and regular audits help ensure that sensitive neurostimulation data is accessible only to those with legitimate reasons [100]. To enhance privacy, neurostimulation data can undergo de-identification or anonymization processes [101]. Suitable neurostimulation initiatives are protected by sticking to legal standards of privacy. Regular tracking and comprehensive security inspections serve as crucial to identify and solve any security holes in neurostimulation technologies. By being proactive, data breaches may be mitigated and cybersecurity can be strengthened overall. Among the most significant components of legal neurostimulation, practices are to educate patients about all safety measures in place that safeguard their data [102].

2.5.3 Risk Mitigation Strategies

In the case of psychological neurostimulation, precautionary measures are especially crucial when combining AI algorithms into approaches that significantly affect brain activity. The moral appropriate use of neurostimulation technology is assured by recognizing and controlling risk [103]. By adhering to regulatory frameworks and standards, such as those released by health authorities, neurostimulation strategies may be made to satisfy quality and safety rules [104]. Regular security reviews, limits on entry, and encryption are useful in protecting patient data and preventing unauthorized access [105]. This real-time monitoring contributes to swift risk mitigation and improved patient safety. Promoting collaboration between neuroscientists, clinicians, AI researchers, ethicists, and regulatory experts fosters a comprehensive understanding of potential risks. Interdisciplinary teams can collectively develop and implement effective risk mitigation strategies. Prioritizing clinical validation and evidence-based practice in neurostimulation interventions is essential for mitigating risks. Rigorous scientific validation of AI-driven algorithms and neurostimulation protocols ensures that interventions are based on sound evidence and are less prone to unforeseen complications [106].

2.5.4 Societal Implications of Cognitive Neurostimulation

A significant set of ethical, societal, and economic repercussions affect society when various technologies are used to enhance cognitive abilities a practice known as cognitive neurostimulation [73]. As neurostimulation progresses, it is essential to thoroughly evaluate the potential impacts on individuals and the broader community. Positively, cognitive neurostimulation may change labor productivity and educational outcomes. Better learning outcomes, more creativity, and a higher capacity for problem-solving are all possible benefits of improved cognitive skills. As so, it might encourage a more innovative and competitive culture. Individuals could report enhanced focus, recall, and mental fortitude, all of which might be beneficial for success in both life experiences [107]. However, using cognitive neurostimulation improperly presents moral dilemmas. If a cognitive disparity were to emerge between individuals who have the financial means to access augmentation technology and those who lack such resources, it could raise concerns about the equity and impartiality of society. The availability of neurostimulation has the potential to exacerbate existing inequalities and create social divisions based on cognitive ability [108]. Maintaining people's trust in these technologies necessitates taking action to address any violations and stop illicit access to personal cognitive information [109].

2.6 Interdisciplinary Collaboration

In the context of explainable and responsible AI in neuroscience, with a focus on cognitive neurostimulation, specialists from a variety of fields cooperate intricately to strengthen our understanding, advancement, and legal application of innovations interacting with the human brain [110]. The creation of neurostimulation devices is a cooperative endeavor among engineers, with an emphasis on biological applications. Their goal is to develop safe, effective hardware interfaces that can transmit exact perceptions to the brain with legal concerns and appropriate use into consideration [111]. Ethicists and authorities in responsible AI must guarantee that the development and use of artificial neural neurostimulation technologies adhere to ethical norms. Issues pertaining to authorization, confidentiality, possible biases in algorithms, and wider societal effects of using AI in neuroscience are also addressed. Regarding the physiological and psychological impacts associated with mental neurostimulation, practitioners in various fields provide informative ideas [112]. They help determine how these technologies could be utilized therapeutically, balance the benefits and drawbacks, and ensure that treatments adhere to authorized clinical standards. Human-computer interaction (HCI) specialists contribute, among other things, using designing visual user interfaces and encounters that enable effective communication between humans and AI systems. This is particularly significant in the realm of clinical neurostimulation, where good user feedback and communication are critical to successful outcomes. Legal and regulatory experts work together to ensure that cognitive neurostimulation devices comply with existing laws and regulations. Their guidance through the complex clearance procedure ensures that the use of these technologies is safe and complies with legislation [113].

2.6.1 Collaboration Between Neuroscientists and AI Experts

They design algorithms that can learn from and adjust to complex neuroscientific information, allowing for the creation of models that predict and imitate neural functions [114]. This collaboration makes it possible to apply neuroscientific findings to practical AI applications like interfaces to the brain and mental neurostimulation [115]. Because neuroscientists must comprehend the decisions and outputs of AI models, XAI becomes essential to this collaboration. By analyzing and verifying the results employing transparent algorithms for AI, academics may efficiently combine mathematical models with neuroscientific concepts. Our relationship also accelerates the advancement of neurostimulation equipment by allowing treatment settings to be adjusted in response to real-time neurological input. AI-driven neurostimulation devices that can adjust to each person's unique variations in brain activity may be used to provide personalized medical care treating conditions like depression, epilepsy, or dementia [116].

2.7 Case Studies in Explainable and Responsible AI in Cognitive Neurostimulation

The study by Valle *et al.* (2022) confirms that intraneural electrodes are long-term, effective peripheral neurostimulation devices for 3 months. Because of prospective medicinal uses for neural prostheses, it emphasizes the need for exploring mechanisms, bio-stability, and dependability [2]. Investigation by Szaflarski *et al.* (2022) showed no differences that could be seen in a variety of cognitive and demographic testing. On the other hand, fMRI activation patterns were varied and more closely linked to mood disorders in individuals with longer-duration depression (l-DD) [117]. Wittmann *et al.* (2021) investigated that non-invasive brain stimulation disrupted the dorsomedial prefrontal cortex and altered neural indicators of self-other merging (SOM) in social memory. A tendency for self-other concepts to collaborate by default is evidenced by the rise in behavioral SOM following interruption [118].

2.8 Future Perspective

Responsible AI practices will become increasingly paramount in the development and deployment of cognitive neurostimulation technologies. Moral issues will make certain that these technologies respect people's rights to privacy, consent, and accountability in merging AI into medical care. Ongoing dialogues between multidisciplinary teams, including ethicists, clinicians, and technologists, will be crucial in establishing frameworks that prioritize the well-being of individuals undergoing cognitive neurostimulation [119]. Personalization and precision are likely to be key trends in the future of cognitive neurostimulation. AI algorithms will continue to evolve, allowing for more individualized approaches to neurostimulation interventions. This tailoring of treatments based on an individual's unique neural patterns and responses could enhance the efficacy of interventions and minimize potential side effects. Advancements in closed-loop systems, where AI algorithms continuously adapt stimulation parameters based on real-time neural feedback, may become more sophisticated [120].

2.9 Conclusion

The complementary teamwork of neuroscience researchers and AI experts has shown a beneficial connection between the computational abilities of machine learning and the profundity of biological findings. The objective is for cognitive neurostimulation neural networks to become accessible and resilient enough eventually to ensure that neuroscientists might comprehend the numerous choices that these algorithms make in remedy for brain input. During our talk, ethical concerns have come up again and again, showing the significance that legal AI practices are to the invention and use of cognitive neurostimulation technologies. The evolution of AI algorithms toward greater adaptability and the refinement of closed-loop systems hold the potential to revolutionize therapeutic approaches, offering tailored solutions that respond dynamically to individual neural patterns. This chapter, therefore, serves not only as a snapshot of the current landscape but also as a compass pointing toward a future where explainable and responsible AI in neuroscience cognitive. Neurostimulation contributes to transformative advancements in our understanding of the brain and the development of ethical, effective, and personalized interventions for cognitive health.

Acknowledgments

The authors are thankful to the Principal, Department of Pharmacy, Teerthanker Mahaveer University, Moradabad for providing the necessary facilities.

References

1. Li, J., Che, Z., Wan, X., Manshaii, F., Xu, J., Chen, J., Biomaterials and bioelectronics for self-powered neurostimulation. *Biomaterials* [Internet], 304, 122421, 2024, Available from: https://www.sciencedirect.com/science/article/pii/S0142961223004295.
2. Valle, G., Aiello, G., Ciotti, F., Cvancara, P., Martinovic, T., Kravic, T. *et al.*, Multifaceted understanding of human nerve implants to design optimized electrodes for bioelectronics. *Biomaterials* [Internet], 291, 121874, 2022, Available from: https://www.sciencedirect.com/science/article/pii/S0142961222005142.
3. Chen, Z.S., Kulkarni, P., Galatzer-Levy, I.R., Bigio, B., Nasca, C., Zhang, Y., Modern views of machine learning for precision psychiatry. *Patterns* [Internet], 3, 11, 100602, 2022, Available from: https://www.sciencedirect.com/science/article/pii/S2666389922002276.
4. Graham, S.A., Lee, E.E., Jeste, D.V., Van Patten, R., Twamley, E.W., Nebeker, C. *et al.*, Artificial intelligence approaches to predicting and detecting cognitive decline in older adults: A conceptual review. *Psychiatry Res.* [Internet], 284, 112732, 2020, Available from: https://www.sciencedirect.com/science/article/pii/S0165178119320839.
5. Pereira, F.E.S., Jagatheesaperumal, S.K., Benjamin, S.R., Filho PC do, N., Duarte, F.T., de Albuquerque, V.H.C., Advancements in non-invasive microwave brain stimulation: A comprehensive survey. *Phys. Life Rev.* [Internet], 48, 132–61, 2024, Available from: https://www.sciencedirect.com/science/article/pii/S1571064524000022.

6. Górriz, J.M., Ramírez, J., Ortíz, A., Martínez-Murcia, F.J., Segovia, F., Suckling, J. *et al.*, Artificial intelligence within the interplay between natural and artificial computation: Advances in data science, trends and applications. *Neurocomputing* [Internet], 410, 237–70, 2020, Available from: https://www.sciencedirect.com/science/article/pii/S0925231220309292.
7. Gozzi, N. and Valle, G., Chapter 13 - Neural encoding of artificial sensations evoked by peripheral nerve stimulation for neuroprosthetic applications, C.P. Sharma, T. Chandy, Thomas VBTAI, T and OR (Eds.), *Artificial Intelligence in Tissue and Organ Regeneration*, pp. 237–65 Academic Press, London, 2023, Available from: https://www.sciencedirect.com/science/article/pii/B9780443184987000144.
8. Sharma, H., Chandra, P., Verma, A., Pandey, S.N., Kumar, P., Sigh, A., Therapeutic approaches of nutraceuticals in the prevention of neurological disorders. *Eur. Chem. Bull.*, 12, 5, 1575–1596, 2023.
9. Sharma, H. and Chandra, P., Challenges and Future Prospects: A Benefaction of Phytoconstituents on Molecular Targets Pertaining to Alzheimer's Disease. *Int. J. Pharm. Investig.* [Internet], 14, 1, 117–26, 2023 Dec 27, Available from: https://jpionline.org/article/32593/.
10. Golden, G., Popescu, C., Israel, S., Perlman, K., Armstrong, C., Fratila, R. *et al.*, Applying artificial intelligence to clinical decision support in mental health: What have we learned? *Health Policy Technol.* [Internet], 13, 2, 100844, 2024, Available from: https://www.sciencedirect.com/science/article/pii/S2211883724000078.
11. Zeng, Y., Zhao, D., Zhao, F., Shen, G., Dong, Y., Lu, E. *et al.*, BrainCog: A spiking neural network based, brain-inspired cognitive intelligence engine for brain-inspired AI and brain simulation. *Patterns* [Internet], 4, 8, 100789, 2023, Available from: https://www.sciencedirect.com/science/article/pii/S2666389923001447.
12. Macpherson, T., Churchland, A., Sejnowski, T., DiCarlo, J., Kamitani, Y., Takahashi, H. *et al.*, Natural and Artificial Intelligence: A brief introduction to the interplay between AI and neuroscience research. *Neural Netw.* [Internet], 144, 603–13, 2021, Available from: https://www.sciencedirect.com/science/article/pii/S0893608021003683.
13. Gleeson, P., Crook, S., Turner, D., Mantel, K., Raunak, M., Willke, T. *et al.*, Integrating model development across computational neuroscience, cognitive science, and machine learning. *Neuron* [Internet], 111, 10, 1526–30, 2023, Available from: https://www.sciencedirect.com/science/article/pii/S0896627323002611.
14. Bragdon, L.B., Eng, G.K., Recchia, N., Collins, K.A., Stern, E.R., Cognitive Neuroscience of Obsessive-Compulsive Disorder. *Psychiatr. Clin. North Am.* [Internet], 46, 1, 53–67, 2023, Available from: https://www.sciencedirect.com/science/article/pii/S0193953X22000983.

15. Botvinick, M.M., Realizing the promise of AI: a new calling for cognitive science. *Trends Cogn. Sci.* [Internet], 26, 12, 1013–4, 2022, Available from: https://www.sciencedirect.com/science/article/pii/S1364661322001863.
16. Liu, S., Wang, L., Gao, R.X., Cognitive neuroscience and robotics: Advancements and future research directions. *Robot. Comput. Integr. Manuf.* [Internet], 85, 102610, 2024, Available from: https://www.sciencedirect.com/science/article/pii/S0736584523000856.
17. Kok, A., Cognitive control, motivation and fatigue: A cognitive neuroscience perspective. *Brain Cogn.* [Internet], 160, 105880, 2022, Available from: https://www.sciencedirect.com/science/article/pii/S0278262622000380.
18. Chen, R.M., A rough-set and AI based approach for hierarchical cognitive processing of perceptions. *Appl. Soft Comput.* [Internet], 136, 110143, 2023, Available from: https://www.sciencedirect.com/science/article/pii/S1568494623001618.
19. Gopinath, N., Artificial intelligence and neuroscience: An update on fascinating relationships. *Process Biochem.* [Internet], 125, 113–20, 2023, Available from: https://www.sciencedirect.com/science/article/pii/S1359511322004512.
20. Liljenström, H., Review for Cognitive Systems Research of the book The Brain and AI, by authors Karl Schlagenhauf and Fanji Gu. *Cognit. Syst. Res.* [Internet], 64, 29–36, 2020, Available from: https://www.sciencedirect.com/science/article/pii/S1389041720300437.
21. Hasson, U. and Nusbaum, H.C., Emerging Opportunities for Advancing Cognitive Neuroscience. *Trends Cognit. Sci.* [Internet], 23, 5, 363–5, 2019, Available from: https://www.sciencedirect.com/science/article/pii/S1364661319300622.
22. Badrulhisham, F., Pogatzki-Zahn, E., Segelcke, D., Spisak, T., Vollert, J., Machine learning and artificial intelligence in neuroscience: A primer for researchers. *Brain Behav. Immun.* [Internet], 115, 470–9, 2024, Available from: https://www.sciencedirect.com/science/article/pii/S0889159123003380.
23. Wiese, W. and Friston, K.J., AI ethics in computational psychiatry: From the neuroscience of consciousness to the ethics of consciousness. *Behav. Brain Res.* [Internet], 420, 113704, 2022, Available from: https://www.sciencedirect.com/science/article/pii/S0166432821005921.
24. Visentini, G. and Andler, D., Psychanalyse et neurosciences cognitives. Un entretien avec Daniel Andler. *Anal.* [Internet], 5, 3, 222–36, 2021, Available from: https://www.sciencedirect.com/science/article/pii/S2542360621000743.
25. Astle, D.E., Johnson, M.H., Akarca, D., Toward computational neuroconstructivism: a framework for developmental systems neuroscience. *Trends Cognit. Sci.* [Internet], 27, 8, 726–44, 2023, Available from: https://www.sciencedirect.com/science/article/pii/S1364661323000992.
26. Ebner, N.C., Horta, M., El-Shafie, D., New directions for studying the aging social-cognitive brain. *Curr. Opin. Psychol.* [Internet], 56, 101768,

2024, Available from: https://www.sciencedirect.com/science/article/pii/S2352250X23002130.

27. Taniguchi, T., Yamakawa, H., Nagai, T., Doya, K., Sakagami, M., Suzuki, M. *et al.*, A whole brain probabilistic generative model: Toward realizing cognitive architectures for developmental robots. *Neural Netw.* [Internet], 150, 293–312, 2022, Available from: https://www.sciencedirect.com/science/article/pii/S0893608022000673.
28. Lindsay, G.W., Grounding neuroscience in behavioral changes using artificial neural networks. *Curr. Opin. Neurobiol.* [Internet], 84, 102816, 2024, Available from: https://www.sciencedirect.com/science/article/pii/S0959438823001411.
29. Baughman, N.R., Wilhelm, R.A., Spechler, P.A., McNaughton, B.A., Demuth, M.J., Lawrence, G.L. *et al.*, Cognitive control as a potential neural mechanism of protective role of spirituality in anxiety disorders among American Indian people: An ERP study. *Psychiatry Res. Neuroimaging* [Internet], 335, 111712, 2023, Available from: https://www.sciencedirect.com/science/article/pii/S0925492723001221.
30. Platek, S.M., Hasicic, A., Krill, A.L., Boldly going where no brain has gone: Futures of evolutionary cognitive neuroscience. *Futures* [Internet], 43, 8, 771–6, 2011, Available from: https://www.sciencedirect.com/science/article/pii/S0016328711001273.
31. Astle, D.E., Bassett, D.S., Viding, E., Understanding divergence: Placing developmental neuroscience in its dynamic context. *Neurosci. Biobehav. Rev.* [Internet], 157, 105539, 2024, Available from: https://www.sciencedirect.com/science/article/pii/S0149763424000071.
32. Richards, B., Tsao, D., Zador, A., The application of artificial intelligence to biology and neuroscience. *Cell* [Internet], 185, 15, 2640–3, 2022, Available from: https://www.sciencedirect.com/science/article/pii/S0092867422007991.
33. Dajani, D.R. and Uddin, L.Q., Demystifying cognitive flexibility: Implications for clinical and developmental neuroscience. *Trends Neurosci.* [Internet], 38, 9, 571–8, 2015, Available from: https://www.sciencedirect.com/science/article/pii/S016622361500154X.
34. Mumuni, F. and Mumuni, A., Improving deep learning with prior knowledge and cognitive models: A survey on enhancing explainability, adversarial robustness and zero-shot learning. *Cognit. Syst. Res.* [Internet], 84, 101188, 2024, Available from: https://www.sciencedirect.com/science/article/pii/S1389041723001225.
35. Jiang, Q., Lin, W., Pan, Y., Li, D., Wang, Q., The cognitive neural mechanism of trait anxiety influences mind wandering: An ERP study. *Neurosci. Lett.* [Internet], 822, 137648, 2024, Available from: https://www.sciencedirect.com/science/article/pii/S0304394024000259.
36. Lokare, V.T. and Jadhav, P.M., An AI-based learning style prediction model for personalized and effective learning. *Think. Skills Creat.* [Internet], 51,

101421, 2024, Available from: https://www.sciencedirect.com/science/article/pii/S187118712300189X.
37. Wien, A.H. and Peluso, A.M., Influence of human versus AI recommenders: The roles of product type and cognitive processes. *J. Bus. Res.* [Internet], 137, 13–27, 2021, Available from: https://www.sciencedirect.com/science/article/pii/S0148296321005774.
38. Garza-Ulloa, J., Chapter 7 - Cognitive learning and reasoning models applied to biomedical engineering, J. Garza-Ulloa and C.M. (Eds.), *Applied Biomedical Engineering Using Artificial Intelligence and Cognitive Models*, pp. 609–76 Academic Press, London, 2022, Available from: https://www.sciencedirect.com/science/article/pii/B9780128207185000052.
39. Kay, K., Bonnen, K., Denison, R.N., Arcaro, M.J., Barack, D.L., Tasks and their role in visual neuroscience. *Neuron* [Internet], 111, 11, 1697–713, 2023, Available from: https://www.sciencedirect.com/science/article/pii/S0896627323002180.
40. Stevens, F. and Taber, K., The neuroscience of empathy and compassion in pro-social behavior. *Neuropsychologia* [Internet], 159, 107925, 2021, Available from: https://www.sciencedirect.com/science/article/pii/S0028393221001767.
41. Hall, P.A., Burhan, A.M., MacKillop, J.C., Duarte, D., Next-generation cognitive assessment: Combining functional brain imaging, system perturbations and novel equipment interfaces. *Brain Res. Bull.* [Internet], 204, 110797, 2023, Available from: https://www.sciencedirect.com/science/article/pii/S0361923023002228.
42. Machado, P.M., Carmo, A.C.N., Leal, L.B.L.G., de Souza, R.P., Rocha, P.R.S., Funez, M.I., A systematic review of the added value of perioperative pain neuroscience education. *Patient Educ. Couns.* [Internet], 117, 107984, 2023, Available from: https://www.sciencedirect.com/science/article/pii/S0738399123003646.
43. Baker, B., Lansdell, B., Kording, K.P., Three aspects of representation in neuroscience. *Trends Cognit. Sci.* [Internet], 26, 11, 942–58, 2022, Available from: https://www.sciencedirect.com/science/article/pii/S1364661322002108.
44. Mohan, V., Bhat, A., Morasso, P., Muscleless motor synergies and actions without movements: From motor neuroscience to cognitive robotics. *Phys. Life Rev.* [Internet], 30, 89–111, 2019, Available from: https://www.sciencedirect.com/science/article/pii/S1571064518300587.
45. Watanabe, T., Chen, X., Yunoki, K., Matsumoto, T., Horinouchi, T., Ito, K. *et al.*, Differential Effects of Transcranial Static Magnetic Stimulation Over Left and Right Dorsolateral Prefrontal Cortex on Brain Oscillatory Responses During a Working Memory Task. *Neuroscience* [Internet], 517, 50–60, 2023, Available from: https://www.sciencedirect.com/science/article/pii/S0306452223001227.
46. Philippen, S., Hanert, A., Schönfeld, R., Granert, O., Yilmaz, R., Jensen-Kondering, U. *et al.*, Transcranial direct current stimulation of the right

temporoparietal junction facilitates hippocampal spatial learning in Alzheimer's disease and mild cognitive impairment. *Clin. Neurophysiol.* [Internet], 157, 48–60, 2024, Available from: https://www.sciencedirect.com/science/article/pii/S138824572300771X.

47. Eser, P., Kocabicak, E., Bekar, A., Temel, Y., Insights into neuroinflammatory mechanisms of deep brain stimulation in Parkinson's disease. *Exp. Neurol.* [Internet], 374, 114684, 2024, Available from: https://www.sciencedirect.com/science/article/pii/S0014488624000104.
48. Décarie-Spain, L., Hayes, A.M.R., Lauer, L.T., Kanoski, S.E., The gut-brain axis and cognitive control: A role for the vagus nerve. *Semin. Cell Dev. Biol.* [Internet], 156, 201–9, 2024, Available from: https://www.sciencedirect.com/science/article/pii/S1084952123000320.
49. Subramanian, S., Lopez, R., Zorumski, C.F., Cristancho, P., Electroconvulsive therapy in treatment resistant depression. *J. Neurol. Sci.* [Internet], 434, 120095, 2022, Available from: https://www.sciencedirect.com/science/article/pii/S0022510X21027970.
50. DuBreuil, D.M., Chiang, B.M., Zhu, K., Lai, X., Flynn, P., Sapir, Y. *et al.*, A high-content platform for physiological profiling and unbiased classification of individual neurons. *Cell Rep. Methods* [Internet], 1, 1, 100004, 2021, Available from: https://www.sciencedirect.com/science/article/pii/S2667237521000047.
51. Weber, L.A., Ethofer, T., Ehlis, A.C., Predictors of neurofeedback training outcome: A systematic review. *NeuroImage Clin.* [Internet], 27, 102301, 2020, Available from: https://www.sciencedirect.com/science/article/pii/S2213158220301388.
52. Mathias, B. and von Kriegstein, K., Enriched learning: behavior, brain, and computation. *Trends Cognit. Sci.* [Internet], 27, 1, 81–97, 2023, Available from: https://www.sciencedirect.com/science/article/pii/S1364661322002686.
53. Webler, R.D., Oathes, D.J., van Rooij, S.J.H., Gewirtz, J.C., Nahas, Z., Lissek, S.M. *et al.*, Causally mapping human threat extinction relevant circuits with depolarizing brain stimulation methods. *Neurosci. Biobehav. Rev.* [Internet], 144, 105005, 2023, Available from: https://www.sciencedirect.com/science/article/pii/S0149763422004948.
54. Chai, Y., Sheline, Y.I., Oathes, D.J., Balderston, N.L., Rao, H., Yu, M., Functional connectomics in depression: insights into therapies. *Trends Cognit. Sci.* [Internet], 27, 9, 814–32, 2023, Available from: https://www.sciencedirect.com/science/article/pii/S1364661323001237.
55. Chikhi, S., Matton, N., Sanna, M., Blanchet, S., Mental strategies and resting state EEG: Effect on high alpha amplitude modulation by neurofeedback in healthy young adults. *Biol. Psychol.* [Internet], 178, 108521, 2023, Available from: https://www.sciencedirect.com/science/article/pii/S0301051123000388.
56. Pagani, M., Gutierrez-Barragan, D., De Guzman, E., Gozzi, A., 2 - Resting state fMRI connectivity mapping across species: Challenges and

opportunities, in: *Neuroimaging Methods and Applications* [Internet], J. Chen, C.B.T.A. Chang, RSFMRI (Eds.), *Advances in Resting-State Functional MRI,* pp. 21–57, Academic Press, 2023, Available from: https://www.sciencedirect.com/science/article/pii/B9780323916882000096.

57. Tager, D., Panjeti-Moore, D., Yang, J.C., Rivera-Cruz, A., Loring, D.W., Staikova, E. *et al.*, The effect of responsive neurostimulation (RNS) on neuropsychiatric and psychosocial outcomes in drug-resistant epilepsy. *Epilepsy Behav.* [Internet], 142, 109207, 2023, Available from: https://www.sciencedirect.com/science/article/pii/S1525505023001269.
58. Zugliani, M.M., Fidry, M., Steffen, R.E., Lan, K., Brietzke, E., Milev, R. *et al.*, Clinical effectiveness of non-TMS neurostimulation in depression: Clinical trials from 2010 to 2020. *Prog. Neuro-Psychopharmacol. Biol. Psychiatry* [Internet], 110, 110287, 2021, Available from: https://www.sciencedirect.com/science/article/pii/S0278584621000464.
59. McIntyre, R.S., Lee, Y., Rodrigues, N.B., Nasri, F., Lao, G., Zeng, W. *et al.*, Repetitive transcranial magnetic stimulation for cognitive function in adults with bipolar disorder: A pilot study. *J. Affect. Disord.* [Internet], 293, 73–7, 2021, Available from: https://www.sciencedirect.com/science/article/pii/S016503272100519X.
60. Mamaril-Davis, J., Vessell, M., Ball, T., Palade, A., Shafer, C., Aguilar-Salinas, P. *et al.*, Combined Responsive Neurostimulation and Focal Resection for Super Refractory Status Epilepticus: A Systematic Review and Illustrative Case Report. *World Neurosurg.* [Internet], 167, 195–204.e7, 2022, Available from: https://www.sciencedirect.com/science/article/pii/S1878875022010956.
61. Neacsiu, A.D., Beynel, L., Graner, J.L., Szabo, S.T., Appelbaum, L.G., Smoski, M.J. *et al.*, Enhancing cognitive restructuring with concurrent fMRI-guided neurostimulation for emotional dysregulation–A randomized controlled trial. *J. Affect. Disord.* [Internet], 301, 378–89, 2022, Available from: https://www.sciencedirect.com/science/article/pii/S016503272200057X.
62. Grimaldi, D., Papalambros, N.A., Zee, P.C., Malkani, R.G., Neurostimulation techniques to enhance sleep and improve cognition in aging. *Neurobiol. Dis.* [Internet], 141, 104865, 2020, Available from: https://www.sciencedirect.com/science/article/pii/S0969996120301406.
63. Klooster, D.C.W., de Louw, A.J.A., Aldenkamp, A.P., Besseling, R.M.H., Mestrom, R.M.C., Carrette, S. *et al.*, Technical aspects of neurostimulation: Focus on equipment, electric field modeling, and stimulation protocols. *Neurosci. Biobehav. Rev.* [Internet], 65, 113–41, 2016, Available from: https://www.sciencedirect.com/science/article/pii/S0149763415301482.
64. Guerrero Moreno, J., Biazoli, C.E., Baptista, A.F., Trambaiolli, L.R., Closed-loop neurostimulation for affective symptoms and disorders: An overview. *Biol. Psychol.* [Internet], 161, 108081, 2021, Available from: https://www.sciencedirect.com/science/article/pii/S0301051121000740.

65. Bonifazi, G., Cauteruccio, F., Corradini, E., Marchetti, M., Terracina, G., Ursino, D. *et al.*, A model-agnostic, network theory-based framework for supporting XAI on classifiers. *Expert Syst. Appl.* [Internet], 241, 122588, 2024, Available from: https://www.sciencedirect.com/science/article/pii/S0957417423030907.
66. Bouazizi, S. and Ltifi, H., Enhancing accuracy and interpretability in EEG-based medical decision making using an explainable ensemble learning framework application for stroke prediction. *Decis. Support Syst.* [Internet], 178, 114126, 2024, Available from: https://www.sciencedirect.com/science/article/pii/S0167923623002014.
67. Saeed, W., Omlin, C., Explainable, A.I., (XAI): A systematic meta-survey of current challenges and future opportunities. *Knowl.-Based Syst.* [Internet], 263, 110273, 2023, Available from: https://www.sciencedirect.com/science/article/pii/S0950705123000230.
68. Borys, K., Schmitt, Y.A., Nauta, M., Seifert, C., Krämer, N., Friedrich, C.M. *et al.*, Explainable AI in medical imaging: An overview for clinical practitioners – Beyond saliency-based XAI approaches. *Eur. J. Radiol.* [Internet], 162, 110786, 2023, Available from: https://www.sciencedirect.com/science/article/pii/S0720048X23001006.
69. Jang, H., Kim, S., Yoon, B., An eXplainable, A.I., (XAI) model for text-based patent novelty analysis. *Expert Syst. Appl.* [Internet], 231, 120839, 2023, Available from: https://www.sciencedirect.com/science/article/pii/S0957417423013416.
70. Loring, D.W., Jarosiewicz, B., Meador, K.J., Kanner, A.M., Skarpaas, T.L., Morrell, M.J., Mood and quality of life in patients treated with brain-responsive neurostimulation: The value of earlier intervention. *Epilepsy Behav.* [Internet], 117, 107868, 2021, Available from: https://www.sciencedirect.com/science/article/pii/S1525505021001025.
71. Maran, M., Friederici, A.D., Zaccarella, E., Syntax through the looking glass: A review on two-word linguistic processing across behavioral, neuroimaging and neurostimulation studies. *Neurosci. Biobehav. Rev.* [Internet], 142, 104881, 2022, Available from: https://www.sciencedirect.com/science/article/pii/S0149763422003700.
72. Moseley, P., Fernyhough, C., Ellison, A., Auditory verbal hallucinations as atypical inner speech monitoring, and the potential of neurostimulation as a treatment option. *Neurosci. Biobehav. Rev.* [Internet], 37, 10, Part 2, 2794–805, 2013, Available from: https://www.sciencedirect.com/science/article/pii/S014976341300225X.
73. De Raedt, R., Vanderhasselt, M.A., Baeken, C., Neurostimulation as an intervention for treatment resistant depression: From research on mechanisms towards targeted neurocognitive strategies. *Clin. Psychol. Rev.* [Internet], 41, 61–9, 2015, Available from: https://www.sciencedirect.com/science/article/pii/S0272735814001524.

74. Deer, T.R., Mekhail, N., Provenzano, D., Pope, J., Krames, E., Thomson, S. *et al.*, The Appropriate Use of Neurostimulation: Avoidance and Treatment of Complications of Neurostimulation Therapies for the Treatment of Chronic Pain. *Neuromodulation Technol. Neural Interface* [Internet], 17, 6, 571–98, 2014, Available from: https://www.sciencedirect.com/science/article/pii/S1094715914601252.
75. Neacsiu, A.D., Beynel, L., Gerlus, N., LaBar, K.S., Bukhari-Parlakturk, N., Rosenthal, M.Z., An experimental examination of neurostimulation and cognitive restructuring as potential components for Misophonia interventions. *J. Affect. Disord.* [Internet], 350, 274–85, 2024, Available from: https://www.sciencedirect.com/science/article/pii/S0165032724001368.
76. Spagna, A., Hajhajate, D., Liu, J., Bartolomeo, P., Visual mental imagery engages the left fusiform gyrus, but not the early visual cortex: A meta-analysis of neuroimaging evidence. *Neurosci. Biobehav. Rev.* [Internet], 122, 201–17, 2021, Available from: https://www.sciencedirect.com/science/article/pii/S0149763420307041.
77. Hirjak, D., Meyer-Lindenberg, A., Fritze, S., Sambataro, F., Kubera, K.M., Wolf, R.C., Motor dysfunction as research domain across bipolar, obsessive-compulsive and neurodevelopmental disorders. *Neurosci. Biobehav. Rev.* [Internet], 95, 315–35, 2018, Available from: https://www.sciencedirect.com/science/article/pii/S0149763418302148.
78. Dolcos, F., Katsumi, Y., Moore, M., Berggren, N., de Gelder, B., Derakshan, N. *et al.*, Neural correlates of emotion-attention interactions: From perception, learning, and memory to social cognition, individual differences, and training interventions. *Neurosci. Biobehav. Rev.* [Internet], 108, 559–601, 2020, Available from: https://www.sciencedirect.com/science/article/pii/S0149763418310005.
79. Reh, R., Williams, L.J., Todd, R.M., Ward, L.M., Warped rhythms: Epileptic activity during critical periods disrupts the development of neural networks for human communication. *Behav. Brain Res.* [Internet], 399, 113016, 2021, Available from: https://www.sciencedirect.com/science/article/pii/S0166432820307154.
80. Garcia-Cairasco, N., Podolsky-Gondim, G., Tejada, J., Searching for a paradigm shift in the research on the epilepsies and associated neuropsychiatric comorbidities. From ancient historical knowledge to the challenge of contemporary systems complexity and emergent functions. *Epilepsy Behav.* [Internet], 121, 107930, 2021, Available from: https://www.sciencedirect.com/science/article/pii/S1525505021001645.
81. Rossetti, M.G., Delvecchio, G., Calati, R., Perlini, C., Bellani, M., Brambilla, P., Structural neuroimaging of somatoform disorders: A systematic review. *Neurosci. Biobehav. Rev.* [Internet], 122, 66–78, 2021, Available from: https://www.sciencedirect.com/science/article/pii/S014976342030693X.
82. Ferraro, S., Klugah-Brown, B., Tench, C.R., Bazinet, V., Bore, M.C., Nigri, A. *et al.*, The central autonomic system revisited – Convergent evidence

for a regulatory role of the insular and midcingulate cortex from neuroimaging meta-analyses. *Neurosci. Biobehav. Rev.* [Internet], 142, 104915, 2022, Available from: https://www.sciencedirect.com/science/article/pii/S0149763422004043.

83. Deuschl, G., Becktepe, J.S., Dirkx, M., Haubenberger, D., Hassan, A., Helmich, R.C. *et al.*, The clinical and electrophysiological investigation of tremor. *Clin. Neurophysiol.* [Internet], 136, 93–129, 2022, Available from: https://www.sciencedirect.com/science/article/pii/S1388245722000207.
84. Cecula, P., Yu, J., Dawoodbhoy, F.M., Delaney, J., Tan, J., Peacock, I. *et al.*, Applications of artificial intelligence to improve patient flow on mental health inpatient units - Narrative literature review. *Heliyon* [Internet], 7, 4, e06626, 2021, Available from: https://www.sciencedirect.com/science/article/pii/S2405844021007295.
85. Mattioli, F., Maglianella, V., D'Antonio, S., Trimarco, E., Caligiore, D., Non-invasive brain stimulation for patients and healthy subjects: Current challenges and future perspectives. *J. Neurol. Sci.* [Internet], 456, 122825, 2024, Available from: https://www.sciencedirect.com/science/article/pii/S0022510X23022876.
86. Sharma, H., Rani, T., Khan, S., An insight into neuropathic pain: a systemic and up-to-date review. *IJPSR*, 14, 2, 607–21, 2023.
87. Cimolato, A., Ciotti, F., Kljajić, J., Valle, G., Raspopovic, S., Symbiotic electroneural and musculoskeletal framework to encode proprioception via neurostimulation: ProprioStim. *iScience* [Internet], 26, 3, 106248, 2023, Available from: https://www.sciencedirect.com/science/article/pii/S2589004223003255.
88. Shlobin, N.A., Campbell, J.M., Rosenow, J.M., Rolston, J.D., Ethical considerations in the surgical and neuromodulatory treatment of epilepsy. *Epilepsy Behav.* [Internet], 127, 108524, 2022, Available from: https://www.sciencedirect.com/science/article/pii/S152550502100785X.
89. Perrin, A.J. and Pariante, C.M., Endocrine and immune effects of non-convulsive neurostimulation in depression: A systematic review. *Brain Behav. Immun.* [Internet], 87, 910–20, 2020, Available from: https://www.sciencedirect.com/science/article/pii/S0889159119314060.
90. Yan, H. and Ibrahim, G.M., Resective epilepsy surgery involving eloquent cortex in the age of responsive neurostimulation: A value-based decision-making framework. *Epilepsy Behav.* [Internet], 99, 106479, 2019, Available from: https://www.sciencedirect.com/science/article/pii/S1525505019306171.
91. Shlobin, N.A. and Rosenow, J.M., Ethical Considerations in the Implantation of Neuromodulatory Devices. *Neuromodulation Technol. Neural Interface* [Internet], 25, 2, 222–31, 2022, Available from: https://www.sciencedirect.com/science/article/pii/S1094715921069750.
92. Reed, K.L., Will, K.R., Conidi, F., Bulger, R., Concordant Occipital and Supraorbital Neurostimulation Therapy for Hemiplegic Migraine; Initial Experience; A Case Series. *Neuromodulation Technol. Neural Interface*

[Internet], 18, 4, 297–304, 2015, Available from: https://www.sciencedirect.com/science/article/pii/S1094715921017001.

93. Winter, Y., Sandner, K., Bassetti, C.L.A., Glaser, M., Ciolac, D., Ziebart, A. *et al.*, Vagus nerve stimulation for the treatment of narcolepsy. *Brain Stimul.* [Internet], 17, 1, 83–8, 2024, Available from: https://www.sciencedirect.com/science/article/pii/S1935861X24000020.
94. Ojemann, W.K.S., Scheid, B.H., Mouchtaris, S., Lucas, A., LaRocque, J.J., Aguila, C. *et al.*, Resting-state background features demonstrate multidien cycles in long-term EEG device recordings. *Brain Stimul.* [Internet], 16, 6, 1709–18, 2023, Available from: https://www.sciencedirect.com/science/article/pii/S1935861X23019484.
95. Stephens, J.A. and Berryhill, M.E., Older Adults Improve on Everyday Tasks after Working Memory Training and Neurostimulation. *Brain Stimul.* [Internet], 9, 4, 553–9, 2016, Available from: https://www.sciencedirect.com/science/article/pii/S1935861X16300511.
96. Gil-López, F., Boget, T., Manzanares, I., Donaire, A., Conde-Blanco, E., Baillés, E. *et al.*, External trigeminal nerve stimulation for drug resistant epilepsy: A randomized controlled trial. *Brain Stimul.* [Internet], 13, 5, 1245–53, 2020, Available from: https://www.sciencedirect.com/science/article/pii/S1935861X20301236.
97. Smyth, C., Anjum, M.F., Ravi, S., Denison, T., Starr, P., Little, S., Adaptive Deep Brain Stimulation for sleep stage targeting in Parkinson's disease. *Brain Stimul.* [Internet], 16, 5, 1292–6, 2023, Available from: https://www.sciencedirect.com/science/article/pii/S1935861X23018776.
98. Russo, R., Wallace, D., Fitzgerald, P.B., Cooper, N.R., Perception of Comfort During Active and Sham Transcranial Direct Current Stimulation: A Double Blind Study. *Brain Stimul.* [Internet], 6, 6, 946–51, 2013, Available from: https://www.sciencedirect.com/science/article/pii/S1935861X13001678.
99. Klein, E., Montes Daza, N., Dasgupta, I., MacDuffie, K., Schönau, A., Flynn, G. *et al.*, Views of stakeholders at risk for dementia about deep brain stimulation for cognition. *Brain Stimul.* [Internet], 16, 3, 742–7, 2023, Available from: https://www.sciencedirect.com/science/article/pii/S1935861X23017485.
100. Hogeveen, J., Grafman, J., Aboseria, M., David, A., Bikson, M., Hauner, K.K., Effects of High-Definition and Conventional tDCS on Response Inhibition. *Brain Stimul.* [Internet], 9, 5, 720–9, 2016, Available from: https://www.sciencedirect.com/science/article/pii/S1935861X16300912.
101. Faller, J., Doose, J., Sun, X., Mclntosh, J.R., Saber, G.T., Lin, Y. *et al.*, Daily prefrontal closed-loop repetitive transcranial magnetic stimulation (rTMS) produces progressive EEG quasi-alpha phase entrainment in depressed adults. *Brain Stimul.* [Internet], 15, 2, 458–71, 2022, Available from: https://www.sciencedirect.com/science/article/pii/S1935861X22000365.
102. Chaudhry, S.R., Lendvai, I.S., Muhammad, S., Westhofen, P., Kruppenbacher, J., Scheef, L. *et al.*, Inter-ictal assay of peripheral circulating inflammatory mediators in migraine patients under adjunctive cervical non-invasive

vagus nerve stimulation (nVNS): A proof-of-concept study. *Brain Stimul.* [Internet], 12, 3, 643–51, 2019, Available from: https://www.sciencedirect.com/science/article/pii/S1935861X19300397.
103. Wei, K., Luo, Y., Bai, Y., Chen, T., Bi, B., Toward a neurocircuit-based sequential bilateral transcranial magnetic stimulation for treatment of obsessive-compulsive disorder. *Brain Stimul.* [Internet], 16, 6, 1585–7, 2023, Available from: https://www.sciencedirect.com/science/article/pii/S1935861X2301940X.
104. Leahu, P., Bange, M., Ciolac, D., Scheiter, S., Matei, A., Gonzalez-Escamilla, G. *et al.*, Increased migraine-free intervals with multifocal repetitive transcranial magnetic stimulation. *Brain Stimul.* [Internet], 14, 6, 1544–52, 2021, Available from: https://www.sciencedirect.com/science/article/pii/S1935861X2100629X.
105. Badran, B.W., Gruber, E.M., O'Leary, G.H., Austelle, C.W., Huffman, S.M., Kahn, A.T. *et al.*, Electrical stimulation of the trigeminal nerve improves olfaction in healthy individuals: A randomized, double-blind, sham-controlled trial. *Brain Stimul.* [Internet], 15, 3, 761–8, 2022, Available from: https://www.sciencedirect.com/science/article/pii/S1935861X22000845.
106. Naro, A., Leo, A., Russo, M., Cannavò, A., Milardi, D., Bramanti, P. *et al.*, Does Transcranial Alternating Current Stimulation Induce Cerebellum Plasticity? Feasibility, Safety and Efficacy of a Novel Electrophysiological Approach. *Brain Stimul.* [Internet], 9, 3, 388–95, 2016, Available from: https://www.sciencedirect.com/science/article/pii/S1935861X16300195.
107. Powers, J.P. and LaBar, K.S., Regulating emotion through distancing: A taxonomy, neurocognitive model, and supporting meta-analysis. *Neurosci. Biobehav. Rev.* [Internet], 96, 155–73, 2019, Available from: https://www.sciencedirect.com/science/article/pii/S0149763418300368.
108. Hudson, V.E., Elniel, A., Ughratdar, I., Zebian, B., Selway, R., Lin, J.P., A comparative historical and demographic study of the neuromodulation management techniques of deep brain stimulation for dystonia and cochlear implantation for sensorineural deafness in children. *Eur. J. Paediatr. Neurol.* [Internet], 21, 1, 122–35, 2017, Available from: https://www.sciencedirect.com/science/article/pii/S1090379816301246.
109. Szabo, Y.Z., Burns, C.M., Lantrip, C., Understanding associations between rumination and inflammation: A scoping review. *Neurosci. Biobehav. Rev.* [Internet], 135, 104523, 2022, Available from: https://www.sciencedirect.com/science/article/pii/S0149763422000094.
110. Deer, T.R., Mekhail, N., Provenzano, D., Pope, J., Krames, E., Leong, M. *et al.*, The Appropriate Use of Neurostimulation of the Spinal Cord and Peripheral Nervous System for the Treatment of Chronic Pain and Ischemic Diseases: The Neuromodulation Appropriateness Consensus Committee. *Neuromodulation Technol. Neural Interface* [Internet], 17, 6, 515–50, 2014, Available from: https://www.sciencedirect.com/science/article/pii/S1094715914601239.

111. Yücel, M., Carter, A., Allen, A.R., Balleine, B., Clark, L., Dowling, N.A. *et al.*, Neuroscience in gambling policy and treatment: an interdisciplinary perspective. *Lancet Psychiatry* [Internet], 4, 6, 501–6, 2017, Available from: https://www.sciencedirect.com/science/article/pii/S2215036616303698.
112. Vitale, F., Gelinas, J.N., Cabrera, L.Y., Neurotechnology: Bridging the dialogue between engineers, material scientists, clinicians, and ethicists. *iScience* [Internet], 25, 11, 105432, 2022, Available from: https://www.sciencedirect.com/science/article/pii/S2589004222017047.
113. Hitti, F.L., Widge, A.S., Riva-Posse, P., Malone, D.A., Okun, M.S., Shanechi, M.M. *et al.*, Future directions in psychiatric neurosurgery: Proceedings of the 2022 American Society for Stereotactic and Functional Neurosurgery meeting on surgical neuromodulation for psychiatric disorders. *Brain Stimul.* [Internet], 16, 3, 867–78, 2023, Available from: https://www.sciencedirect.com/science/article/pii/S1935861X23017771.
114. Bell, E. and Racine, E., Chapter 26 - Ethics guidance for neurological and psychiatric deep brain stimulation, in: *Brain Stimulation* [Internet], A.M. Lozano, M.B.T.H. Hallett, C.N. (Eds.), *Handbook of Clinical Neurology*, pp. 313–25, Elsevier, 2013, Available from: https://www.sciencedirect.com/science/article/pii/B9780444534972000267.
115. Tolchin, B., Hirsch, L.J., LaFrance, W.C., Neuropsychiatric Aspects of Epilepsy. *Psychiatr. Clin. North Am.* [Internet], 43, 2, 275–90, 2020, Available from: https://www.sciencedirect.com/science/article/pii/S0193953X20300022.
116. Konsman, J.P., Expanding the notion of mechanism to further understanding of biopsychosocial disorders? Depression and medically-unexplained pain as cases in point. *Stud. Hist. Philos. Sci.* [Internet], 103, 123–36, 2024, Available from: https://www.sciencedirect.com/science/article/pii/S0039368123001693.
117. Szaflarski, J.P., Allendorfer, J.B., Goodman, A.M., Byington, C.G., Philip, N.S., Correia, S. *et al.*, Diagnostic delay in functional seizures is associated with abnormal processing of facial emotions. *Epilepsy Behav.* [Internet], 131, 108712, 2022, Available from: https://www.sciencedirect.com/science/article/pii/S1525505022001615.
118. Wittmann, M.K., Trudel, N., Trier, H.A., Klein-Flügge, M.C., Sel, A., Verhagen, L. *et al.*, Causal manipulation of self-other mergence in the dorsomedial prefrontal cortex. *Neuron* [Internet], 109, 14, 2353–2361.e11, 2021, Available from: https://www.sciencedirect.com/science/article/pii/S0896627321003809.
119. Matisz, C.E. and Gruber, A.J., Neuroinflammatory remodeling of the anterior cingulate cortex as a key driver of mood disorders in gastrointestinal disease and disorders. *Neurosci. Biobehav. Rev.* [Internet], 133, 104497, 2022, Available from: https://www.sciencedirect.com/science/article/pii/S0149763421005686.

120. Xu, L., Gong, H., Zhong, Y., Wang, F., Wang, S., Lu, L. *et al.*, Real-time monitoring of manual acupuncture stimulation parameters based on domain adaptive 3D hand pose estimation. *Biomed. Signal Process. Control* [Internet], 83, 104681, 2023, Available from: https://www.sciencedirect.com/science/article/pii/S1746809423001143.

3

Diagnostic and Surgical Uses of Explainable AI (XAI)

Roja Rani Budha[1], Saba Wahid A.M. Khan[1*], Tushar Lokhande[1], G.S.N. Koteswara Rao[2] and Shams Aaghaz[3]

[1]*H.K. College of Pharmacy, Oshiwara, Jogeshwari (W), Mumbai, Maharashtra, India*

[2]*Shobhaben Pratapbhai Patel School of Pharmacy and Technology Management, SVKM's NMIMS, Vile Parle (W), Mumbai, Maharashtra, India*

[3]*Baylor University, Waco, Texas, USA*

Abstract

In current years, the field of artificial intelligence (AI) has exhibited a significant impact potential in the view of medicine. Nevertheless, the implementation of AI in clinical applications is blocked by challenges associated with explainability. Particularly in techniques like deep learning, the inherent black-box nature of AI methods possesses difficulties in comprehending decision-making processes. Researchers have delved into the reality of explainable AI (XAI) to overcome this limitation, which offers dual insights into the model's rationale and decision-making capabilities. In this chapter, the current scenario in the combined effect of XAI in medical diagnosis and surgical applications is discussed. The focus of this discussion is to provide a valuable reference for medical professionals and AI scientists involved in the design and implementation of medical XAI applications. In domains like healthcare, the explainability and interpretability of machine learning and AI systems are foremost concerns. Reliance in the outcomes of these systems are significant, especially in medical field where errors can lead to severe consequences. Identifying the need for transparency, XAI has bloomed as a pivotal area of research in this medical domain. Its main objective is to unravel the intricacies of complex machine learning models, addressing the challenges possessed by their translucent nature. XAI algorithms such as Local Interpretable Model-Agnostic Explanations and SHapley Additive exPlanations machine learning models have gained prominence to build trust. These algorithms provide explanations for the

**Corresponding author*: khansabawahid@gmail.com; rojampharm@gmail.com

Rishabha Malviya and Sonali Sundram (eds.) Explainable and Responsible Artificial Intelligence in Healthcare, (65–88) © 2025 Scrivener Publishing LLC

black-box models that made prediction, offering perceptions into feature importance and building trust in the system's reliability. This study serves as a comprehensive versatility between machine learning, XAI, and medical applications; the main objective to contribute important insights to both medical professionals and AI researchers toward surgery and diagnosis is extensively reported. The scope of the AI in the surgery and diagnosis is also critically reviewed.

Keywords**:** Artificial intelligence, explainable AI, diagnostic uses, surgical uses, SHAP XAI, algorithms, deep learning, automated robots

List of Abbreviation

Age-Related Macular Degeneration	AMD
American Dental Education Association	ADEA
American Society of Anesthesiologists	ASA
Artificial Intelligence	AI
Artificial Neural Network	ANN
Augmented Reality	AR
Bilingual Evaluation Understudy	BLEU
Bone Mineral Density	BMD
Categorical Boosting	CatBoost
Class Activation Mapping	CAM
Clinical Decision Support	CDS
Computer-Aided Design	CAD
Computed Tomography	CT
Cone-Beam Computed Tomography	CBCT
Conference on Computer Vision and Pattern Recognition	CVPR
Coronavirus Disease 2019	COVID-19
Deep Convolutional Neural Networks	DCNNs
Deep Learning	DL
Deep Learning Important Features	LIFT
Deep Neural Network	DNN
Defense Advanced Research Projects Agency	DARPA
Diabetic Retinopathy	DR
Digital Image Processing	DCP
Dual-Energy Computed Tomography	DECT
Dual-Energy X-ray Absorptiometry	DEXA
Electronic Health Record	EHR
Empirical Methods in Natural Language Processing	EMNLP

European Conference on Computer Vision	ECCV
Explainable Artificial Intelligence	XAI
Explainable Neural Network	XNN
Expressive Gradients	EG
Generative Adversarial Network	GAN
Global Vectors for Word Representation	GloVe
Gradient Boosting Classifier	GBC
Gradient Boosting Machine	GBM
Gradient-Weighted Class Activation Mapping	Grad-CAM
Guided Backpropagation	GBP
Guided Smooth Inquire	GSInquire
Harris Hawks Optimization	HHO
Health Insurance Portability and Accountability Act	HIPAA
Hounsfield Units	HU
Integrated Gradients	IG
International Conference on Computer Vision	ICCV
International Conference on Image Processing	ICP
International Conference on Machine Learning	ICML
Layer-wise Relevance Propagation	LRP
Light Gradient Boosting Machine	LGBM
Local Interpretable Model-Agnostic Explanations	LIME
Long Short-Term Memory	LSTM
Machine Learning	ML
Magnetic Resonance Imaging	MRI
Medical Diagnosis Network	MDNet
Medical Image Computing and Computer Assisted Intervention	MICCAI
Natural Language Processing	NLP
Neural Network	NN
Optical Coherence Tomography	OCT
Oral and Maxillofacial Surgery	OMFS
Periodontal Screening Index	PSI
Random Forest	RF
Randomized Input Sampling for Explanation of Black-Box	Models RISE
Regions of Interest	ROIs
Responsible Artificial Intelligence	RAI
Scientific Explainable Artificial Intelligence	sXAI
Shapley Additive Explanations	SHAP
Standard Deviation	SD
Support Vector Machine	SVM

Temporomandibular Joint	TMJ
Testing with Concept Activation Vectors	TCAV
Ultrasound	US
Variational Autoencoder	VAE
Visual Question Answering	VQA
World Health Organization	WHO
X-radiation	X-ray

3.1 Introduction

In the field of artificial intelligence (AI) applied to medical system, a significant progress is currently seen. This progress has led to a spike in the implementation of AI in medical field with the objective of aiding healthcare professionals in their decision-making processes [1]. AI has found applications ranging from disease diagnosis among all the diverse medical domains [2] to surgical procedures [3]. However, the implementation of AI in medicine faces obstacles, notably originating from the opaque nature of certain AI models. The opacity in these models compromises trust among medical practitioners and difficulty in understanding the reasoning behind AI-generated decisions. Characterization of deep learning models by their vast number of parameters frequently produces final decisions without proper explanations, exacerbating the issue. Advancing the opacity of AI systems in medicine is essential to imbibe trust among healthcare providers. For medical AI to gain acceptance and become seamlessly integrated into clinical workflows, the implementation of opaque and interpretable AI systems through XAI methodologies is essential [4].

Creating copy of human-like intelligence in machines is associated with the AI in the field of computer science [5], allowing them to tackle problems and make decisions related to human cognition [5]. AI systems undergo training on extensive datasets to acquire task-solving capabilities, and this is valuable in circumstances such as COVID-19, in which it helps in identifying infections, subsequently by applying this learned knowledge to analyze new inputs and generate desired outcomes autonomously [7, 8]. Furthermore, AI-generated models showed comparable CT scans to that of the radiologists [9]. The arrival of deep learning, propelled by improvement in hardware technology, has driven AI into various applications, including expert systems, natural language processing (NLP), computer vision, and image classification [10]. As hardware toward neuromorphic designs evolved, struggling for energy efficiency related to the human brain [11], there is a continuous revolutionization of AI problem-solving and decision-making processes.

AI and XAI have made noteworthy struggle in offering solutions to complex challenges. XAI, in particular, addresses the critical need for opacity in AI models, removing the gap of trust between AI-generated results and clinicians. XAI facilitates the effortless combination of AI into human decision-making processes.

Healthcare includes a diverse field of activities, including diagnosis, prevention, and treatment of diseases. Clinicians often struggle with challenges associated with manually analyzing complex data, such as medical imagery from X-rays, MRI, CT scans, and ultrasounds. Beyond imagery, diagnosis extends to textual data analysis, incorporating the identification of mental health issues like depression [5–8]. Furthermore, prevention and treatment necessitate timely and accurate diagnoses, which can be expedited through the utilization of transparent and trustworthy AI models. AI and XAI hold significant potential in increasing the burdens associated with medical decision-making, thereby revolutionizing the practices of healthcare professional.

3.2 Uncertainty of CNN Model Prediction by Leveraging XAI

In recent scenario, noticeable effectiveness in different medical domain is observed from convolutional neural networks (CNNs). Despite this, it is vital to recognize the inherent uncertainty in CNN's forecasts to ensure trustworthy and dependable outcome. This segment explores the critical significance of CNN models that account for uncertainty in the medical and healthcare industry.

A novel CNN model that is cognizant of uncertainty carried out by Gour *et al.* is noteworthy to understand. In this domain, identifying the utmost significance of uncertainty estimation, the authors have formulated an all-encompassing framework that not only places attention at the forefront but also measures the degree of uncertainty connected to each forecast. By involving uncertainty into the model, their principal objective is to provide medical practitioners with results that are more dependable and understandable.

In 2021, Shamsi *et al.* published a perceptive research article. Focusing on the difficulties presented by the shortage of data, the authors' expertise employs transfer learning methodologies to advance the model performance. The primary aim is to provide healthcare professionals with thorough information, as well as accurate and precise diagnosis regarding the uncertainties that may associated with those diagnoses.

The predictions made by CNN models are inherently uncertain due to a multiple of factors like complex characteristics of medical data; another noticeable feature that could increase is due to significant divergent identified during the training.

Ensemble methods, Monte Carlo dropout, and Bayesian neural network advanced models are used to identify the level of uncertainty. It is capable of producing numerous predictions or probability distributions, which, in turn, include ultimate prediction and indication of uncertainty.

In summary, the involvement of CNN model studies aids for the collaborative endeavors that seek classification. Incorporating uncertainty-aware advanced methodologies while maintaining the integrity and openness of their prognostications can effectively utilize CNN models.

3.3 Algorithms of XAI Techniques

3.3.1 Interpretable AI of LIME (Local Interpretable Model-Agnostic Explanations)

Significant innovation in explainable AI (XAI) is presented by LIME by Ribeiro *et al.* in 2016 [12]. To interpret factors contributing to a single prediction specific by machine learning (ML), the core principle involves approximating the behavior of the original complex model within a more interpretable model, customized for the prediction under scrutiny.

The versatility of LIME renders it suitable for diverse models. Notably, LIME deliberately focuses on individual predictions, coupled with its seamless integration with various models.

3.3.2 Enhanced Interpretability with SHAP (SHapley Additive exPlanations)

In response to the challenge of model interpretability, Lundberg *et al.* introduced SHAP, a pioneering methodology aimed at unifying XAI [13]. SHAP seeks to assist researchers in understanding the internal mechanisms of AI models.

Operating within the complex domain of XAI, SHAP assigns features, elucidating the significance of each feature in the context of a specific prediction. This approach facilitates the identification of crucial factors influencing a prediction, transcending the constraints of model intricacies and types.

Its effectiveness extends to scenarios involving multifaceted features, where SHAP's ability to unravel complex relationships and offer nuanced insights sets it apart from alternative methodologies.

3.3.3 Enlightening Deep Learning Insights with CAM (Class Activation Mapping)

Interpretability requirements of deep learning–based computer vision models CAM are specially used to meet the desired requirement [14], specifically crafted for the intricacies of computer vision tasks.

CAM's utility extends beyond computer vision to encompass medical imaging, where its elucidative prowess enhances the better understanding and enhanced decision making progress.

3.3.4 Grad-CAM (Gradient-Weighted Class Activation Mapping)

To enhance interpretability for complex predictions from deep learning models, Grad-CAM is used [15] in circumstances such as high-resolution images. This technique combines gradient and visual analysis and significant insights to deep learning.

3.3.5 Counterfactual Explanations

Counterfactual explanations, termed as "what-if" explanations, offer insights into the outcomes of AI or ML algorithms by analyzing alternative scenarios [16].

Counterfactual explanations help in identifying influential features and factors driving predictions by systematically altering input features and observing resulting changes in output. Particularly in automated decision-making systems, this approach fosters a deeper understanding of model decision-making processes.

3.3.6 Anchors

ML algorithms implicates important feature by anchor rule-based explanations [17]. By identifying minimal sets of conditions guaranteeing specific predictions, anchors offer intuitive and accessible explanations for individual predictions.

Generation of concise "if-then" rules is focused by anchors. This localized approach enhances understanding without delving into overall model behavior.

3.3.7 Influence Functions

The impact of individual training samples or parameters on model outcomes is quantified by influence functions and statistical tools [18]. By measuring sensitivity to changes in training data, influence functions identify influential training examples, shaping model behavior.

Analyzing the derivatives of model prediction because of the changes in individual training will enable the computation of influence functions and reveal the impact of each example on model behavior, offering valuable insights into decision-making processes.

These techniques collectively contributing to provide transparent and understandable.

3.4 Need for Using XAI

Superior accuracy is achieved by deep learning–based models compared to those conducted by human doctors. A growing consensus among experts among AI and healthcare suggests that the explainability of an AI model holds a greater significance than its accuracy for practical implementation in clinical practice. Therefore, a thorough comprehension of the functioning of medical AI applications is essential before their adoption and deployment. Consequently, there is a pressing need to conduct comprehensive surveys of medical XAI, as the transparency provided by XAI is indispensable for the acceptance of AI applications in the field of medicine [19].

3.4.1 Applications

Different applications of XAI techniques and SHAP XAI algorithms discussion are presented in Tables 3.1 and 3.2 respectively.

Table 3.1 Applications of XAI techniques (algorithms) [20–22].

Anatomical location	Modality	Main XAI technique employed
Bladder	Histology	CAM
Brain	MRI	CAM
Cardiovascular	X-ray	Grad-CAM
Dental	X-ray	Grad-CAM
Female reproductive system	Histology	Grad-CAM

Table 3.2 SHAP XAI algorithms discussion—literature [23, 24].

Disease of chronic obstructive pulmonary	Gradient boosting machine (GBM)	The study here focused on essential attributes to the GBM model, which indicates the influence of each feature on a prediction, based on their average absolute GBM.
Prediction of COVID-19	XGboost model, RF, LGBM, gradient boosting classifier (GBC), and categorical boosting (CatBoost)	To optimize the hyperparameters of several state-of-the-art classifiers, such as HHO-RF, HHOXGB, and HHO-LGB, as well as ensemble techniques, with the aim of enhancing classification accuracy, Harris Hawks Optimization (HHO) method is utilized.
Prioritization of COVID-19 vaccine	Random Forest, XGBoost classifiers, and XAI	CovidXAI employs XGBoost classifiers and random forest to forecast an individual's risk group.

3.4.2 Application of Artificial Intelligence (AI) in Surgery [25]

1. Preoperative Planning

Objective:
The objective of preoperative planning is to ensure accuracy, privacy, and speed in surgical procedures.

Challenges:
Preoperative planning—multimodal input integration, complex symptomatology, and limited diagnostic data with reduced informativeness.

Sub-areas:
This domain encompasses classification, detection, segmentation, and registration techniques.

2. Guidance to intraoperative

Objective:
Intraoperative guidance aims to provide real-time, high-precision assistance during surgical procedures.

Challenges:
The challenges associated with intraoperative guidance include visual acceptability issues and environmental variations.

Sub-areas:
Sub-fields include 3D shape instantiation and endoscopic navigation.

3. Surgical Robots

Objective:
The aim of surgical robotics is to deliver real-time, precise, and robust performance during surgical interventions.

Challenges:
The challenges in surgical robotics revolve around achieving accurate kinematic and dynamic modeling to ensure optimal functionality.

Sub-areas:
Key areas within surgical robotics encompass robot perception.

3.5 Scope of AI Surgery [25]

Scope of AI surgery during preoperative, intraoperative stages with their ethical and legal issues are presented in Table 3.3.

Table 3.3 Scope of surgery.

Preoperative planning	**Intraoperative guidance**	**Surgical robot**	**Ethical and legal issues**
Enhanced through the availability of extensive public datasets for training deep convolutional neural networks (DCNNs)	Transition from static image displays to dynamic visualization of organ function	Continued development toward more flexible, lightweight, and economical robotic systems	Emphasis on protecting patient privacy and securing sensitive medical data in AI-driven healthcare environments

(Continued)

Table 3.3 Scope of surgery. (*Continued*)

Preoperative planning	Intraoperative guidance	Surgical robot	Ethical and legal issues
Federated learning meta-learning and explainable AI	Integration of advanced augmented reality	Advancement in robot autonomy to enhance surgical precision and efficiency	Implementation of support systems to address potential failures in AI during surgery, ensuring continuity of care
Utilization of multimodal information for timely identification and intervention in medical conditions	Facilitated communication and cooperation among multidisciplinary teams for complex surgical procedures	Nanorobots: Exploration of nanoscale devices for precise diagnosis and targeted drug delivery in healthcare applications	Establishment of trust between patients and AI systems to ensure ethical use and decision-making

3.5.1 AI/ML Applications Across Surgical Specialties

The integration of AI/ML paradigms is poised to revolutionize preoperative risk assessment across surgical disciplines due to their capacity to swiftly process vast datasets. By analyzing patient data encompassing factors such as weight, vital signs, comorbidities, and more, sophisticated algorithms can predict preoperative risk levels accurately. This predictive capability not only enables the identification of potential risks but also facilitates the formulation of tailored strategies to mitigate them effectively [4, 15].

Categorizing by specific surgical procedures and clinical contexts and incorporating large data sets, this approach advances in precision medicine by precise risk stratification, receiving objective preoperative risk assessments, and inputting patient-specific data [20].

Recent studies have significantly focused in diverse ranging from identifying and predicting complications of cardiac preoperatively to estimate different intervention risk–benefit ratios These techniques work better when properly designed and implemented, hence facilitating risk assessment and preparation for adverse outcomes post-surgery, with ongoing advancements with the objective at increasing their predictive accuracy [21–24].

Furthermore, preoperative risk assessment with ML analysis of radiologic imaging shows significant promise, showing a comparable performance to expert radiologists [20, 24].

The differentiation of cancer subtypes is enabled by radiomics based on distinctive imaging features, enabling more accurate tailored and prognostication management strategies [25].

Based on patient characteristics, prediction of waitlist mortality and post-transplant results is significantly impacted by AI-driven algorithms. These algorithms enhance patient outcome by optimizing organ allocation and recipient matching. Additionally, ML models can minimize complications associated with graft size mismatch and estimate graft weight [26].

3.5.2 Intraoperative Surgical Decision-Making

Because AI/ML algorithms excel in preoperative risk assessment, their greatest potential lies in enhancing intraoperative care. ML algorithms also hold potential in classifying complex disease states like increasing decision-making by providing insights into optimal treatment strategies, frailty, or sepsis [27].

Moreover, AI-driven algorithms can identify patterns associated with adverse outcomes during surgery, enabling proactive interventions to mitigate risks and optimize patient care. By increasing ML training on large datasets by led by experts, these algorithms for surgical teams contribute to improved patient outcomes by advancing decision-making support [28–31].

Minimizing delays in diagnosis and enhancing surgical precision can optimize intraoperative pathology and histology determination. Interpretation of histology, potentially improving outcomes in oncologic surgeries and other procedures requiring intraoperative tissue analysis, can be utilized by computer vision algorithm [32–36].

3.5.3 Advancement of Minimally Invasive Surgery and Laparoscopic

Additionally, combination of surgery offers opportunities to enhance procedural efficiency and accuracy. Identifying critical anatomical landmarks and surgical outcomes and reducing the risk of complications can be improved by use of real-time image processing that can improve laparoscopic visibility [37].

Orthopedic and neurosurgical procedures are benefitted by AI with augmented reality (AR). By overlaying 3D models, AR-guided surgery is advanced, derived from preoperative imaging onto the surgical field, potentially revolutionizing surgical navigation and precision [38].

3.5.3.1 Surgical Education

Enhancement in medical education, particularly in the field of surgery, holds potential due to AR technology. AR facilitates engrossing learning experiences in anatomy and surgical procedures utilizing head-mounted devices. In the future, reducing cognitive load and enhancing sustained practice sessions AR may allow surgeons to practice various techniques. AR could serve as a valuable educational tool, allow surgeons to manipulate personalized organ models derived from patient data, and serve as an educational tool within the operating room [39].

Machine learning (ML) algorithms are near to revolutionizing surgical education by tailoring learning experiences to individual students' proficiency levels. Algorithms can generate learning curves, predicting the number of trials needed for each student to attain proficiency in specific surgical tasks by analyzing students' performance data. Additionally, ML can address the current lack of objective assessments of surgical proficiency and dexterity and targeted feedback on specific skills [40].

Recent advancements in computer vision technology enable video-based learning with certain limitation and accurate identification of distinct surgical phases, allowing for rapid retrieval of specific stages for review. AI-driven algorithms enhance the effectiveness of surgical education and skill development by providing actionable insights into surgical proficiency [40].

3.5.3.2 Postoperative Risk Assessment

By analyzing pre- and perioperative data alongside intraoperative variables, AI models can accurately predict postoperative outcomes, enabling proactive interventions to mitigate risks. ML and AI technologies offer hopeful prospects for postoperative risk assessment. Facilitating prompt adjustments to treatment plans involving these predictive models into electronic health records (EHRs) can synchronize patient care by delivering mobile alerts to physicians [41].

Additionally, ML models excel in addressing concerns regarding opioid overuse and addiction, predicting postoperative pain management needs. Although further validation is warranted, these models grip a significant potential in optimizing strategies of postoperative pain management [42].

Additionally, ML algorithms offer a novel approach to providing objective insights into patients' functional outcomes following surgery and postoperative gait analysis. Leveraging computer vision technology, future ML algorithms may enhance the accuracy and efficiency of gait analysis, enabling stratification of patients based on their postoperative functional recovery and identifying those at higher risk of recurrent issues or falls [42, 43].

3.5.4 Autonomous Robots and Artificial Intelligence

The evolution of AI applications promises significant advancements in surgical outcomes, yet the most transformative breakthroughs are anticipated through the development of autonomous robots. Presently, surgical machines predominantly fall within levels 0 or 1, which require direct operator control. However, there are emerging applications at level 2, where robots offer some degree of autonomy, such as autonomous suturing. While current automatons are limited to simple tasks, experiments demonstrate potential for higher-level autonomy, as seen in successful phantom tissue experiments like tissue ablation and small bowel anastomosis. Future autonomous robots are envisioned to integrate various sensory modalities, including computer vision and tactile feedback, to execute complex surgical tasks autonomously.

As AI complexity increases, so does the intricacy of training methods, particularly in visual-based learning. Three primary learning methods exist. However, its applicability in surgery is hindered by challenges in generalizing behaviors across diverse surgical environments. Reinforcement learning, on the other hand, relies on trial-and-error, allowing the agent to update actions based on outcomes. While powerful, it requires numerous trials for optimization and poses risks in real surgical settings. Transfer learning offers a solution by training agents in simulated environments and transferring knowledge to real-world scenarios. Despite challenges in discordance between simulation and reality, improvements in simulation quality and adaptive policies enhance transfer learning outcomes. By leveraging transfer learning models, autonomous surgical robots of the future are poised to navigate complex surgical tasks with adaptability and efficiency [44–49]. Different studies on automated robots are presented in Table 3.4.

Table 3.4 Studies on automated robots.

Studied algorithm	Findings	Reference
Automation	A self-governing robotic system equipped with computer vision capabilities and an automated suturing algorithm demonstrated proficiency in performing suturing procedures on both *ex vivo* and live porcine tissue samples.	Shademan *et al.* [50]
Automation	An autonomous robot employing computer vision algorithms achieved the creation of a 3D surgical cavity.	Hu *et al.* [51]
Automation	A proprioceptive stretch sensor made of liquid metal successfully reconstructed the deformation of soft actuators in real time.	Tapia *et al.* [45]
Automation	The primary methods for instructing autonomous robots include deep reinforcement learning.	Hua *et al.* [46]
Automation	Utilizing machine learning via primitive imitation resulted in enhanced performance.	Rivera *et al.* [48]
Automation	While imitation learning algorithms demonstrate considerable efficacy in ideal scenarios, reinforcement learning proves more advantageous when the dataset contains ample noise and encompasses diverse learning policies and tasks.	Kumar *et al.* [52]
Automation	A reinforcement learning algorithm was employed to develop a program with the ability to learn and enhance performance across chess, shogi, and Go.	Silver *et al.* [44]
Automation	Transfer learning algorithms that leverage pre-learned skill latents have demonstrated successful application in accomplishing novel tasks, such as drawing and object pushing.	He *et al.* [47]

3.6 Limitations and Concerns

While AI holds significant potential to revolutionize, it is crucial to acknowledge its limitations. The development of ML algorithms heavily relies on large datasets to create generalizable models, requiring substantial annotation, manpower, and time for both training and test datasets. Furthermore, ML algorithms may exhibit biases inherent in the input data, potentially leading to disproportionate outcomes for underrepresented groups due to biases in clinical trial participation. Additionally, minute fluctuations in input data or poor data quality can significantly impact model performance, emphasizing the importance of standardizing imaging techniques and data quality for efficacy [52–57].

Deliberate manipulation of input data can bias outputs and compromise model integrity. Additionally, the risk of adversarial attacks poses a significant concern. AI usage involves implementing oversight and liability frameworks, as current regulations lack governing bodies for reviewing approval processes. ML algorithms in clinical care, particularly in autonomous surgery settings present a significant threat due to adversarial attacks [58].

In deep learning algorithms, the "black-box" effect in further complicates matters. Legal considerations, including liability issues, are paramount, with a devoid of precedent in case law related to legality of AI in clinical settings having significant challenges. AI recommendations diverge from established standards of care, potentially discouraging widespread adoption Physicians may face increased liability risks [59, 60].

Additionally, data privacy concerns arise, especially in cloud-based or crowd-sourced data storage scenarios, necessitating clear delineation of medicolegal terms, data ownership, and monetization policies for each AI application while safeguarding patient rights and ensuring ethical and legal compliance. Addressing these complex challenges is essential to realizing the full potential of AI in healthcare [61, 62].

3.7 Conclusion and Future Implications for Surgeons and Future Perspective

Algorithms helps in identifying risk for patient and hence making surgeries safer option for patients [63]. The need for human-human interaction and surgeon patient relationship is not vanished with AI [64].

Total dependency on AI can lead to less skilled healthcare professional and may lead to allowance of mistake made by algorithms [65].

During surgery, AI can significantly aid in anesthetic evaluations to detect abnormalities before clinical signs appear and hold promise for surgical tasks such as identifying, classifying, and visualizing anatomical structures. Moreover, AI algorithms have demonstrated utility in predicting bleeding risks both during and after surgery. AI can also contribute to postoperative pain evaluation, diagnostics, and planning of postoperative care [66–77].

AI can support the development of diagnostic and treatment decision support systems, aiding in recommending best practices and streamlining the diagnostic and treatment processes [78–87].

Future advancements in robotics will address current limitations, aiming for smaller designs to enhance versatility, particularly in single-port and natural orifice surgeries. Microbots, operated via external electromagnetic fields, offer potential for untethered use within delicate spaces like the vitreous. Haptic feedback, currently limited in surgical robots, is expected to improve significantly in future iterations, along with enhanced visual feedback, including the use of fluorophores. AI-powered robots may assist in specific surgical tasks, allowing surgeons to focus on critical aspects, although fully autonomous surgical robots are not foreseeable in the near term [88–95].

Telemedicine, including robotic surgery, can extend healthcare accessibility, particularly in underserved areas, with AI supporting patient care delivery. These platforms can provide personalized, interactive learning experiences and real-time feedback, complementing traditional teaching methods rather than replacing them entirely [96–100].

Ensuring competency is crucial in surgical training, with AI offering valuable resources for knowledge and skill development. However, defining and measuring competency, especially with AI integration, requires attention, as does fostering the right attitude and willingness to learn among surgical learners. Modern curricula should embrace AI as a tool with extensive potential.

In summary, AI holds promise for improving patient care by enhancing surgical training. Systematic analysis of current literature and careful consideration of large datasets are necessary to leverage AI effectively. While AI augments cognitive abilities, it should be used judiciously, complementing human learning rather than replacing it entirely.

References

1. Alloghani, M., Al-Jumeily, D., Aljaaf, A.J., Khalaf, M., Mustafina, J., Tan, S.Y., The application of artificial intelligence technology in healthcare: a systematic review. *Commun. Comput. Inf. Sci.*, 1174, 248–61, 2020.
2. Loh, E., Medicine and the rise of the robots: a qualitative review of recent advances of artificial intelligence in health. *BMJ Lead.*, 2, 59–63, 2018.
3. Zhou, X., Guo, Y., Shen, M., Yang, G.-Z., Application of artificial intelligence in surgery. *Front. Med.*, 14, 417–30, 2020.
4. Adadii, A. and Mohammed, B., Peeking inside the black-box: a survey on explainable artificial intelligence (XAI). *IEEE Access*, 6, 52138–60, 2018.
5. William, D. and Suhartono, D., Text-based depression detection on social media posts: a systematic literature review. *Procedia Comput. Sci.*, 179, 582–9, 2021.
6. Havigerová, J.M., Haviger, J., Kučera, D., Hoffmannová, P., Text-based detection of the risk of depression. *Front. Psychol.*, 10, 513, 2019.
7. Al Hanai, T., Ghassemi, M.M., Glass, J.R., Detecting depression with audio/text sequence modeling of interviews, in: *Interspeech*, pp. 1716–20, 2018.
8. Ye, J., Yu, Y., Wang, Q., Li, W., Liang, H., Zheng, Y. *et al.*, Multi-modal depression detection based on emotional audio and evaluation text. *J. Affect Disord.*, 295, 904–13, 2021.
9. Rathod, P. and Naik, S., Review on epilepsy detection with explainable artificial intelligence, in: *10th International Conference on Emerging Trends in Engineering and Technology-Signal and Information Processing (ICETET-SIP-22)*, pp. 1–6, IEEE, 2022.
10. Miró-Nicolau, M., Moyà-Alcover, G., Jaume-i-Capó, A., Evaluating explainable artificial intelligence for X-ray image analysis. *Appl. Sci.*, 12, 9, 4459, 2022.
11. Yang, C.C., Explainable artificial intelligence for predictive modeling in healthcare. *J. Healthc. Inform. Res.*, 6, 2, 228–39, 2022.
12. Ribeiro, M.T., Singh, S., Guestrin, C., "Why should I trust you?" Explaining the predictions of any classifier, in: *Proceedings of the 22nd ACM SIGKDD International Conference on Knowledge Discovery and Data Mining*, pp. 1135–44, 2016.
13. Lundberg, S.M. and Lee, S.I., A unified approach to interpreting model predictions, in: *Advances in neural information processing systems*, vol. 30, 2017.
14. Zhou, B., Khosla, A., Lapedriza, A., Oliva, A., Torralba, A., Learning deep features for discriminative localization, in: *Proceedings of the IEEE conference on computer vision and pattern recognition*, pp. 2921–29, 2016.
15. Selvaraju, R.R., Cogswell, M., Das, A., Vedantam, R., Parikh, D., Batra, D., Grad-CAM: visual explanations from deep networks via gradient-based localization, in: *Proceedings of the IEEE international conference on computer vision*, pp. 618–26, 2017.

16. Wachter, S., Mittelstadt, B., Russell, C., Counterfactual explanations without opening the black box: automated decisions and the GDPR. *Harv. JL Tech.*, 31, 841, 2017.
17. Ribeiro, M.T., Singh, S., Guestrin, C., Anchors: high-precision model-agnostic explanations, in: *Proceedings of the AAAI conference on artificial intelligence*, vol. 32, no. 1, 2018.
18. Koh, P.W. and Liang, P., Understanding black-box predictions via influence functions, in: *International conference on machine learning*, pp. 1885–94, 2017.
19. Nazar, M., Alam, M.M., Yafi, E., Mazliham, M.S., A systematic review of human-computer interaction and explainable artificial intelligence in health.
20. Hashimoto, D.A., Rosman, G., Rus, D., Meireles, O.R., Artificial intelligence in surgery: promises and perils. *Ann. Surg.*, 268, 1, 70–76, 2018.
21. Loftus, T.J. *et al.*, Artificial intelligence and surgical decision-making. *JAMA Surg.*, 155, 2, 148–58, 2020.
22. Pereira, S.S., Guimarães, M., Monteiro, M.P., Towards precision medicine in bariatric surgery prescription. *Rev. Endocr. Metab. Disord.*, 24, 961–77, 2023 2023.
23. Topart, P., Obesity surgery: which procedure should we choose and why? *J. Visc. Surg.*, 160, 2, S30–7, 2023.
24. Bihorac, A. *et al.*, MySurgeryRisk: development and validation of a machine-learning risk algorithm for major complications and death after surgery. *Ann. Surg.*, 269, 4, 652, 2019.
25. Koçak, B., Durmaz, E.Ş., Ateş, E., Kılıçkesmez, Ö., Radiomics with artificial intelligence: a practical guide for beginners. *Diagn. Interv. Radiol.*, 25, 6, 485, 2019.
26. Guijo-Rubio, D., Gutiérrez, P.A., Hervás-Martínez, C., Machine learning methods in organ transplantation. *Curr. Opin. Organ. Transplant.*, 25, 4, 399–405, 2020.
27. Loftus, T.J., Upchurch, G.R., Bihorac, A., Use of artificial intelligence to represent emergent systems and augment surgical decision-making. *JAMA Surg.*, 154, 9, 791–792, 2019.
28. Yang, Q., Steinfeld, A., Zimmerman, J., Unremarkable AI: Fitting intelligent decision support into critical, clinical decision-making processes, in: *Proceedings of the 2019 CHI Conference on Human Factors in Computing Systems*, Association for Computing Machinery Special Interest Group on Computer-Human Interaction in Glasgow, Scotland, UK, pp. 1–11, 2019.
29. Stawicki, S., *Fundamentals of Patient Safety in Medicine and Surgery*, Wolters Kluwer (India) Pvt. Ltd, New Delhi, India, 2015.
30. Laessig, M.A. *et al.*, Potential implementations of blockchain technology in patient safety: A high-level overview, in: *Blockchain in Healthcare: From Disruption to Integration*, pp. 117–140, Springer, Cham, Switzerland, 2023.
31. Pappada, S.M. *et al.*, Evaluation of a model for glycemic prediction in critically ill surgical patients. *PLoS One*, 8, 7, e69475, 2013.

32. Barth, N. and Seamon, M.J., Situation awareness in patient safety, in: *Fundamentals of Patient Safety in Medicine and Surgery*, vol. 15, p. 105, 2015.
33. Komorowski, M., Celi, L.A., Badawi, O., Gordon, A.C., Faisal, A.A., The artificial intelligence clinician learns optimal treatment strategies for sepsis in intensive care. *Nat. Med.*, 24, 11, 1716–1720, 2018.
34. Ehrmann, D.E. *et al.*, Evaluating and reducing cognitive load should be a priority for machine learning in healthcare. *Nat. Med.*, 28, 7, 1331–1333, 2022.
35. De Melo, C.M., Kim, K., Norouzi, N., Bruder, G., Welch, G., Reducing cognitive load and improving warfighter problem solving with intelligent virtual assistants. *Front. Psychol.*, 11, 554706, 2020.
36. Lee, L.W., Dabirian, A., McCarthy, I.P., Kietzmann, J., Making sense of text: Artificial intelligence-enabled content analysis. *Eur. J. Mark.*, 54, 615–644, 2020.
37. Ofli, F. *et al.*, Combining human computing and machine learning to make sense of big (aerial) data for disaster response. *Big Data*, 4, 1, 47–59, 2016.
38. Xia, W., Chen, E., Pautler, S., Peters, T., Laparoscopic image enhancement based on distributed retinex optimization with refined information fusion. *Neurocomputing*, 483, 460–473, 2022.
39. Ruiz-Fernández, D., Galiana-Merino, J.J., de Ramón-Fernández, A., Vives-Boix, V., Enríquez-Buendía P. A DCP-based method for improving laparoscopic images. *J. Med. Syst.*, 44, 1–9, 2020.
40. Peden, R.G., Mercer, R., Tatham, A.J., The use of head-mounted display eyeglasses for teaching surgical skills: A prospective randomised study. *Int. J. Surg.*, 34, 169–173, 2016.
41. Barteit, S., Lanfermann, L., Bärnighausen, T., Neuhann, F., Beiersmann, C., Augmented, mixed, and virtual reality-based head-mounted devices for medical education: Systematic review. *JMIR Serious Games*, 9, 3, e29080, 2021.
42. Cao, Z., Simon, T., Wei, S.-E., Sheikh, Y., Realtime multi-person 2D pose estimation using part affinity fields, in: *Proceedings of the IEEE Conference on Computer Vision and Pattern Recognition*, Honolulu, HI, USA, pp. 7291–7299, IEEE, 2017.
43. Chen, B. *et al.*, Computer vision and machine learning-based gait pattern recognition for fall prediction. *Sensors*, 22, 20, 7960, 2022.
44. Silver, D. *et al.*, A general reinforcement learning algorithm that masters chess, shogi, and go through self-play. *Science*, 362, 6419, 1140–1144, 2018.
45. Tapia, J., Knoop, E., Mutný, M., Otaduy, M.A., Bächer, M., Makesense: Automated sensor design for proprioceptive soft robots. *Soft Rob.*, 7, 3, 332–345, 2020.
46. Hua, J., Zeng, L., Li, G., Ju, Z., Learning for a robot: Deep reinforcement learning, imitation learning, transfer learning. *Sensors*, 21, 4, 1278, 2021.
47. He, Z. *et al.*, Zero-shot skill composition and simulation-to-real transfer by learning task representations, arXiv, vol. abs/1810.02422, 2018.

48. Rivera, C., Popek, K.M., Ashcraft, C., Staley, E.W., Katyal, K.D., Paulhamus, B.L., Learning generalizable behaviors from demonstration. *Front. Neurorobot.*, 16, 932652, 2022.
49. Saeidi, H. *et al.*, Autonomous robotic laparoscopic surgery for intestinal anastomosis. *Sci. Robot.*, 7, 62, eabj2908, 2022.
50. Shademan, A., Decker, R.S., Opfermann, J.D., Leonard, S., Krieger, A., Kim, P.C., Supervised autonomous robotic soft tissue surgery. *Sci. Transl. Med.*, 8, 337, 337ra64, 2016.
51. Hu, D., Gong, Y., Seibel, E.J., Sekhar, L.N., Hannaford, B., Semi-autonomous image-guided brain tumour resection using an integrated robotic system: A bench-top study. *Int. J. Med. Robot. Comput. Assist. Surg.*, 14, 1, e1872, 2018.
52. Kumar, A., Hong, J., Singh, A., Levine, S., When should we prefer offline reinforcement learning over behavioral cloning? arXiv, 2022, abs/2204.05618.
53. Khalsa, R.K., Khashkhusha, A., Zaidi, S., Harky, A., Bashir, M., Artificial intelligence and cardiac surgery during COVID-19 era. *J. Card. Surg.*, 36, 5, 1729–1733, 2021.
54. Rampat, R. *et al.*, Artificial intelligence in cornea, refractive surgery, and cataract: Basic principles, clinical applications, and future directions. *Asia-Pac. J. Ophthalmol. (Phila)*, 10, 3, 268, 2021.
55. Murphy, D. and Saleh, D., Artificial intelligence in plastic surgery: What is it? Where are we now? What is on the horizon? *Ann. R. Coll. Surg. Engl.*, 102, 8, 577–580, 2020.
56. Crawford, K. and Calo, R., There is a blind spot in AI research. *Nature*, 538, 7625, 311–313, 2016.
57. Wang, D.D. *et al.*, 3D printing, computational modeling, and artificial intelligence for structural heart disease. *Cardiovasc. Imaging*, 14, 1, 41–60, 2021.
58. Biggio, B. and Roli, F., Wild patterns: Ten years after the rise of adversarial machine learning, in: *Proceedings of the 2018 ACM SIGSAC Conference on Computer and Communications Security*, Association for Computing Machinery, New York, NY, USA, pp. 2154–2156, 2018.
59. Gumbs, A.A. *et al.*, Artificial intelligence surgery: How do we get to autonomous actions in surgery? *Sensors*, 21, 16, 5526, 2021.
60. Cutillo, C.M. *et al.*, Machine intelligence in healthcare—Perspectives on trustworthiness, explainability, usability, and transparency. *npj Digital Med.*, 3, 1, 47, 2020.
61. Pecqueux, M. *et al.*, The use and future perspective of artificial intelligence—A survey among German surgeons. *Front. Public Health*, 10, 982335, 2022.
62. Price, W.N., Gerke, S., Cohen, I.G., Potential liability for physicians using artificial intelligence. *JAMA*, 322, 18, 1765–1766, 2019.
63. Bahl, M., Barzilay, R., Yedidia, A.B., Locascio, N.J., Yu, L., Lehman, C.D., High-risk breast lesions: A machine learning model to predict pathologic upgrade and reduce unnecessary surgical excision. *Radiology*, 286, 3, 810–818, 2018.

64. Hashimoto, D.A., Witkowski, E., Gao, L., Meireles, O., Rosman, G., Artificial intelligence in anesthesiology: Current techniques, clinical applications, and limitations. *Anesthesiology*, 132, 2, 379–394, 2020.
65. Myers, T.G., Ramkumar, P.N., Ricciardi, B.F., Urish, K.L., Kipper, J., Ketonis, C., Artificial intelligence and orthopaedics: An introduction for clinicians. *J. Bone Joint Surg. Am.*, 102, 9, 830, 2020.
66. Bedrikovetski, S., Dudi-Venkata, N.N., Kroon, H.M., Seow, W., Vather, R., Carneiro, G., Moore, J.W., Sammour, T., Artificial intelligence for preoperative lymph node staging in colorectal cancer: A systematic review and meta-analysis. *BMC Cancer*, 21, 1058, 2021.
67. Feng, Y., Wang, Z., Cui, R., Xiao, M., Gao, H., Bai, H., Delvoux, B., Zhang, Z., Dekker, A., Romano, A. *et al.*, Clinical analysis and artificial intelligence survival prediction of serous ovarian cancer based on preoperative circulating leukocytes. *J. Ovarian Res.*, 15, 64, 2022.
68. Xue, B., Li, D., Lu, C., King, C.R., Wildes, T., Avidan, M.S., Kannampallil, T., Abraham, J., Use of machine learning to develop and evaluate models using preoperative and intraoperative data to identify risks of postoperative complications. *JAMA Netw. Open*, 4, e212240, 2021.
69. Zhang, H., Wang, A.Y., Wu, S., Ngo, J., Feng, Y., He, X., Zhang, Y., Wu, X., Hong, D., Artificial intelligence for the prediction of acute kidney injury during the perioperative period: Systematic review and meta-analysis of diagnostic test accuracy. *BMC Nephrol.*, 23, 405, 2022.
70. Hashimoto, D.A., Witkowski, E., Gao, L., Meireles, O., Rosman, G., Artificial intelligence in anesthesiology: Current techniques, clinical applications, and limitations. *Anesthesiology*, 132, 379–394, 2020.
71. Matava, C., Pankiv, E., Ahumada, L., Weingarten, B., Simpao, A., Artificial intelligence, machine learning and the pediatric airway. *Paediatr. Anaesth.*, 30, 264–268, 2020.
72. Wijnberge, M., Geerts, B.F., Hol, L., Lemmers, N., Mulder, M.P., Berge, P., Schenk, J., Terwindt, L.E., Hollmann, M.W., Vlaar, A.P. *et al.*, Effect of a machine learning-derived early warning system for intraoperative hypotension vs standard care on depth and duration of intraoperative hypotension during elective noncardiac surgery: The HYPE randomized clinical trial. *JAMA*, 323, 1052–1060, 2020.
73. Lee, S., Lee, H.C., Chu, Y.S., Song, S.W., Ahn, G.J., Lee, H., Yang, S., Koh, S.B., Deep learning models for the prediction of intraoperative hypotension. *Br. J. Anaesth.*, 126, 808–817, 2021.
74. Carson, T., Ghoshal, G., Cornwall, G.B., Tobias, R., Schwartz, D.G., Foley, K.T., Artificial Intelligence-enabled, Real-time Intraoperative Ultrasound Imaging of Neural Structures Within the Psoas: Validation in a Porcine Spine Model. *Spine*, 46, E146–E152, 2021.
75. Massalimova, A., Timmermans, M., Esfandiari, H., Carrillo, F., Laux, C.J., Farshad, M., Denis, K., Fürnstahl, P., Intraoperative tissue classification

methods in orthopedic and neurological surgeries: A systematic review. *Front. Surg.*, 9, 952539, 2022.
76. Zhou, S., Zhou, F., Sun, Y., Chen, X., Diao, Y., Zhao, Y., Huang, H., Fan, X., Zhang, G., Li, X., The application of artificial intelligence in spine surgery. *Front. Surg.*, 9, 885599, 2022.
77. Lonsdale, H., Jalali, A., Ahumada, L., Matava, C., Machine Learning and Artificial Intelligence in Pediatric Research: Current State, Future Prospects, and Examples in Perioperative and Critical Care. *J. Pediatr.*, 221S, S3–S10, 2020.
78. Chen, D., Afzal, N., Sohn, S., Habermann, E.B., Naessens, J.M., Larson, D.W., Liu, H., Postoperative bleeding risk prediction for patients undergoing colorectal surgery. *Surgery*, 164, 1209–1216, 2018.
79. Huang, R.S., Nedelcu, E., Bai, Y., Wahed, A., Klein, K., Tint, H., Gregoric, I., Patel, M., Kar, B., Loyalka, P., Post-operative bleeding risk stratification in cardiac pulmonary bypass patients using artificial neural network. *Ann. Clin. Lab. Sci.*, 45, 181–186, 2015.
80. Fontaine, D., Vielzeuf, V., Genestier, P., Limeux, P., Santucci-Sivilotto, S., Mory, E., Darmon, N., Lanteri-Minet, M., Mokhtar, M., Laine, M. *et al.*, Artificial intelligence to evaluate postoperative pain based on facial expression recognition. *Eur. J. Pain*, 26, 1282–1291, 2022.
81. Lotsch, J., Ultsch, A., Mayer, B., Kringel, D., Artificial intelligence and machine learning in pain research: A data scientometric analysis. *Pain Rep.*, 7, e1044, 2022.
82. Bian, Y., Xiang, Y., Tong, B., Feng, B., Weng, X., Artificial Intelligence-Assisted System in Postoperative Follow-up of Orthopedic Patients: Exploratory Quantitative and Qualitative Study. *J. Med. Internet Res.*, 22, e16896, 2020.
83. Obata, S., Ichiyama, Y., Kakinoki, M., Sawada, O., Saishin, Y., Ito, T., Tomioka, M., Ohji, M., Prediction of postoperative visual acuity after vitrectomy for macular hole using deep learning-based artificial intelligence. *Graefe's Arch. Clin. Exp. Ophthalmol.*, 260, 1113–1123, 2022.
84. Chidambaram, S., Sounderajah, V., Maynard, N., Markar, S.R., Diagnostic Performance of Artificial Intelligence-Centred Systems in the Diagnosis and Postoperative Surveillance of Upper Gastrointestinal Malignancies Using Computed Tomography Imaging: A Systematic Review and Meta-Analysis of Diagnostic Accuracy. *Ann. Surg. Oncol.*, 29, 1977–1990, 2022.
85. Stam, W.T., Goedknegt, L.K., Ingwersen, E.W., Schoonmade, L.J., Bruns, E.R.J., Daams, F., The prediction of surgical complications using artificial intelligence in patients undergoing major abdominal surgery: A systematic review. *Surgery*, 171, 1014–1021, 2022.
86. Hemachandran, K., Verma, P., Pareek, P., Arora, N., Rajesh Kumar, K.V., Ahanger, T.A., Audumbar Pise, A., Ratna, R., Artificial Intelligence: A Universal Virtual Tool to Augment Tutoring in Higher Education. *Comput. Intell. Neurosci.*, 2022, 1410448, 2022.

87. Troussas, C., Krouska, A., Kabassi, K., Sgouropoulou, C., Cristea, A.I., Editorial: Artificial intelligence techniques for personalized educational software. *Front. Artif. Intell.*, 5, 988289, 2022.
88. Chaudhry, M.A. and Kazim, E., Artificial Intelligence in Education (AIEd): A high-level academic and industry note 2021. *AI Ethics*, 2, 157–165, 2022.
89. Park, J.J., Tiefenbach, J., Demetriades, A.K., The role of artificial intelligence in surgical simulation. *Front. Med. Technol.*, 4, 1076755, 2022.
90. Bhandari, M., Zeffiro, T., Reddiboina, M., Artificial intelligence and robotic surgery: Current perspective and future directions. *Curr. Opin. Urol.*, 30, 48–54, 2020.
91. Yang, J.H., Goodman, E.D., Dawes, A.J., Gahagan, J.V., Esquivel, M.M., Liebert, C.A., Kin, C., Yeung, S., Gurland, B.H., Using AI and computer vision to analyze technical proficiency in robotic surgery. *Surg. Endosc.*, 37, 4, 3010–3017, 2023.
92. Nema, S. and Vachhani, L., Surgical instrument detection and tracking technologies: Automating dataset labeling for surgical skill assessment. *Front. Robot. AI*, 9, 1030846, 2022.
93. Zhao, B., Waterman, R.S., Urman, R.D., Gabriel, R.A., A Machine Learning Approach to Predicting Case Duration for Robot-Assisted Surgery. *J. Med. Syst.*, 43, 32, 2019.
94. Loftus, T.J., Tighe, P.J., Filiberto, A.C., Efron, P.A., Brakenridge, S.C., Mohr, A.M., Rashidi, P., Upchurch, G.R., Jr, Bihorac, A., Artificial Intelligence and Surgical Decision-making. *JAMA Surg.*, 155, 148–158, 2020.
95. Alip, S.L., Kim, J., Rha, K.H., Han, W.K., Future Platforms of Robotic Surgery. *Urol. Clin. N. Am.*, 49, 23–38, 2022.
96. Ullrich, F., Bergeles, C., Pokki, J., Ergeneman, O., Erni, S., Chatzipirpiridis, G., Pané, S., Framme, C., Nelson, B.J., Mobility experiments with microrobots for minimally invasive intraocular surgery. *Investig. Ophthalmol. Vis. Sci.*, 54, 2853–2863, 2013.
97. Jamjoom, A.A.B., Jamjoom, A.M.A., Thomas, J.P., Palmisciano, P., Kerr, K., Collins, J.W., Vayena, E., Stoyanov, D., Marcus, H.J., iRobotSurgeon Collaboration. Autonomous surgical robotic systems and the liability dilemma. *Front. Surg.*, 9, 1015367, 2022.
98. Li, J., Yang, X., Chu, G., Feng, W., Ding, X., Yin, X., Zhang, L., Lv, W., Ma, L., Sun, L. *et al.*, Application of Improved Robot-assisted Laparoscopic Telesurgery with 5G Technology in Urology. *Eur. Urol.*, 83, 41–44, 2023.
99. Egert, M., Steward, J.E., Sundaram, C.P., Machine Learning and Artificial Intelligence in Surgical Fields. *Ind. J. Surg. Oncol.*, 11, 573–577, 2020.
100. Vohra, P., khan, S. *et al.*, Artificial Intelligence: A Manifested Leap in Psychiatric Rehabilitation. *Int. J. Pharm. Biol. Arch.*, 14, 4, 143–150, 2023.

4

Osteoporosis Risk Assessment and Individualized Feature Analysis Using Interpretable XAI and RAI Techniques

Shivam Rajput[1], Rishabha Malviya[1]* and Sathvik Belagodu Sridhar[2]

[1]Department of Pharmacy, School of Medical and Allied Sciences, Galgotias University, Greater Noida, Uttar Pradesh, India
[2]Department of Clinical Pharmacy and Pharmacology, RAK College of Pharmacy, RAK Medical and Health Sciences University, Ras Al Khaimah, United Arab Emirates

Abstract
"Osteoporosis," an important health issue, is marked by a drop in bone mineral density (BMD) and a higher risk of breaking a bone. The use of medical imaging techniques, like computed tomography (CT) scanning, has led to new ways to test for and identify osteoporosis. Mostly in the form of clinical decision support systems that help doctors make better decisions, artificial intelligence (AI) is being used more and more in the healthcare business. In addition to accurately finding and locating lesions through magnetic resonance imaging, it is their job to analyze the data that radiologists and pathologists give them. Many people think of AI as a mysterious technology that makes them doubt how reliable it is, which is a major cause for worry. When one choice could mean the difference between someone's life and death, the level of worry is much higher. Recently, there has been a lot of talk about responsible AI (RAI) and explainable AI (XAI). Both XAI and RAI want to set ethical standards for AI to make sure that people can understand AI algorithms and their effects. The goal of RAI is to create AI that is ethical, open, and responsible throughout all of its stages, such as creation, deployment, and use. The main goal is to make healthcare outcomes more clear and understandable while also reducing discrimination and promoting ethical ideals of fairness and justice. Still, the ongoing research into health AI raises important moral and social questions that apply to the field of RAI as a whole. At times when sensitive

**Corresponding author*: rishabhamalviya19@gmail.com

Rishabha Malviya and Sonali Sundram (eds.) Explainable and Responsible Artificial Intelligence in Healthcare, (89–114) © 2025 Scrivener Publishing LLC

problems come up and lives are at stake, this is a lot more of a worry than when it is not related to health. So, it is very important to do a full review of health AI that follows the rules for RAI. This chapter will look at the big picture of AI in healthcare, with a focus on osteoporosis. This chapter will talk about how XAI and RAI help in giving clear outlines to important ideas.

***Keywords*:** XAI, RAI, artificial intelligence, osteoporosis, biomarkers, fragility fracture

4.1 Introduction

Osteoporosis causes bone mineral density (BMD) to drop and bone tissue structure to break down. This makes bones more likely to break and become weak [1]. Research [2] shows that 23.1% of women and 11.7% of men around the world had osteoporosis in 2021. There were big differences in how common osteoporosis was in different countries [3]. Fragility fractures are the main problem that can happen because of osteoporosis. They have high rates of both death and illness [4, 5]. A lot of research has already shown that major osteoporotic fractures have important effects on the body, mind, society, and the economy [6]. Independence goes down, costs for health care go up, death rates go up, and quality of life goes down [7, 8]. Finding osteoporotic fractures and the problems that they cause early on can help make prevention and treatment plans work better [9, 10].

The World Health Organization (WHO) says that dual-energy X-ray absorption (DEXA) is a common way to measure BMD and diagnose osteoporosis [11]. DEXA scans can be used to turn BMD numbers into T-scores. The BMD of the person is divided by the BMD of the reference group to get this value. Following that, it is split by the group mean's standard deviation (SD) [12]. A T-score of −2.5 or less means that someone has osteoporosis, whereas a T-score between −1.0 and −2.5 means that an individual has osteopenia [13].

Even though DEXA is widely used as a cheap and painless way to measure bone mass [14], there are some important issues that need to be addressed [15]. One problem is that DEXA can only find BMD [16], and reports of low screening rates [17] have been made. Another problem is that a flat method, which only works in two dimensions [18], makes it hard to figure out BMD and estimate the risk of fracture. Also, changes that happen over time may change DEXA data, which could lead to an overestimation of BMD [19]. Other things that might affect BMD tests are structural or surface changes on the bone, like atherosclerosis [20], metallic devices, or problems that happen after a laminectomy [21].

One radiographic method for reliably determining BMD is dual-energy computed tomography DECT. BMD evaluation using DECT was initially investigated over 40 years ago [22]. As X-rays pass through bone, they get weaker, but DECT can detect this. Because attenuation is density dependent, DECT may measure the BMD of a targeted region by capturing images on multiple energy levels [23].

With DECT, the microstructure of trabecular bone may be studied with great precision because of how well it differentiates between cortical and trabecular bone. This investigation involves the examination of specific local characteristics, such as the spacing and connectivity of trabeculae. The thorough evaluation of bone health significantly depends on these crucial attributes [24]. One drawback of DECT's unique diagnostic capabilities is the higher radiation dose that it produces, which has limited its potential for osteoporosis screening [25]. Moreover, an in-scan calibration phantom is usually required [26], which can be troublesome when employed for routine BMD measurements in computed tomography (CT) scans performed for purposes other than BMD evaluation [27] or for evaluating BMD retrospectively [28].

Potentially replacing DEXA and DECT scans with CT scans alone to assess BMD is one upcoming development. This has various significant implications in the field of medicine. To begin with, it enables the display of both quantitative data and anatomical visualizations at the same time [29]. People who have had CT scans for regular checkups or other medical reasons may also be able to undergo automated evaluations [30]. A complete CT database could also be used to find people who might need to be referred or treated [30]. Last but not least, this approach may reduce expenses [31] and radiation exposure [32] because patients would not need further radiological testing for osteoporosis diagnosis and treatment.

Attenuation or radiodensity values [in Hounsfield Units (HUs)] at various locations on the CT scans were positively correlated with the corresponding BMD values from DEXA scans acquired as early as 2013 [33], which served as the foundation for the BMD values obtained from CT scans. Later studies confirmed that trabecular HU values from CT scans can be used to diagnose osteoporosis [34]. Due to limitations in computational resources, human intervention, and other factors, the majority of research have relied on manual or semi-automatic segmentation approaches, which have their advantages but also their disadvantages, such as being time-consuming [35].

Artificial intelligence (AI) technology has recently emerged, and it can be applied to identify and classify osteoporosis using ML and DL models. These utilizations include the prediction of osteoporosis risk [37] and the evaluation of risk of fracture [38]. The complex processing of CT images has been made easier with the use of AI, which has also improved automatic segmentation [39]. BMD has been measured and put into groups using this method in many studies [40–42]. It is possible to look at a lot of quantitative data that is taken from medical pictures like CT scans using radiomics. By revealing tiny features that cannot be seen with the naked eye, these traits help in gaining a deeper understanding of the basic traits of tissue. The trabecular bone structure in CT scans has been looked at by mixing deep learning (DL), texture analysis, and radiomics. Using this method instead of just DEXA or optical readings gives a lot more useful information about the bone's microstructure and health. This makes it easier to find people who have osteoporosis [43, 44]. There have been many studies that try to classify or identify osteoporosis using AI. However, these studies often have problems, like only including a few patients or only using AI in one medical facility. These studies also lack practical clinical validation.

4.2 Responsible Artificial Intelligence (RAI)

RAI, which is a relatively new field of study, looks into the moral issues that come up with new technologies. The main focus of this study is on the moral effects of AI [45]. Because many people do not understand important problems related to AI, RAI has become necessary. New research and examples from real life have brought attention to the unintended effects of AI, which include biases, mistakes, revelations that were not predicted, and prejudices. Because the process was not clear, these effects came about [46]. It is very important to set the right AI standards in healthcare settings [47] because the data is private and there are big responsibilities that come with it. The goals of RAI include reducing bias, promoting fairness, making results easier to understand and more open, and guaranteeing that the system is strong and safe. Human ideals and morals should be followed so that these goals can be reached more easily [68]. As long as responsible principles are followed, the main goal of AI growth should be to keep people and society from suffering severe damage [48].

The ways that AI can be used in healthcare are greatly limited by these problems. An example of AI being used in healthcare is the collection and study of large amounts of clinical data to help with decision-making, personalized treatment, and evaluation. AI, known as "artificial intelligence," is a system's capacity to learn and adapt to new situations by analyzing data, understanding it, drawing conclusions, and acquiring new information [49]. If AI is ethically incorporated and employed in healthcare, then it has the capacity to greatly improve the welfare of individuals involved in providing care. While AI has many potential benefits, it is also capable of making ethically inappropriate decisions that compromise ethical standards and infringe upon human rights and dignity [50]. Several recent research studies have brought attention to the moral questions raised by AI. Individuals or patients, who can be seen as "walking data generators," typically lack awareness regarding the utilization, objectives, and users of their medical data [51, 52]. The integration of AI in the field of healthcare presents notable constraints pertaining to equity, accountability, and protection of human rights. Moreover, it has the capacity to lead to unparalleled levels of exclusion from essential public services [52, 53].

However, the growing utilization of AI in healthcare gives rise to concerns over the implementation and acceptance of RAI practices that currently lack a unified and integrated area of research. Investigating the theoretical foundations of ethical AI in healthcare helps researchers map out their future studies and promotes collaboration on knowledge creation [54].

4.3 Explainable Artificial Intelligence (XAI)

AI is an area of science and technology that focuses on making computers smart enough to do things that normally require human intelligence, like understanding what they see, making decisions, recognizing speech, and translating languages [55]. Machine learning (ML), DL, and neural networks (NN) are all forms of AI. Many fields make use of AI, including econometrics for stock market trend prediction, biometry for face recognition, e-commerce for recommendation systems, and the automotive sector for self-driving automobiles. Biomedicine [56] and healthcare [57] are two areas that use AI more and more. With its aid, specialists will be able to filter through vast data sets in pursuit of greater precision medicine [58] and improved patient care [59]. AI programs have the potential to greatly improve medical decision-making in numerous ways, including providing clinical decision support (CDS), assisting with the detection of cancer in magnetic resonance (MR) pictures, and analyzing reports authored by radiologists and pathologists, among numerous others. It may soon be easier to generate reports that people can readily understand by utilizing generative AI and NLP technologies, particularly Chat Generative Pre-trained Transformer (ChatGPT) [60].

Nevertheless, there exist several obstacles that impede the efficient utilization of AI in the healthcare sector. The initial category is referred to as "small" data, which leads to a biased outcome [61]. Findings from studies conducted on homogeneous populations may not be generalizable to patients with varying characteristics. Avoiding bias in trial design and creating datasets with larger and more diverse patient populations are the most direct routes to fixing this problem. Another obstacle arises in the form of privacy and security concerns. Tough laws like the European General Data Protection Regulation, Health Insurance Portability and Accountability Act (HIPAA) in the US, and the Chinese Personal Information Protection Law limit how personal data can be used and make it illegal to share it without permission. People who do this will face harsh punishments. Using global or federated learning is one way to solve these problems. The way can be used to both get data and send it to a central repository. It is best not to send the information to anyone else to protect privacy and safety [62]. Another choice to think about is synthetic data, which can be made from raw materials or used as a base for data that already exists. Usually, advanced AI methods like Generative Adversarial Networks [63] are used to do this. Another problem is that medical workers and patients may not have a lot of faith in AI systems. They can be regarded as an enigmatic entity: input is provided, and output is produced, without comprehension of the internal processes. In a field where a decision could affect the patient's life or death, the lack of trust in AI algorithms, their accuracy, and reliability is a major worry. A potential solution to this ambiguity is the concept of XAI [64], which has been gaining popularity. The goal of XAI is to make algorithms and the results that they generate understandable to humans.

4.4 Key Principles of Explainable Artificial Intelligence (XAI)

4.4.1 Transitioning from a "Black Box" to a "(Translucent) Glass Box"

The objective of XAI is to reframe AI as a transparent and comprehensible "glass box" (sometimes referred to as a "white box") rather than an enigmatic and incomprehensible "black box" [65, 66]. The decision-making process is completely transparent in glass box models like decision trees or linear regressions, where all parameters are explicitly defined. Ideally, the model is entirely transparent. However, in specific cases, such as with DL models, the model may possess just partial explicability. This can be compared to a "translucent glass box" that has a variable level of opacity, ranging from 0% to 100%. Increased transparency in the model's glass box can improve understanding and potentially promote better trust. Researchers propose that trust can be classified into two tiers: confidence in the model and reliance on the forecast. There are a lot of people with varying information demands in the healthcare industry [67]. Users, who are typically clinicians but can also be patients, pay greater attention to the model's predictions than data scientists do. However, confidence in data scientists primarily concerns the reliability and accuracy of the model, whereas confidence in physicians and patients mostly concerns the dependability and accuracy of its forecasts. In order to tackle the matter of "placing trust in a prediction," one can provide justifications for each specific forecast. Alternatively, in order to address the issue of "trusting the model," one can opt for many predictions (along with their reasons) [B18]. Additional research can pinpoint when each of these two methods is most appropriate.

4.4.2 Explainability: Transparent or *Post-Hoc*

Studies on XAI have been categorized into two methods by researchers. While some studies focus on constructing transparent models (Figure 4.1) [68], most research aims at upgrading black-box models with an extra layer of explainability, which are dubbed *post-hoc* models. The transparent models are constructed using a variety of methods, including k-nearest neighbors, rule-based learning, general additive models, logistic or linear regression, decision trees, and Bayesian models. Because of their intrinsic comprehensibility, these models are thought of as transparent. Neural networks, random forests, and DL are just a few of the methods that can make *post-hoc* models more understandable. The approaches encompassed in this set include offering textual explanations, visual explanations, explanations localized to a specific context, explanations through the use of examples, explanations achieved by simplification, and ways for clarifying the relevance of features. Researchers have formulated four principles to delineate XAI systems: (1) Explainability: AI systems that are explainable offer corroborating evidence or rationales for their results and procedures. (2) Clarity: These explanations should be easily comprehensible to individual

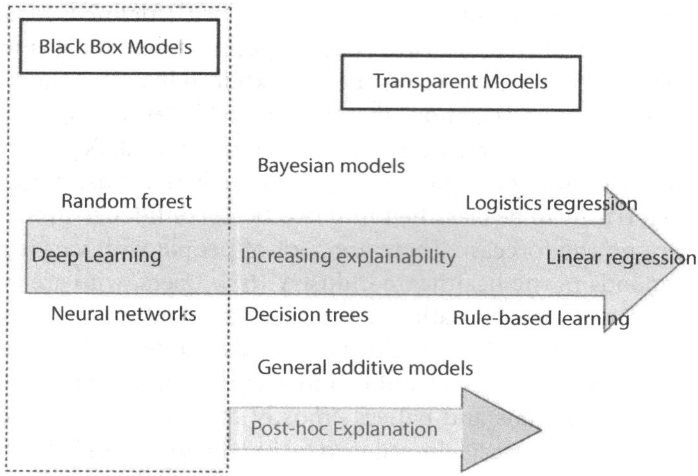

Figure 4.1 Examining naturally transparent models as comparison to black box models that necessitate post hoc explanations.

consumers. (3) Explanations must precisely depict the system's method for producing the output. (4) Limitations of knowledge: The system functions within the parameters that it was specifically created for and only when it possesses sufficient certainty in its results [69]. Researchers have shown that ML *post-hoc* explanation methodologies do not offer reliable findings. Thus, they cannot be exclusively relied upon to guarantee equity in critical decision-making processes, such as those related to healthcare [70].

4.4.3 Cooperation Between AI and Humans

Recognizing the necessity of not supplanting humans with AI algorithms is crucial for clinicians, researchers, patients, and others [71]. An AI system has the capacity to outperform humans in particular tasks, but humans now offer added value through their expertise in a particular field, vast experience, and ability to think creatively. The AI system may surpass the physician in terms of accuracy when evaluating their performance on a specific task. However, it is crucial to assess the AI model not just on its own but also in combination with a person, as they usually work together in clinical environments. Usually, when AI is used to assist in decision making, it can lead to the best possible results [72]. Integrating an AI model with human expertise improves the clarity of the decision-making process. By integrating explainable with the clinician's expertise in the field, the decision-making process becomes more visible and comprehensible. Clinical decision support (CDS) that is easy to understand helps developers find bugs and provides clinicians faith in AI to make smart decisions [73]. Researchers have found that patients may inadvertently become bystanders to their doctors' decision-making when CDS systems use opaque algorithms [74]. Figure 4.2 depicts the distinct characteristics that a person and an AI model contribute to healthcare decision-making, emphasizing that the best results are obtained by utilizing both of them together. In the future, there may be a propensity for the figure to incline toward the right side. Nevertheless, the distinctive attributes of humans are anticipated to confirm that collaborative decision-making will continue to be the most advantageous option in the foreseeable future.

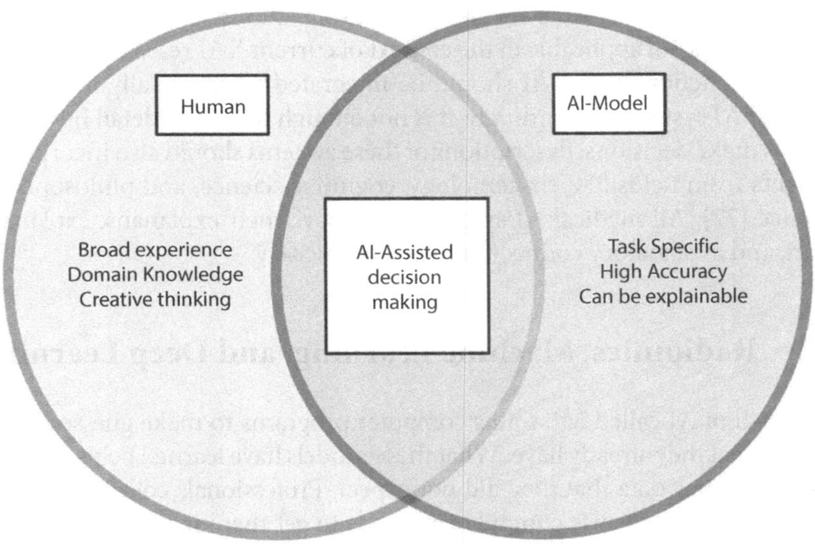

Figure 4.2 Incorporating human knowledge into AI models can improve the quality of AI-assisted decision-making.

4.4.4 Scientific Explainable Artificial Intelligence (sXAI)

Scientists differentiate sXAI from other forms of XAI [75]. Current XAI methods, according to researchers, are based on a bottom-up notion. This necessitates classifying all types of XAI in accordance with state-of-the-art computational approaches and technologies. Nevertheless, employing this method may lead to explanations that are perplexingly comparable to categorizations, commonly referred to as "how-explanations." However, researchers offer an authentic scientific elucidation within the realm of medical. This explanation covers three basic points: firstly, the establishment of sXAI, which encompasses the "explanans" (the entity accountable for delivering an explanation), the "explanandum" (the entity requiring an explanation), and the "explanatory relation" (the objective connection between the two). Furthermore, sXAI incorporates both human beings and non-epistemic beliefs. Furthermore, the method through which human agents can proficiently assess the caliber of an explanation. There will be major changes to the way that medical XAI is designed and understood, as well as a transition from traditional XAI to sXAI. The researchers [76] conduct a thorough analysis of this methodology and conclude that current XAI approaches fail to meet the requirements for authentic explanations. Consequently, their framework is not applicable in the context of current XAI research. To ensure optimal functionality, sXAI should be integrated hierarchically into future medical AI systems. Accordingly, it is not enough to simply detail how algorithms make decisions; descriptions of these systems should also incorporate insights from fields like epistemology, cognitive science, and philosophy of science [77]. All medical AI systems must have their explanans, explanandum, and explanatory connection defined precisely.

4.5 Radiomics, Machine Learning, and Deep Learning

A branch of AI called ML trains computer programs to make guesses based on data that they already have. What these models have learned helps them do tasks with new data that they did not expect. Professionals collect and organize data sources or use computer methods to get them in order to use ML. Supervised ML algorithms use data that has already been labeled by people to make guesses or put data into groups. Unsupervised models, on the other hand, learn from data that has not been labeled and find patterns and connections in it. It is better to use unsupervised models to understand the structure of datasets and give correct descriptions. This representation can be used as the first step before training a supervised model to make it work better.

The goal of the "deep learning" subfield of ML is to simulate the operation of NNs similar to those found in the human brain. The system employs complex artificial NNs with numerous hidden layers to handle challenging problems efficiently and rapidly. Because these layers are secret, the system can keep learning more and getting better. Deep learning systems, such as convolutional NNs (CNNs), can learn features directly from images, which is different from traditional ML methods. With this method, DL algorithms not only can find a link between features of a picture and its results but also can learn more about those features. Deep learning makes a lot of data, some of which is used for image classification, object placement recognition, and pixel label segmentation. Radiomics is a new area that grew out of DL. The researchers in this field use computer analysis to uncover hidden patterns by removing a number of quantitative features from medical pictures (such as CT scans). When used to the study of bone health, DL algorithms and radiomics can reveal imaging features associated with key pathological and histological aspects of bone trabeculae. These traits might be able to do better at diagnosing problems than people and even regular imaging methods when used together. At present, the most common ML methods include CNNs that automatically extract crucial picture features to directly categorize data from input images [108] and radiomics-based feature analysis, which is shown in Figure 4.3 and which entails manually extracting predetermined features

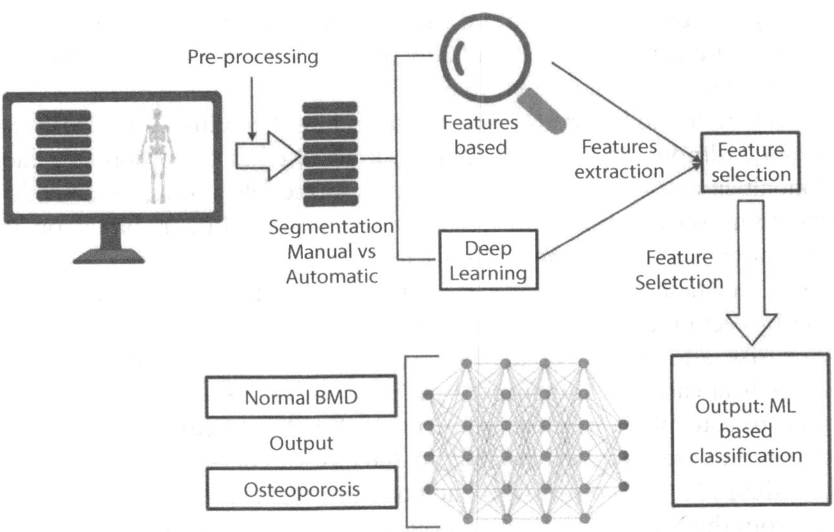

Figure 4.3 A diagram showing the fundamental steps and general architecture of radiomics, including input data selection, segmentation, feature extraction inside ROIs, exploratory analysis, and modeling.

integrated into DL training datasets [107]. When compared to human abilities, CNNs can detect diagnostic patterns and characteristics with greater precision. They are especially valuable in the domain of identifying and categorizing osteoporosis [78, 107].

4.6 Diagnosis of Osteoporosis

Osteoporosis is primarily found in postmenopausal women, but it is also a growing concern for older males. Compared to people of other races, Caucasians have a higher risk of developing this illness [79]. Bone mineral density (BMD) tests employing DEXA are usually performed on the proximal femur, lumbar spine, and, on rare occasions, the forearm to diagnose osteoporosis. The diagnostic procedure involves comparing the measured BMD to a reference sample of healthy, premenopausal persons of the same sex and ethnicity. The T-score or SDs that quantify the degree of the decrease in BMD [80] are utilized for the comparison. The WHO states that a BMD below 2.5 on the T-score is indicative of osteoporosis. When measuring BMD, a T-score above 1.0 is considered normal, whereas a T-score between 1 and 2.5 indicates osteopenia. Diminished bone density increases the probability of suffering fractures that are easily triggered by small injuries [81]. Aside from the BMD requirement, the existence of fragility fractures in a patient indicates the presence of severe osteoporosis [82]. Fifty percent of women and 20% of men will develop an osteoporotic fracture at some point in their lives [83].

Weak bones and more fragility fractures have been linked to BMD testing [84]. Although DEXA uses X-rays, it also makes use of ionizing radiation, albeit at a low dose. When it comes to models, though, DEXA does have some serious limitations. The DEXA examination is based on the assumption that only bone and muscle are present; hence, the presence of fat will inevitably affect the accuracy of the results. In addition, because it is a 2D-projection approach, it is unable of precisely assessing the entire bone shape, size, and microstructure [85]. Hence, a lot of people have not gotten the medical care that they need. BMD testing has also led to the identification of osteopenia in most women with fragility fractures, according to population-based research [86, 87]. In 2004, researchers in the US surveyed more than 150,000 women who had gone through menopause, drawing on data from the National Osteoporosis Risk Assessment. The study found that 82% of the fractures caused by osteoporosis occurred in women who did not meet the DEXA diagnostic criteria for the illness [88].

4.6.1 ML- and DL-Based Osteoporosis Diagnosis

There is a vast and ever-expanding variety of AI techniques available [89–91]. There are primarily two types of algorithms: supervised and unsupervised. A common type of supervised model involves connecting input variables with a corresponding output metric. The weights that can be given to the input parameters to change their relevance in producing the output are determined by whether the prediction distance from the result rises or decreases during the training phase. Instead of focusing on generating predetermined output metrics, unsupervised models characterize the clusters of inputs. Semi-supervised algorithms can operate in both types of scenarios. The process is known as regression or classification based on the outcome type prediction. Regression occurs when the output is a numerical value. This is the scenario where the model needs to predict the BMD of each individual in dataset linked to osteoporosis. If the result is categorical, then the task is referred to as categorization. This scenario occurs when the model needs to categorize a set of research participants into two groups: those who have osteoporosis and those who do not. Assigning individuals to one of three T-score categories—normal, osteopenia, or osteoporosis—is an instance of the third approach, which involves forecasting ordered categorical variables as results.

4.6.2 The AI-Based Diagnosis

Linear and logistic regressions, which have a lengthy track record, are still utilized in prediction modeling. However, there has been a substantial increase in the variety of models that are now accessible in the market in the past few decades. The choice of an ML method is contingent upon several aspects, such as the particular task being performed (e.g., classification, regression, or clustering), the intricacy of the data, and the limitations on computational time. When it comes to classification, Naive Bayes is a very basic model that tends to be very biased toward certain results and not very dynamic. So, even though it is quick and easy to use for smaller datasets, it might not work well with more complicated ones. The k-nearest neighbors (kNN) algorithm utilizes the distances between data points as a simple way to categorize or make predictions. It can work as a link classifier. The support vector machine (SVM) is a classification method that separates data into two classes by utilizing hyperplanes. These hyperplanes are geometric subspaces with a dimension of $n - 1$, contained in a space with a dimension of n. For example, in a 2D data space, the hyperplane can be a line, whereas, in a 3D data space, it can be a plane. The SVMs are proficient at managing intricate and non-linear situations without succumbing to overfitting. Decision between classification or regression trees utilizes a hierarchical decision-making mechanism, commencing with the root and continuing to the branches. Random forests are better than kNN at getting rid of traits that are not important, but they can become too good at what they do, which can be fixed with ensemble learning. Ensemble learning takes advantage of a set of smaller base models to improve the final outcome. Boosting is a technique where learners progressively enhance their performance and ultimately generate a result that is weighted. Instead, the forecast is computed by averaging the outcomes acquired from a set of bootstrap samples of decision trees when bootstrap aggregation (bagging) is employed in conjunction with decision trees.

Deep learning is a collection of techniques that rely on NNs. In this approach, learning takes place at multiple levels of abstraction [92–94]. Scientists have created ANNs, also known as NNs, to mimic the data processing methods of neurons in the brain. These networks utilize nonlinear statistical algorithms. The model is determined by the strength and direction of the connections between the network's components. Basically, this learning approach creates new parameters by mixing the input parameters in a linear fashion, and then it uses a nonlinear function of these new parameters to describe the result. Despite their exceptional performance with massive inputs, they can be very costly due to the vast quantity of processing resources they demand. As said before, the CNN is a well-liked DL method that makes use of convolved weights [95].

4.7 General Workflow of AI-Based BMD Classification in CT

CT imaging can be used to extract BMD data by converting the HUs measured within the bones. In CT scans, the radiodensity of specific bodily tissues or substances is evaluated using a quantitative metric called the HU. The data presented here pertain to the fact that X-rays undergo tissue attenuation. The air and water densities are used as reference points for calibrating the results.

There are two primary methods for assessing BMD after collecting HU measurements from bones:

1. **Phantom-Based Calibration:** During the process of obtaining images, phantoms with pre-determined densities (such as rods of calcium hydroxyapatite or dipotassium phosphate)

are placed beneath the body [96, 97]. These apparitions are utilized to correlate observed HU values with BMD through the use of linear equations. An obstacle arises from the lack of uniform positioning of phantoms in clinical CT images [98]. Nevertheless, this challenge can be overcome by asynchronously scanning the density phantom, which means conducting the scan without the patient being present, utilizing the same scanner and scan methods.

2. **Phantomless Internal Calibration:** This method utilizes internal reference regions, such as skeletal muscle and adipose tissue, to ascertain the highest HU values. Images calibrated with patient phantoms are used to compute the BMD density values for these internal benchmarks. A standard calibration curve is generated from the extrapolated data by applying scan-specific equations to the trabecular HU to BMD conversion.

Another well-established approach for assessing BMD using CT images involves utilizing HU parameters to evaluate the presence of osteoporosis [99, 100]. This approach is not trustworthy, though, because it cannot handle things like different locations, different X-ray intensities, beam hardening artefacts, and hardware differences, such as scan models and protocols [101, 102].

DL and AI are increasingly being utilized to enhance the categorization and precision of BMD forecasts. Using these methods, one can obtain CT scans, bone attenuation (HU) values, and textural features for use in model construction [103, 104]. The standard stages in constructing an AI model include acquiring images and data, segmenting them, extracting features from regions of interest (ROIs), conducting exploratory analysis using feature selection, and ultimately establishing the model [105, 106]. Test sets, which ideally consist of both internal and external data, are utilized to validate the models and assess their performance and ability to generalize [107]. There are two primary techniques for ML:

1. **Feature-Based Imaging Feature Analysis:** This process includes the manual extraction of many attributes and their integration into a training dataset to enable AI-based image categorization [108].
2. **Deep Learning-Based Analysis (e.g., CNNs):** By directly gaining patterns from input photos, CNNs use DL to automatically extract valuable visual information [109]. This has

the potential to improve BMD categorization by enabling the detection and examination of distinct diagnostic patterns and imaging properties that are beyond the understanding of a human reader [110, 111].

4.8 Conclusion

Artificial intelligence (AI) has become more and more incorporated into the healthcare industry, assisting healthcare professionals in making better-informed decisions by providing CDS. Additionally, it aids in the identification of cancer locations in MR imaging, the analysis of reports authored by radiologists and pathologists, and the completion of numerous other activities. However, AI presents a substantial danger due to its nature as an inscrutable system, hence eroding trust in its reliability. This issue is especially crucial in fields where a solitary decision might result in life-or-death outcomes. The terms XAI and RAI have been gaining prominence as a consequence. The purpose of XAI and RAI is to guarantee that AI algorithms, along with the consequent decisions that they make, can be comprehended by people. This chapter has examined essential principles in XAI and RAI that are applicable to various challenges in the healthcare field. Additionally, it investigates the capacity of XAI and RAI to promote progress in the field of healthcare, particularly in relation to osteoporosis. In order to screen for and classify osteoporosis, this chapter emphasizes the expanding corpus of research that validates the potential of combining XAI with RAI. The use of AI algorithms in conjunction with state-of-the-art imaging technologies has the potential to completely transform osteoporosis evaluation and diagnosis.

References

1. Ensrud, K.E. and Crandall, C.J., Bisphosphonates for postmenopausal osteoporosis. *Jama*, 322, 20, 2017–8, 2019 Nov 26.
2. Salari, N., Ghasemi, H., Mohammadi, L., Behzadi, M.H., Rabieenia, E., Shohaimi, S., Mohammadi, M., The global prevalence of osteoporosis in the world: a comprehensive systematic review and meta-analysis. *J. Orthop. Surg. Res.*, 16, 1–20, 2021 Dec.
3. Xiao, P.L., Cui, A.Y., Hsu, C.J., Peng, R., Jiang, N., Xu, X.H., Ma, Y.G., Liu, D., Lu, H.D., Global, regional prevalence, and risk factors of osteoporosis according to the World Health Organization diagnostic criteria: a systematic review and meta-analysis. *Osteoporos. Int.*, 33, 10, 2137–53, 2022 Oct.

4. Center, J.R., Nguyen, T.V., Schneider, D., Sambrook, P.N., Eisman, J.A., Mortality after all major types of osteoporotic fracture in men and women: an observational study. *Lancet*, 353, 9156, 878–82, 1999 Mar 13.
5. Melton III, L.J., Adverse outcomes of osteoporotic fractures in the general population. *J. Bone Miner. Res.*, 18, 6, 1139–41, 2003 Jun 1.
6. Gold, D.T., The nonskeletal consequences of osteoporotic fractures: psychologic and social outcomes. *Rheum. Dis. Clin. North Am.*, 27, 1, 255–62, 2001 Feb 1.
7. Gold, D.T., Williams, S.A., Weiss, R.J., Wang, Y., Watkins, C., Carroll, J., Middleton, C., Silverman, S., Impact of fractures on quality of life in patients with osteoporosis: a US cross-sectional survey. *J. Drug Assess.*, 8, 1, 175–83, 2019 Jan 1.
8. Williams, S.A., Chastek, B., Sundquist, K., Barrera-Sierra, S., Leader Jr, D., Weiss, R.J., Wang, Y., Curtis, J.R., Economic burden of osteoporotic fractures in US managed care enrollees. *Am. J. Manag. Care*, 26, 5, e142–9, 2020 May 1.
9. Stanghelle, B., Bentzen, H., Giangregorio, L., Pripp, A.H., Bergland, A., Associations between health-related quality of life, physical function and pain in older women with osteoporosis and vertebral fracture. *BMC Geriatr.*, 19, 1–0, 2019 Dec.
10. Tucci, J.R., Importance of early diagnosis and treatment of osteoporosis to prevent fractures. *Am. J. Manag. Care*, 12, 7, S181, 2006 May 1.
11. Kanis, J.A., Melton III, L.J., Christiansen, C., Johnston, C.C., Khaltaev, N., The diagnosis of osteoporosis. *J. Bone Miner. Res.*, 9, 8, 1137–41, 1994 Aug.
12. Sheu, A. and Diamond, T., Diagnostic tests: bone mineral density: testing for osteoporosis. *Aust. Prescr.*, 39, 2, 35, 2016 Apr.
13. Porter, J.L., Varacallo, M., Castano, M., Osteoporosis (Nursing), in: *StatPearls* [Internet], StatPearls Publishing, Treasure Island, Florida, USA, 2023 Aug 4.
14. Adams, J.E., Quantitative computed tomography. *Eur. J. Radiol.*, 71, 3, 415–24, 2009 Sep 1.
15. Ito, K., Cost-effectiveness of screening for osteoporosis in older men with a history of falls. *JAMA Netw. Open*, 3, 12, e2027584–, 2020 Dec 1.
16. Miller, P.D., Zapalowski, C., Kulak, C.A., Bilezikian, J.P., Bone densitometry: the best way to detect osteoporosis and to monitor therapy. *J. Clin. Endocrinol. Metab.*, 84, 6, 1867–71, 1999 Jun 1.
17. Gillespie, C.W. and Morin, P.E., Trends and disparities in osteoporosis screening among women in the United States, 2008-2014. *Am. J. Med.*, 130, 3, 306–16, 2017 Mar 1.
18. Williams, S., Khan, L., Licata, A.A., DXA and clinical challenges of fracture risk assessment in primary care. *Cleve. Clin. J. Med.*, 88, 11, 615–22, 2021 Nov 1.
19. Chirvi, S., Pintar, F.A., Yoganandan, N., Stemper, B., Kleinberger, M., Trabecular bone mineral density correlations using QCT: Central and peripheral human skeleton. *J. Mech. Behav. Biomed. Mater.*, 112, 104076, 2020 Dec 1.

20. Jørgensen, H.S., Borghs, H., Heye, S., Smout, D., Claes, K., Evenepoel, P., Vascular calcification of the abdominal aorta has minimal impact on lumbar spine bone density in patients with chronic kidney disease. *Bone*, 162, 116482, 2022 Sep 1.
21. Garg, M.K. and Kharb, S., Dual energy X-ray absorptiometry: Pitfalls in measurement and interpretation of bone mineral density. *Indian J. Endocrinol. Metab.*, 17, 2, 203–10, 2013 Mar 1.
22. Vetter, J.R., Perman, W.H., Kalender, W.A., Mazess, R.B., Holden, J.E., Evaluation of a prototype dual-energy computed tomographic apparatus. II. Determination of vertebral bone mineral content. *Med. Phys.*, 13, 3, 340–3, 1986 May.
23. Booz, C., Noeske, J., Albrecht, M.H., Lenga, L., Martin, S.S., Yel, I., Huizinga, N.A., Vogl, T.J., Wichmann, J.L., Diagnostic accuracy of quantitative dual-energy CT-based bone mineral density assessment in comparison to Hounsfield unit measurements using dual x-ray absorptiometry as standard of reference. *Eur. J. Radiol.*, 132, 109321, 2020 Nov 1.
24. Roski, F., Hammel, J., Mei, K., Baum, T., Kirschke, J.S., Laugerette, A., Kopp, F.K., Bodden, J., Pfeiffer, D., Pfeiffer, F., Rummeny, E.J., Bone mineral density measurements derived from dual-layer spectral CT enable opportunistic screening for osteoporosis. *Eur. Radio.*, 29, 6355–63, 2019 Nov.
25. Ghasemi Shayan, R., Oladghaffari, M., Sajjadian, F., Fazel Ghaziyani, M., Image quality and dose comparison of single-energy CT (SECT) and dual-energy CT (DECT). *Radiol. Res. Pract.*, 2020, 1403957, 2020 Apr 20.
26. Koch, V., Hokamp, N.G., Albrecht, M.H., Gruenewald, L.D., Yel, I., Borggrefe, J., Wesarg, S., Eichler, K., Burck, I., Gruber-Rouh, T., Lenga, L., Accuracy and precision of volumetric bone mineral density assessment using dual-source dual-energy versus quantitative CT: a phantom study. *Eur. Radio. Exp.*, 5, 1–0, 2021 Dec.
27. Mussmann, B., Andersen, P.E., Torfing, T., Overgaard, S., Bone density measurements adjacent to acetabular cups in total hip arthroplasty using dual-energy CT: an *in vivo* reliability and agreement study. *Acta Radiol. Open*, 7, 9, 2058460118796539, 2018 Aug.
28. Kang, J.W., Park, C., Lee, D.E., Yoo, J.H., Kim, M., Prediction of bone mineral density in CT using deep learning with explainability. *Front. Physiol.*, 13, 1061911, 2023 Jan 10.
29. Schreiber, J.J., Anderson, P.A., Rosas, H.G., Buchholz, A.L., Au, A.G., Hounsfield units for assessing bone mineral density and strength: a tool for osteoporosis management. *JBJS*, 93, 11, 1057–63, 2011 Jun 1.
30. Yasaka, K., Akai, H., Kunimatsu, A., Kiryu, S., Abe, O., Prediction of bone mineral density from computed tomography: application of deep learning with a convolutional neural network. *Eur. Radio.*, 30, 3549–57, 2020 Jun.

31. Cheng, X., Zhao, K., Zha, X., Du, X., Li, Y., Chen, S., Wu, Y., Li, S., Lu, Y., Zhang, Y., Xiao, X., Opportunistic screening using low-dose CT and the prevalence of osteoporosis in China: a nationwide, multicenter study. *J. Bone Miner. Res.*, 36, 3, 427–35, 2020 Dec 1.
32. Gausden, E.B., Nwachukwu, B.U., Schreiber, J.J., Lorich, D.G., Lane, J.M., Opportunistic use of CT imaging for osteoporosis screening and bone density assessment: a qualitative systematic review. *Jbjs*, 99, 18, 1580–90, 2017 Sep 20.
33. Pickhardt, P.J., Pooler, B.D., Lauder, T., del Rio, A.M., Bruce, R.J., Binkley, N., Opportunistic screening for osteoporosis using abdominal computed tomography scans obtained for other indications. *Ann. Internal Med.*, 158, 8, 588–95, 2013 Apr 16.
34. Zhu, Y., Triphuridet, N., Yip, R., Becker, B.J., Wang, Y., Yankelevitz, D.F., Henschke, C.I., Opportunistic CT screening of osteoporosis on thoracic and lumbar spine: a meta-analysis. *Clin. Imaging*, 80, 382–90, 2021 Dec 1.
35. Bott, K.N., Matheson, B.E., Smith, A.C., Tse, J.J., Boyd, S.K., Manske, S.L., Addressing Challenges of Opportunistic Computed Tomography Bone Mineral Density Analysis. *Diagnostics*, 13, 15, 2572, 2023 Aug 2.
36. Yushkevich, P.A., Piven, J., Hazlett, H.C., Smith, R.G., Ho, S., Gee, J.C., Gerig, G., User-guided 3D active contour segmentation of anatomical structures: significantly improved efficiency and reliability. *Neuroimage*, 31, 3, 1116–28, 2006 Jul 1.
37. Yoo, T.K., Kim, S.K., Kim, D.W., Choi, J.Y., Lee, W.H., Oh, E., Park, E.C., Osteoporosis risk prediction for bone mineral density assessment of postmenopausal women using machine learning. *Yonsei Med. J.*, 54, 6, 1321–30, 2013 Nov 1.
38. Lis-Studniarska, D., Lipnicka, M., Studniarski, M., Irzmański, R., Applications of Artificial Intelligence Methods for the Prediction of Osteoporotic Fractures. *Life*, 13, 8, 1738, 2023 Aug 13.
39. Lessmann, N., Van Ginneken, B., De Jong, P.A., Išgum, I., Iterative fully convolutional neural networks for automatic vertebra segmentation and identification. *Med. Image Anal.*, 53, 142–55, 2019 Apr 1.
40. Huang, C.B., Hu, J.S., Tan, K., Zhang, W., Xu, T.H., Yang, L., Application of machine learning model to predict osteoporosis based on abdominal computed tomography images of the psoas muscle: a retrospective study. *BMC Geriatr.*, 22, 1, 796, 2022 Oct 13.
41. Naghavi, M., De Oliveira, I., Mao, S.S., Jaberzadeh, A., Montoya, J., Zhang, C., Atlas, K., Manubolu, V., Montes, M., Li, D., Atlas, T., Opportunistic AI-enabled automated bone mineral density measurements in lung cancer screening and coronary calcium scoring CT scans are equivalent. *Eur. J. Radiol. Open*, 10, 100492, 2023 Jan 1.

42. Sebro, R. and De la Garza-Ramos, C., Utilizing machine learning for opportunistic screening for low BMD using CT scans of the cervical spine. *J. Neuroradiol.*, 50, 3, 293–301, 2023 May 1.
43. Wang, J., Zhou, S., Chen, S., He, Y., Gao, H., Yan, L., Hu, X., Li, P., Shen, H., Luo, M., You, T., Prediction of osteoporosis using radiomics analysis derived from single source dual energy CT. *BMC Musculoskelet. Disord.*, 24, 1, 100, 2023 Feb 7.
44. Jiang, Y.W., Xu, X.J., Wang, R., Chen, C.M., Radiomics analysis based on lumbar spine CT to detect osteoporosis. *Eur. Radio.*, 32, 11, 8019–26, 2022 Nov.
45. Tigard, D.W. and Responsible, A.I., and moral responsibility: a common appreciation. *AI Ethics*, 1, 2, 113–7, 2021 May.
46. Stahl, B.C. and Coeckelbergh, M., Ethics of healthcare robotics: Towards responsible research and innovation. *Rob. Auton. Syst.*, 86, 152–61, 2016 Dec 1.
47. Morley, J., Machado, C., Burr, C., Cowls, J., Taddeo, M., Floridi, L., The debate on the ethics of AI in health care: a reconstruction and critical review, 2019 Nov 13, Available at SSRN 3486518.
48. Dignum, V., *Responsible artificial intelligence: how to develop and use AI in a responsible way*, Springer, Cham, 2019 Nov 4.
49. Mikalef, P. and Gupta, M., Artificial intelligence capability: Conceptualization, measurement calibration, and empirical study on its impact on organizational creativity and firm performance. *Inf. Manage.*, 58, 3, 103434, 2021 Apr 1.
50. Martin, K., Ethical implications and accountability of algorithms. *J. Bus. Ethics*, 160, 4, 835–50, 2019 Dec.
51. Newell, S. and Marabelli, M., Strategic opportunities (and challenges) of algorithmic decision-making: A call for action on the long-term societal effects of 'datification'. *J. Strategic Inf. Syst.*, 24, 1, 3–14, 2015 Mar 1.
52. Floridi, L. and Taddeo, M., What is data ethics? *Philos. Trans. R. Soc. A: Math. Phys. Eng. Sci.*, 374, 2083, 20160360, 2016 Dec 28.
53. Stahl, B.C. and Markus, M.L., Let's claim the authority to speak out on the ethics of smart information systems.
54. Chen, L., Baird, A., Straub, D.W., An analysis of the evolving intellectual structure of health information systems research in the information systems discipline. *J. Assoc. Inf. Syst.*, 20, 8, 5, 2019.
55. Adesina, A.S. and Zubairu, A.N., Contemporary Library and Artificial Intelligence Technology. *Alexandria*, 33, 1–3, 18–30, 2024 Feb 5, 09557490241231483.
56. Hulsen, T., Literature analysis of artificial intelligence in biomedicine. *Ann. Trans. Med.*, 10, 23, 1–15, 2022 Dec.
57. Rajput, S., Sharma, P.K., Malviya, R., Artificial intelligence for emergency medical care. *Health Care Sci.*, 2, 1–16, 2023.

58. Hulsen, T., Jamuar, S.S., Moody, A.R., Karnes, J.H., Varga, O., Hedensted, S., Spreafico, R., Hafler, D.A., McKinney, E.F., From big data to precision medicine. *Front. Med.*, 6, 34, 2019 Mar 1.
59. Hulsen, T., Friedecký, D., Renz, H., Melis, E., Vermeersch, P., Fernandez-Calle, P., From big data to better patient outcomes. *Clin. Chem. Lab. Med. (CCLM)*, 61, 4, 580–6, 2023 Mar 28.
60. Biswas, S., ChatGPT and the future of medical writing. *Radiology*, 307, 2, e223312, 2023 Feb 2.
61. Celi, L.A., Cellini, J., Charpignon, M.L., Dee, E.C., Dernoncourt, F., Eber, R., Mitchell, W.G., Moukheiber, L., Schirmer, J., Situ, J., Paguio, J., Sources of bias in artificial intelligence that perpetuate healthcare disparities—A global review. *PLOS Digital Health*, 1, 3, e0000022, 2022 Mar 31.
62. Hulsen, T., Sharing is caring—data sharing initiatives in healthcare. *Int. J. Environ. Res. Public Health*, 17, 9, 3046, 2020 May.
63. Vega-Márquez, B., Rubio-Escudero, C., Riquelme, J.C., Nepomuceno-Chamorro, I., Creation of synthetic data with conditional generative adversarial networks, in: *14th International Conference on Soft Computing Models in Industrial and Environmental Applications (SOCO 2019)*, Seville, Spain, May 13–15, 2019, Proceedings 14, Springer International Publishing, pp. 231–240, 2020.
64. Gunning, D., Stefik, M., Choi, J., Miller, T., Stumpf, S., Yang, G.Z., XAI—Explainable artificial intelligence. *Sci. Rob.*, 4, 37, eaay7120, 2019 Dec 18.
65. Rai, A., Explainable AI: From black box to glass box. *J. Acad. Mark. Sci.*, 48, 137–41, 2020 Jan.
66. Loyola-Gonzalez, O., Black-box vs. white-box: Understanding their advantages and weaknesses from a practical point of view. *IEEE Access*, 7, 154096–113, 2019 Oct 24.
67. Gerlings, J., Jensen, M.S., Shollo, A., Explainable AI, but explainable to whom? An exploratory case study of xAI in healthcare, in: *Handbook of Artificial Intelligence in Healthcare*, Vol 2: Practicalities and Prospects, pp. 169–98, 2022.
68. Arrieta, A.B., Díaz-Rodríguez, N., Del Ser, J., Bennetot, A., Tabik, S., Barbado, A., García, S., Gil-López, S., Molina, D., Benjamins, R., Chatila, R., Explainable Artificial Intelligence (XAI): Concepts, taxonomies, opportunities and challenges toward responsible AI. *Inf. Fusion*, 58, 82–115, 2020 Jun 1.
69. Phillips, P.J., Phillips, P.J., Hahn, C.A., Fontana, P.C., Yates, A.N., Greene, K., Broniatowski, D.A., Przybocki, M.A., Four principles of explainable artificial intelligence.
70. Vale, D., El-Sharif, A., Ali, M., Explainable artificial intelligence (XAI) post-hoc explainability methods: Risks and limitations in non-discrimination law. *AI Ethics*, 2, 4, 815–26, 2022 Nov.

71. Malviya, R., Rajput, S., Vaidya, M., *Artificial Intelligence for Bone Disorder: Diagnosis and Treatment*, John Wiley & Sons, Hoboken, New Jersey, USA, 2024 Feb 28.
72. Zhang, Y., Liao, Q.V., Bellamy, R.K., Effect of confidence and explanation on accuracy and trust calibration in AI-assisted decision making, in: *Proceedings of the 2020 conference on fairness, accountability, and transparency*, 2020 Jan 27, pp. 295–305.
73. Antoniadi, A.M., Du, Y., Guendouz, Y., Wei, L., Mazo, C., Becker, B.A., Mooney, C., Current challenges and future opportunities for XAI in machine learning-based clinical decision support systems: a systematic review. *Appl. Sci.*, 11, 11, 5088, 2021 May 31.
74. Amann, J., Blasimme, A., Vayena, E., Frey, D., Madai, V.I., Precise4Q Consortium. Explainability for artificial intelligence in healthcare: a multidisciplinary perspective. *BMC Med. Inf. Decis. Making*, 20, 1–9, 2020 Dec.
75. Durán, J.M., Dissecting scientific explanation in AI (sXAI): A case for medicine and healthcare. *Artif. Intell.*, 297, 103498, 2021 Aug 1.
76. Cabitza, F., Campagner, A., Malgieri, G., Natali, C., Schneeberger, D., Stoeger, K., Holzinger, A., Quod erat demonstrandum?-Towards a typology of the concept of explanation for the design of explainable AI. *Expert Syst. Appl.*, 213, 118888, 2023 Mar 1.
77. Hulsen, T., Explainable Artificial Intelligence (XAI): Concepts and challenges in healthcare. *AI*, 4, 3, 652–66, 2023 Aug 10.
78. Kaka, H., Zhang, E., Khan, N., Artificial intelligence and deep learning in neuroradiology: exploring the new frontier. *Can. Assoc. Radiol. J.*, 72, 1, 35–44, 2021 Feb.
79. US Preventive Services Task Force*, Screening for osteoporosis: US preventive services task force recommendation statement. *Ann. Internal Med.*, 154, 5, 356–64, 2011 Mar 1.
80. Kanis, J.A. and Kanis, J.A., Assessment of fracture risk and its application to screening for postmenopausal osteoporosis: synopsis of a WHO report. *Osteoporos. Int.*, 4, 368–81, 1994 Nov.
81. WA P, Consensus development conference: diagnosis, prophylaxis, and treatment of osteoporosis. *Am. J. Med.*, 94, 6, 646–50, 1993.
82. Kanis, J.A., Diagnosis of osteoporosis and assessment of fracture risk. *Lancet*, 359, 9321, 1929–36, 2002 Jun 1.
83. US Department of Health and Human Services, *Bone health and osteoporosis: a report of the Surgeon General*, vol. 87, US Department of Health and Human Services, Office of the Surgeon General, Rockville, MD, 2004 Oct 14.
84. Marshall, D., Johnell, O., Wedel, H., Meta-analysis of how well measures of bone mineral density predict occurrence of osteoporotic fractures. *Bmj*, 312, 7041, 1254–9, 1996 May 18.
85. Chang, G., Honig, S., Brown, R., Deniz, C.M., Egol, K.A., Babb, J.S., Regatte, R.R., Rajapakse, C.S., Finite element analysis applied to 3-T MR imaging of

proximal femur microarchitecture: lower bone strength in patients with fragility fractures compared with control subjects. *Radiology*, 272, 2, 464–74, 2014 Aug.
86. Schuit, S.C., Van der Klift, M., Weel, A.E., De Laet, C.E., Burger, H., Seeman, E., Hofman, A., Uitterlinden, A.G., Van Leeuwen, J.P., Pols, H.A., Fracture incidence and association with bone mineral density in elderly men and women: the Rotterdam Study. *Bone*, 34, 1, 195–202, 2004 Jan 1.
87. Wainwright, S.A., Marshall, L.M., Ensrud, K.E., Cauley, J.A., Black, D.M., Hillier, T.A., Hochberg, M.C., Vogt, M.T., Orwoll, E.S., Study of Osteoporotic Fractures Research Group. Hip fracture in women without osteoporosis. *J. Clin. Endocrinol. Metab.*, 90, 5, 2787–93, 2005 May 1.
88. Siris, E.S., Chen, Y.T., Abbott, T.A., Barrett-Connor, E., Miller, P.D., Wehren, L.E., Berger, M.L., Bone mineral density thresholds for pharmacological intervention to prevent fractures. *Arch. Internal Med.*, 164, 10, 1108–12, 2004 May 24.
89. Bishop, C.M. and Nasrabadi, N.M., *Pattern recognition and machine learning*, Springer, New York, 2006 Aug 17.
90. Hastie, T., Tibshirani, R., Friedman, J., *The elements of statistical learning*, Springer series in statistics, Springer, New York, NY, USA, 2001.
91. Michie, D., Spiegelhalter, D.J., Taylor, C.C., Campbell, J. (Eds.), *Machine learning, neural and statistical classification*, Ellis Horwood, Chichester, West Sussex, England, 1995 Jun 1.
92. Le, Q.V., A tutorial on deep learning part 1: Nonlinear classifiers and the backpropagation algorithm, Mountain View, CA, 2015 Dec 13.
93. Le, Q.V., A tutorial on deep learning part 2: Autoencoders, convolutional neural networks and recurrent neural networks, vol. 20, Google Brain, pp. 1–20, 2015 Oct 20.
94. LeCun, Y., Bengio, Y., Hinton, G., Deep learning. *Nature*, 521, 7553, 436–44, 2015 May 28.
95. Ferizi, U., Honig, S., Chang, G., Artificial intelligence, osteoporosis and fragility fractures. *Curr. Opin. Rheumatol.*, 31, 4, 368–75, 2019 Jul 1.
96. Issever, A.S., Link, T.M., Kentenich, M., Rogalla, P., Schwieger, K., Huber, M.B., Burghardt, A.J., Majumdar, S., Diederichs, G., Trabecular Bone Structure Analysis in the Osteoporotic Spine Using a Clinical *In Vivo* Setup for 64-Slice MDCT Imaging: Comparison to μCT Imaging and μFE Modeling. *J. Bone Miner. Res.*, 24, 9, 1628–37, 2009 Sep 1.
97. Pickhardt, P.J., Nguyen, T., Perez, A.A., Graffy, P.M., Jang, S., Summers, R.M., Garrett, J.W., Improved CT-based osteoporosis assessment with a fully automated deep learning tool. *Radiol. Artif. Intell.*, 4, 5, e220042, 2022 Aug 31.
98. Resmi, S.L., Hashim, V., Mohammed, J., Dileep, P.N., Bone Mineral Density Prediction from CT Image: A Novel Approach using ANN. *Appl. Bionics Biomech.*, 2023, 1123953, 2023 Apr 28.

99. Sarker, I.H., Machine learning: Algorithms, real-world applications and research directions. *SN Comput. Sci.*, 2, 3, 160, 2021 May.
100. Rajkomar, A., Dean, J., Kohane, I., Machine learning in medicine. *N. Engl. J. Med.*, 380, 14, 1347–58, 2019 Apr 4.
101. Hosny, A., Parmar, C., Quackenbush, J., Schwartz, L.H., Aerts, H.J., Artificial intelligence in radiology. *Nat. Rev. Cancer*, 18, 8, 500–10, 2018 Aug.
102. Alhajeri, M., Aldosari, H., Aldosari, B., Evaluating latest developments in PACS and their impact on radiology practices: A systematic literature review. *Inf. Med. Unlocked*, 9, 181–90, 2017 Jan 1.
103. Gore, J.C., Artificial intelligence in medical imaging. *Magn. Reson. Imaging*, 68, A1–4, 2020 May 1.
104. Doi, K., Computer-aided diagnosis in medical imaging: historical review, current status and future potential. *Comput. Med. Imaging Graphics*, 31, 4-5, 198–211, 2007 Jun 1.
105. Nagoev, Z.V., Sundukov, Z.A., Pshenokova, I.A., Denisenko, V.A., Architecture of CAD for distributed artificial intelligence based on self-organizing neuro-cognitive architectures. *News Kabardin–Balkar Sci. Center RAS*, 2, 40–7, 2020.
106. Kriegeskorte, N., Deep neural networks: a new framework for modeling biological vision and brain information processing. *Annu. Rev. Vision Sci.*, 1, 417–46, 2015 Nov 24.
107. Liu, Z., Wang, S., Dong, D., Wei, J., Fang, C., Zhou, X., Sun, K., Li, L., Li, B., Wang, M., Tian, J., The applications of radiomics in precision diagnosis and treatment of oncology: opportunities and challenges. *Theranostics*, 9, 5, 1303, 2019.
108. Ciresan, D.C., Meier, U., Masci, J., Gambardella, L.M., Schmidhuber, J., Flexible, high performance convolutional neural networks for image classification, in: *Twenty-second international joint conference on artificial intelligence*, 2011 Jun 28.
109. Zaharchuk, G., Gong, E., Wintermark, M., Rubin, D., Langlotz, C.P., Deep learning in neuroradiology. *Am. J. Neuroradiol.*, 39, 10, 1776–84, 2018 Oct 1.

110. Uemura, K., Fujimori, T., Otake, Y., Shimomoto, Y., Kono, S., Takashima, K., Hamada, H., Takenaka, S., Kaito, T., Sato, Y., Sugano, N., Development of a system to assess the two-and three-dimensional bone mineral density of the lumbar vertebrae from clinical quantitative CT images. *Arch. Osteoporosis*, 18, 1, 22, 2023 Jan 21.
111. Ong, W., Liu, R.W., Makmur, A., Low, X.Z., Sng, W.J., Tan, J.H., Kumar, N., Hallinan, J.T., Artificial Intelligence Applications for Osteoporosis Classification Using Computed Tomography. *Bioengineering*, 10, 12, 1364, 2023 Nov 27.

5

Spinal Metastasis—Imaging Using XAI and RAI Techniques

Arti A. Bagada* **and Priya V. Patel**

Department of Pharmaceutical Sciences, Saurashtra University, Rajkot, Gujarat, India

Abstract

The most frequent malignant condition of the spine is spinal metastases. Artificial intelligence (AI) and machine learning have seen significant advancements recently, which has enhanced their application in oncological imaging. In medicine, AI has shown a lot of promise. With a high degree of learning performance (prediction accuracy), explainable AI (XAI) seeks to "produce explainable models and allow individuals to figure out appropriately, faith, and adeptly govern the rising generation of artificially intelligent companions." The bulk of studies on the application of AI approaches in primary malignant tumors implementing oncological radiography, such as brain, liver, kidney, and breast cancers, have demonstrated remarkable prediction outcomes; however, only a small number of these studies have been verified in an actual clinical environment. Utilizing multimodal imaging, research on computer-aided interpretation, radiomics, and machine learning has been conducted recently to maximize therapy choices for spinal metastases. Radiomics is a new field of AI that deals with the measurement and quantification of features or information found in digital medical pictures that pertain to tumor pathophysiology. Medical managerial decisions are capable of being strengthened by integrating these data with clinically and a qualitative imaging-derived data. This chapter includes a brief about spinal metastasis and various imaging using XAI and responsible AI (RAI) techniques for spinal metastasis with their wide spectrum application, prospects, and limitations.

Keywords: Spinal metastasis, XAI techniques, RAI techniques

**Corresponding author*: arti910@Gmail.Com; ORCID: 0000-0003-2908-6058

Rishabha Malviya and Sonali Sundram (eds.) Explainable and Responsible Artificial Intelligence in Healthcare, (115–144) © 2025 Scrivener Publishing LLC

List of Abbreviations

SMT	Spinal Metastasis
MRI	Magnetic Resonance Imaging
PET	Positron Emission Tomography
CT	Computed Tomography
AI	Artificial Intelligence
DNNS	Deep Neural Networks
XAI	Explainable Artificial Intelligence
RAI	Responsible Artificial Intelligence
ML	Machine Learning
DL	Deep Learning
PROIS	Patient-Reported Outcome Instruments
CAD	Computer-Aided Diagnostic
CS	Compressed Sensing
GAN	Generative Adversarial Network
T2WI	T2-Weighted Imaging
STB	Spinal Tuberculosis
LR	Linear Regression
LIME	Local Interpretable Model-Agnostic Explanations
COMI	Core Outcome Measures Index
SAI	Sustainable Artificial Intelligence
NGOS	Non-Governmental Organizations
HAI	Humancentric Artificial Intelligence
IAI	Inclusive Artificial Intelligence
FAI	Fair Artificial Intelligence
TAI	Transparent Artificial Intelligence

5.1 Introduction

Spinal metastasis (SMT) is a tumor-forming disorder that develops through the spinal column as well as is up to 35 times more common than any other primary malignant sickness, making it the third most common site of tumors. SMT has the potential to have a significant impact on quality of life due to complications such as fracture pain, spinal cord compression, neurological deficits, decreased mobility, bone marrow aplasia, and hypercalcemia, which can cause symptoms such as constipation, polyuria, polydipsia, fatigue, cardiac arrhythmias, and acute renal failure. As a result, early diagnosis, assessment, and the best possible medical treatment of SMT are crucial to avoid difficulties and enhance the quality of life for patients [1]. The most prevalent location of bone metastases is the cervical cord in cancer sufferers, accounting for as many as 40% of cases, including a maximum of 20% developing symptoms from their spinal cord compressing [2, 3]. The yearly frequency of symptomatic SMT is projected to range from around between 3% and 5% with the thoracic spine comprising particularly frequently implicated. In almost 20% of cases, it is the initial indication of malignancy. Spine metastases may originate from a variety of fundamental malignancies; lung, prostate, and breast cancers are the most common types [4].

Radiological studies are essential for diagnosing and treating SMT. While simple radiography is a swift along manageable first testing, higher-technology methods for image acquisition such as bone scintigraphy, magnetic resonance imaging (MRI), positron emission tomography (PET), and computed tomography (CT) are more useful in recognizing and classifying SMT [5].

Distinguished imaging methods provide distinct benefits for detecting SMT. CT has a sensitivity of 79.2% and a specificity of 92.3% for guiding interventional operations and systemic staging. MRI provides a higher than 90% in terms of specificity and sensitivity, correspondingly, and requires no radiation. The sensitivity of 18F FDG-PET is 89.8% and 63.3%, respectively [5–9].

Advances in enormous amounts of data fetching as well as expressive attribute assessments have rendered artificial intelligence (AI) increasingly prevalent throughout a multitude of areas of contemporary society. AI is particularly useful for medical image analysis. Deep neural networks (DNNs) are computational techniques that let an algorithm program by itself by analyzing an enormous number of data samples showing the desired behavior. This eliminates the need for rules to be explicitly stated [10–14]. AI usage in radiation therapy seeks to strengthen radiologist workflow, assisting consequently referring clinicians and patients. AI can boost the diagnostic process across the board. Radiology involves picture capture, post-processing, and automated report production. AI algorithms in spine imaging can improve picture quality; mark vertebral levels; and detect, segment, and characterize lesions [15].

The basic AI techniques are explainable AI (XAI) and responsible AI (RAI) as shown in Figure 5.1. XAI is a term used to denote the campaigns, initiatives, and events undertaken to address concerns about AI transparency and trust, rather than a specific technological concept. XAI has been called "interpretable" or just "readily apparent AI." The goal of AI is to uphold a high level of computational efficiency while building

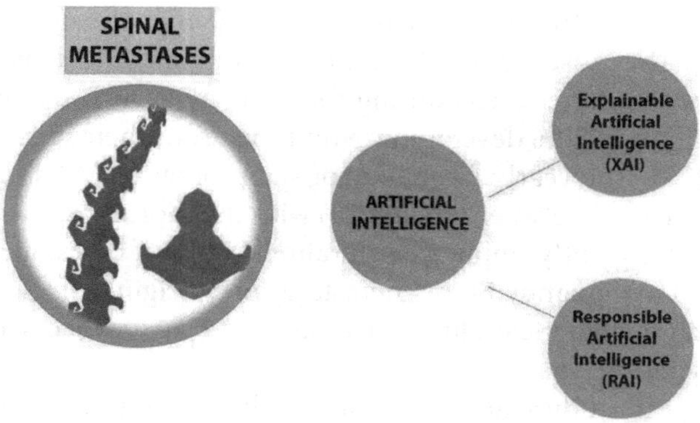

Figure 5.1 Spinal metastases of AI techniques.

explainable algorithms, permitting individuals to grasp, be well reliable, and proficiently oversee the forthcoming generation of collaborators with AI (Defense Advanced Research and Protection Agency). XAI is created with consumers in mind, empowering them to examine AI. Overall, XAI aims to analyze, enhance, learn from, and justify AI to someday manage it [16]. Responsible AI, or RAI, is a field that applies ethics to AI development and usage, ensuring systems benefit humanity. Truthfulness, resilience, accountability, openness, and confidentiality alongside security are the primary issues that it faces. A vital aspect of RAI is XAI, which gives people a perception of how AI models behave while executing judgments. Explainability is a fundamental component of RAI, and XAI approaches enhance transparency [17].

Radiomics-based approaches need the extraction of numerous handmade features, which are afterward utilized to construct a set of exercises for grouping imagery and applying deep learning (DL). A flaw in the method is that certain customized features are restricted to the clinician's or radiologist's experience, which lowers the generated algorithm's correctness. Without the need for manual feature selection, machine learning (ML), and DL approaches may be able to quickly identify pertinent picture properties for categorization. Convolutional neural networks are typically used for this because research has shown them to improve accuracy in forecasting lesion identification, division, and therapeutic response in oncological imaging [18–23].

Current XAI algorithms for image analysis may be classified into two types: attribution-based and non-attribution–based. Whereas non-attribution–based methodologies investigate, debug, and explain model behavior, attribution-based methods provide heat maps that illustrate the decision-making area of an image. Numerous uses of medical imaging, including the diagnosis of COVID-19, evaluation of knee discomfort, classification of Alzheimer's illness, and MS diagnosis, have made use of attribution-based methodologies. Choosing therapeutically meaningful concepts for MRI segmentation, tweaking images to gauge the degree of osteoarthritis in the knee, and categorizing cancer using archetypal images are a few examples of non-attribution–based methods [24].

Because there are so many different medical data sources involved, the multifunctional XAI technique has grown increasingly prevalent in healthcare applications. It highlights the roles of different types of data, elucidates their connections, and provides information on the most significant data points from different modalities [25–27]. This chapter discusses several XAI strategies for medical data, with an emphasis on RAI principles, explainability, and future research directions. Understanding explainability is critical for creating transparent, robust, fair, and repeatable AI.

5.2 Spinal Metastasis: Need of Artificial Intelligence for Imaging

5.2.1 The Fiscal Impact of Spine Surgery: Overseeing Cascading Monetary Implications and Price Hikes

Spine treatment is expensive; in the US, annual direct costs are roughly $110 billion on average [28, 29]. The average amount spent on health care is predicted to reach $5.3 trillion by 2025 or about 20% of the US gross domestic product (GDP) [29]. Moreover, the costs are steadily rising; a spinal fusion done today will probably cost 12 times as much as one done thirty years ago. In 2014, total hip and total knee arthroplasty expenses were surpassed by the aggregate cost of spinal fusions during a hospital stay in the United States. It is easy to believe that supply and demand economics, or more specifically, the idea that the existing patterns in spine care expenditure are unsustainable, are the driving forces behind this surge in spending. But the contrary has really been what we have seen [30].

Medicare reimbursements are expected to be reduced by billions of dollars over the next several years due to the rapidly rising cost of healthcare. Furthermore, as a result of health care reform, payer rejections have increased, reimbursements have decreased, and hospitals and doctors are being profiled based on the amount and caliber of treatment they provide [29]. In the absence of innovation or substantial reduction, the present trend of spine surgery expenses is unsustainable [31].

5.2.2 Diverseness in Medical Care Administration and Investigation

There are many distinct surgical approaches for treating a particular issue in spine surgery, which are frequently based on training and experience [32]. Sixty-nine percent of US neurosurgery and orthopedic spine surgeons surveyed in 2014 disagreed about the best course of action for surgically treating recurrent lumbar disc herniations [33]. Another poll conducted in 2016 found that 75% of spine surgeons disagreed on the best ways to treat patients with persistent low back pain [34]. Treatment options and costs vary as a result of this heterogeneity of care. Alvin and colleagues' cross-sectional analysis supported this by demonstrating a clear correlation between therapy expenses and patient count along with the years of expertise in treating recurrent lumbar disc herniations [32]. Furthermore, it has been demonstrated that spine surgeons in private practice are more cost-conscious than their academic counterparts [32].

Patient-reported outcome instruments (PROIs), which can be utilized to figure out the worth of a particular surgical procedure and gauge the performance of surgeons, exhibit heterogeneity, and add to the complexity of the situation. Even though they are not ideal indicators of success, they are nonetheless required to address any disparities in care. Nevertheless, it is crucial to recognize the limits of patient reporting. For example, about 206 unique PROIs were found in a new cross-sectional investigation that examined the use of PROIs in spine surgery, with specialists having limited consensus on outcome measurements [35]. Considering these aspects, there are several domains in which AI techniques may be applied to enhance patient care and foster consensus among surgeons.

5.2.3 AI in Spine Surgery

AI system–based benefits and how they apply to surgical procedures for the spine have drawn more and more interest [36–38]. AI may enhance outcomes, reduce downrange financial risks to the institution and to payers, and assist doctors and hospital centers in defining the quality and cost of treatment [1–3]. Although AI has generated criticism as well, properly applied, it has the potential to transform the standard of care in spine surgery, save costs and waste, and enhance patient care and efficiency [37–39].

The phrase "artificial intelligence" (AI) describes a machine's computational capacity to carry out activities that are similar to those carried out by humans. This is accomplished by using distinctive inputs to produce outputs with a high added value [40].

Global interest in AI for medical imaging is growing as a result of recent advancements in the field and the ever-growing volume of digital image and report data. The original idea behind the use of AI and computer-aided diagnostic (CAD) systems was to help radiologists or doctors identify cancers or lesions, which would boost productivity, improve detection, and lower mistake rates [41, 14]. Therefore, efforts are being made to improve AI's capacity for diagnosis as well as its efficiency so that it may be effectively used in clinical settings. With the development of artificial neural networks, a class of structures that are somewhat inspired by the functioning of the human brain [42]. AI in radiology has grown significantly as a result of the development of several computational learning models, particularly ML and DL algorithms. The implementation of AI in oncology imaging workflow can be broadly categorized into three areas: (1) abnormality detection; (2) abnormality characterization, encompassing image processing techniques such as segmentation, differentiation, and classification; and (3) integrated diagnostics, encompassing prognosis prediction, treatment response, and decision support for treatment planning and decision-making.

5.2.4 Artificial Intelligence Applications in the Spine

One of the first anatomical locations for which specific AI algorithms were used in imaging investigations was the spine. As the spine is commonly included in the field of view for several other imaging examinations (such as neck, thorax, and abdomen), a significant amount of extra information may be captured or missed. The creation of automated AI technologies that may be used to evaluate the spinal cord and vertebrae during these non-spine exams is becoming more and more popular as a result. Furthermore, automated vertebral body labeling methods for CT and MRI are now readily accessible [42].

AI techniques have been created recently that reliably detect vertebral fractures and diagnose osteoporosis on plain and CT radiographs, showing promising early findings [44, 45]. Additionally, algorithms have been used on CT and MRI scans to attempt to produce automated reporting and grading of degenerative abnormalities in the lumbar spine [46]. Additionally, particular AI instruments have been created to identify SMT [47] and the identification of hematological malignancies [15].

5.2.5 Principal ML Approaches Used in Spine Care

Numerous presentations have been made on the entirety of how modern ML and AI functions are created and exploited, including the thorough analysis by Galbusera *et al.* from 2019 [48, 49]. The application of ML in medicine, specifically in the treatment of spinal illnesses, may be characterized based on how the learning process takes shape. Three major categories are recognized and described in the following subsections.

5.2.5.1 Supervised Learning

Using training datasets, supervised learning makes predictions about results that are previously known. Determining the link between an original dataset and the associated outcome is the aim. By reducing the discrepancy between the expected and actual outcome, the prediction is maximized. The term "loss of function" refers to this distinction. After it is minimized, a useful prediction is produced that may be used on similar datasets with undetermined outcomes. The complexity of the issue and the caliber of the data have a significant impact on how many datasets are required to make a reliable forecast.

5.2.5.2 Reinforcement Learning

It is a particular type of supervised learning. There are no known outcomes in this application. Rather, the output is assessed outside, and a modification to the output manufacturing process is then implemented.

5.2.5.3 Unsupervised Learning

The phrase "unsupervised learning" describes dataset analysis done without drawing any predefined inferences. But here, the objective is to identify patterns, groups, and characteristics to extract additional information from the available data—rather than to forecast a certain outcome. Big data analytics are the primary usage of this type in the applications that are currently released, and they provide new perspectives [50].

5.2.6 Obtaining and Reconstructing Images: Accelerate Medical Imaging

One of the key elements that have attracted a lot of consideration throughout the clinical medical diagnostic imaging procedure has always been imaging speed. Patients may experience pain and imaging departments' daily average circulation will be reduced by prolonged scanning times. Relevant worldwide research mostly concentrates on MRI acceleration when it comes to fast imaging. Mardani *et al.* [50] suggested a compressed sensing (CS) quick imaging approach based on a generative adversarial network (GAN) for magnetic resonance (MR) compression. This technique uses a GAN to represent a lower-degree array of superior MR images. Dr. Good fellow presented the GAN to the scientific community [51]. The GAN is composed of a generator and a discriminator. The generator creates a manifold of high-quality images by mapping low-quality magnetic resonance images onto it. To ensure the reliability and correctness of the generated images, the author adds the k-space data fidelity item to the network. The imaging results are noticeably better than those of conventional CS algorithms, and experimental findings demonstrate that this approach can reach at least five times the scanning acceleration [52].

5.3 Artificial Intelligence Imaging Using XAI and RAI Technique

Spinal MRI may see the spine, spinal cord, and surrounding soft tissues in a range of planes, sequences, and parameters [53]. Because of its exceptionally sensitive nature to shifts in tissue signal, this approach is a superb instrument to assist with identifying and characterizing soft tissue lesions. It is currently the method of choice for diagnosing spinal conditions [54]. Nonetheless, in certain instances, it may be challenging to make an early differential diagnosis between spinal tuberculosis (STB) and SM. For instance, when a paravertebral abscess or intervertebral disc involvement does not occur, when the lesion presents as an atypical form of vertebral involvement, or when both tuberculosis and a tumor have a history [55]. Despite having a high degree of selectivity, PET/CT is not widely used in clinical settings because of its high cost and radiation exposure [56]. DL approaches were just recently utilized to extract visual attributes from photos and turn them into high-dimensional features. These traits might therefore be used to customize, assess, and distinguish disorders, especially in the realm of imaging for healthcare purposes [57]. Previous research has demonstrated the effectiveness of convolutional neural network models for identifying lesions in the brain, kidney, prostate, and breast using MRI data. These models achieve excellent levels of sensitivity and specificity [58]. Diagnostic technologies aided by AI have the potential to enhance clinical practice by providing a sophisticated, accurate, and user-friendly solution for diagnosis, hence decreasing the need for invasive and painful biopsies. In this work, we assessed DL algorithms' capacity to distinguish between STB and SM using T2-weighted imaging (T2WI), and we contrasted their efficacy with two spinal surgeons' diagnoses of these illnesses, whose degrees of expertise varied [53, 59].

AI robots offer a lot of promise to help medical practitioners with a variety of regular duties [60]. Additionally, AI algorithms from the field of DL [61]. These DNNs are incredibly effective and can perform almost as well as humans [62]. Unfortunately, there is a major drawback to these most popular models. Because of their tremendous dimensionality, extreme nonlinearity, and complexity, human specialists can no longer understand them [63]. Transparency, retraceability, and explainability, however, are crucial and even required in the medical industry for lawful reasons [64] as well as for moral concerns [65]. Frequently, the question of why has greater significance than the AI's actual output. Explainable artificial intelligence (XAI) is a subfield in computing science concerned with the implementation of transparency, traceability, and accessibility in designated black box strategies. This is becoming increasingly important as medical AI solutions are expected to achieve greater quality requirements. A human expert must be able to justify and comprehend a machine's decision-making process rather than merely depending on conventional metrics like accuracy and precision [66, 67].

Responsible AI (RAI), also known as ethical or trustworthy AI, is a collection of normative statements and guidelines that specify how AI systems must be created, implemented, and managed in order to abide by the law and ethical standards. To put it another way, companies trying to use AI models ethically first create a framework that includes pre-established ethics, regulations, and principles [68].

5.3.1 XAI Technique

According to [69], the capacity to communicate the reasoning behind an AI decision in a way that is clear to humans and a wider variety of end users is known as explainability. The many end users concentrate on the various explainability vantage points. The explainability of the model or algorithm is of more relevance to data scientists or AI specialists. Physicians and medical professionals, however, are more focused on clinical inference and prediction. Interpretability is the other concept associated with explainability. Interpretability is the ability to give an abstract idea meaning [70]. While interpretability refers to the model's representation formed from the training data, explainability is concerned with the analysis of forecasts created in the context of fresh instances [71]. Moreover, there are two categories of XAI techniques: post-hoc and intrinsic. An intrinsic approach is one in which we can comprehend a technique's foundation or a decision-making process without the need for more knowledge. Common intrinsic techniques consist of linear regression (LR) [72], including statistical regression, k-nearest neighbor, rule-based learners, generic additive models, and decision trees. Machine learning is a subset of AI, whereas DL is a subset of ML. Furthermore, we believe that XAI is a subset of AI, with ML acting as the underlying approach. Using this method, users can figure out which fraction of the input data affects the classifier's categorization choice. Additional ad hoc techniques include Shapley additive explanations [73], class activation mapping [74], and principle component analysis [75]. Dimensional lowering, focus mechanism, limited neural network design, visual clarification, local justification, example-based clarification, description by straightforwardness, and feature impact are the several types of post-hoc explainability techniques [76].

5.3.1.1 Switched from "Black Box" to "(Translucent) Glass Box"

We wish to go from a "black box" to a transparent "glass box" with XAI [77] also referred to as a "white box" [78]. A glass box model provides perfect transparency because all of the parameters are known, and we can see exactly how the model comes to its conclusion. The model is completely transparent in an ideal scenario, but, in many other scenarios (such as DL models), the model may only be partially explainable; in these cases, it may be thought of as a "translucent glass box" with an opacity level that ranges from 0% to 100%. A transparent glass box with a low opacity (or a high transparency model) might help people comprehend the model better, which can boost confidence. This trust may be separated into two categories: faith in the forecast and faith in the model, as explained in one of the studies [79]. Different participants related to healthcare deserve different justifications [80]. In order instance: users—often physicians, but

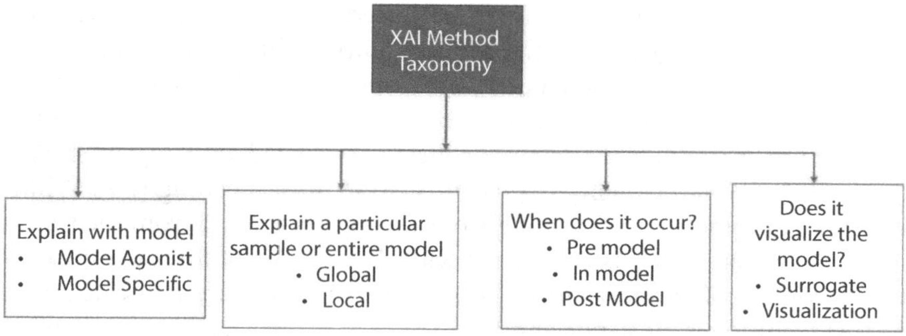

Figure 5.2 The XAI techniques taxonomy.

occasionally patients as well—are primarily interested in the predictions made by the model, whereas data professionals tend to be more interested in the model itself. Consequently, trust in a data scientist often refers to faith in the model itself, but trust in a doctor or patient normally refers to trust in the model's predictions. While the "confidence in the model" problem may be overwhelmed by picking numerous such forecasts, the "confidence in a forecast" problem may be resolved by providing explanations for each prognosis [79]. Which of these two techniques should be used in which situation might be determined by future study [81].

Whereas the "confidence in the model" problem may be overwhelmed by picking numerous such forecasts, the "confidence in a forecast" problem may be resolved by providing explanations for each prognosis.

Classification approaches, in general, are not absolute; they may concurrently be classified into several overlapping or non-overlapping classes and vary significantly depending on the properties of the methods [82]. Figure 5.2 displays the XAI techniques taxonomy.

5.3.1.2 Interpretation Types

XAI models are divided into two categories: intrinsic and post-hoc models. The two XAI domains work differently. Model-based interpretability, often referred to as intrinsic interpretability, allows the model to be understood by changing its components and/or structure. To explain a trained model, post-hoc models look at both the original and additional models. Although post-hoc investigation is generally employed, some extra work is required to make it beneficial before it can be deployed in the medical area [83]. The following is an overview of the post-hoc and intrinsic explanations.

5.3.1.2.1 Intrinsic Explanation

This type of model has a structure that is simple to comprehend. Despite having a relatively simple structure, conventional models—like LR models—may be understood in this context. For example, a model explains relevant to the language interpreter together with the answer [84].

5.3.1.2.2 Post-Hoc Explanation

It refers to the intelligible data obtained by external procedures during model analysis. For example, back propagation [85], class activation mapping [74], and layer-wise relevance propagation [86] are all post-hoc interpretation strategies.

5.3.1.3 Model Accuracy

XAI models are either concept-specific or concept-agnostic, contingent upon whether the technique applies to several concept types.

5.3.1.3.1 Model-Specific Description

A model-specific approach is useful for certain kinds of scenarios. For example, a technique needs to use some kind of model feature or architecture. Furthermore, intrinsic models are all model-specific as they all utilize the structure of the model [87].

5.3.1.3.2 Model-Agnostic Description

Model-agnostic approaches have no model-specific requirements. Rather, it is employed by the majority of XAI models. For instance, the perturbation-based technique known as local interpretable model-agnostic explanations (LIME) [79]. Modifying the model inputs yields and interprets many outcomes. This may be categorized as post-hoc in nature.

5.3.1.4 Explanation Areas

XAI can be defined for specific both inputs and outcomes or for the whole framework. There are a couple of explanations for this scenario: (1) universal explanations and (2) regional explanations.

5.3.1.4.1 Regional Explanation

This type of analysis treats the framework as a black box, focusing on the regional variables affecting the choice. As a result, qualities that influence the decision-making process are identified. Regional explanations frequently focus on a particular data set of input and the specific properties associated with it [88].

5.3.1.4.2 Universal Explanation

The model is utilized to understand this type of explanation. Understanding the manner of interaction between the framework's elements, for example, highlights and acknowledges the contribution made to the conclusion. One way to put it is, "How does the model predict?" The model's performance decides whether it is interpreted globally. To provide an appropriate global interpretation of the model, one might generalize the regional version [88, 89].

The diagnosis of spinal diseases, the suggestion of treatments, and the prediction of patient outcomes have all benefited greatly from using AI and ML. In the work of Jujjavarapu *et al.*, one notable case study uses a DL model to predict surgical outcomes in patients with lumbar disc herniation and lumbar spinal stenosis [90]. With an area under curve (AUC) of 0.725 as opposed to 0.597, the study showed that the AI model Predicted early surgery more accurately compared to a benchmark model (logistic regression).

Halicka *et al.* provided another interesting case study, whereby they created an AI program that could forecast the results that patients would report after lumbar spine surgery [91]. The goal of the project was to use multivariate regression and random-forest techniques to create and externally evaluate prediction models for the results of spine surgery. Individuals undergoing surgery on the lumbar spine for detrimental pathologies were included throughout the study. The Core Outcome Measures Index scores and variations in the severity of leg and back pain were used to assess the models. The models explained the discrepancies in the validation data and showed satisfactory calibration. The range of the discriminating ability was 0.62 to 0.72, which suggests a modest level of prediction accuracy. Age, baseline scores, the kind of degenerative disease, prior operations, cigarette smoking situation, mortality, and time spent in hospitalization were the most significant predictors. The created models were robust, but their discriminating skills were only marginally satisfactory, indicating the need for further prognostic variables [92].

The capacity of AI and ML to precisely and consistently aid their potential in the field of spine care is built on their ability to identify and treat spinal diseases. Table 5.1 lists the drawbacks of AI and ML in spinal care as well as ways to enhance it. These AI-driven systems' authenticity and

Table 5.1 Challenges and the development approaches to AI and ML in spinal care.

Limitations	Improvement measures
Lack of diverse data of excellent quality	Make sure you gather data with appropriate labeling and annotation; increase the number of data sources and partnerships; use data augmentation methods to broaden the diversity of datasets.
Possible issues involving justice and partiality	Provide methods for detecting and mitigating prejudice; put in place algorithms that consider fairness; perform a thorough assessment of the models' fairness and bias.
Explainability and comprehensibility	Create comprehensible and transparent AI and ML models; develop interpretability strategies independent of models; explain the judgments and predictions made by the model.
Transferability and generalizability	Gather information from various contexts and demographics; examine domain adaptability and transfer learning strategies; perform external validation research in various medical environments.

dependability are not assured, though. To guarantee the correctness and dependability of their outputs, they must be carefully examined and validated by rigorous testing, validation, and ongoing evaluation [93].

An AI system is said to be reliable if it can reliably provide the same outcomes under the same circumstances. This is especially significant in medical contexts because accurate forecasts are essential for making therapeutic decisions. Various assessments and therapeutic approaches for the same patient may result from variations in AI system performance, which might have detrimental effects on patient care [94]. External validation is an additional technique for promising the efficacy and dependability of AI systems in spine care. This kind of testing investigates the usefulness of models using datasets that were not used in the training phase or primary validity. It is an essential stage in determining if AI models are generalizable and ready for use in actual healthcare settings [95, 96].

5.3.2 RAI (Responsible Artificial Intelligence) Technique

The healthcare industry is focusing on RAI development, deployment, management, and governance. Responsible AI is an approach that emphasizes justice, model explainability, and responsibility when using AI technologies in real-world organizations. While there are AI ethical frameworks and norms available, they may not apply to healthcare [97].

Most AI systems, particularly DL networks, which are already playing an important role, look like a black box to an outside user [98]. While techniques for visualizing the internal workings and characteristics of AI systems have been introduced [85]. Despite the introduction of more accessible to humans gadgets like decision trees, AI projections seem to be made based on a mysterious logic that is incomprehensible to outside observers [99]. The issue of managerial responsibility, whose is currently being dealt with at the regulatory level, is promptly dealt with through this restriction. Stated differently, in the event that a prediction turns into wrong, like wrong diagnosis, it is crucial to ascertain if the blame rests with the manufacturer, the AI system itself, or the radiologists who utilized it. Because establishing AI tools require more thorough examination and verification compared to competing tools, their concealed aspect has a substantial impact on marketing approval and could result in lengthier the introduction and greater expenses [49].

Potential biases in the forecasts, which might be purposeful (fraudulent) or inadvertent, provide another challenge. A decision support tool (DST) that encourages the use of medications or equipment manufactured by a particular company is an example of an intentional bias. Another example is a tool that is intended to maximize certain quality indicators that are beneficial to the hospital but may not always optimize patient care [99]. The lack of data on some uncommon diseases or phenotypes, which may be underrepresented in the training dataset compared to more common disorders, or the lack of records, or restricted records, for some ethnicities, may be the cause of unintentional biases [98]. Inadequate data collection strategies, involving giving a preference to additional readily available data sources, might also unintentionally introduce bias. In an effort to lessen the effects of these difficulties, efforts are being made to regulate AI, with the ultimate objective being the establishment of strong public trust [100]. It should be emphasized that cultural differences among East Asian nations, the United States, and the European Union might lead to markedly different perspectives on governance and regulation [49].

Because so much medical along with photographic information needed the use of AI in healthcare raises concerns regarding security and confidentiality. By implementing opt-in regulations, the General Data Protection Regulation of the European Union increased rights for patients. This rule differs from the less stringent US one, which may lead to more US participation in AI innovation [101].

5.3.2.1 RAI Principles

The ethical literature on AI has identified six key characteristics: equality, openness, trustworthiness, credibility, anonymity, and compassion. These characteristics are considered important in healthcare AI research and are most frequently cited in order to develop our initial understanding of RAI, even though there is no generally recognized ethical a foundation [97]. The basic RAI principles are sown in Table 5.2.

Table 5.2 RAI principles [97].

RAI principles	Concept
SAI	Promoting responsible local leadership for more sustainable AI solutions and AI for social sustainability
HAI	Improving AI agents to fulfill ethical care criteria, maintaining public confidence by including health professionals, and developing artificial wisdom through multidisciplinary collaboration
IAI	Equitable interaction and engagement in the management of AI
FAI	Reducing computational and information bias, information representation, and equity plus health inequalities in environments with limited resources
TAI	Protecting individual confidentiality explication of models built on AI and choices and tackling the deprivation of confidentiality via law user autonomy and well-informed agreement to use information

5.3.2.1.1 Sustainable AI (SAI)

Two subthemes emerged in the topic of SAI: (1) promoting responsible local leadership for more sustainable AI solutions and (2) AI for social sustainability.

AI healthcare technology must be created with responsible local leadership; it includes business as well as non-governmental organizations, scientific centers educational institutions, foreign agencies, and grassroots organizations in addition to local governments.

A framework is made up of four components: educating local experts, strong monitoring mechanisms, a systems-based approach, and accountable and inclusive local leadership [102, 103]. Collaboration and the empowerment of local actors are essential for advancing SAI. Local AI expertise must be established and nurtured, while international organizations may develop governance methods and discover investment opportunities. This guarantees that AI satisfies industry requirements while also supporting local infrastructure and knowledge [104].

Academics and practitioners alike have expressed an interest in AI for sustainability. However, the social implications for human and environmental well-being must be recognized. Healthcare organizations must use AI ethically, balancing stakeholder requirements, reducing ethical issues, and producing long-term profitability. Misuse of AI can exacerbate health inequities [105–108]. Establish collaborations between educational establishments and healthcare practitioners to use complementary skills in AI technology, pedagogy, morality, legislation, and medical practice. These courses ought to be included in medical schools' curriculum to teach aspiring medical professionals about the use of AI and ethical data collection [109].

5.3.2.1.2 Humancentric AI (HAI)

It mostly focuses on three concepts: (a) improving AI agents to fulfil ethical care criteria, (b) maintaining public confidence by including health professionals, and (c) creating AI by working across disciplines. The revolutionary impact of AI in healthcare may result in people being regarded as commodities, with health insurance firms coercing care seekers to use AI-driven systems devoid of individual substitutes. This might result in a shift away from patient-centered care and interaction processes in psychological care provided in the United Kingdom, such as psychotherapy [97, 110].

Provide clinical context to computer and data scientist, (2) guarantee data quality; and (3) interpret AI black-box solutions for patient recommendations are the three ethical duties of medical practitioners adopting AI tools [111]. In a study, one researcher concluded that AI falls short of society's technological goals and that artificial wisdom (AW) should be the primary emphasis of AI technology. Wisdom is associated with lifespan, health, happiness, and well-being in both people and society [112].

5.3.2.1.3 Inclusive AI (IAI)

Digitalization is altering the interactions between patients and providers. Patients fear AI-powered health systems might alter their interactions with doctors, which would impact the cost and quality of care [113].

5.3.2.1.4 Fair AI (FAI)

Biases such as label, cohort, minority, missing data, and privilege can all have an impact on AI model design, training data, clinician-patient interactions, and more. To reduce these biases, experts recommend generalizing prediction tasks, taking contextual elements into account, and assessing AI models and algorithms regularly through algorithm stewardship programs. Identifying label choice bias in algorithms might help to alleviate structural inequities [114–117].

To overcome AI bias, a data governance body should be formed that includes patients, healthcare specialists, and AI experts. To guarantee their objectivity and representativeness, the committee will examine datasets and algorithms. Transparency in monitoring communities and people is critical, with community leaders taking part in reporting unpleasant situations [99, 118].

5.3.2.1.5 Transparent AI (TAI)

AI and analytical algorithms are altering healthcare by gathering and exploiting personal health data, resulting in identity theft, a scam, computational discrimination, privacy issues, and information leaks. AI carebots may overcome limits in traditional psychological therapies. However, ethical implications and a road plan for responsible innovation are critical, particularly in light of privacy concerns and regulatory control advances [119–122].

5.4 Challenges and Future Directions and Research Needs

The use of AI in biomechanical investigations represents a new horizon in spinal surgery research. Although AI is nevertheless in its nascent stages, it offers various exciting potential in this discipline. AI may be effective in two domains: the study of position and locomotion patterns, and the recognition of aberrant gait in spinal illnesses [52]. In an assortment of modeling, investigators imposed arbitrary stresses toward a tiny portion of bone trabecular tissue employing a proven biomechanical computer model that predicted bone tissue reacting to mechanical loading based on regional strains. An artificial neural network was trained with the simulation outputs, or reestablished segmental skeletal density, to predict the pressures that lead to this kind of remodeling. Calculating stresses in patient-specific research is another application of AI that reduces a demand for cognitively expensive finite element designs [123]. The challenges coming from the large quantity of processing will slow the growth of AI [124, 125]. To have a more comprehensive picture of ethical AI in healthcare, future studies should look at studies from other languages or continents. Using XAI models can improve the understanding of illnesses and their causes, making them more useful for diagnosis [126]. Using the RAI techniques, the responsible medical the five principles of sustainability, inclusivity, human-centeredness, justice, and openness are all incorporated into AI development. Policymakers and legislators can assess these initiatives to mitigate inherent risks and biases and improve AI adoption [97].

5.5 Conclusion

AI application in radiation therapy attempts to enhance radiologist workflow, hence benefiting referring doctors and patients. AI can enhance diagnostic procedures across the board. Radiology involves picture capture, post-processing, and automated report production. AI algorithms in spine imaging can improve picture quality, identify vertebral levels, and locate, segment, and characterize lesions. XAI aims to evaluate, enhance, learn from, and justify AI so that it may someday be managed. Responsible AI (RAI) is a field that applies ethics to AI development and use, ensuring that systems benefit humanity. It prioritizes justice, robustness, openness, accountability, privacy, and safety. Explainable AI (XAI) is a key component of RAI, providing humans with visibility into AI models' reasoning throughout decision-making processes. XAI techniques increase transparency, making explainability an important aspect of RAI. The current chapter focuses on the various XAI and RAI procedures for spinal metastases. A glass box approach, like a decision tree or LR model, is one of the XAI models. It offers complete transparency as all of the parameters are exposed, and we can see precisely how the model comes to its conclusions. It also incorporates the intrinsic and post-hoc models of XAI. It contains XAI model specifics and explanations. Equality, honesty, accountability, confidence secrecy, and affection are important and often mentioned in healthcare AI research to advance our fundamental understanding of RAI, according to the literature on AI ethics. More models based on this principle are necessary for both methods.

References

1. Ong, W., Zhu, L., Zhang, W., Kuah, T., Lim, D.S.W., Low, X.Z. *et al.*, Application of artificial intelligence methods for imaging of spinal metastasis. *Cancers*, 14, 16, 4025, 2022.
2. Laur, O., Nandu, H., Titelbaum, D.S., Nunez, D.B., Khurana, B., Nontraumatic spinal cord compression: MRI primer for emergency department radiologists. *Radiographics*, 39, 6, 1862–80, 2019.
3. Barzilai, O., Fisher, C.G., Bilsky, M.H., State of the art treatment of spinal metastatic disease. *Neurosurgery*, 82, 6, 757–69, 2018.
4. Kuah, T., Vellayappan, B.A., Makmur, A., Nair, S., Song, J., Tan, J.H. *et al.*, State-of-the-art imaging techniques in metastatic spinal cord compression. *Cancers*, 14, 13, 3289, 2022.
5. O'Sullivan, G.J., Carty, F.L., Cronin, C.G., Imaging of bone metastasis: an update. *World J. Radiol.*, 7, 8, 202, 2015.
6. Liu, T., Wang, S., Liu, H., Meng, B., Zhou, F., He, F. *et al.*, Detection of vertebral metastases: a meta-analysis comparing MRI, CT, PET, BS and BS with SPECT. *J. Cancer Res. Clin. Oncol.*, 143, 457–65, 2017.
7. Wallace, A.N., Greenwood, T.J., Jennings, J.W., Use of imaging in the management of metastatic spine disease with percutaneous ablation and vertebral augmentation. *Am. J. Roentgenol.*, 205, 2, 434–41, 2015.
8. Schiff, D., O'neill, B., Wang, C.H., O'Fallon, J.R., Neuroimaging and treatment implications of patients with multiple epidural spinal metastases. *Cancer: Interdiscip. Int. J. Am. Cancer Soc.*, 83, 8, 1593–601, 1998.
9. Moynagh, M.R., Colleran, G.C., Tavernaraki, K., Eustace, S.J., Kavanagh, E.C. (Eds.), Whole-body magnetic resonance imaging: assessment of skeletal metastases. *Semin. Musculoskelet. Radiol.*, 022–036, 2010, © Thieme Medical Publishers.

10. Dong, M., Huang, X., Xu, B., Unsupervised speech recognition through spike-timing-dependent plasticity in a convolutional spiking neural network. *PLoS One*, 13, 11, e0204596, 2018.
11. Frank, D.-A., Chrysochou, P., Mitkidis, P., Ariely, D., Human decision-making biases in the moral dilemmas of autonomous vehicles. *Sci. Rep.*, 9, 1, 13080, 2019.
12. Moravčík, M., Schmid, M., Burch, N., Lisý, V., Morrill, D., Bard, N. *et al.*, Deepstack: Expert-level artificial intelligence in heads-up no-limit poker. *Science*, 356, 6337, 508–13, 2017.
13. Nensa, F., Demircioglu, A., Rischpler, C., Artificial intelligence in nuclear medicine. *J. Nucl. Med.*, 60, Supplement 2, 29S–37S, 2019.
14. Hosny, A., Parmar, C., Quackenbush, J., Schwartz, L.H., Aerts, H.J., Artificial intelligence in radiology. *Nat. Rev. Cancer*, 18, 8, 500–10, 2018.
15. Martín-Noguerol, T., Miranda, M.O., Amrhein, T.J., Paulano-Godino, F., Xiberta, P., Vilanova, J.C. *et al.*, The role of Artificial intelligence in the assessment of the spine and spinal cord. *Eur. J. Radiol.*, 161, 110726, 2023.
16. Meske, C., Abedin, B., Klier, M., Rabhi, F., Explainable and responsible artificial intelligence. *Electron. Mark.*, 32, 4, 2103–6, 2022.
17. Baker, S. and Xiang, W., Explainable AI is Responsible AI: How Explainability Creates Trustworthy and Socially Responsible Artificial Intelligence, 2023, arXiv preprint arXiv:231201555.
18. Tran, K.A., Kondrashova, O., Bradley, A., Williams, E.D., Pearson, J.V., Waddell, N., Deep learning in cancer diagnosis, prognosis and treatment selection. *Genome Med.*, 13, 1–17, 2021.
19. Liu, Z., Wang, S., Dong, D., Wei, J., Fang, C., Zhou, X. *et al.*, The applications of radiomics in precision diagnosis and treatment of oncology: opportunities and challenges. *Theranostics*, 9, 5, 1303, 2019.
20. Parekh, V.S. and Jacobs, M.A., Deep learning and radiomics in precision medicine. *Expert Rev. Precis. Med. Drug Dev.*, 4, 2, 59–72, 2019.
21. Esteva, A., Kuprel, B., Novoa, R.A., Ko, J., Swetter, S.M., Blau, H.M. *et al.*, Dermatologist-level classification of skin cancer with deep neural networks. *Nature*, 542, 7639, 115–8, 2017.
22. Kermany, D.S., Goldbaum, M., Cai, W., Valentim, C.C., Liang, H., Baxter, S.L. *et al.*, Identifying medical diagnoses and treatable diseases by image-based deep learning. *Cell*, 172, 5, 1122–31.e9, 2018.
23. De Fauw, J., Ledsam, J.R., Romera-Paredes, B., Nikolov, S., Tomasev, N., Blackwell, S. *et al.*, Clinically applicable deep learning for diagnosis and referral in retinal disease. *Nat. Med.*, 24, 9, 1342–50, 2018.
24. Hossain, M.I., Zamzmi, G., Mouton, P.R., Salekin, M.S., Sun, Y., Goldgof, D., Explainable AI for Medical Data: Current Methods, Limitations, and Future Directions. *ACM Comput. Surv.*, 1–41, 2023.
25. Kamal, M.S., Northcote, A., Chowdhury, L., Dey, N., Crespo, R.G., Herrera-Viedma, E., Alzheimer's patient analysis using image and gene

expression data and explainable-AI to present associated genes. *IEEE Trans. Instrum. Meas.*, 70, 1–7, 2021.
26. Wang, S., Yin, Y., Wang, D., Wang, Y., Jin, Y., Interpretability-based multimodal convolutional neural networks for skin lesion diagnosis. *IEEE Trans. Cybern.*, 52, 12, 12623–37, 2021.
27. Yang, G., Ye, Q., Xia, J., Unbox the black-box for the medical explainable AI via multi-modal and multi-centre data fusion: A mini-review, two showcases and beyond. *Inf. Fusion*, 77, 29–52, 2022.
28. Deyo, R.A., Mirza, S.K., Martin, B.I., Kreuter, W., Goodman, D.C., Jarvik, J.G., Trends, Major Medical Complications, and Charges Associated With Surgery for Lumbar Spinal Stenosis in Older Adults. *JAMA*, 303, 13, 1259–65, 2010.
29. Parker, S.L., Chotai, S., Devin, C.J., Tetreault, L., Mroz, T.E., Brodke, D.S. *et al.*, Bending the Cost Curve—Establishing Value in Spine Surgery. *Neurosurgery*, 80, 3S, S61–S9, 2017.
30. Rasouli, J.J., Shao, J., Neifert, S., Gibbs, W.N., Habboub, G., Steinmetz, M.P. *et al.*, Artificial Intelligence and Robotics in Spine Surgery. *Global Spine J.*, 11, 4, 556–64, 2020.
31. Waterman, B.R., Belmont, P.J., Schoenfeld, A.J., Low back pain in the United States: incidence and risk factors for presentation in the emergency setting. *Spine J.*, 12, 1, 63–70, 2012.
32. Alvin, M.D., Lubelski, D., Alam, R., Williams, S.K., Obuchowski, N.A., Steinmetz, M.P. *et al.*, Spine Surgeon Treatment Variability: The Impact on Costs. *Global Spine J.*, 8, 5, 498–506, 2017.
33. Mroz, T.E., Lubelski, D., Williams, S.K., O'Rourke, C., Obuchowski, N.A., Wang, J.C. *et al.*, Differences in the surgical treatment of recurrent lumbar disc herniation among spine surgeons in the United States. *Spine J.*, 14, 10, 2334–43, 2014.
34. Lubelski, D., Williams, S.K., O'Rourke, C., Obuchowski, N.A., Wang, J.C., Steinmetz, M.P. *et al.*, Differences in the Surgical Treatment of Lower Back Pain Among Spine Surgeons in the United States. *Spine*, 41, 11, 978–86, 2016.
35. Guzman, J.Z., Cutler, H.S., Connolly, J., Skovrlj, B., Mroz, T.E., Riew, K.D. *et al.*, Patient-Reported Outcome Instruments in Spine Surgery. *Spine*, 41, 5, 429–37, 2016.
36. Janssen, D.M.C., van Kuijk, S.M.J., d'Aumerie, B.B., Willems, P.C., External validation of a prediction model for surgical site infection after thoracolumbar spine surgery in a Western European cohort. *J. Orthop. Surg. Res.*, 13, 1, 114, 2018.
37. Ames, C.P., Smith, J.S., Pellisé, F., Kelly, M., Alanay, A., Acaroğlu, E. *et al.*, Artificial Intelligence Based Hierarchical Clustering of Patient Types and Intervention Categories in Adult Spinal Deformity Surgery: Towards a New Classification Scheme that Predicts Quality and Value. *Spine*, 44, 13, 915–26, 2019.

38. Ghogawala, Z., Dunbar, M., Essa, I., Artificial Intelligence for the Treatment of Lumbar Spondylolisthesis. *Neurosurg. Clin. North Am.*, 30, 3, 383–9, 2019.
39. Durand, W.M., DePasse, J.M., Daniels, A.H., Predictive Modeling for Blood Transfusion After Adult Spinal Deformity Surgery: A Tree-Based Machine Learning Approach. *Spine*, 43, 15, 1058–66, 2018.
40. Rajkomar, A., Dean, J., Kohane, I., Machine Learning in Medicine. *N. Engl. J. Med.*, 380, 14, 1347–58, 2019.
41. Ong, W.Z., L., Zhang, W., Kuah, T., Lim, D.S.W., Low, X.Z., Thian, Y.L., Teo, E.C., Tan, J.H., Kumar, N. *et al.*, Artificial Intelligence Methods for Spinal Metastasis Imaging, Encyclopedia, Available online: https://encyclopedia.pub/entry/27921 (accessed on 13 March 2024).
42. Kriegeskorte, N., Deep Neural Networks: A New Framework for Modeling Biological Vision and Brain Information Processing. *Annu. Rev. Vis. Sci.*, 1, 417–46, 2015.
43. Stern, D., Likar, B., Pernus, F., Vrtovec, T., Automated detection of spinal centrelines, vertebral bodies and intervertebral discs in CT and MR images of lumbar spine. *Phys. Med. Biol.*, 55, 1, 247–64, 2010.
44. Zhang, B., Y.K., Ning, Z., Wang, K., Dong, Y., Liu, X., Liu, S., Wang, J., Zhu, C., Yu, Q., Duan, Y., Deep learning of lumbar spine X-ray for osteopenia and osteoporosis screening: A multicenter retrospective cohort study. *Bone*, 140, 115561, 2020 Nov 1.
45. Gorelik, N. and Gyftopoulos, S., Applications of Artificial Intelligence in Musculoskeletal Imaging: From the Request to the Report. *Can. Assoc. Radiol. J.*, 72, 1, 45–59, 2021.
46. Han, Z., Wei, B., Xi, X., Chen, B., Yin, Y., Li, S., Unifying neural learning and symbolic reasoning for spinal medical report generation. *Med. Image Anal.*, 67, 101872, 2021.
47. Wang, J., Fang, Z., Lang, N., Yuan, H., Su, M.-Y., Baldi, P., A multi-resolution approach for spinal metastasis detection using deep Siamese neural networks. *Comput. Biol. Med.*, 84, 137–46, 2017.
48. Wirries, A., Geiger, F., Oberkircher, L., Jabari, S., An Evolution Gaining Momentum—The Growing Role of Artificial Intelligence in the Diagnosis and Treatment of Spinal Diseases. *Diagnostics*, 12, 4, 836, 2022.
49. Galbusera, F., Casaroli, G., Bassani, T., Artificial intelligence and machine learning in spine research. *JOR Spine*, 2, 1, e1044, 2019 Mar.
50. Mardani, M., Gong, E., Cheng, J.Y., Vasanawala, S.S., Zaharchuk, G., Xing, L. *et al.*, Deep Generative Adversarial Neural Networks for Compressive Sensing MRI. *IEEE Trans. Med. Imaging*, 38, 1, 167–79, 2019.
51. Goodfellow, I., Pouget-Abadie, J., Mirza, M., Xu, B., Warde-Farley, D., Ozair, S. *et al.*, Generative adversarial networks. *Commun. ACM*, 63, 11, 139–44, 2020.
52. Cui, Y., Zhu, J., Duan, Z., Liao, Z., Wang, S., Liu, W., Artificial intelligence in spinal imaging: current status and future directions. *Int. J. Environ. Res. Public Health*, 19, 18, 11708, 2022.

53. Eweje, F.R., Bao, B., Wu, J., Dalal, D., Liao, W.-h., He, Y. *et al.*, Deep Learning for Classification of Bone Lesions on Routine MRI. *EBioMedicine*, 68, 103402, 2021.
54. Patel, A., James, S.L., Davies, A.M., Botchu, R., Spinal imaging update. *Bone Joint J.*, 97-B, 12, 1683–92, 2015.
55. Ur-Rahman, N., El-Bakry, A., Jamjoom, A., Jamjoom, Z.A.-A., Kolawole, T.M., Atypical forms of spinal tuberculosis: case report and review of the literature. *Surg. Neurol.*, 51, 6, 602–7, 1999.
56. Vorster, M., Sathekge, M.M., Bomanji, J., Advances in imaging of tuberculosis: the role of: 18: F-FDG PET and PET/CT. *Curr. Opin. Pulm. Med.*, 20, 3, 287–93, 2014.
57. Biamonte, E., Levi, R., Carrone, F., Vena, W., Brunetti, A., Battaglia, M. *et al.*, Artificial intelligence-based radiomics on computed tomography of lumbar spine in subjects with fragility vertebral fractures. *J. Endocrinol. Invest.*, 45, 10, 2007–17, 2022.
58. Xi, I.L., Zhao, Y., Wang, R., Chang, M., Purkayastha, S., Chang, K. *et al.*, Deep Learning to Distinguish Benign from Malignant Renal Lesions Based on Routine MR Imaging. *Clin. Cancer Res.*, 26, 8, 1944–52, 2020.
59. Duan, S., Dong, W., Hua, Y., Zheng, Y., Ren, Z., Cao, G. *et al.*, Accurate Differentiation of Spinal Tuberculosis and Spinal Metastases Using MR-Based Deep Learning Algorithms. *Infect. Drug Resist.*, 16, 4325–34, 2023.
60. O'Sullivan, S., Leonard, S., Holzinger, A., Allen, C., Battaglia, F., Nevejans, N. *et al.*, Operational framework and training standard requirements for AI-empowered robotic surgery. *Int. J. Med. Rob. Comput. Assisted Surg.*, 16, 5, 1–13, 2020.
61. Piccialli, F., Di Somma, V., Giampaolo, F., Cuomo, S., Fortino, G., A survey on deep learning in medicine: Why, how and when? *Inf. Fusion*, 66, 111–37, 2021.
62. Bengio, Y., Lecun, Y., Hinton, G., Deep learning for AI. *Commun. ACM*, 64, 7, 58–65, 2021.
63. Holzinger, A., Langs, G., Denk, H., Zatloukal, K., Müller, H., Causability and explainability of artificial intelligence in medicine. *Wiley Interdiscip. Rev.: Data Min. Knowl. Discov.*, 9, 4, e1312, 2019.
64. Schneeberger, D., Stöger, K., Holzinger, A. (Eds.), The European legal framework for medical AI. *International Cross-Domain Conference for Machine Learning and Knowledge Extraction*, Springer, Cham, 2020.
65. Müller, H., Mayrhofer, M.T., Van Veen, E.-B., Holzinger, A., The Ten Commandments of Ethical Medical AI. *Computer*, 54, 7, 119–23, 2021.
66. London, A.J., Artificial intelligence and black-box medical decisions: accuracy versus explainability. *Hastings Center Rep.*, 49, 1, 15–21, 2019.
67. O'Sullivan, S., Janssen, M., Holzinger, A., Nevejans, N., Eminaga, O., Meyer, C.P. *et al.*, Explainable artificial intelligence (XAI): closing the gap between image analysis and navigation in complex invasive diagnostic procedures. *World J. Urol.*, 40, 5, 1125–34, 2022.

68. https://www.altexsoft.com/blog/responsible-ai/.
69. Doshi-Velez, F. and Kim, B., Towards a rigorous science of interpretable machine learning, 2017, arXiv preprint arXiv:170208608.
70. Vilone, G. and Longo, L., Notions of explainability and evaluation approaches for explainable artificial intelligence. *Inf. Fusion*, 76, 89–106, 2021.
71. Kim, M.-Y., Atakishiyev, S., Babiker, H.K.B., Farruque, N., Goebel, R., Zaïane, O.R. *et al.*, A multi-component framework for the analysis and design of explainable artificial intelligence. *Mach. Learn. Knowl. Extr.*, 3, 4, 900–21, 2021.
72. Kleinbaum, D.G., Dietz, K., Gail, M., Klein, M., Klein, M., *Logistic regression*, Springer, New York Dordrecht Heidelberg London, 2002.
73. Lundberg, S.M. and Lee, S.-I., A unified approach to interpreting model predictions. *Advances in neural information processing systems*, vol. 30, 2017.
74. Zhou, B., Khosla, A., Lapedriza, A., Oliva, A., Torralba, A. (Eds.), Learning deep features for discriminative localization. *Proceedings of the IEEE conference on computer vision and pattern recognition*, 2016.
75. Selvaraju, R.R., Cogswell, M., Das, A., Vedantam, R., Parikh, D., Batra, D. (Eds.), Grad-cam: Visual explanations from deep networks via gradient-based localization. *Proceedings of the IEEE international conference on computer vision*, 2017.
76. Zhang, Y., Weng, Y., Lund, J., Applications of Explainable Artificial Intelligence in Diagnosis and Surgery. *Diagnostics. (Basel)*, 12, 2, 1–18, 2022.
77. Rai, A., Explainable AI: From black box to glass box. *J. Acad. Marketing Sci.*, 48, 137–41, 2020.
78. Loyola-Gonzalez, O., Black-box vs. white-box: Understanding their advantages and weaknesses from a practical point of view. *IEEE Access*, 7, 154096–113, 2019.
79. Ribeiro, M.T., Singh, S., Guestrin, C. (Eds.), "Why should i trust you?" Explaining the predictions of any classifier. *Proceedings of the 22nd ACM SIGKDD international conference on knowledge discovery and data mining*, 2016.
80. Gerlings, J., Jensen, M.S., Shollo, A., Explainable AI, but explainable to whom? An exploratory case study of xAI in healthcare, in: *Handbook of Artificial Intelligence in Healthcare*, Vol 2: Practicalities and Prospects, pp. 169–98, 2022.
81. Hulsen, T., Explainable Artificial Intelligence (XAI): Concepts and Challenges in Healthcare. *AI*, 4, 3, 652–66, 2023.
82. Singh, A., Sengupta, S., Lakshminarayanan, V., Explainable Deep Learning Models in Medical Image Analysis. *J. Imaging*, 6, 6, 52, 2020.
83. Ghassemi, M., Oakden-Rayner, L., Beam, A.L., The false hope of current approaches to explainable artificial intelligence in health care. *Lancet Digital Health*, 3, 11, e745–e50, 2021.
84. Wu, J. and Mooney, R.J., Faithful multimodal explanation for visual question answering, 2018, arXiv preprint arXiv:180902805.

85. Simonyan, K., Vedaldi, A., Zisserman, A., Deep inside convolutional networks: Visualising image classification models and saliency maps, 2023, arXiv preprint arXiv:13126034.
86. Bach, S., Binder, A., Montavon, G., Klauschen, F., Müller, K.-R., Samek, W., On pixel-wise explanations for non-linear classifier decisions by layer-wise relevance propagation. *PLoS One*, 10, 7, e0130140, 2015.
87. Adadi, A. and Berrada, M., Peeking inside the black-box: a survey on explainable artificial intelligence (XAI). *IEEE Access*, 6, 52138–60, 2018.
88. Das, A. and Rad, P., Opportunities and challenges in explainable artificial intelligence (xai): A survey, 2020, arXiv preprint arXiv:200611371.
89. Chaddad, A., Peng, J., Xu, J., Bouridane, A., Survey of Explainable AI Techniques in Healthcare. *Sensors. (Basel)*, 23, 2, 1–19, 2023.
90. Jujjavarapu, C., Suri, P., Pejaver, V., Friedly, J., Gold, L.S., Meier, E. *et al.*, Predicting decompression surgery by applying multimodal deep learning to patients' structured and unstructured health data. *BMC Med. Inf. Decis. Making*, 23, 1, 2, 2023.
91. Halicka, M., Wilby, M., Duarte, R., Brown, C., Predicting patient-reported outcomes following lumbar spine surgery: development and external validation of multivariable prediction models. *BMC Musculoskelet. Disord.*, 24, 1, 333, 2023.
92. Yagi, M., Yamanouchi, K., Fujita, N., Funao, H., Ebata, S., Revolutionizing Spinal Care: Current Applications and Future Directions of Artificial Intelligence and Machine Learning. *J. Clin. Med.*, 12, 13, 4188, 2023.
93. Park, S.H. and Han, K., Methodologic guide for evaluating clinical performance and effect of artificial intelligence technology for medical diagnosis and prediction. *Radiology*, 286, 3, 800–9, 2018.
94. Cabitza, F., Rasoini, R., Gensini, G.F., Unintended Consequences of Machine Learning in Medicine. *Jama*, 318, 6, 517–8, 2017.
95. Norgeot, B., Glicksberg, B.S., Butte, A.J., A call for deep-learning healthcare. *Nat. Med.*, 25, 1, 14–5, 2019.
96. Yagi, M., Y, K., Fujita, N., Funao, H., Ebata, S., Artificial Intelligence in Spinal Care, Encyclopedia, Available online: https://encyclopedia.pub/entry/46192 (accessed on 15 March 2024).
97. Siala, H. and Wang, Y., SHIFTing artificial intelligence to be responsible in healthcare: A systematic review. *Soc. Sci. Med.*, 296, 114782, 2022.
98. Pesapane, F., Volonté, C., Codari, M., Sardanelli, F., Artificial intelligence as a medical device in radiology: ethical and regulatory issues in Europe and the United States. *Insights Imaging*, 9, 745–53, 2018.
99. Char, D.S., Shah, N.H., Magnus, D., Implementing machine learning in health care—addressing ethical challenges. *New Engl. J. Med.*, 378, 11, 981, 2018.
100. Winfield, A.F. and Jirotka, M., Ethical governance is essential to building trust in robotics and artificial intelligence systems. *Philos. Trans. R. Soc. A: Math. Phys. Eng. Sci.*, 376, 2133, 20180085, 2018.

101. Thierer, A.D., Castillo O'Sullivan, A., Russell, R., Artificial intelligence and public policy. *Mercatus Res. Pap.*, 2017.
102. Alami, H., Gagnon, M.-P., Fortin, J.-P., Digital health and the challenge of health systems transformation. *Mhealth.*, 3, 1–5, 2017.
103. Alami, H., Rivard, L., Lehoux, P., Hoffman, S.J., Cadeddu, S.B.M., Savoldelli, M. *et al.*, Artificial intelligence in health care: laying the Foundation for Responsible, sustainable, and inclusive innovation in low-and middle-income countries. *Global. Health*, 16, 1–6, 2020.
104. Hosny, A. and Aerts, H.J., Artificial intelligence for global health. *Science*, 366, 6468, 955–6, 2019.
105. Guidance, W., *Ethics and governance of artificial intelligence for health*, World Health Organization, WHO, 2021.
106. Carter, S.M., Rogers, W., Win, K.T., Frazer, H., Richards, B., Houssami, N., The ethical, legal and social implications of using artificial intelligence systems in breast cancer care. *Breast*, 49, 25–32, 2020.
107. Abràmoff, M.D., Leng, T., Ting, D.S., Rhee, K., Horton, M.B., Brady, C.J. *et al.*, Automated and computer-assisted detection, classification, and diagnosis of diabetic retinopathy. *Telemed. e-Health*, 26, 4, 544–50, 2020.
108. Powell, J., Trust Me, I'ma chatbot: how artificial intelligence in health care fails the turing test. *J. Med. Internet Res.*, 21, 10, e16222, 2019.
109. McCoy, L.G., Nagaraj, S., Morgado, F., Harish, V., Das, S., Celi, L.A., What do medical students actually need to know about artificial intelligence? *npj Digit. Med.*, 3, 1, 86, 2020.
110. Quinn, T.P., Senadeera, M., Jacobs, S., Coghlan, S., Le, V., Trust and medical AI: the challenges we face and the expertise needed to overcome them. *J. Am. Med. Inf. Assoc.*, 28, 4, 890–4, 2021.
111. Miller, D.D., Machine intelligence in cardiovascular medicine. *Cardiol. Rev.*, 28, 2, 53–64, 2020.
112. Jeste, D.V., Graham, S.A., Nguyen, T.T., Depp, C.A., Lee, E.E., Kim, H.-C., Beyond artificial intelligence: exploring artificial wisdom. *Int. Psychogeriatr.*, 32, 8, 993–1001, 2020.
113. Luxton, D.D., Recommendations for the ethical use and design of artificial intelligent care providers. *Artif. Intell. Med.*, 62, 1, 1–10, 2014.
114. Eaneff, S., Obermeyer, Z., Butte, A.J., The case for algorithmic stewardship for artificial intelligence and machine learning technologies. *JAMA*, 324, 14, 1397–8, 2020.
115. Shameer, K., Johnson, K.W., Glicksberg, B.S., Dudley, J.T., Sengupta, P.P., Machine learning in cardiovascular medicine: are we there yet? *Heart*, 104, 14, 1156–64, 2018.
116. Vollmer Dahlke, D. and Ory, M.G., Emerging issues of intelligent assistive technology use among people with dementia and their caregivers: A US Perspective. *Front. Public Health*, 8, 506205, 2020.

117. Obermeyer, Z., Powers, B., Vogeli, C., Mullainathan, S., Dissecting racial bias in an algorithm used to manage the health of populations. *Science*, 366, 6464, 447–53, 2019.
118. Reddy, S., Allan, S., Coghlan, S., Cooper, P., A governance model for the application of AI in health care. *J. Am. Med. Inf. Assoc.*, 27, 3, 491–7, 2020.
119. Toh, T.S., Dondelinger, F., Wang, D., Looking beyond the hype: applied AI and machine learning in translational medicine. *EBioMedicine*, 47, 607–15, 2019.
120. Wearn, O.R., Freeman, R., Jacoby, D.M., Responsible AI for conservation. *Nat. Mach. Intell.*, 1, 2, 72–3, 2019.
121. Drew, L., The ethics of brain-computer interfaces. *Nature*, 571, 7766, S19–S, 2019.
122. Benke, K. and Benke, G., Artificial intelligence and big data in public health. *Int. J. Environ. Res. Public Health*, 15, 12, 2796, 2018.
123. Zadpoor, A.A., Campoli, G., Weinans, H., Neural network prediction of load from the morphology of trabecular bone. *Appl. Math. Modell.*, 37, 7, 5260–76, 2013.
124. Grace, K., Salvatier, J., Dafoe, A., Zhang, B., Evans, O., When will AI exceed human performance? Evidence from AI experts. *J. Artif. Intell. Res.*, 62, 729–54, 2018.
125. Kuang, L., He, L., Yili, R., Kai, L., Mingyu, S., Jian, S. *et al.*, Application and development trend of artificial intelligence in petroleum exploration and development. *Pet. Explor. Dev.*, 48, 1, 1–14, 2021.
126. Madanu, R., Abbod, M.F., Hsiao, F.-J., Chen, W.-T., Shieh, J.-S., Explainable ai (xai) applied in machine learning for pain modeling: A review. *Technologies*, 10, 3, 74, 2022.

6

Explainable Artificial Intelligence and Responsible Artificial Intelligence for Dentistry

Tamanna Rai[1], Rishabha Malviya[2*] and Sathvik Belagodu Sridhar[3]

[1]United College of Engineering and Research, Greater Noida, U.P, India
[2]Department of Pharmacy, School of Medical and Allied Sciences, Galgotias University, Greater Noida, India
[3]Department of Clinical Pharmacy and Pharmacology, RAK College of Pharmacy, RAK Medical and Health Sciences University, Ras Al Khaimah, United Arab Emirates

Abstract

New ideas like responsible artificial intelligence (RAI) and explainable artificial intelligence (XAI) are being used in dentistry to make care for patients better and solve ethical and practical problems. This chapter looks at the ideas behind RAI and XAI and how they are used in dentistry. It discusses much about how important these tools are and how they might affect oral health. Diagnostic tools driven by AI can help dentists find oral problems, look at dental images, and guess how treatment will work. To sum up, XAI and RAI offer good chances for making AI applications in dentistry more useful, clear, and morally sound.

***Keywords*:** Expendable AI, responsible AI, dentistry, diagnosis, ethical AI, dental imaging

6.1 Introduction

About 2.3 billion people around the world are thought to have permanent tooth caries. This means that their teeth will always be damaged. Caries, which is another name for tooth decay, is damage to the tooth, mostly the

**Corresponding author*: rishabhamalviya19@gmail.com

Rishabha Malviya and Sonali Sundram (eds.) Explainable and Responsible Artificial Intelligence in Healthcare, (145–164) © 2025 Scrivener Publishing LLC

enamel layer, that comes from bacteria that make lactic acid [1]. Untreated, this can ultimately result in dental malocclusion, leading to discomfort, infection, and eventual tooth extraction [2–4]. Not all dental caries lesions can be detected using visual and tactile examination. As a result, imaging techniques are commonly employed to enhance the rate of detection [5–7]. Nevertheless, despite the use of medical imaging, dentists may still overlook first caries lesions. Thus, the accuracy of diagnosis and effectiveness of treatment rely on the technological capabilities and the expertise of the reading specialist [8]. Moreover, the analysis of X-ray pictures contributes to the doctors' burden. A highly reliable and precise automatic detection method is required to aid clinical stomatologists in making objective caries diagnoses. In computer science, artificial intelligence (AI) refers to the study of intelligent media, which includes any system that can perceive its environment and behave in a manner that optimizes its chances of accomplishing its goals [9]. Artificial intelligence (AI) is pivotal in contemporary healthcare, presenting exceptional prospects for enhancing diagnostic capabilities, therapeutic efficacy, patient involvement, and operational effectiveness. The introduction of such innovations holds the ability to significantly revolutionize healthcare delivery, leading to improvements in the performance, mobility, and economic viability of healthcare services on an international scale [10]. Artificial intelligence (AI) is swiftly transforming the dentistry industry by providing a wide range of cutting-edge solutions designed to enhance patient care and optimise dental practice procedures. AI is very effective in diagnostic imaging analysis, namely, in examining dental radiographs like Cone-beam computed tomography (CBCT) scans and X-ray imaging. Algorithms may carefully analyze these images to assist dentists in detecting caries, periodontal disease, and structural problems at an early stage [11]. Moreover, integrating AI into computer-Aided Design (CAD) and computer-aided manufacturing (CAM) dentistry enables the accurate creation of dental restorations, reducing the occurrence of human mistakes and enhancing the quality of the restorations. AI drastically improves treatment planning and simulation, allowing dentists to properly replicate different procedures and effectively discuss treatment options with patients. Predictive analytics, driven by AI, leverage patient data to evaluate the likelihood of oral illnesses permitting tailored preventive approaches and prompt therapies [12]. To further encourage patient participation in their own oral health care, AI-powered patient engagement systems provide interactive resources for teaching proper oral hygiene and receiving post-treatment care instructions [13]. Although fully autonomous medical robotic systems are now unattainable, the primary component utilized in dentistry is the virtual aspect of AI, specifically software-type algorithms. Due to their robust data analysis capabilities, these virtual algorithms are anticipated to enhance the precision and effectiveness of dental diagnosis. They will also offer visualized anatomical guidance for treatment, simulate and evaluate potential outcomes, and predict the occurrence and prognosis of oral diseases. AI has transformed dentistry by improving diagnostic precision, treatment results, and practice effectiveness, through techniques such as robotic assistance during surgeries and automated practice management solutions [14]. The current advancement in AI studies presents a significant opportunity to enhance patient outcomes and transform the delivery of oral healthcare in dentistry [15].

6.2 The Scope of AI in Healthcare

When compared to traditional analytic approaches and clinical judgment, AI provides several advantages. Programs that use AI will be more accurate and simple to understand, letting medical professionals treat patients in ways that have never been seen before [16].

- Patient observation and examination, accumulation of patient information, and application of the clinician's expertise and experience to the interpretation of information gathered from the patient.
- Formulation of a diagnosis.

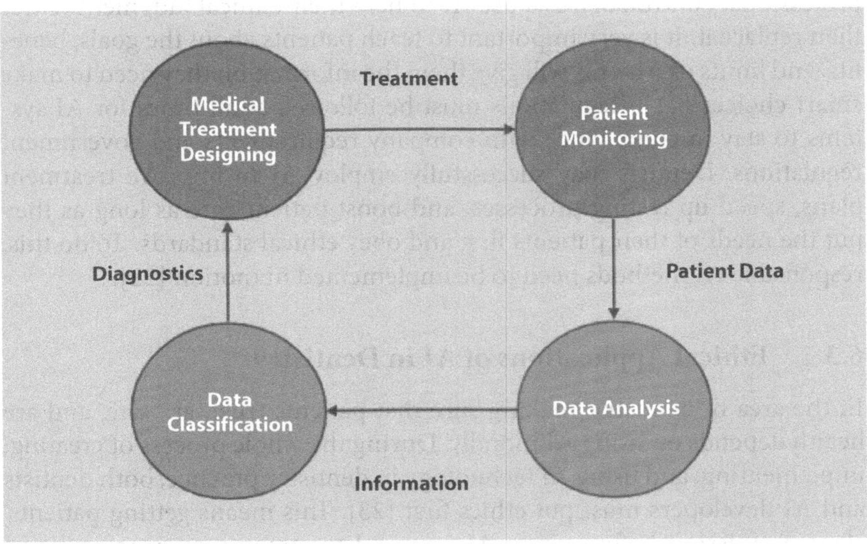

Figure 6.1 Medical diagnostic cycle.

- Therapeutic plan by the physician [17].

If this diagnostic cycle is conceptualized as an intelligent agent system, then the clinician serves as the intelligent agent, receives patient data as input, and generates the diagnosis as a result [18] (Figure 6.1).

6.3 Responsible Artificial Intelligence (AI) in Dentistry

Responsible AI in dentistry underscores the importance of integrating AI technology into dental practices in a transparent, secure, and ethical manner. Ethical considerations must be of the utmost importance to both dentists and AI developers when implementing AI-driven treatments; they must ensure that patient autonomy, privacy, and data confidentiality are maintained [19]. Making sure things are clear is very important, which means giving clear information about how AI algorithms work and how they are used to encourage responsibility and build trust. To make sure that all patients get fair and unbiased care, it is important to work to reduce bias. This involves picking training data with great care and following a strict plan, as well as constantly checking for and fixing any possible flaws. Before they can be used in healthcare settings, AI systems need to be thoroughly tested to make sure they are safe, effective, and accurate [20]. Also, it is important to keep an eye out for progress all the time. As part of their professional control, dentists use AI to help their clinical judgment rather than replace it. It is very important to teach patients about the goals, benefits, and limits of AI. This will give them the information they need to make smart choices [21]. Regulations must be followed at all times for AI systems to stay in compliance with company requirements and government regulations. Dentists may successfully employ AI to improve treatment plans, speed up testing processes, and boost patient care as long as they put the needs of their patients first and obey ethical standards. To do this, responsible AI methods need to be implemented in motion [22].

6.3.1 Ethical Applications of AI in Dentistry

In the area of dentistry, making sure that patients trust, are safe, and are health depends on using AI morally. During the whole process of creating, implementing, and using AI technology in dentistry practice, both dentists and AI developers must put ethics first [23]. This means getting patients' clear permission before using AI-powered treatments or processes and making sure that patients' privacy and confidentiality are protected at all times. A very important thing is to make sure that people understand exactly what AI is used for and how it works in their medical care [24]. This makes things easier for people to understand and develops trust. To make sure that all patients receive equitable care, dentists have to recognize and fix any holes in AI systems. It is also dentists' professional responsibility to employ AI to improve their clinical skills rather than fully substituting them. In this manner, people may still monitor the decision-making process by adhering to ethical norms; the dentistry business can maximize the promise of AI while still preserving patients' rights to security, privacy, and dignity [25].

6.3.2 Guidelines from Dental Associations

The American Dental Association (ADEA) has created an advisory group or task delegation to focus on AI. This is because AI is growing so quickly in the dentistry field. The people in this group would be in charge of giving dental educators the tools they need to make an AI-based program that works along with is also ethical [26]. The team's purpose is to monitor AI news that may affect dentistry schools and provide a toolbox or compilation of micro-credentialing courses to assist teachers, among other things. ADEA should conduct a survey and develop proposals regarding the use of AI in dentistry education in collaboration with its Councils and other relevant organizations to gain a more comprehensive understanding of the application of AI. ADEA members can work together to draft and discuss policy statements and position papers. If the ADEA subgroup on AI and the new standards working group on AI in dentistry work together, then they can achieve major results [27]. To stay current with the latest advancements in the healthcare field and to ensure equitable healthcare delivery, this collaboration entails implementing regular continuing education mandates in AI and establishing governing bodies at both national and state levels to ensure the algorithm's ongoing reassessment, modification, and renewal.

6.4 Explainable Artificial Intelligence (XAI) in Dentistry

Artificial intelligence that can be explained (XAI) is critical in dentistry because it can aid in professional decision-making, trust, and transparency in the dental office. When it comes to dentistry, where accuracy and precision are critical, both patients and dentists must thoroughly comprehend how any AI-generated concepts or diagnoses operation [28]. "Explainable artificial intelligence" (XAI) is a way for people to learn about how AI systems make decisions. This level of openness makes it easier for people to check and understand the data that highly clever systems give them. This builds trust between dentists and their customers and in the dental community as a whole. When dentists use explainable AI, they can carefully look over and confirm the AI's suggestions, especially if those suggestions are different from what they already know from clinical experience. "Explainable artificial intelligence" (XAI) is a way for people to learn about how AI systems make decisions. This level of openness makes it easier for people to check and understand the data that highly clever systems give them. This builds trust between dentists and their customers and in the dental community as a whole. When dentists use explainable AI, they can carefully look over and confirm the AI's suggestions, especially if those suggestions are different from what they already know from clinical experience [29]. Making sure that the patient is safe and getting the best results from the treatment is important. Extendable artificial intelligence (XAI) helps dentists make better decisions by giving them more information. It also encourages professionals and AI systems to work together, which eventually raises the quality of dental care by making things more clear [30].

6.5 Application of AI in Dentistry

Artificial intelligence (AI) has been widely used in dentistry to improve the accuracy and efficiency of diagnostic procedures. This is critical to achieving optimal treatment outcomes and providing high-quality care to patients [31]. Dentists must use their broad knowledge to diagnose and choose the best course of treatment. In addition, accurate clinical decision-making abilities are required to forecast the prognosis. However, there are times when dentists lack the necessary skills to make an appropriate clinical decision within a limited timeframe [32]. AI apps can help individuals make more informed decisions and perform better. The objective of this chapter was to monitor the expansion of extensively utilized AI applications in dentistry and assess their effectiveness concerning the prognosis of treatment outcomes, clinical decision-making, and diagnosis [33]. Figure 6.2 showcases several AI applications within the realm of dentistry.

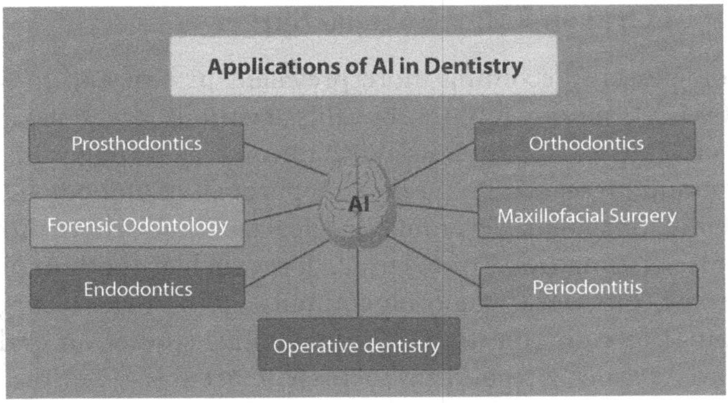

Figure 6.2 Various application of AI in dentistry.

6.5.1 AI in Periodontitis

Periodontitis is among the most pervasive illnesses. This condition affects a substantial number of people, in the billions, and failure to treat it may result in tooth displacement or complete tooth loss [34]. Preventing severe periodontitis requires prompt diagnosis and intervention. When diagnosing periodontal disease in clinical practice, gingival recession and pocket probing depths are evaluated. Use of the PSI regularly to measure clinical attachment loss. Nevertheless, the dependability of this clinical assessment is compromised: the detection of periodontal disease remains contingent on the judgment of dentists, who might fail to detect specific instances of periodontal tissue atrophy [35].

Scientist developed a system that detects premolar and molar periodontitis using a digital convolution neural network. This network contains 16 convolution layers and two completely linked layers. Furthermore, ANN can be used to effectively diagnose individuals with chronic or aggressive periodontitis based on the profile of their immune response [36]. The dental chair, which is utilized extensively by dentists for medical care for patients, is the most widespread and fundamental instance of an AI application. Artificial intelligence has altered the dental chair from a standard hydraulic chair to one that is completely automated and powered by sensors. The most current and advanced invention is a dental chair that can be controlled by voice and does not require manual work from the practitioner. Shortly, it will be possible for a dental chair to monitor a patient's weight, psychological state, and health while they are sitting for therapy [37].

6.5.2 AI in Oral and Maxillofacial Surgery

AI technologies are becoming more prevalent in oral and maxillofacial surgery (OMFS), offering multiple benefits at various stages of patient care. Artificial intelligence is mostly used in oral surgery through the advancement of robotic surgery, which seeks to replicate human body movements and reasoning. Image-guided cranial surgical techniques have shown effective in clinical settings for various procedures such as tooth implantation, chemotherapy, biopsies, temporomandibular joint (TMJ) surgery, and elimination of foreign objects [38]. Comparative studies on oral implant surgery have revealed a significant increase in accuracy over the freehand approach, even when performed by competent surgeons. Furthermore, there was no discernible difference between proficient surgeons and apprentices. According to reports, faster operation times, increased intraoperative precision, and improved safety are common when working with sensitive structures. Image guidance permits more comprehensive surgical resection, perhaps reducing the need for additional surgical revisions [39]. AI has changed the field of surgery, resulting in the development of numerous robotic surgeons. These robots can execute semi-automated surgical procedures with greater efficiency while being closely overseen by a skilled physician [40]. Furthermore, AI-driven communication tools, such as chatbots, help to educate patients by delivering important information on medical conditions, treatment options, and postoperative care instructions. Overall, AI offers enormous potential in the field of OMFS, as it has the potential to significantly improve diagnostic accuracy, surgical precision, treatment planning, and, ultimately, patient outcomes. However, it is critical that AI be incorporated into clinical practice ethically and safely [41].

6.5.3 AI in Orthodontics

A convolutional neural network (CNN) model was built and evaluated on a dataset of 156 lateral cephalograms to accurately identify the specific teeth that require extraction in the context of orthodontic planning [42]. Predicting extractions produced a higher success rate for the model than properly identifying the particular combination of premolar teeth that required extraction. Orthodontists frequently utilize medical outcomes, dental models, photographs, and radiology to determine the necessity of extractions during the process of arranging orthodontic treatment. To successfully support clinical decision-making, ML models should include all of these inputs. Other orthodontic treatment planning research has used cephalograms to apply automated landmark tracing, cervical vertebral stage, and skeletal categorization methods [43–45].

6.5.4 AI in Operative Dentistry

Operative dentistry is the branch of dentistry that focuses on detecting, treating, and preventing dental caries (cavities) and other tooth problems. It includes a variety of treatments aimed at restoring teeth to their proper shape, functionality, and attractiveness [46]. Artificial intelligence has the potential to significantly impact surgical dentistry through a variety of techniques like vertical root fractures, dental caries, pulp space volume, apical lesions, and tooth attrition has all been studied in the context of operation. In 2D radiograph, the intensity of each grayscale pixel represents an item's density. By absorbing the aforementioned qualities, an AI computer can learn about the pattern and make predictions to categorize the tooth, locate cavities, and so on. Lee *et al.* [47] created a CNN approach for identifying dental caries on periapical radiographs. Kühnisch *et al.* [48] introduced a CNN method to detect caries in intraoral pictures. Schwendicke *et al.* [49] evaluated the cost-effectiveness of AI and dentists' proximal caries diagnoses. The results showed that AI was both more effective and less expensive.

6.5.5 AI in Prosthodontics

In the field of prosthodontics, the standard procedure for creating a dental crown consists of several steps: tooth preparation, taking an impression, refining the model, devising the design, building the crown, executing a trial fitting, and finally securely affixing the crown. The application of AI in prosthodontics is mostly focused on improving restorative design. AI-powered software can help with the digital fabrication of smiles, allowing prosthodontists to visualize and customize the aesthetic outcome of prosthodontic procedures. Patients can preview their potential smile modifications before undergoing therapy, which increases communication and satisfaction. The design process for commercial items such as CEREC, Sirona, and 3Shape has been digitized using CAD/CAM technology. Although the use of a tooth library in crown design has dramatically improved the efficiency of the design process, it is still incapable of producing a tailored design for each particular patient [50]. As a result of advances in AI, Hwang *et al.* [51] and Tian *et al.* [52] suggested new ways that use 2D-GAN models to build crowns by acquiring insights from technicians' designs. The training data was collected from three-dimensional tooth models and represented as two-dimensional depth maps. Ding [53] developed a crown generation network dubbed 3D-DCGAN, which included 3D data directly into the creation process. The molded crowns were aesthetically identical to real teeth. Artificial intelligence (AI) can be combined with CAD/CAM or 3D/4D printing to improve workflow efficiency [54]. Additionally, AI has been used to forecast debonding for CAD/CAM restorations and colour matching [39].

6.5.6 In Forensic Odontology

Artificial intelligence is a scientific advancement that has been extensively utilized in the domain of forensic medicine. It has shown significant efficacy in determining the biological age and gender of both healthy and ill people. Furthermore, it is used to examine bite marks and predict mandibular shape. Dentistry is positioned to benefit significantly from the introduction of cutting-edge AI technologies [55]. The dental chair, a fundamental component of dental clinics, has seen a significant evolution, from physiologic hydraulic pressure chairs with a manual pump to electronic chairs with numerous associated sensors. The most recent improvement is a voice-activated dental chair, which eliminates the need for the doctor to perform any physical tasks. All activities are carried out using voice commands. Dental chairs will eventually be able to monitor a patient's vital signs, weight, anxiety level, duration of operation, and weight. All activities are carried out using voice commands. Dental chairs will eventually be able to monitor a patient's vital signs, anxiety level, weight, and duration of operation. Additionally, they will calm the patient and notify the operating doctors if any irregularities are discovered. This is because all extremely intelligent people are constantly working to improve AI [56]. One of the most exciting AI applications is "bioprinting," which is the process of stacking cells to create living tissue and organs. This method offers the ability to restore oral hard and soft tissues that have been destroyed due to disease or trauma [57].

6.5.7 Artificial Intelligence in Endodontics

Artificial intelligence is becoming increasingly important in the field of endodontics [58]. It is currently playing a bigger part in endodontic treatment planning and disease diagnosis [59]. AI-based networks can detect even the smallest changes at the level of a single pixel, which may go unnoticed by human sight [60]. Figure 6.3 mentions and provides detailed descriptions of some of its applications in endodontics.

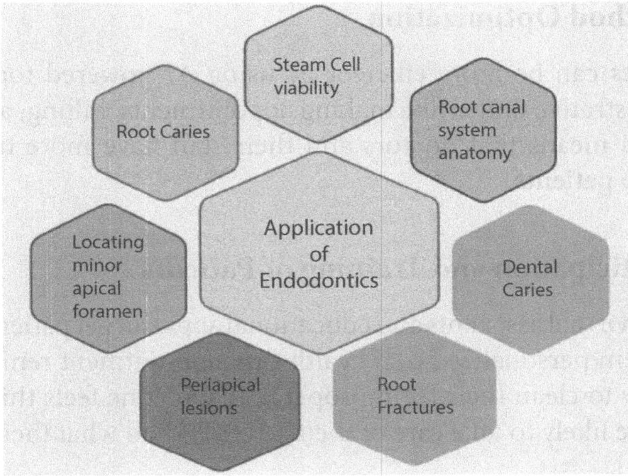

Figure 6.3 Application of artificial intelligence in endodontics.

6.6 Benefits of AI in Dentistry

6.6.1 Improved Diagnosis

Artificial intelligence algorithms possess the ability to examine dental pictures, such as X-rays and scans, with superior precision and efficiency compared to human dentists. This results in enhanced identification of oral illnesses, dental caries, and irregularities in their initial phases, facilitating prompt intervention and therapy [61].

6.6.2 Predicted Data Analytics

Artificial intelligence can analyze patient data to forecast possible oral health problems or consequences. Dentists can promote preventive care by proactively detecting patterns and risk factors to intervene and prevent dental issues before they emerge [62].

6.6.3 Therapy Planning Assistance

AI systems can aid dentists in formulating customized treatment plans for patients by examining their dental records, medical history, and other pertinent data. This contributes to the optimization of treatment outcomes and the reduction of dangers.

6.6.4 Method Optimization

Dental offices can be more efficient by using AI-powered tools to automate administrative duties like making appointments, billing, and keeping records. This means that doctors and their staff have more time to give better care to patients.

6.6.5 Participation and Training of Patients

AI-powered virtual assistants and educational apps can get patients involved by giving them personalized oral health tips, appointment reminders, and steps on how to clean their teeth properly. If someone feels this way, then they are more likely to take care of themselves and do what their treatment plans say [63].

6.6.6 Research and Development

AI algorithms can analyze massive volumes of dental data derived from research articles, clinical studies, and patient records. This allows researchers to identify trends, correlations, and potential therapy improvements. This facilitates research and contributes significantly to the field of dental care.

6.6.7 Digital Dentistry

It employs AI to enable remote consultations and diagnostics through digital dentistry systems, allowing patients to receive dental care regardless of where they are. People who reside in rural or underdeveloped areas may have limited access to dental treatment, making this especially valuable for them [64].

6.6.8 Prosthetics and Orthodontics

Dental replacements like crowns, bridges, and dentures can be designed and made better with AI technology because it makes the process more accurate and customizable. AI-powered software can help plan dental treatment for braces and aligners better, which can lead to more accurate results [65].

6.6.9 Economical

The application of AI technology in dentistry can assist reduce patient consumption. Improving efficiency, precision, and preventive care can assist achieve this goal, resulting in savings for both patients and dental clinics.

If you discover dental problems early, then you may avoid having to undergo more extensive and costly operations in the future. Also, efficient processes save money [66].

6.7 Challenges of AI in Dentistry

Using AI in dentistry presents various potential benefits, but it also brings forth a multitude of new obstacles. Many people have worries about the security and confidentiality of their data because AI systems need significant access to medical records. This creates apprehensions regarding the confidentiality and security of data regarding unlawful intrusion. Moreover, maintaining the quality and uniformity of the data provided is difficult because of the diverse data collection techniques used by various dental organisations [67]. To uphold patient confidence and promote equitable decision-making, it is imperative to address ethical considerations such as obtaining patient consent, enhancing transparency, and mitigating algorithmic biases. Moreover, the seamless incorporation of AI tools into existing clinical procedures, along with guaranteeing adherence to medical equipment and software standards, is crucial yet intricate undertakings [68]. AI is not widely used in dentistry because algorithms can be biased and hard to understand; there is not a lot of training data available, and it costs a lot to get started. Dentists, AI researchers, lawmakers, and regulatory bodies need to work together to solve these problems. Their goal should be to set moral standards, technological benchmarks, and rules that will encourage the fair and right use of AI in oral healthcare. Aside from that, they need to deal with problems of privacy, security, ethics, and accessibility [69].

6.8 Conclusion

In conclusion, combining the ideas of XAI and RAI holds a lot of promise for improving dental care and dealing with important ethical and practical issues. RAI frameworks emphasize fairness, responsibility, and openness to make sure that AI systems used in dentistry are ethical and responsible. With these models, algorithms are sure to make decisions clearly and fairly. These steps build trust and dependability between people and dentists. At the same time, using XAI techniques helps doctors understand and evaluate the reasoning behind suggestions made by AI. They can then make well-informed clinical choices and come up with new ways to improve patient care. The XAI and RAI tools work together to make sure that AI technology is used in dentistry safely and ethically. This step protects patients' privacy and makes sure that everyone has equal access to high-quality dental care. As time goes on, dental workers, AI researchers, policymakers, and regulatory groups must continue to work together to improve the principles of XAI and RAI and make sure they are used effectively in dental practice.

References

1. James, S.L., Abate, D., Abate, K.H., Abay, S.M., Abbafati, C., Abbasi, N., Abbastabar, H., Abd-Allah, F., Abdela, J., Abdelalim, A., Abdollahpour, I., Global, regional, and national incidence, prevalence, and years lived with disability for 354 diseases and injuries for 195 countries and territories, 1990–2017: a systematic analysis for the Global Burden of Disease Study 2017. *Lancet*, 392, 10159, 1789–858, 2018 Nov 10.
2. Oztekin, F., Katar, O., Sadak, F., Yildirim, M., Cakar, H., Aydogan, M., Ozpolat, Z., Talo Yildirim, T., Yildirim, O., Faust, O., Acharya, U.R., An explainable deep learning model to prediction dental caries using panoramic radiograph images. *Diagnostics*, 13, 2, 226, 2023 Jan 7.
3. Pitts, N.B., Zero, D.T., Marsh, P.D., Ekstrand, K., Weintraub, J.A., Ramos-Gomez, F., Tagami, J., Twetman, S., Tsakos, G., Ismail, A., Dental caries. *Nat. Rev. Dis. Primers*, 3, 17030, 2017 May.
4. Paulose-Ram, R., Graber, J.E., Woodwell, D., Ahluwalia, N., The National Health and Nutrition Examination Survey (NHANES), 2021–2022: adapting data collection in a COVID-19 environment. *Am. J. Public Health*, 111, 12, 2149–56, 2021 Dec.
5. Gomez, J., Detection and diagnosis of the early caries lesion. *BMC Oral Health*, 15, Suppl 1, S3, 2015 Sep 15.
6. Metzger, Z., Colson, D.G., Bown, P., Weihard, T., Baresel, I., Nolting, T., Reflected near-infrared light versus bite-wing radiography for the detection of proximal caries: A multicenter prospective clinical study conducted in private practices. *J. Dent.*, 116, 103861, 2022 Jan 1.
7. Michou, S., Vannahme, C., Bakhshandeh, A., Ekstrand, K.R., Benetti, A.R., Intraoral scanner featuring transillumination for proximal caries detection. An *in vitro* validation study on permanent posterior teeth. *J. Dent.*, 116, 103841, 2022 Jan 1.
8. Topping, G.V. and Pitts, N.B., Clinical visual caries detection. Detection, assessment, diagnosis and monitoring of caries. 21, 15–41, 2009.
9. Javaid, M., Haleem, A., Singh, R.P., Suman, R., Artificial intelligence applications for industry 4.0: A literature-based study. *J. Ind. Integr. Manage.*, 7, 01, 83–111, 2022 Mar 21.

10. Carrillo-Perez, F., Pecho, O.E., Morales, J.C., Paravina, R.D., Della Bona, A., Ghinea, R., Pulgar, R., Pérez, M.D., Herrera, L.J., Applications of artificial intelligence in dentistry: A comprehensive review. *J. Esthet. Restor. Dent.*, 34, 1, 259–80, 2022 Jan.
11. Shan, T., Tay, F.R., Gu, L., Application of artificial intelligence in dentistry. *J. Dent. Res.*, 100, 3, 232–44, 2021 Mar.
12. Gupta, R.S., Lal, B., Bhagat, A.C., Alagarsamy, R., Medical Imaging for Patient-Specific Implants, in: *Biomedical Implants*, pp. 39–60, CRC Press, Boca Raton, Florida, United States, 2024.
13. Agrawal, P., Nikhade, P., Nikhade, P.P., Artificial intelligence in dentistry: past, present, and future. *Cureus J. Med. Sci.*, 14, 7, e27405, 2022 Jul 28.
14. Schwendicke, F.A., Samek, W., Krois, J., Artificial intelligence in dentistry: chances and challenges. *J. Dent. Res.*, 99, 7, 769–74, 2020 Jul.
15. Dhopte, A. and Bagde, H., Smart smile: revolutionizing dentistry with artificial intelligence. *Cureus*, 15, 6, e41227, 2023 Jun 30.
16. Bush, J., How AI is taking the scut work out of health care. *Harv Bus Rev.*, 2018, https://hbr.org/2018/03/how-ai-is-taking-the-scut-work-out-of-health-care.
17. Murff, H.J., Patel, V.L., Hripcsak, G., Bates, D.W., Detecting adverse events for patient safety research: a review of current methodologies. *J. Biomed. Inf.*, 36, 1-2, 131–43, 2003 Feb 1.
18. Li, J.P., Liu, H., Ting, D.S., Jeon, S., Chan, R.P., Kim, J.E., Sim, D.A., Thomas, P.B., Lin, H., Chen, Y., Sakomoto, T., Digital technology, tele-medicine and artificial intelligence in ophthalmology: A global perspective. *Prog. Retin. Eye Res.*, 82, 100900, 2021 May 1.
19. Fitzek, S. and Choi, K.E., Potential Impact and Challenges of Implementing Artificial Intelligence in the Romanian Healthcare System. *Postmodernism Probl.*, 13, 2, 148–92, 2023 Aug 7.
20. Diakopoulos, N., Accountability, transparency, and algorithms, in: *The Oxford handbook of ethics of AI*, vol. 17(4), p. 197, 2020 Jun 30.
21. Kelly, C.J., Karthikesalingam, A., Suleyman, M., Corrado, G., King, D., Key challenges for delivering clinical impact with artificial intelligence. *BMC Med.*, 17, 1–9, 2019 Dec.
22. Dobrzański, L.A., Dobrzański, L.B., Dobrzańska-Danikiewicz, A.D., Dobrzańska, J., The concept of sustainable development of modern dentistry. *Processes*, 8, 12, 1605, 2020 Dec 6.
23. Saudagar, N., Jabeen, R., Sharma, P., Mong, S., Vaderhobli, R.M., Ethical Implications with the Utilization of Artificial Intelligence in Dentistry. *Ethics Biol. Eng. Med.: Int. J.*, 12, 1, 161–174, 2021.
24. Park, W.J. and Park, J.B., History and application of artificial neural networks in dentistry. *Eur. J. Dent.*, 12, 04, 594–601, 2018 Oct.
25. Lin, G.S., Ng, Y.S., Ghani, N.R., Chua, K.H., Revolutionising dental technologies: a qualitative study on dental technicians' perceptions of Artificial intelligence integration. *BMC Oral Health*, 23, 1, 690, 2023 Sep 25.

26. Kalkwarf, K.L., Haden, N.K., Valachovic, R.W., ADEA commission on change and innovation in dental education. *J. Dental Educ.*, 69, 10, 1085, 2005 Oct 1.
27. Tabish, S.A. and Nabil, S., Future of healthcare delivery: Strategies that will reshape the healthcare industry landscape. *Int. J. Sci. Res.*, 4, 2, 727–58, 2015 Feb.
28. Nor, A.K., Pedapati, S.R., Muhammad, M., Leiva, V., Overview of explainable artificial intelligence for prognostic and health management of industrial assets based on preferred reporting items for systematic reviews and meta-analyses. *Sensors*, 21, 23, 8020, 2021 Dec 1.
29. Batra, A.M. and Reche, A., A new era of dental care: harnessing artificial intelligence for better diagnosis and treatment. *Cureus*, 15, 11, e49319, 2023 Nov 23.
30. Thurzo, A., Urbanová, W., Novák, B., Czako, L., Siebert, T., Stano, P., Mareková, S., Fountoulaki, G., Kosnáčová, H., Varga, I., Where is the artificial intelligence applied in dentistry? Systematic review and literature analysis. *Healthcare*, 10, 7, 1269, 2022 Jul 8, MDPI.
31. Ahmed, N., Abbasi, M.S., Zuberi, F., Qamar, W., Halim, M.S., Maqsood, A., Alam, M.K., Artificial intelligence techniques: analysis, application, and outcome in dentistry—a systematic review. *Biomed Res. Int.*, 2021, 9751564, 2021 Jun 22.
32. Tandon, D., Rajawat, J., Banerjee, M., Present and future of artificial intelligence in dentistry. *J. Oral Biol. Craniofac. Res.*, 10, 4, 391–6, 2020 Oct 1.
33. Fatima, A., Shafi, I., Afzal, H., Díez, I.D., Lourdes, D.R., Breñosa, J., Espinosa, J.C., Ashraf, I., Advancements in dentistry with artificial intelligence: current clinical applications and future perspectives. *Healthcare*, 10, 11, 2188, 2022 Oct 31, MDPI.
34. Naylor, C.D., On the prospects for a (deep) learning health care system. *JAMA*, 320, 11, 1099–1100, 2018.
35. Tonetti, M.S., Jepsen, S., Jin, L., Otomo-Corgel, J., Impact of the global burden of periodontal diseases on health, nutrition and wellbeing of mankind: a call for global action. *J. Clin. Periodontol.*, 44, 5, 456–62, 2017, doi: 10.1111/jcpe.12732.
36. Zheng, L., Wang, H., Mei, L., Chen, Q., Zhang, Y., Zhang, H., Artificial intelligence in digital cariology: a new tool for the diagnosis of deep caries and pulpitis using convolutional neural networks. *Ann. Transl. Med.*, 9, 9, 763, 2021 May.
37. Jackson, J., Data mining: a conceptual overview. *Commun. Assoc. Inf. Syst.*, 8, 267–296, 2002.
38. Rokhshad, R., Keyhan, S.O., Yousefi, P., Artificial intelligence applications and ethical challenges in oral and maxillo-facial cosmetic surgery: a narrative review. *Maxillofac. Plast. Reconstr. Surg.*, 45, 1, 14, 2023 Mar.
39. Khanna, S.S. and Dhaimade, P.A., Artificial intelligence: transforming dentistry today. *Indian J. Basic Appl. Med. Res.*, 6, 3, 161–7, 2017 Jun.

40. Heo, M.S., Kim, J.E., Hwang, J.J., Han, S.S., Kim, J.S., Yi, W.J., Park, I.W., Artificial intelligence in oral and maxillofacial radiology: what is currently possible? *Dentomaxillofac. Radiol.*, 50, 3, 20200375, 2021 Mar 1.
41. Jung, S.K. and Kim, T.W., New approach for the diagnosis of extractions with neural network machine learning. *Am. J. Orthod. Dentofacial Orthop.*, 149, 1, 127–33, 2016 Jan 1.
42. Kök, H., Acilar, A.M., İzgi, M.S., Usage and comparison of artificial intelligence algorithms for determination of growth and development by cervical vertebrae stages in orthodontics. *Prog. Orthod.*, 20, 1–0, 2019 Dec.
43. Yu, H.J., Cho, S.R., Kim, M.J., Kim, W.H., Kim, J.W., Choi, J., Automated skeletal classification with lateral cephalometry based on artificial intelligence. *J. Dent. Res.*, 99, 3, 249–56, 2020 Mar.
44. Kazimierczak, N., Kazimierczak, W., Serafin, Z., Nowicki, P., Nożewski, J., Janiszewska-Olszowska, J., AI in Orthodontics: Revolutionizing Diagnostics and Treatment Planning—A Comprehensive Review. *J. Clin. Med.*, 13, 2, 344, 2024 Jan 7.
45. Huang, Y.P. and Lee, S.Y., An Effective and Reliable Methodology for Deep Machine Learning Application in Caries Detection, medRxiv, 21256502, 2021.
46. Lee, J.H., Kim, D.H., Jeong, S.N., Choi, S.H., Detection and diagnosis of dental caries using a deep learning-based convolutional neural network algorithm. *J. Dent.*, 77, 106–11, 2018 Oct 1.
47. Kühnisch, J., Meyer, O., Hesenius, M., Hickel, R., Gruhn, V., Caries detection on intraoral images using artificial intelligence. *J. Dent. Res.*, 101, 2, 158–65, 2022 Feb.
48. Schwendicke, F., Rossi, J.G., Göstemeyer, G., Elhennawy, K., Cantu, A.G., Gaudin, R., Chaurasia, A., Gehrung, S., Krois, J., Cost-effectiveness of artificial intelligence for proximal caries detection. *J. Dent. Res.*, 100, 4, 369–76, 2021 Apr.
49. Chen, Y., Lee, J.K., Kwong, G., Pow, E.H., Tsoi, J.K., Morphology and fracture behavior of lithium disilicate dental crowns designed by human and knowledge-based AI. *J. Mech. Behav. Biomed. Mater.*, 131, 105256, 2022 Jul 1.
50. Hwang, J.J., Azernikov, S., Efros, A.A., Yu, S.X., Learning beyond human expertise with generative models for dental restorations, arXiv preprint arXiv:1804.00064, 2018 Mar 30.
51. Tian, S., Wang, M., Dai, N., Ma, H., Li, L., Fiorenza, L., Sun, Y., Li, Y., DCPR-GAN: dental crown prosthesis restoration using two-stage generative adversarial networks. *IEEE J. Biomed. Health. Inf.*, 26, 1, 151–60, 2021 Oct 12.
52. Ding, H., Cui, Z., Maghami, E., Chen, Y., Matinlinna, J.P., Pow, E.H., Fok, A.S., Burrow, M.F., Wang, W., Tsoi, J.K., Morphology and mechanical performance of dental crown designed by 3D-DCGAN. *Dent. Mater.*, 39, 3, 320–32, 2023 Mar 1.
53. Wei, J., Peng, M., Li, Q., Wang, Y., Evaluation of a novel computer color matching system based on the improved back-propagation neural network model. *J. Prosthodont.*, 27, 8, 775–83, 2018 Oct.

54. Yamaguchi, S., Lee, C., Karaer, O., Ban, S., Mine, A., Imazato, S., Predicting the debonding of CAD/CAM composite resin crowns with AI. *J. Dent. Res.*, 98, 11, 1234–8, 2019 Oct.
55. Deshmukh, S.V., Artificial intelligence in dentistry. *J. Int. Clin. Dent. Res. Organ.*, 10, 2, 47–8, 2018 Jul 1.
56. Khanagar, S.B., Vishwanathaiah, S., Naik, S., Al-Kheraif, A.A., Divakar, D.D., Sarode, S.C., Bhandi, S., Patil, S., Application and performance of artificial intelligence technology in forensic odontology–A systematic review. *Legal Med.*, 48, 101826, 2021 Feb 1.
57. Asiri, A.F. and Altuwalah, A.S., The role of neural artificial intelligence for diagnosis and treatment planning in endodontics: A qualitative review. *Saudi Dent. J.*, 34, 4, 270–81, 2022 May 1.
58. Patel, B., *Endodontic diagnosis, pathology and treatment planning*. Classification of pulp and perio-apical disease, Springer International Publishing, Switzerland, 2015.
59. Nawresh, A. and Sasikala, S., Application of Artificial Intelligence in Image Processing, in: *Empowering Artificial Intelligence Through Machine Learning*, pp. 187–215, Apple Academic Press, Palm Bay, Florida, USA, 2022 Jun 16.
60. Dixit, S., Kumar, A., Srinivasan, K., A Current Review of Machine Learning and Deep Learning Models in Oral Cancer Diagnosis: Recent Technologies, Open Challenges, and Future Research Directions. *Diagnostics*, 13, 7, 1353, 2023 Apr 5.
61. Shen, K.L., Huang, C.L., Lin, Y.C., Du, J.K., Chen, F.L., Kabasawa, Y., Chen, C.C., Huang, H.L., Effects of artificial intelligence-assisted dental monitoring intervention in patients with periodontitis: a randomized controlled trial. *J. Clin. Periodontol.*, 49, 10, 988–98, 2022 Oct.
62. Ayad, N., Schwendicke, F., Krois, J., van den Bosch, S., Bergé, S., Bohner, L., Hanisch, M., Vinayahalingam, S., Patients' perspectives on the use of artificial intelligence in dentistry: a regional survey. *Head Face Med.*, 19, 1, 23, 2023 Jun 22.
63. Joda, T., Yeung, A.W., Hung, K., Zitzmann, N.U., Bornstein, M.M., Disruptive innovation in dentistry: what it is and what could be next. *J. Dent. Res.*, 100, 5, 448–53, 2021 May.
64. Cerghizan, D., Iulia, N.A., Maris, M., Laura, B.D., Condurache, G., Gabriela, T., Matei, M., Interrelation between Prosthetic and Orthodontic Treatment. *Rom. J. Oral Rehabil.*, 12, 145–56, 2020 Jul.
65. Blatz, M.B., Chiche, G., Bahat, O., Roblee, R., Coachman, C., Heymann, H.O., Evolution of aesthetic dentistry. *J. Dent. Res.*, 98, 12, 1294–304, 2019 Nov.
66. Babu, A., Onesimu, J.A., Sagayam, K.M., Artificial intelligence in dentistry: concepts, applications and research challenges. *E3S Web Conf.*, 297, 01074, 2021, EDP Sciences.

67. Sikstrom, L., Maslej, M.M., Hui, K., Findlay, Z., Buchman, D.Z., Hill, S.L., Conceptualising fairness: three pillars for medical algorithms and health equity. *BMJ Health Care Inf.*, 29, 1, e100459, 2022.
68. Graskemper, J.P., *Professional responsibility in dentistry: a practical guide to law and ethics*, John Wiley & Sons, Hoboken, New Jersey, United States, 2023 Jan 31.
69. Baniya, P., Agrawal, A., Gupta, B.B., The Impact of Artificial Intelligence and Machine Learning in Medical Imaging, in: *Enhancing Medical Imaging with Emerging Technologies*, pp. 221–249, IGI Global, Pennsylvania, United States, 2024.

7

Explainable Artificial Intelligence Technique in Deep Learning–Based Medical Image Analysis

Babita Gupta[1], Rishabha Malviya[1*], Sonali Sundram[1] and Sathvik Belagodu Sridhar[2]

[1]Department of Pharmacy, School of Medical and Allied Sciences, Galgotias University, Greater Noida, Uttar Pradesh, India
[2]Department of Clinical Pharmacy and Pharmacology, RAK College of Pharmacy, RAK Medical and Health Sciences University, Ras Al Khaimah, United Arab Emirates

Abstract
Artificial intelligence (AI) and explainable AI (XAI) have made substantial progress in the fields of medicine and healthcare to reduce the lack of trust in AI outcomes among doctors. XAI offers justifications for the outcomes and choices made by AI models to develop AI platforms that are easily understood, transparent, and reliable and can be easily included in human decision-making processes. However, XAI is a new concept; it has garnered substantial attention for its potential applications across multiple fields. The study provides a thorough examination of several medical imaging disciplines, including both practical applications and methodological approaches. The chapter focuses on image analysis using deep learning and XAI. It provides a comprehensive examination of XAI as it relates to the diagnosis of medical imaging, encompassing textual, visual, example-based, and conceptual explanation approaches. In addition, this study examines the current healthcare imaging databases and the standards used to evaluate the accuracy of explanations.

***Keywords*:** Artificial intelligence, explainable AI, deep learning, image analysis

**Corresponding author*: rishabhamalviya19@gmail.com; rishabha.malviya@galgotiasuniversity.edu.in

Rishabha Malviya and Sonali Sundram (eds.) Explainable and Responsible Artificial Intelligence in Healthcare, (165–190) © 2025 Scrivener Publishing LLC

7.1 Introduction

Over the last decade, there have been distinguished advancements in the area of AI, which have assisted many applications for computer vision to become much more accurate. Medical image interpretation is a field of study that has achieved significant advancements in precisely categorizing many forms of medical data, such as chest X-rays and corneal pictures [1, 2], with a degree of accuracy comparable to that of humans. The use of automated medical imaging is still quite rare in actual healthcare facilities, nevertheless, Despite this progress. Zachary Lipton explains that clinicians would not accept algorithm decisions without knowing their decision process. This feature has increased the need for developing approaches that can reveal the decision-making process of AI systems, which has resulted in the development of a completely novel field of study known as explainable artificial intelligence (XAI).

Recent advancements in deep learning (DL), together with the growing computing capabilities and creative algorithms, have facilitated the progress of DL-based techniques across multiple healthcare domains. Medical imaging is an important illustration including multiple methods used to observe the human being and prevent or treat a healthcare disorder. Radiographs, X-rays, and other imaging methods including computed tomography (CT) and magnetic resonance imaging (MRI) each give distinctive details into the nature and extent of injuries, illnesses, and treatment outcomes in the investigated body area. Evaluating this data often involves carrying out medical imaging tasks, such as categorization, identification, division, and arrangement. AI-medical imaging studies aim to simplify time-consuming procedures using efficient and acceptable DL-based approaches [3, 4].

Defense advanced research projects agency (DARPA) defines XAI as the objective of creating easier-to-understand models while yet retaining a high degree of learning efficacy in terms of prediction precision. The goal is to allow human beings to understand, trust, and properly control the next generation of AI partnerships. Even though XAI can be used in many situations, it is especially useful when determining important choices, like in the hospital process, where an incorrect decision could kill someone. This is further supported by the General Data Protection Regulation of the European Union, which mandates the disclosure of the algorithm's process of determining decisions, enhancing its transparency before its use on patients [5].

AI has become more accessible to the general public, which has made it feasible for professionals to use algorithms based on machine learning without the requirement for a greater understanding of the techniques that are being used. AI may enhance biomedical imaging by providing extra and more complete data on tumor dimension, shape, texture, and other characteristics, exceeding the capabilities of human radiologists [6]. AI has the possibility of bringing about a revolutionary change in the system of health condition diagnosis via the use of images in radiology [7]. XAI is a relatively new area that aims to resolve the difficulties associated with the complex nature of AI algorithms. It includes a variety of tools and frameworks designed to assist humans in understanding and interpreting the operations of AI models.

XAI offers substantial knowledge of AI algorithms, particularly in medicinal and healthcare sectors where individual lives are at risk. XAI approaches improve confidence in model decisions by providing more information. An explainable model explains its predictions that are understandable to humans, specifically for a particular purpose. An interpretable model is a model that allows for the extraction of conclusions on its internal workings and predictions. The model's predictions and human-understandable explanations, however, often have different explainability gaps. Several methodologies and instruments have been created to enhance the comprehensibility of the model.

A comprehension of DNNs can be achieved by utilizing the online application [8] to visualize the activations and characteristics of trained networks on a layer-by-layer basis. The study examined the relationship between machine vision and natural language processing for AI using picture-annotated images and visual query responses [9]. XAI competition for financial services intends to improve models via cooperation between organizers, Google, and academic institutions.

7.2 Deep Learning (DL) in the Analysis of Medical Images

Because DL came along, there have been big changes in the field of computer vision. Previously, the process of manually extracting features has been substituted with end-to-end learning via convolutional neural networks (CNNs). Litjens *et al.* [10] conducted an initial examination of the progress made in medical image analysis since the introduction of DL. Their study concluded that, in 2017, CNNs surpassed conventional handcrafted feature extraction for the majority of body parts as the preferred method in medical imaging studies. The scientists found that data pretreatment and augmentation approaches are crucial for better outcomes and that combining medical pictures with textual information (health-related records) may enhance image categorization specificity [11]. Rehman *et al.* [12] presented a comprehensive summary of the recent progress in using DL for the analysis of medical images.

The survey included several pattern recognition tasks, including picture classification, segmentation, and registrations. To enhance the outcomes of the image classification challenge, the authors proposed performing data augmentation using generative models. Further studies to address the most prevalent difficulties indicated by Litjens *et al.* [10] were also provided by the survey. The combination of transfer learning and synthetic data creation may overcome difficulties and enhance the generalization capabilities of existing algorithms. However, the investigators concluded that the lack of extensive annotations is still a significant obstacle in medical imaging. This challenge has a negative influence on the effectiveness of DL models, as they are susceptible to overfitting and bias problems caused by the limited data available.

The medical imaging analysis sector has acknowledged these significant advancements. However, there has been a gradual shift from systems that depend on manually crafted aspects to methods for extracting data characteristics. Before the development of AlexNet, numerous methods for learning features were prevalent. Bengio *et al.* [13] provide a comprehensive examination of various strategies. These methods include principal component analysis, picture patch clustering, dictionary techniques, and more. This study focuses on deep models, excluding typical feature-learning techniques for medical pictures.

Ravi *et al.* [14] provide a detailed assessment of DL applications in health informatics, including a brief consideration of medical image processing. DL applications to medical image analysis appeared in workshops, conferences, and publications. The evaluation of DL by Shen *et al.* [15] in medical imaging analysis was detailed, although it excluded retinal image processing. In addition, the document comprised summary tables to facilitate rapid evaluation and a discussion sequence that addressed current developments, unresolved issues, and prospective approaches for advancement in investigation.

7.3 Guidelines for Clinical XAI

Using comprehensive knowledge of AI, medical practice, and examination of human factors, they have created the clinical XAI guidelines. These guidelines were generated based on extensive research including physicians, as well as preliminary experiments in XAI assessment [16], and a survey of relevant literature (Table 7.1). Physicians provided quantitative evaluations of the graphical explanation and qualitative input on the XAI system via conversations and an open-ended survey. The recommendations for the therapeutic side were based on the qualitative data. The guidelines for clinical XAI include a checklist of five assessment criteria aimed at optimizing a clinical XAI approach. The categorization of these factors is based on three approaches: clinical usefulness, assessment, and operation. Each target in the guidelines is accompanied by its main resources derived

Table 7.1 The guidelines for designing and assessing XAI. Assessment procedures provide established evaluation techniques as sources of reference to determine if a guideline requirement has been fulfilled. These recommendations were developed with the help of essential sources. G stands for guidelines, and U refers to the outcomes of the physician user survey (which may be found in Supplementary Material S1).

Consideration	Clinical XAI guidelines	Methods of evaluation	References
Clinical Usability	G1: Comprehensibility: Clinical users must be able to comprehend the explanations without technical understanding.	Create and present schematic diagrams to clinical users.	U3: Enhancing the transparency of AI systems by revealing details about their performance, training dataset, and judgment confidence [18, 19]
	G2: Significance in clinical practice: The explanation should be related to how doctors make clinical decisions and help them with their clinical conceptualization.	Consult with clinical users to ensure explanations align with their conceptual process.	U2: Managing disagreements; U3: Clinical needs of AI that can be explained.

(*Continued*)

Table 7.1 The guidelines for designing and assessing XAI. Assessment procedures provide established evaluation techniques as sources of reference to determine if a guideline requirement has been fulfilled. These recommendations were developed with the help of essential sources. G stands for guidelines, and U refers to the outcomes of the physician user survey (which may be found in Supplementary Material S1). (*Continued*)

Consideration	Clinical XAI guidelines	Methods of evaluation	References
Evaluation	G3: Truthfulness. The explanations should accurately represent the decision-making method of AI technology. This is the requirement for G4.	The study conducted a cumulative feature removal/ addition test using various sources.	Confirming AI decision and trust calibration [19, 20].
	G4: Evaluating the reliability of information: Users' evaluations of the probability of explanations may provide an understanding of the quality of AI decisions, including potential defects or biases.	A statistical test was conducted to ascertain the level of correlation between the quality of the AI decision and the plausibility of the explanation.	U2: The practical applicability of explainable AI; U5: The evaluation of explainable AI in a healthcare environment [21].

from user surveys or literature. The evaluation procedures are described as well to facilitate the identification of whether the target has been achieved. The rules and their main aspects are given in Table 7.1 [17].

7.4 Factors to Examine about the Feasibility and Efficacy of Using the Product in the Clinical Environment

Guideline 1: Comprehensibility

An explanation should be simple enough for clinical users to clearly understand both the structure and the context. Users might understand the explanation without requiring training in machine learning, AI, or programming.

Guideline 2: Clinical Significance

Physicians utilize explanations by examining the AI-generated evidence presented in the explanation. They then integrate this evidence into their analytical approach for activities like evaluating the accuracy of AI decisions, reaching a final decision on a case, enhancing abilities to solve issues, or achieving advancements in technology (U2: Clinical usefulness of explainable AI; U1: Clinical utility of AI). The explanatory content should relate to the physicians' clinical decision-making process and should be able to help their clinical reasoning process for XAI to be clinically beneficial.

Two main phases comprise a process of interpreting images by a physician when dealing with diagnostic or predictive tasks using medical images: 1) Feature extraction involves the initial application of pattern recognition by physicians to localize significant features and determine the pattern of this characteristic. 2) Medical reasoning is then conducted on the features extracted, and physicians formulate diagnostic hypotheses (differential diagnosis) using the evidence provided by the image features. To meet the clinical criteria of explainable AI, an explanation should include information that corresponds to the method described above. This allows doctors to integrate the explanation into their process of interpreting medical images.

7.5 Factors to Consider During the Evaluation

Guideline 3: Trustworthiness

The explanation needs to give a precise overview of the procedure for making decisions that the model employs. The initial requirement for a clinically focused explanation is to meet the criteria of honesty before considering G4: Possibility with information. Medicinal users assessing the plausibility of the explanation is one of the explanation's most significant clinical applications (G4). to determine whether or not to accept the AI proposal. They then calibrate their faith in the AI's present predictions on the case or the AI model in general by this evaluation (U2). Users often assume that the explanation provided accurately describes the model's decision-making procedure. There are main implications that might result from a violation of transparency during the use of explanation by doctors: "There is a possibility that clinical users would incorrectly reject the accurate suggestion made by AI simply because of the unsuccessful execution of the XAI approach, which demonstrates an irrational explanation."

Guideline 4: Informational plausibility

The primary purpose of description is to be understood and evaluated by medicinal users. Physicians depend on the evaluation of justification plausibility or acceptability (i.e., the extent to which the explanation corresponds with human previous knowledge) as a means of determining the quality of AI decisions. Thus, XAI enables many practical applications, such as validating AI's assessments (U2.3), establishing trust in AI (U2.3), assuring the safe use of AI, deciding conflicts with AI (U2.2), detecting possible biases, and facilitating medical advances (U2.4). Possibility with information evaluates the ability of an XAI technique to effectively assist users in identifying any faults and biases in AI decision-making. This involves providing a credible explanation for correct decisions and an unappealing explanation for incorrect decisions made by the AI system. G3: Truthfulness serves as a representative of G4: Ensuring informative plausibility is essential to accurately depict the AI decision-making process.

7.5.1 A Framework for XAI

This section provides a concise introduction to the XAI method used in DL for the interpretation of medical images. The XAI methodologies may be classified based on three parameters discussed below. The framework of all three of these factors is based on the surveys done by Adadi and Berrada [22] and Murdoch *et al.* [23].

7.5.2 Comparison Between Model-Based and Post-Hoc Explanation

The first differentiation established is between model-based explanation and post-hoc explanation.

7.5.2.1 Model-Based Explanation

It is related to conceptual frameworks, such as the support vector machine or a linear regression model, which possess the dual qualities of simplicity and sophistication to accurately represent a connection between the two variables, input, and output [23]. Typically, this comprises the models used in classical machine learning. Model-based explanations may restrict the number of characteristics used (sparsity) or need humans to comprehend how the model makes decisions (simulation) [24]. Thus, a certain collection of characteristics produces an output, explaining the model's underlying structure. It is not possible to provide an explanation based on models via the use of sparsity or reproducibility because the primary emphasis of our study is on XAI approaches for DL. DL employs a complex neural network that consists of several weights, ranging from hundreds to millions. This network is not sparse and is not conducive for a person to internally replicate and analyze the whole of its decision-making process. Murdoch *et al.* [23] stated model-based feature engineering, which uses automated methodologies to create explainable features.

7.5.2.2 Post-Hoc Explanation

It refers to the procedure of analyzing a trained model, specifically a neural network in the context of DL, to get a better understanding of its functioning. A key difference between model-based explanation and post-hoc explanation is that the former tries to explain the black box network behavior that is created by training a neural network, whereas the latter requires the network to be explainable. This method includes inspecting learned features, analyzing their importance and interaction, and using saliency maps [25, 26].

7.5.3 Comparing Model-Specific and Model-Agnostic Explanations

Analyzing the differences between model-specific and model-agnostic explanations is similar to comparing model-based and post-hoc explanations [22], but there are also small distinctions.

7.5.3.1 Model-Specific Explanation

It is a way of explaining can only be used with certain types of models. This approach may use neural network-specific features. One potential limitation is that an exploration of model-specific explanations inhibits the selection of neural networks, which may result in the exclusion of a network whose output more closely matches the input data. According to Adadi [22], the model-specific explanation is fundamentally model-specific; nevertheless, it is not necessarily model-based. Certain CNN approaches, such as post-hoc saliency mapping, are not model-based explanation methods, but rather particular methodologies [23].

7.5.3.2 Model-Agnostic Explanation

It acts exclusively on the input and output of the neural network, irrespective of the specific type of neural network employed. Through manipulating the input, the user can observe the transformation that occurs in the neural network's output. This helps to clarify which areas are driving the production. Model-agnostic reasoning is usually after the fact.

7.6 XAI in Medical Image Analysis

Medical image analysis uses XAI techniques, which are adapted from computer vision approaches. There are three main kinds of explanation methods: visual, textual, and example-based. It can further divide each technique into subtypes depending on the following criteria: model-specific vs. model-agnostic, global versus local, and model-based versus post-hoc (Figure 7.1).

7.6.1 Visual Explanation

Tandem Net is a comprehensive framework that was introduced by Zhang *et al.* [27]. It is comparable to image captioning [28] in that it generates visible attention mapping that matches textual explanations on pictures. Lee *et al.* [29] combined radiology reports and visual saliency maps to provide

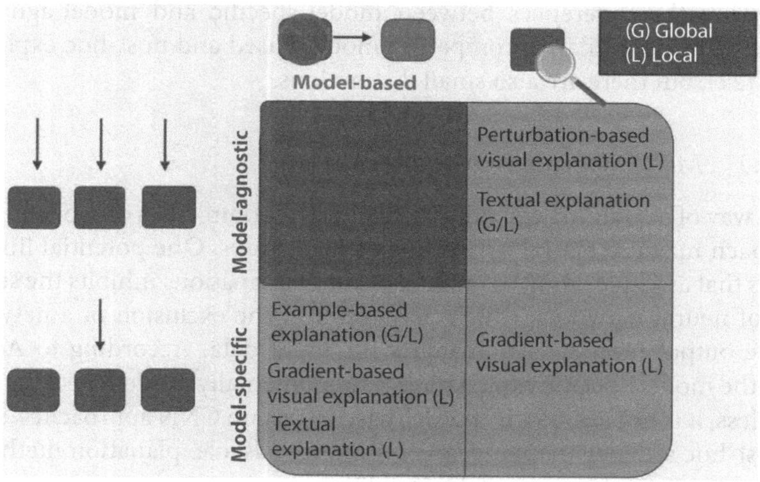

Figure 7.1 The proposed XAI framework.

visual explanations for breast mammograms using image captioning. Wang *et al.* [40] demonstrated a comparable method, TieNet, using chest X-rays. The authors made a significant observation: they demonstrated how various textual explanations contributed to distinct saliency maps on the input picture that corresponded to radiological results. In general, it is important to emphasize that systems such as visual question answering (VQA) or image captioning are not considered XAI approaches. Instead, they demonstrate how the combination of semantic and visual aspects may be used to improve the diagnostic process. Furthermore, the use of these techniques does not need a thorough comprehension or interpretation particular to the approach. Saliency maps represent the crucial regions of an image that are significant when deciding a choice. While certain saliency mapping methods make use of perturbation or multiple instance learning, the majority rely on backpropagation. These methods provide localized, model-specific (exclusive to CNNs), retrospective explanation. These approaches were employed in the examination of medical images. De Vos *et al.* [30] assessed the quantity of coronary artery calcium measured on each slice of the heart or chest CT picture using deconvolution to determine the determination point.

7.6.2 Textual Explanation

A common limitation of computer-aided diagnostic methods is the inability to provide meaningful explanations for model predictions. This concludes that textual XAI methods try to show extra information through textual descriptions produced using normal language [31]. Various approaches have been suggested to acquire context-related knowledge from images, including semantic annotation and AI-based conversation simulation. Mutuality involves expanding the accessible information base (images) with other sources of knowledge on the visual content. An advantageous characteristic of such systems is the ability to have inquiries that are unconstrained and unrestricted, allowing users to ask questions that go beyond simple yes-or-no inquiries. The field of VQA is often considered a sample application of automated image comprehension. VQA incorporates knowledge and insights from several fields, including computer vision, natural language processing, and information representation [32, 33].

The VQA project has made a substantial impact by adding more pictures to the Microsoft Common Objects in Context (COCO) library [34]. Approximately 0.25 million pictures, 0.76 million questions, and 10 million responses comprise the final VQA dataset. Textual descriptions constitute a type of XAI known as "textual explanation." The explanations may encompass fundamental attributes (e.g., "spiculated substantial value") or exhaustive scientific investigations. There are three distinct categories of text explanation: completing tests including idea attribution, as well as generating picture captions accompanied by visual explanations.

7.6.3 Image Description

Vinyals *et al.* [28] used a comprehensive image captioning system to give textual explanations for pictures. A CNN was utilized to encode the image, whereas a recurrent neural network, more precisely a long-short-term memory net [34], was employed to encode the text. For training purposes, used human-generated phrases, and, for assessment, they employed the bilingual evaluation understudy (BLEU) metric. The BLEU metric is a system that describes the accuracy of word N-grams, which are sequences of N words, between produced sentences and reference sentences [35]. Singh *et al.* [36] provided textual explanations for chest X-rays using an image captioning system. The LSTM model was trained using word embedding databases Global Vectors (GloVe) and the radiology variant RadGloVe [37, 38]. The usage of both Rad-GloVe and GloVe resulted in a greater level of performance in the produced radiology report, as anticipated, compared to using alone GloVe.

7.6.4 Captioning Images with Accompanying Visual Description

Several studies used a hybrid approach, combining visual explanation with image captioning. Zhang *et al.* [39] proposed an approach that included dual attention mechanisms for both textual and visual information. They used the same method as when they captioned images, with an encoder for the picture and an LSTM for the text, but they paid extra attention to both at the same time. This enabled advanced connections between picture and text predictions, resulting in visual attention maps that corresponded with textual explanations in histology images.

In their study, Wang *et al.* [40] used a similar methodology and demonstrated that different portions of the textual explanation corresponded to distinct regions of saliency mapping in the chest X-ray picture. A saliency map of the chest was shown, highlighting many locations that corresponded to various radiological results. Lee *et al.* [41] demonstrated the use of visual explanation in image screening for breast cancer with mammography. They demonstrated that including this loss function enhances the production of superior textual explanations. In addition, they connected the radiological results to visual saliency maps.

7.6.5 Testing Using Concept Activation Vectors (TCAVs)

According to Kim *et al.* [42], it provides an explanation that corresponds to advanced ideas that are simple for humans to comprehend. Kim *et al.* [42] utilized TCAV to generate linear explanations that are comprehensible to humans regarding the condition of neural networks internally. This approach resulted in a complete understanding of the networks in relation to ideas that are easily understandable by humans. The TCAV method utilizes user-specified sets of idea examples and random non-concept examples. Some examples of such a notion include the use of "stripes" to determine whether or not a picture included a zebra, or the use of "spiculated bulk" to determine whether or not an image had a malignancy. TCAV measured the responsiveness of a trained model to specific ideas by using CAVs.

The sensitivity of that idea was then measured by using the reaction of test cases to these CAVs as the basis for the measurement. The authors demonstrated the practicality of TCAV via an application in medical image processing. They achieved this by establishing a connection between physician annotations, such as "microaneurysm," and the presence of diabetic retinal degeneration in fundus imaging. Clough *et al.* [43] detected heart illness in cine-MRI by categorizing the hidden area of a VAE. TCAV was used to demonstrate the correlation between cardiac disease and clinically established biomarkers. A characteristic that may be associated with reconstructing images exhibiting cardiac disease, they implemented a low maximal ejection rate through the incorporation of the CAV into the latent space.

7.7 Non-Visual XAI Techniques in Medical Imaging

Visual XAI techniques, such as identification and heat maps, are often used in explanation approaches for medical imaging due to their visual nature [44]. While visual XAI techniques are considered to be simple to understand and instinctive, some studies have shown important drawbacks. Adebayo *et al.* [45] conducted a significant investigation to determine if saliency approaches are insensitive. This undesired impact shows that an explanation is detached from the model or data and provides no explanation. Edge detectors are a good example of this kind of tool as they do nothing more than identify regions of a picture with very noticeable color changes; they have no bearing on the accuracy of model predictions. Furthermore, Ghorbani *et al.* [46] provided evidence of the susceptibility of saliency maps to image perturbations and adversarial harm, which raises concern regarding how to ensure the resilience of visual XAI methods.

Tomsett *et al.* [47] found inconsistent assessment measures in sanity-check experiments, highlighting the difficulty of completely evaluating visual explanations despite the increased effort. Furthermore, visually XAI approaches include just a small portion of the whole range of available methods. Thus, it is crucial to investigate a variety of XAI methods to completely understand and utilize their potential in the medical imaging field, even though non-visual XAI methods may appear more specialized and visually depend on knowledge specific to the method to achieve precise interpretation.

Therefore, in addition to visual explanations, three different groups of non-visual XAI approaches were defined based on the specific outcome that a user might anticipate when using an XAI methodology [48]: supplementary explanations, case-based explanations, and textual explanations. The subsequent parts will offer a comprehensive introduction to these categories. Additionally, they may serve as a system for categorizing XAI approaches based on their result. Determining the appropriate type of informational image for a specific application depends on factors such as the end-users, technical conditions, the desired level of explainability, and, most importantly, what is considered advantageous in terms of interpretability within the medical field. End-users are defined as physicians, radiologists, and clinicians in this paper. Presumably, their primary concern lies in the correlation of information and verification of diagnoses. A radiologist using a malignancy detection model may seek visual interpretations of the original picture to assess the model's focus and predictability. However, a predictive model that estimates a patient's overall probability of death might have advantages by including counterfactuals. However, artificial representations and auxiliary values could be more illuminating when developing such models [48]. In conclusion, each approach can provide useful explanatory insight. There are no guidelines or limitations on selecting acceptable ways. Selecting an effective XAI approach for employment is challenging due to end-user perceptions, particular demands, and limited evaluation criteria [49].

7.8 Challenges and Future Directions

XAI methods could assist in comprehending predictions made by a DL model. However, some obstacles must be addressed before these methods are widely used for healthcare purposes. This section presents an analysis of the utilization and obstacles associated with XAI methods in the field of biomedical applications. Additionally, it summarizes recent advances that could transform XAI applications in the field of biomedical imaging.

7.8.1 Understanding and Enhancing Explanation

In XAI, the word "explanation" is not properly defined [50, 51]. There is currently no universally accepted definition of explanations; however, some progress has been made in this area through the development of mathematical methodologies [52]. "Explanation" is defined differently by different people [53]. Some research institutes and regulatory agencies are working to define and use explainable AI and related concepts. The views of patients, clinicians, and engineers vary, and existing definitions are inconsistent, making explainable AI a false promise for patient-level decision assistance. The relevance of the model's emphasized aspects to human-identified variables and conclusions may also vary [54]. Therefore, the use of AI in medical practice would need further efforts to be made to make the XAI approaches more understandable. The advancement of deep neural networks (DNNs) and subsequent attempts to understand their basic mechanisms and decision-making processes resulted in the development of several valuable approaches. However, it would be beneficial to include explainability in the model.

The majority of tumor detection investigations use post-hoc explainability methodologies; however, it would be beneficial to establish intrinsic explanation strategies for adoption and explainability [55]. To enhance the comprehensibility of the multi-task capsule network, X-Caps, explainability was improved by utilizing the high-level visual features of capsule networks. They generate malignancy scores, which are utilized by specialists to assess and diagnose tumor cases. To identify biased models caused by activations with incorrect pixels in test pictures, automated heatmap analysis was included as a building step in the MLOps (machine learning operations) pipeline for vision AI [55]. White-box modeling techniques with little accuracy cost for interpretability include monotonic gradient boosting machine (GBM), scalable Bayesian rule lists, and explainable neural network (XNN) [56]. Initiating the development of a comprehensible model from the initial stages will facilitate the process of providing explanations and conducting fairness evaluations. Future approaches may combine intrinsic, rule-extraction, and attribute techniques to respond to human-friendly language [57].

7.8.2 Application of XAI in Medical Imaging

Medical imaging involves a wide range of techniques for capturing images in both time and space, to obtain the most relevant data to assist in diagnosing the underlying medical disease. Image modalities and their observable features differ. The most used XAI approach for medical imaging is Grad-CAM, followed by layer-wise relevance propagation (LRP), local interpretable model-agnostic explanations (LIME), SHapley Additive exPlanations (SHAP), and others. XAI methods are being used in the fields of neurology, respiratory, and ophthalmic assessments. MRI is the most often used imaging modality in the field of neurology. Chest X-ray (CXR) images are highly preferred for respiratory examinations because they may be easily produced. Among the several ways of XAI, Grad-CAM is the most commonly used. Fundus visuals are the most often used modality in ophthalmic investigations. Various methodologies have been suggested and are currently being developed to facilitate the wide integration of DNN and XAI approaches into clinical practice. DNNs facilitate the selection of ROIs automatically, eliminating the need for laborious manual annotations [58, 59]. It is crucial to link the uncertainty of the model's predictions to help the physician focus more on these specific cases [60, 61].

The predictability and explainability of the model may be enhanced by including additional data in the model training process [62, 63]. XAI approaches leveraging multimodal DNN models provide insights into hidden patterns in segmentation and classification problems. Utilizing various scales may enhance the precision and comprehensibility [64–66]. XAI approaches to support clinicians may improve diagnostic outcomes compared to models or clinicians alone [67–70]. Due to limited medical data, research focuses on tackling related difficulties [71]. A smartphone application using a DNN model for segmentation and categorization enhances accessibility for mass glaucoma screening [72].

The explainability methods mostly use visuals that give a qualitative signal by showing how important the picture areas are to the decision-making process. While the model may provide some level of confidence, its reliability for medical imaging cannot be depended on without a standardized method for evaluating several models and their results. Developing quantifiable measures for model comparison will enable the effective implementation of explainability approaches across many visual modalities. Metrics may be used to evaluate and approve XAI procedures for clinical use, addressing regulatory requirements. DNN models must be developed to be both accurate and interpretable. XAI systems should be integrated into clinical processes with simple interfaces. Model-agnostic approaches have the potential to improve explainability.

7.8.3 Data-Focused XAI

The quality and amount of training data significantly impact model performance and explainability. For optimal outcomes, DNN requires large, high-quality data to avoid overfitting and aligning with a few data points [73]. This may provide a problem for imaging datasets because there are fewer image samples available than in normal circumstances, which makes acquiring them difficult. Noise and inaccurate labeling may have an impact on the quality of the data [74]. Additionally, the outcomes of explanation by examples may be hampered by low-quality data [75]. By enhancing the edges and outlines, denoising approaches may make the DNN less susceptible to tiny perturbations and quality degradations [76]. To increase the DNN performance, images were pre-processed using a contrast-to-noise ratio, unnecessary parts were removed, etc. [77].

The effectiveness of DNN algorithms in accurately forecasting a disease is improved by the quality of the images, which may consequently lead to a reduction in the apparent explainability gap. It may be simpler for the model to understand or interpret the data if there is less noise in it [78].

Training data is essential for DL models to provide repeatable and valuable results [79]. Insufficient data may lead to overfitting in AI models, as data-collecting policies and processes vary between hospitals. Small datasets were often used in certain research claiming DNN medical imaging performance outperformed radiologists, which is a major disadvantage [74]. Considering additional parameters like age, race, and ethnicity, it is challenging to acquire data on breast cancer that covers all picture variants. Noise may occur in biomedical imaging datasets and CT images [73]. Due to variations in data quality and random model initialization for MRI images, DNNs with identical architectures may provide varied predictions [80].

Methods to overcome the difficulties of limited datasets in AI model training have been investigated in studies. Data augmentation, GANs, LRP pruning, decontextualized hierarchical representation learning, few-shot learning, and labeled datasets from many sources or organizations are among the techniques used. Nevertheless, the majority of data lacks adequate diversity, interoperability, and representation. Only the systems of individual departments are allowed to store imaging data utilized in clinical situations, except radiology.

The integration of data from various sources has the potential to yield novel insights. Federated learning improves global DNN model development using local data. This reduces various biases in the model and data and enables the evaluation of DNN's explainability and accuracy using the same dataset. Federated learning has the potential to promote the creation of a worldwide library of standardized datasets for evaluating performance in biomedical imaging. This would allow for the evaluation of the precision and explainability of DNNs compared to the same dataset, as well as the mitigation of various biases that may exist in both the model and the data.

7.8.4 Fusion/Hybrid Imaging for XAI

A multi-modal approach integrates several imaging modalities into a single report, for example, PET, MRI, and CT. A growing number of medical imaging applications are beginning to include patient characteristics or time-series data in their workflow, in addition to other image modalities used for diagnosis. It is possible to integrate the previous electrocardiogram with cardiac MRI and CT [81]. Combining data kinds, mapping, and fusion is a key challenge in data science. Combining multi-modal data might provide new insights [82]. Information fusion and mixed systems can work much better than systems with only one type of data [83].

Image data from X-rays, CT scans, and PET scans were mixed with blood pressure, cough sounds, and body temperature in a cloud-based medical facility for COVID-19–like pandemics [84]. The examination and diagnosis of a disease may be substantially simplified by hybrid imaging, which offers extra data from the many image modalities [85]. Two major challenges in multimodal imaging are class imbalances and insufficient labeled data [85]. The lack of transparency and functionality of DNNs renders them impractical, notwithstanding the remarkable performance exhibited by multimodal approaches [86]. A multimodal diagnostic model for Alzheimer's disease was developed based on the association between MRI and gene expression data [86]. The multimodality approach was shown to be more specific than individual modalities [86]. The fusion of imaging and non-imaging data, as well as multi-modality approaches, might help get AI methods accepted in healthcare facilities. The challenges associated with multimodality include data representation, translation, alignment, and fusion [86]. Aggregating visual explanations may improve model comprehension and boost system certainty.

7.9 Conclusion

The use of XAI approaches to visualize segmentation and classification problems for biomedical imaging is studied. XAI and DNN models may help physicians diagnose diseases. Currently, image-based diagnosis in biomedical imaging fields requires the experience of overloaded practitioners. XAI methods can make things better by automating translation and explainability, which makes it faster for medical professionals to make decisions. Clinical XAI guidelines have been established for designing and evaluating clinically focused XAI systems. The clinical necessity for explanations from physicians and user studies and the technological knowledge from prior XAI assessment studies and XAI literature formed the basis for the recommendation's suggestion. The guidelines G1: Understandability and G2: Clinical Relevance give clinicians information that enables them to select the explanation. The recommendations G3: Truthfulness, G4: Informative plausibility, and G5: Computational Efficiency address the specific requirements for providing accurate and reliable explanations in a therapeutic field. To classify them according to anatomical region and imaging methodology, the study examined the use of XAI in DL-based medical image analysis. It also included assessment techniques, contemporary concerns, and future perspectives on XAI in medical image analysis.

References

1. Xu, K., Ba, J., Kiros, R., Cho, K., Courville, A., Salakhudinov, R., Zemel, R., Bengio, Y., Show, attend, and tell: Neural image caption generation with visual attention, in: *International Conference on Machine Learning (ICML)*, pp. 2048–2057, 2015.
2. Majkowska, A., Mittal, S., Steiner, D.F., Reicher, J.J., McKinney, S.M., Duggan, G.E., Eswaran, K., Chen, P.-H.C., Liu, Y., Kalidindi, S.R. *et al.*, Chest Radiograph Interpretation with Deep Learning Models: Assessment with Radiologist-adjudicated Reference Standards and Population-adjusted Evaluation. *Radiology*, 294, 2, 421–431, 2020.
3. Hosch, R., Kroll, L., Nensa, F., Koitka, S., Differentiation Between Anteroposterior and Posteroanterior Chest X-Ray View Position With Convolutional Neural Networks. *Rofo*, 193, 2, 168–176, Feb. 2021.
4. Koitka, S., Kim, M.S., Qu, M., Fischer, A., Friedrich, C.M., Nensa, F., Mimicking the radiologists' workflow: Estimating pediatric hand bone age with stacked deep neural networks. *Med. Image Anal.*, 64, 101743, Aug. 2020.
5. Goodman, B. and Flaxman, S., European Union Regulations on Algorithmic Decision-Making and a "Right to Explanation", 2017.
6. Sorantin, E., Grasser, M.G., Hemmelmayr, A., Tschauner, S., Hrzic, F., Weiss, V., Lacekova, J., Holzinger, A., The augmented radiologist: artificial intelligence in the practice of radiology. *Pediatr. Radiol.*, 19, 1–3, 2021 Oct.
7. Folke, T., Yang, S., Anderson, S., Shafto, P., Explainable AI for medical imaging: explaining pneumothorax diagnoses with Bayesian teaching. *Artificial*

Intelligence and Machine Learning for Multi-Domain Operations Applications III, vol. 11746, pp. 644–664, 2021.

8. Yosinski, J., Clune, J., Nguyen, A., Fuchs, T., Lipson, H., Understanding neural networks through deep visualization, arXiv preprint arXiv:1506.06579, 2015 Jun 22.
9. Oussalah, M., AI explainability. A bridge between machine vision and natural language processing, in: *Pattern Recognition. ICPR International Workshops and Challenges: Virtual Event, January 10–15, 2021, Proceedings, Part III*, pp. 257–273, 2021.
10. Litjens, G., Kooi, T., Bejnordi, B.E., Setio, A.A.A., Ciompi, F., Ghafoorian, M., Van Der Laak, J.A., Van Ginneken, R., Sánchez, C.I., A survey on deep learning in medical image analysis. *Med. Image Anal.*, 42, 60–88, 2017.
11. Schlegl, T., Waldstein, S.M., Vogl, W.-D., Schmidt-Erfurth, U., Langs, G., Predicting semantic descriptions from medical images with convolutional neural networks, in: *Proceedings of the International Conference on Information Processing in Medical Imaging (IPMI'15)*, pp. 437–448, 2015.
12. Rehman, A., Butt, M.A., Zaman, M., A survey of medical image analysis using deep learning approaches, in: *Proceedings of the IEEE International Conference on Computing Methodologies and Communication (ICCMC'21)*, pp. 1334–1342, 2021.
13. Bengio, Y., Courville, A., Vincent, P., Representation learning: A review and new perspectives. *IEEE Trans. Pattern Anal. Mach. Intell.*, 35, 8, 1798–1828, 2013.
14. Ravi, D., Wong, C., Deligianni, F., Berthelot, M., Andreu-Perez, J., Lo, B., Yang, G.-Z., Deep learning for health informatics. *IEEE J. Biomed. Health Inform.*, 21, 4–21, Jan. 2017.
15. Shen, D., Wu, G., Suk, H.-I., Deep learning in medical image analysis. *Annu. Rev. Biomed. Eng.*, Mar., 221–48, 2017.
16. WJin, W., Li, X., Hamarneh, G., Evaluating explainable AI on a multi-modal medical imaging task: Can existing algorithms fulfill clinical requirements?, in: *Proceedings of the AAAI Conference on Artificial Intelligence*, vol. 36, no. 11, pp. 11945–11953, 2022 Jun 28.
17. Jin, W., Li, X., Fatehi, M., Hamarneh, G., Guidelines and evaluation of clinical explainable AI in medical image analysis. *Med. Image Anal.*, 84, 102684, 2023 Feb 1.
18. Jin, W., Fan, J., Gromala, D., Pasquier, P., Hamarneh, G., EUCA: The end-user-centered explainable AI framework, arXiv preprint arXiv:2102.02437, 2021 Feb 4.
19. Sokol, K. and Flach, P., Explainability fact sheets: A framework for systematic assessment of explainable approaches, in: *Proceedings of the 2020 conference on fairness, accountability, and transparency*, pp. 56–67, 2020 Jan 27.

20. Jacovi, A. and Goldberg, Y., Towards faithfully interpretable NLP systems: How should we define and evaluate faithfulness?, arXiv preprint arXiv:2004.03685, 2020 Apr 7.
21. Doshi-Velez, F. and Kim, B., Considerations for evaluation and generalization in interpretable machine learning, in: *Explainable and interpretable models in computer vision and machine learning*, pp. 3–17, 2018.
22. Adadi, A. and Berrada, M., Peeking Inside the Black Box: A Survey on Explainable Artificial Intelligence (XAI). *IEEE Access*, 6, 52138–52160, 2018.
23. Murdoch, W.J., Singh, C., Kumbier, K., Abbasi-Asl, R., Yu, B., Definitions, methods, and applications in interpretable machine learning. *Proc. Natl. Acad. Sci. U.S.A.*, 116, 22071–22080, 2019.
24. Tibshirani, R., Regression shrinkage and selection via the lasso. *J. R. Stat. Soc.*, 58, 267–288, 1996.
25. Abbasi-Asl, R. and Yu, B., Structural compression of convolutional neural networks, arXiv preprint arXiv:1705.07356, 2017.
26. Tsang, M., Cheng, D., Liu, Y., Detecting statistical interactions from neural network weights, in: *Proceedings of the International Conference on Learning Representations*, 2018.
27. Zhang, Z., Chen, P., Sapkota, M., Yang, L., Tandemnet: Distilling knowledge from medical images using diagnostic reports as optional semantic references, in: *Medical Image Computing and Computer Assisted Intervention–MICCAI 2017: 20th International Conference, Quebec City, QC, Canada, September 11-13, 2017, Proceedings, Part III 20*, pp. 320–328, Springer International Publishing, Salmon Tower Building New York City, 2017.
28. Vinyals, O., Toshev, A., Bengio, S., Erhan, D., Show and tell: A neural image caption generator, in: *Proceedings of the IEEE Conference on computer vision and pattern recognition*, pp. 3156–3164, 2015.
29. Lee, H., Kim, S.T., Ro, Y.M., Generation of multimodal justification using visual word constraint model for explainable computer-aided diagnosis, in: *Interpretability of Machine Intelligence in Medical Image Computing and Multimodal Learning for Clinical Decision Support: Second International Workshop, iMIMIC 2019, and 9th International Workshop, ML-CDS 2019, Held in Conjunction with MICCAI 2019, Shenzhen, China, October 17, 2019, Proceedings 9*, pp. 21–29, Springer International Publishing, Salmon Tower Building, New York City, 2019.
30. de Vos, B.D., Wolterink, J.M., Leiner, T., de Jong, P.A., Lessmann, N., Isgum, I., Direct automatic coronary calcium scoring in cardiac and chest CT. *IEEE Trans. Med. Imaging*, 38, 2127–2138, 2019.
31. Zhang, Z., Xie, Y., Xing, F., McGough, M., Yang, L., Mdnet: A semantically and visually interpretable medical image diagnosis network, in: *Proceedings of the IEEE Conference on Computer Vision and Pattern Recognition*, pp. 6428–6436, 2017.

32. Antol, S., Agrawal, A., Lu, J., Mitchell, M., Batra, D., Zitnick, C.L., Parikh, D., Vqa: Visual question answering, in: *Proceedings of the IEEE international conference on computer vision*, pp. 2425–2433, 2015.
33. Lin, T.Y., Maire, M., Belongie, S., Hays, J., Perona, P., Ramanan, D., Dollár, P., Zitnick, C.L., Microsoft coco: Common objects in context, in: *Computer Vision–ECCV 2014: 13th European Conference, Zurich, Switzerland, September 6-12, 2014, Proceedings, Part V 13*, pp. 740–755, Springer International Publishing, Salmon Tower Building, New York City, 2014.
34. Gers, F.A., Schmidhuber, J., Cummins, F., Learning to forget: Continual prediction with LSTM. *Neural Comput.*, 12, 10, 2451–71, 2000 Oct 1.
35. Papineni, K., Roukos, S., Ward, T., Zhu, W.J., BLEU: a method for automatic evaluation of machine translation, in: *Proceedings of the 40th Annual Meeting of the Association for Computational Linguistics*, pp. 311–318, 2002.
36. Singh, S., Karimi, S., Ho-Shon, K., Hamey, L., From chest X-rays to radiology reports: a multimodal machine learning approach. *2019 International Conference on Digital Image Computing: Techniques and Applications, DICTA 2019*, Institute of Electrical and Electronics Engineers Inc., Department of Computing, Macquarie University, Sydney, Australia, 2019.
37. Pennington, J., Socher, R., Manning, C.D., Glove: global vectors for word representation, in: *Proceedings of the 2014 Conference on Empirical Methods in Natural Language Processing (EMNLP)*, pp. 1532–1543, 2014.
38. Zhang, Y., Ding, D.Y., Qian, T., Manning, C.D., Langlotz, C.P., Learning to summarize radiology findings, in: *Proceedings of the Ninth International Workshop on Health Text Mining and Information Analysis*, Association for Computational Linguistics, Brussels, Belgium, pp. 204–213, 2018.
39. Zhang, Z., Chen, P., Sapkota, M., Yang, L., TandemNet: distilling knowledge from medical images using diagnostic reports as optional semantic references. *Proceedings of the 20th International Conference on Medical Image Computing and Computer-Assisted Intervention. MICCAI 2017*, 2017a, doi:10.1007/ 978-3-319-66179-7_37.
40. Wang, X., Peng, Y., Lu, L., Lu, Z., Summers, R.M., TieNet: text-image embedding network for common thorax disease classification and reporting in chest X-rays, in: *Proceedings of the 31st Meeting of the IEEE/CVF Conference on Computer Vision and Pattern Recognition, CVPR 2018*, IEEE Computer Society, United States, pp. 9049–9058, 2018.
41. Wink, M.H., Wijkstra, H., De La Rosette, J.J., Grimbergen, C.A., Ultrasound imaging and contrast agents: a safe alternative to MRI? *Minim. Invasive Ther. Allied Technol.*, 15, 2, 93–100, 2006 Jan 1.
42. Kim, B., Wattenberg, M., Gilmer, J., Cai, C., Wexler, J., Viegas, F., Sayres, R., Interpretability beyond feature attribution: quantitative testing with concept activation vectors (TCAV), in: *Proceeding of the 35th International Conference on Machine Learning, ICML 2018*, International Machine Learning Society (IMLS), pp. 4186–4195, 2018.

43. Clough, J.R., Oksuz, I., Puyol-Antón, E., Ruijsink, B., King, A.P., Schnabel, J.A., Global and local interpretability for cardiac MRI classification, in: *Proceedings of the 22nd International Conference on Medical Image Computing and Computer-Assisted Intervention MICCAI 2019*, 2019, doi:10.1007/978-3-030-32251-9_72.
44. Van der Velden, B.H., Kuijf, H.J., Gilhuijs, K.G., Viergever, M.A., Explainable artificial intelligence (XAI) in deep learning-based medical image analysis. *Med. Image Anal.*, 79, 102470, 2022 Jul 1.
45. Adebayo, J., Gilmer, J., Muelly, M., Goodfellow, I., Hardt, M., Kim, B., Sanity checks for saliency maps, in: *Advances in neural information processing systems*, vol. 31, 2018.
46. Ghorbani, A., Abid, A., Zou, J., Interpretation of neural networks is fragile, in: *Proceedings of the AAAI conference on artificial intelligence*, vol. 33, no. 01, pp. 3681–3688, 2019 Jul 17.
47. Tomsett, R., Harborne, D., Chakraborty, S., Gurram, P., Preece, A., Sanity checks for saliency metrics, in: *Proceedings of the AAAI conference on artificial intelligence*, vol. 34, no. 04, pp. 6021–6029, 2020 Apr 3.
48. Pocevičiūtė, M., Eilertsen, G., Lundström, C., Survey of XAI in digital pathology, in: *Artificial intelligence and machine learning for digital pathology: state-of-the-art and future challenges*, pp. 56–88, 2020.
49. Arrieta, A.B., Díaz-Rodríguez, N., Del Ser, J., Bennett, A., Tabik, S., Barbado, A., García, S., Gil-López, S., Molina, D., Benjamins, R., Chatila, R., Explainable Artificial Intelligence (XAI): Concepts, taxonomies, opportunities and challenges toward responsible AI. *Inf. Fusion*, 58, 82–115, 2020 Jun 1.
50. Payrovnaziri, S.N., Chen, Z., Rengifo-Moreno, P., Miller, T., Bian, J., Chen, J.H., Liu, X., He, Z., Explainable artificial intelligence models using real-world electronic health record data: a systematic scoping review. *J. Am. Med. Inf. Assoc.*, 27, 7, 1173–85, 2020 Jul.
51. Gillmann, C., Smit, N.N., Gröller, E., Preim, B., Vilanova, A., Wischgoll, T., Ten open challenges in medical visualization. *IEEE Comput. Graphics Appl.*, 41, 5, 7–15, 2021 Sep 10.
52. Samek, W. and Müller, K.R., Towards explainable artificial intelligence, in: *Explainable AI: interpreting, explaining, and visualizing deep learning*, pp. 5–22, 2019.
53. Guidotti, R., Monreale, A., Ruggieri, S., Turini, F., Giannotti, F., Pedreschi, D., A survey of methods for explaining black box models. *ACM Comput. Surv. (CSUR)*, 51, 5, 1–42, 2018 Aug 22.
54. Ghassemi, M., Oakden-Rayner, L., Beam, A.L., The false hope of current approaches to explainable artificial intelligence in health care. *Lancet Digital Health*, 3, 11, e745–50, 2021 Nov 1.
55. Gulum, M.A., Trombley, C.M., Kantardzic, M., A review of explainable deep learning cancer detection models in medical imaging. *Appl. Sci.*, 11, 10, 4573, 2021 May 17.

56. Hall, P. and Gill, N., *An introduction to machine learning interpretability*, O'Reilly Media, Incorporated, Sebastopol, California, 2019.
57. Ras, G., van Gerven, M., Haselager, P., Explanation methods in deep learning: Users, values, concerns, and challenges, in: *Explainable and interpretable models in computer vision and machine learning*, pp. 19–36, 2018.
58. Chen, X., Lin, L., Liang, D., Hu, H., Zhang, Q., Iwamoto, Y., Han, X.H., Chen, Y.W., Tong, R., Wu, J., A dual-attention dilated residual network for liver lesion classification and localization on CT images, in: *2019 IEEE International Conference on Image Processing (ICIP)*, IEEE, pp. 235–239, 2019 Sep 22.
59. Shapira, N., Fokuhl, J., Schultheiß, M., Beck, S., Kopp, F.K., Pfeiffer, D., Dangelmaier, J., Pahn, G., Sauter, A.P., Renger, B., Fingerle, A.A., Liver lesion localization and classification with convolutional neural networks: a comparison between conventional and spectral computed tomography. *Biomed. Phys. Eng. Express*, 6, 1, 015038, 2020 Jan 31.
60. Natekar, P., Kori, A., Krishnamurthi, G., Demystifying brain tumor segmentation networks: interpretability and uncertainty analysis. *Front. Comput. Neurosci.*, 14, 6, 2020 Feb 7.
61. Jang, Y., Son, J., Park, K.H., Park, S.J., Jung, K.H., Laterality classification of fundus images using interpretable deep neural network. *J. Digit. Imaging*, 31, 923–8, 2018 Dec.
62. Tang, Z., Chuang, K.V., DeCarli, C., Jin, L.W., Beckett, L., Keiser, M.J., Dugger, B.N., Interpretable classification of Alzheimer's disease pathologies with a convolutional neural network pipeline. *Nat. Commun.*, 10, 1, 2173, 2019 May 15.
63. Barata, C., Celebi, M.E., Marques, J.S., Explainable skin lesion diagnosis using taxonomies. *Pattern Recognit.*, 110, 107413, 2021 Feb 1.
64. Liz, H., Sánchez-Montañés, M., Tagarro, A., Domínguez-Rodríguez, S., Dagan, R., Camacho, D., Ensembles of convolutional neural network models for pediatric pneumonia diagnosis. *Future Gener. Comput. Syst.*, 122, 220–33, 2021 Sep 1.
65. Liao, W., Zou, B., Zhao, R., Chen, Y., He, Z., Zhou, M., Clinical interpretable deep learning model for glaucoma diagnosis. *IEEE J. Biomed. Health. Inf.*, 24, 5, 1405–12, 2019 Oct 24.
66. El Adoui, M., Drisis, S., Benjelloun, M., Multi-input deep learning architecture for predicting breast tumor response to chemotherapy using quantitative MR images. *Int. J. Comput. Assist. Radiol. Surg.*, 15, 1491–500, 2020 Sep.
67. Qian, X., Pei, J., Zheng, H., Xie, X., Yan, L., Zhang, H., Han, C., Gao, X., Zhang, H., Zheng, W., Sun, Q., Prospective assessment of breast cancer risk from multimodal multiview ultrasound images via clinically applicable deep learning. *Nat. Biomed. Eng.*, 5, 6, 522–32, 2021 Jun.
68. Stieler, F., Rabe, F., Bauer, B., Towards domain-specific explainable AI: model interpretation of a skin image classifier using a human approach, in:

Proceedings of the IEEE/CVF Conference on Computer Vision and Pattern Recognition, pp. 1802–1809, 2021.

59. Heinemann, F., Birk, G., Stierstorfer, B., Deep learning enables pathologist-like scoring of NASH models. *Sci. Rep.*, 9, 1, 18454, 2019 Dec 5.
70. Yi, P.H., Kim, T.K., Wei, J., Shin, J., Hui, F.K., Sair, H.I., Hager, G.D., Fritz, J., Automated semantic labeling of pediatric musculoskeletal radiographs using deep learning. *Pediatr. Radiol.*, 49, 1066–70, 2019 Jul 1.
71. Choi, H., Kim, Y.K., Yoon, E.J., Lee, J.Y., Lee, D.S., Alzheimer's Disease Neuroimaging Initiative. Cognitive signature of brain FDG PET based on deep learning: domain transfer from Alzheimer's disease to Parkinson's disease. *Eur. J. Nucl. Med. Mol. Imaging*, 47, 403–12, 2020 Feb.
72. Martins, J., Cardoso, J.S., Soares, F., Offline computer-aided diagnosis for Glaucoma detection using fundus images targeted at mobile devices. *Comput. Methods Programs Biomed.*, 192, 105341, 2020 Aug 1.
73. Tayarani, M., Applications of artificial intelligence in battling against COVID-19: A literature review. *Chaos, Solitons Fractals*, 3, 110338, 2020 Oct.
74. Le, E.P., Wang, Y., Huang, Y., Hickman, S., Gilbert, F.J., Artificial intelligence in breast imaging. *Clin. Radiol.*, 74, 5, 357–66, 2019 May 1.
75. Kim, B., Khanna, R., Koyejo, O.O., Examples are not enough, learn to criticize! criticism for interpretability, in: *Advances in neural information processing systems*, vol. 29, 2016.
76. Yim, J. and Sohn, K.A., Enhancing the performance of convolutional neural networks on quality degraded datasets, in: *2017 International Conference on Digital Image Computing: Techniques and Applications (DICTA)*, 2017 Nov 29, IEEE, pp. 1–8.
77. Heidari, M., Mirniaharikandehei, S., Khuzani, A.Z., Danala, G., Qiu, Y., Zheng, B., Improving the performance of CNN to predict the likelihood of COVID-19 using chest X-ray images with preprocessing algorithms. *Int. J. Med. Inf.*, 144, 104284, 2020 Dec 1.
78. Paka, A., Gade, K., Farah, D., *Model Performance Management with Explainable AI*, O'Reilly Media, Incorporated, Sebastopol, California, 2021.
79. Singh, R.K., Pandey, R., Babu, R.N., COVIDScreen: explainable deep learning framework for differential diagnosis of COVID-19 using chest X-rays. *Neural Comput. Appl.*, 33, 8871–92, 2021 Jul.
80. Thibeau-Sutre, E., Colliot, O., Dormont, D., Burgos, N., Visualization approach to assessing the robustness of neural networks for medical image classification, in: *Medical Imaging 2020: Image Processing*, 2020 Mar 10, vol. 11313, SPIE, pp. 370–380.
81. McCarthy, N., Dahlan, A., Cook, T.S., O'Hare, N., Ryan, M.L., St John, B., Lawlor, A., Curran, K.M., Enterprise imaging and big data: A review from a medical physics perspective. *Physica Med.*, 83, 206–20, 2021 Mar 1.
82. Holzinger, A., From machine learning to explainable AI. *2018 World Symposium on Digital Intelligence for Systems and Machines (DISA)*, IEEE, pp. 55–66, 2018 Aug 23.

83. Holzinger, A., Malle, B., Saranti, A., Pfeifer, B., Towards multi-modal capability with graph neural networks enabling information fusion for explainable AI. *Inf. Fusion*, 71, 28–37, 2021 Jul 1.
84. Hossain, M.S., Muhammad, G., Guizani, N., Explainable AI and mass surveillance system-based healthcare framework to combat COVID-19-like pandemics. *IEEE Netw.*, 34, 4, 126–32, 2020 Jul 8.
85. O'Sullivan, S., Jeanquartier, F., Jean-Quartier, C., Holzinger, A., Shiebler, D., Moon, P., Angione, C., Developments in AI and machine learning for neuroimaging, in: *Artificial Intelligence and Machine Learning for Digital Pathology: State-of-the-Art and Future Challenges*, pp. 307–20, 2020 Jun 24.
86. Kamal, M.S., Northcote, A., Chowdhury, L., Dey, N., Crespo, R.G., Herrera-Viedma, E., Alzheimer's patient analysis using image and gene expression data and explainable-AI to present associated genes. *IEEE Trans. Instrum. Meas.*, 70, 1–7, 2021 Aug 24.

8

XAI Technique in Deep Learning–Based Medical Image Analysis

Deepak Kumar[1], Sejal Porwal[1], Rishabha Malviya[1]* and Sathvik Belagodu Sridhar[2]

[1]*Department of Pharmacy, School of Medical and Allied Sciences, Galgotias University, Greater Noida, U.P., India*
[2]*RAK College of Pharmacy, RAK Medical and Health Sciences University, Ras Al Khaimah, United Arab Emirates*

Abstract

Medical imaging methods, like magnetic resonance imaging, computed tomography, and X-ray, are essential for diagnosing diseases and for guiding treatment choices. The development of artificial intelligence (AI) and deep learning has led toward an increase in automation in the interpretation of medical images, improving diagnostic efficiency and accuracy. This chapter explores the use of explainable AI (XAI) techniques in improving interpretability and reliability of AI-driven medical picture analysis, focusing on various XAI approaches and their applications. XAI methodologies in medical imaging are examined in this study, with particular emphasis on attribution-based, perturbation-based, and backpropagation-based methods. It draws attention to their potential to enhance interpretability and diagnostic accuracy across a range of imaging modalities. Nonetheless, issues such as model consistency and robustness continue to exist, highlighting the need of ongoing research to guarantee the effective incorporation of XAI into clinical practice for the best possible patient care. The integration of XAI methodologies in medical imaging analysis has significant potential for improving diagnostic precision, requiring continuous research and innovation.

***Keywords*:** Explainable AI, medical image analysis, disease diagnosis, deep learning, convolutional neural networks

**Corresponding author*: rishabhamalviya19@gmail.com; rishabha.malviya@galgotiasuniversity.edu.in

Rishabha Malviya and Sonali Sundram (eds.) Explainable and Responsible Artificial Intelligence in Healthcare, (191–216) © 2025 Scrivener Publishing LLC

8.1 Introduction

Numerous diagnostic imaging methods have been developed as a result of the ongoing advancements in medical technology. Computed tomography (CT), ultrasound, magnetic resonance imaging (MRI), mammography, positron, emission tomography, and X-rays are the medical imaging technologies that are extensively adopted [1, 2]. Advancements in image capturing and bio-medical data collecting have resulted in enormous data volumes. This information is multidimensional (CT, MRI, etc.), variable-rich, and derived from variety of data systems. It makes medical data difficult and unique to analyze, particularly image files. Medical image growth requires significant effort from specialists, which might be subjective, prone to human mistake, and vary considerable from one expert to another expert while analyzing [3]. Because it instantly developed possibility to scan and import diagnostic pictures onto computer, researchers advanced automated analysis tools. Initially, low-level processing of pixel (edge and line detector filters, and region growing) and mathematical modeling (fitting lines, circles, and ellipses) were applied sequentially in medical picture analysis from 1970s to 1990s to advanced compound rule-based systems, which address specific responsibilities [4]. In the late 1990s, supervised method started to gain traction in medical picture analysis. Because these methods are systems built using training data, they grew in popularity. Dynamic shape models, atlas approaches, and statistical classifiers used in combination with feature extraction for computer-aided diagnosis and detection are a few examples [5]. Enabling computers to extract the best characteristics directly from the data is a natural next step in medical picture analysis. Several deep learning (DL) algorithms are grounded on this idea. They use multi-layered models to learn higher-level characteristics repeatedly while converting input data (like photos) into outputs (like presence or absence of an illness). Convolutional neural networks (CNNs) are most popular and effective model among these methods for image processing [6, 7].

In the 1950s, the foundations of artificial intelligence (AI) were established [8]. Artificial neurons, or neural algorithmic systems artificially constructed networks, have prompted the creation of "educated" programs. In 1960s, initial neural networks were created. They were created by layers upon layer of artificial neurons arranged in sets. Statistics was first presented through input layer; then, it was analyzed by intermediate levels, culminating in an output layer that generated a result. Neural networks' capacity for learning was first fully utilized in 1990s with arrival of "deep learning" that concurrently with the development of very huge multi-layered neural network [9]. Creation of a particular type of neural network known as CNNs in 2010 contributed to the growth of DL in addition to the advancements into large data processing and processor power [10]. CNNs are based on the primary visual cortex structure [11]. Image recognition involves automatically extracting visual information from pictures. Automatic extraction is a significant improvement over manual procedures, which were time-consuming and less accurate [12]. Figure 8.1 shows the evidence of "Deep learning has made yearly advances in neural networks, learning algorithms, and computer patterns recognition".

Deep learning models, or AI, have grownup into status over past decade because to their widespread application and high accuracy [13, 14]. Despite its many benefits, AI raises challenges at each step of medical research and development [15]. Obstacles arise due to the need for genuine data in health-related systems, as opposed to synthetic information. As AI models grow in complexity and contain hundreds of layers and over millions of neurons, their algorithms develop into fewer intelligible. In certain cases, lawful permission is conditioned on understanding of system. There is lot of literature on black-box algorithms. Consequently, there exists a compelling need for AI, which is explained [16]. Objective of "explainable AI" (XAI) is to become capable in define the purpose of AI systems, point out their advantages and disadvantages, and forecast future developments. It illustrates how explainability and learning outcomes are related. This relationship introduces a trade-off between strong learning performance (usually shown by the accuracy of the model's performance) and XAI [17]. It is

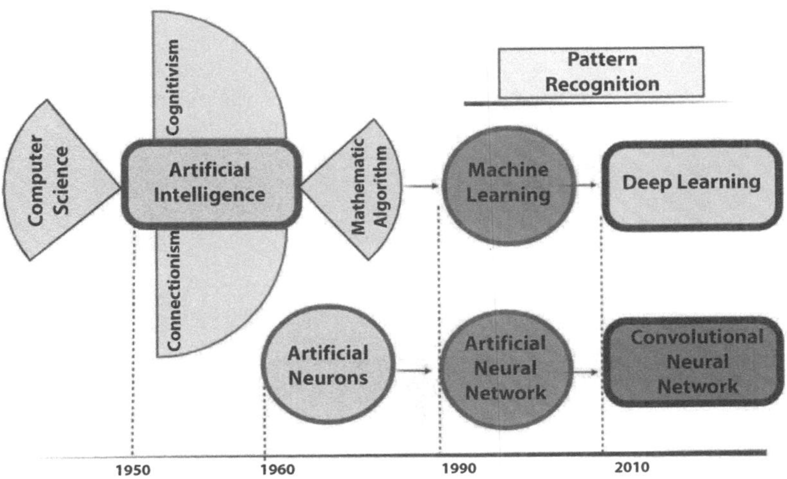

Figure 8.1 Concept and theory behind deep learning.

difficult to track and identify these instances of "right choice, wrong rationale" in the absence of an auditing methodology based on explainability [13]. This decision highlights how explainability is essential to enhancing deep neural network dependability in therapeutic applications [18–20]. Figure 8.2 shown "A flow diagram of XAI-based image analysis".

An explanation in AI is a collection of domain characteristics, such as pixels in a picture, that contribute to the output choice of the model [21]. In order to acquire faith of physicians, regulators, and patients, a medical diagnostic system must possess transparency, simplicity, and explainability. Ideally, it would possess capability to elucidate the whole rationale behind a certain choice to all the parties concerned. Recent legislation, like European General Data Protection Regulation, is increasing difficulty of using black-box models in every company, together with healthcare, due to necessity of traceability in decision-making [22]. AI framework designed to augment medical field must possess level of explainability, enabling human professional to retrace judgements made by the AI and exercise their own judgement. Additionally, some scholars highlight the fact that even people may not consistently possess the capability or want to articulate their judgements [5]. The capacity to provide clear explanations is crucial for ensuring the harmless, reasonable, ethical, and reliable utilization of AI, as well as for facilitating its implementation in practical settings. Dispelling misconceptions around AI may foster trust among end-users by revealing the specific factors that a model considered while making a decision. Demonstrating domain-specific characteristics employed in decision-making process is particularly crucial for non-DL consumer, like majority of healthcare expertise [23].

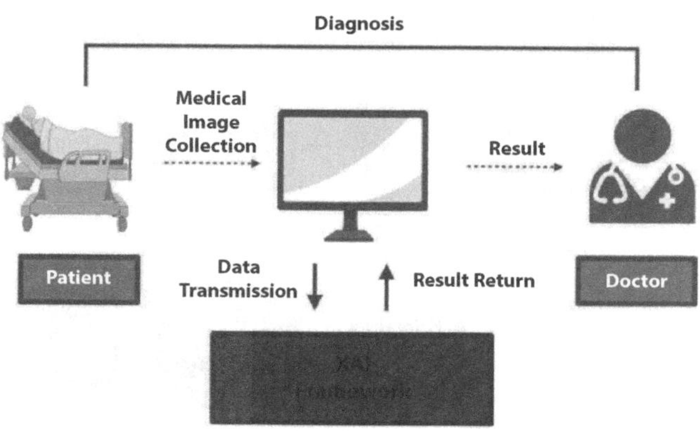

Figure 8.2 XAI-based medical image analysis flow diagram.

8.2 XAI Method in Field of Medical Imaging

Many commonly used explainability strategies in medical image analysis are predicated on visual (saliency-based) explanations pertaining toward the intermediate or ultimate conclusion of the model [24]. The core idea behind saliency-based techniques is to identify portions of a picture that contributes to a final judgement by using spatial data preserved by a model's convolutional layers. The parts of a picture that are conclusively noteworthy and have the greatest attribution to prediction are then emphasized. So-called attribution maps are created when all of the input feature attributions are grouped combined to have the same form as the input sample. These maps frequently appear as heatmaps, where one color reflects a feature's positive contribution to the activation of the target output and another color indicates a suppressing influence [25]. Technically speaking, there are two main ways for creating attribution maps: perturbation-based and backpropagation-based.

8.2.1 Attribution-Based

Attribution-based techniques are commonly employed for elucidate outcomes for deep neural networks (DNNs) in field of medical images. These approaches provide attribution values for input features, aiding in comprehension of each feature's contribution to the network's output. Typically, they produce attribution maps that highlight elements that have a positive impact on the output by marking them in red and features that have a negative impact by marking them in blue. These approaches are often independent of specific models, allowing them to be easily applied to other designs without altering the underlying network [23].

Some frequently employed attribution techniques include DeepTaylor, which exclusively gives positive evidence, and Deep Learning Important FeaTures (LIFT), among other approaches [26]. These techniques are employed on CNNs without modifying the network structure, rendering them convenient and potent tools for XAI [25]. Attribution-based approaches are usually used in diagnostic imaging because they are easy to build, and there are open-source implementations readily available. Researchers can concentrate on developing optimum models for certain tasks while utilizing these approaches to acquire insights about model behavior. These methodologies are especially valuable for works such as illness detection, where comprehending the rationale behind a model's predictions is vital [27]. Table 8.1 shows the list of "Various XAI method with the advantages and disadvantages."

Table 8.1 Various XAI methods with their explanation.

XAI methods	Description	Advantages	Disadvantages
Attribution-based	Allocates attribution values to input features, producing attribution maps that emphasize the features that influence the result. Techniques such as DeepTaylor and LIFT serve as examples.	Model-agnostic and simple to use, it helps interpret model behavior.	Only able to offer feature-level insights; might miss complex interactions.
Perturbation-based	Examines the effects of altering input characteristics through the manipulation of input variables. Some examples of this are Occlusion and LIME.	Model-independent and versatile, its effectiveness lies in its ability to understand the significance of features.	Costly to compute, sensitive to parameters, and capable of producing maps that are sloppy or of low quality.
Backpropagation-based	Utilizes XAI algorithms to create attribution maps by making forward passes through the network. This includes methods such as guided backpropagation and saliency map visualization.	Provides information on the impact of input features, is adaptable, and works with many network designs.	Prone to invariance, may give greater importance to the features of the image than to the explanation of expectations.
Real-time perturbations	Employs a second neural network for saliency detection to improve perturbation strategies.	Enhances the effectiveness and precision of explanations based on perturbations.	Need more processing power in order to detect saliency in real time.

8.2.2 Perturbation-Based Explanations

Analysis of the impact of altering input properties upon output of AI model is done by perturbation. To that end, certain input characteristics are removed, hidden, or changed, and the model's forecast is computed by doing forward pass and then measuring departure from original prediction. Generally speaking, perturbation is ideal if the picture dimensions are independent because it allows one to accurately assess the marginal influence of each dimension. Unfortunately, dimensions and pixels are closely related, especially with regard to picture data. If you have an X-ray of your lungs, then the prediction class of the image would most likely not change much if you removed one pixel. The explanation is that the neighbors of a pixel allow for the reconstruction of its information. As such, it is more successful to produce an impact by eliminating whole patches rather than single pixels. Typical patch dimensions are 5 × 5 or 10 × 10, based on computing capabilities and intended feature sizes [23].

Zeiler and Fergus, for instance, developed the Occlusion method to produce attribution maps that indicate which areas of the picture either favorably or unfavorably affect the score for a certain class [28].

During occlusion, a specified baseline is repeatedly replaced with rectangular patches of a specific size from the input picture. Resolution of attribution map is limited for selected patch size. The effect on the output is to be monitored by methodically perturbing the input picture. This idea takes use of the fact that changing the most important components will have a big effect on result. As the technique does not need access to core components of model, implementation is model-agnostic. In order to understand models created to categorize illnesses from histological slides associated to Alzheimer's disease, like diffuse plaques, cored plaques, and cerebral amyloid angiopathy, Tang *et al.* produced occlusion maps [29]. A possible negative, though, is that the calculation time needed is more expensive than with other techniques [30]. Local Interpretable Model-agnostic Explanations (LIME) is a widely utilized comparative method to occlusion. It entails training secondary, interpretable surrogate designs (such as a decision tree or linear regression) for explaining specific predictions created by primary, opaque model. The way that LIME approaches picture data is to create variants of the images by continuously combining pixels with comparable intensities into so-called superpixels. These arbitrary-shaped superpixels are then repeatedly "switched off" by substituting a user-defined value (such as the median or 0) for the elements in each superpixel. After that, the found pertinent areas might be displayed on the input image delimited or highlighted [31]. Magesh and colleagues produced a model and offered LIME explanations for binary categorization of DaT scanning pictures as having condition Parkinson's disease. Such as occlusion, LIME is a local, model-agnostic technique that works with any kind of model. This technique compensates for the need for a suitable specifying a number of parameters, including the number of produced samples, the similarity function to compare the original and perturbed sample, the surrogate model, and the picture segmentation technique for extract contiguous patches/superpixels [32]. Amount of adjustable factors means that even little changes can provide noticeable consequences. Reproducibility-wise, thus, knowledge of these factors is crucial. Furthermore, because superpixels are coarse, sometimes produced attribution maps might reflect a relatively poor picture quality. Still, alternative approaches can produce better quality. Optimal perturbation masks, for instance, are proposed in meaningful perturbations to minimize picture blurring while maximizing class score reduction, therefore creating an optimization challenge. Utilizing heuristics similar to high positive gradient values as a reliable signal, this is not like other visualization approaches. By using naturalistic effects, including noising, blurring or constant value, they recommended obtaining additional realistic disruption and perceptive explanations rather than filtering off visual portions (which might result in out-of-distribution data) [33]. But Uzunova *et al.* contended that because substituting with constant values is improbable, this method is inappropriate for medical imaging. Unpredictability results from the noise and blur that are inherent in medical imaging. Rather, they suggested, using a variational autoencoder (VAE), to replace diseases on optical coherence tomography (OCT) pictures and brain lesion MRIs by their good looking counterpart and examined the effects on categorization. Results show that, in imaging experiments, OCT and MRI, VAE's perturbations realistically locate pathogenic areas [34].

Various complex perturbation-based methodologies have evolved to boost the quality and efficiency of model explanations in medical imaging. For instance, meaningful perturbations optimize masks to least blur photos while maximizing changing predictions, compared with typical techniques that might block out image portions [35]. However, the replacement with constant values proposed by meaningful perturbations may not be practicable for medical pictures, as they naturally include noise and blur. Instead, technologies such replacing illnesses with healthy-looking equivalents utilizing VAEs have demonstrated potential, giving more realistic perturbations [35, 43].

Real-time perturbations and extremal perturbations (EMs) further advance perturbation approaches by proposing strategies to identify acceptable perturbation masks more effectively. Real-time perturbations deploy a second neural network for saliency detection, whereas EMs aim toward discovering region with maximum outcome on network's output across all perturbations [34, 36]. Meanwhile, SHapley Additive exPlanations (SHAP) applies extra characteristics attribution approach grounded on Shapley values from game theory. However, SHAP's scalability constraints in the quantity of features led to the construction of KernelSHAP, approximate, computationally possible approach influenced through regional surrogate models [37].

In addition, despite its effectiveness, randomized input sampling for explanation of black-box models (RISE) and occlusion have drawbacks such ignoring the shape of objects and depending too much on pre-established parameters [38]. To tackle these challenges, hierarchical perturbation dramatically reduces computing cost without sacrificing quality by concentrating on perturbing the most relevant areas while discarding less influential sections [39].

8.2.3 Backpropagation-Based Explanations

Backpropagation-based techniques, on the other hand, use a XAI algorithm that makes one or extra forward passes through network to produce attribution map. During backpropagation stage, partial derivatives are calculated to quantify the effect of gradients, weights, and activations. Consequently, more saliency maps, relevance maps, and class activation maps (CAMs) are divided under this category [40]. Simonyan *et al.* are the first to suggest saliency map visualization backpropagation method [41]. It determines absolute value of partial derivative with regard to network's incoming picture and intended output class. The concept behind a gradient is that its value represents input characteristics (pixels) that influence the result most significantly. Depending on how much of the positive gradient each pixel in the input picture receives, it is possible to highlight specific pixels in order to indicate their contribution. However, when input toward ReLU activation function is negative while forward pass, there are situations when gradient is cut at zero, which leads for a saturation issue [42]. Known by another name, vanilla gradient, this technique is essentially a generalization of Zeiler and Fergus' later-introduced deconvolution networks (DeconvNets) [28]. The core idea behind DeconvNet is to reverse network flow and set gradients for zero in between backward pass in order to visualize the neural activations of individual layers. Consequently, using filters and unpooling procedures, DeconvNets generate the opposite outcome of a CNN, producing activation map of neural behavior. This technique is restricted to max-pooling layers as unpooling procedure solely uses approximation of convolution features' inverse [43]. Using deconvolution, De Vos *et al.* were able to identify the slice regions that were involved in their prediction of quantity of calcium in coronary arteries on CT images, slice-wise [44]. A revolutionary approach based upon assumption those neurons operate as character detectors is named guided backpropagation (GBP), which was created as a consequence of a refinement of this strategy. The term "guided" refers to the fact that, during the backpropagation process, the neurons that are activated are chosen (directed) by exposing the areas of the image that possess significant attributes by zeroing out negative gradients [40]. GBP is sufficiently adaptable to be employed with a variety of network architectures, including fully connected networks, generative adversarial networks, and CNNs [45].

One drawback was highlighted by Adebayo *et al.* although performing partial input recovery in their assessment, GBP may occasionally be invariant to data and models. This is troublesome because picture characteristics are emphasized rather than predictions being explained by recovering image fragments [46]. An automated technique for measuring perivascular voids on MRIs, which may be indicative of cerebral small artery disease, was presented by Dubost *et al.* [47]. The scientists employed GBP to examine whether neural network picked up on integrated structures or concentrated on the linked aspects of other perivascular regions. Layer-wise relevance propagation (LRP) is other method of pictorial explanation [48]. Intuitively, in each iteration, LRP provides a relevance score to each input neuron from the previous layer and propagates the output back through the network until it reaches the input layer, utilizing the network's weights and activations from the forward pass. In short, LRP is based on the breakdown of the model's decision and generates dispersed significance scores, which indicate relationship between an input neuron's activations. This technique was utilized by Bohle *et al.* to pinpoint areas on brain MRIs that show Alzheimer's disease. In addition, they found that LRP was superior to GBP in finding pertinent regions when comparing saliency maps produced by the two methods. The sensitivity of the heatmaps produced by LRP to particular factors, such as the β value employed in the process, is one possible disadvantage of LRP [49].

8.3 Application of XAI in Medical Imaging

Uses of explainability in diagnostic picture are explored through classifying in two category—one employing pre-existing attribution based approaches and another utilizing alternative, typically precise ways. Techniques are described according to explainability technique and medical imaging application. Figure 8.3 shows "XAI medical image analysis applications."

8.3.1 Attribution-Based

Using attribution-based techniques for interpretability in medical imaging DL research gives numerous advantages. Firstly, these procedures are frequently easier to apply compared to more challenging explainability tactics [50]. Researchers may focus on training effective neural network topologies without added effort of creating them fundamentally explainable.

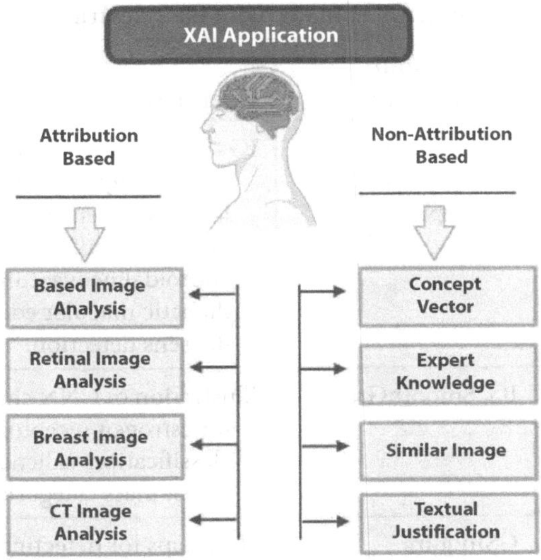

Figure 8.3 Various application of XAI in medical image analysis.

They may just utilize a publicly available attribution approach, speeding the process. This method offers flexibility in model selection. Researchers may opt for either pre-existing DL models, gaining from their established performance and methodologies like transfer learning, or they might construct customized architectures suited to the particular demands of the medical imaging challenge [51]. Pre-existing models simplify implementation and may be fine-tuned for the target dataset, whereas custom structures offer the advantage of focussing on certain data features and maybe reducing overfitting by employing fewer parameters. Given that medical imaging datasets are often smaller compared to publicly recognized benchmarks like ImageNet, both strategies maintain validity. Attribution-based techniques enable researchers to extract insights from these smaller datasets rapidly, driving breakthroughs in medical imaging analysis and diagnosis [52]. Table 8.2 shows the list of various XAI technique with their application, overview and description.

8.3.1.1 *Brain Image Analysis*

A study that used brain MRI to evaluate robustness of several attribution-based CNN techniques for Alzheimer's disease categorization conducted a quantitative examination of various approaches. The methods that were compared were gradient × input, LRP, GBP, and occlusion. To evaluate the

Table 8.2 Application of XAI technique with their description.

Application	Explainability approaches	Overview
Retinal Imaging	IG, expressive gradients (EG), DeepSHAP	IG thermal maps for diabetic retinopathy evaluation, EG for lesion segmentation, evaluation of explainability algorithms for choroidal neovascularization, diabetic macular edema, and drusens detection.
Breast Imaging	IG, SmoothGrad	Illustration of CNN characteristics for estrogen receptor activity classification, saliency maps in breast mass categorization.
X-ray Imaging	GSInquire	Heatmaps for detecting COVID-19 from chest X-rays, saliency map-based interpretation and uncertainty analysis, and guided GradCAM, GBP, and CAM.
CT Imaging	DeepDreams-inspired method	Sensitivity analysis of characteristics, explanation of tumor segmentation from liver CT images, and contrast of actual and artificial tumors.
Skin Imaging	GradCAM, Kernel SHAP	GradCAM and Kernel SHAP are used to compare CNN models for detecting melanoma. CNN characteristics are visualized for skin lesion categorization.
Laparoscopy/ Endoscopy	Shapley Additive Explanations (SHAP)	SHAP attributions aimed at preoperative factor analysis, in-situ parameters, and hypoxemia prediction during surgery.
Brain Imaging	Gradient × input, guided backpropagation, LRP	Analysing CNN feature coherence for brain tumor grading and attribution techniques analysis for Alzheimer's classification.

repeatability of heatmaps for identically trained models, compare L2 norm between average attribution maps of many runs for similar model. Because occlusion covers huge area, it was shown be an order of magnitude lower for the first three strategies when compared to the baseline. Overall, LRP performed the best, indicating that it is preferable to function- and signal-based approaches when using an entirely attribution-based strategy [53]. The highest degree of similarity was also seen for LRP between total, density, and gain (sum/density) for top 10 regions of attributions throughout course of runs. A different study examined medical coherence of features that a CNN educated for the automatic grading of tumors of brain using MRIs using GradCAM and GBP. Both techniques showed greatest activity in the tumor area and stimulated nearby ventricles, which may also specify malignancy, for the suitably rated cases. In some instances, the focus on non-tumor regions combined with a few false alignment in GBP chart might result in error that imply features are not reliable [54].

8.3.1.2 *Retinal Image Analysis*

The application of integrated gradient (IG) heatmap linked by model predictions has been studied as supportive means for assisting ophthalmologists in evaluating diabetic retinopathy (DR). This integrated strategy provides greater grading accuracy compared to unaided expert assessments or model forecasts alone. While initially boosting grading time, user experience led to shorter grading time and greater trust, specifically when both predictions and heatmaps were utilized. However, correctness fell for patients lacking DR when models' help was offered, necessitating the development of an option to toggle support [55].

An variation of IG, named expressive gradients (EG), was created aimed at poorly guided lesion segmentation in age-related macular degeneration (AMD) analysis [56]. EG, which combines input-level attribution maps through advanced attribution maps, outperformed traditional IG and GBP approaches. Additionally, a compact CNN architecture was proven to outperform larger CNNs when partnered with EG, highlighting regions of interest more effectively [57].

8.3.1.3 *Breast Imaging Analysis*

The characteristics of CNN utilized to determine state of oestrogen receptor from breast MRI were shown using IG and SmoothGrad. Significant characteristics for both the spatial and dynamic domains were seen to have been learnt by the model, with varying contributions from each [58].

The pre-processing artefacts led to the learning of some irrelevant features, which the visualizations emphasized. These realizations prompted changes to the training and pre-processing protocols. Saliency maps were used in an earlier research to represent the picture information for the purpose of classifying mammography breast mass utilizing two distinct CNNs: AlexNet [59] and GoogleNet [60]. Evidence was presented that both CNNs were sensitive for context and could learn edges of the mass, that are crucial medical criteria [61].

8.3.1.4 CT Imaging

Innovative attribution strategy, inspired by DeepDreams and developed for explaining tumor segmentation in liver CT images, was given. Leveraging ideas from DeepDreams, this system operates satisfactorily as a black-box neural network explanation. It conducts sensitivity analysis by boosting the activity of target neurons via gradient ascent, exposing significant properties [62]. Assessment between networks accomplished on real and synthetic tumors indicated enhanced sensitivity of the former to clinically relevant characteristics. Notably, the network demonstrated sensitivity to intensity and sphericity, consistent with domain knowledge [63].

8.3.1.5 X-Ray Imaging

A method known as GSInquire was utilized in new work for identify COVID-19 from X-ray of chest pictures. It produced heatmaps that verified the characteristics that the suggested COVID-net model had learned [16]. GSInquire was established as attribution strategy that outpaced other techniques, such as expected gradients and SHAP, in terms of projected new measures, impact coverage, and impact score. Percentage of features that significantly impacted model choice or confidence was definition of the impact score. However, impact coverage was developed with the intention of addressing input components that were subject to hostile influence. An additional study examined the interpretability and ambiguity of COVID-19 detection by use of chest X-rays. Guided GradCAM, saliency maps, GBP, and CAM were used in creation of heatmaps of training model's sample inputs [64].

8.3.1.6 Skin Imaging

Utilizing GradCAM and Kernel SHAP, 30 CNN models that had been trained to detect melanoma were compared based on their attributes. Even the most accurate models were seen to sometimes focus on aspects unrelated to the diagnosis. Both methodologies' attribution maps highlighted differences in models' explanations that produced parallel accuracy. This suggested that numerous neural network topologies acquire distinct learning properties [65]. Convolutional neural networks (CNNs) were shown in additional study for classification of skin lesion. Rescaling feature maps of activations to input size allowed for visualization of the features for last 2 layers. Risk factors counting lighter skin tone or a pink colored texture were noted to be recognized by the layers, along with indicators such as lesion borders and color absence of uniformity [66]. Overfitting was also seen in several bogus features, such as hair and artefacts, which have no real value.

Apart from the commonly used imaging techniques mentioned above, additionally, there are also further studies that use attribution-based methodologies for analysis. To semantically segregate colorectal polyps, a precursor to rectal malignancies, for instance, a study used CNNs and performed uncertainty and interpretability analysis [67]. The edge and shape information was discovered to be used by CNNs to generate predictions when using GBP for heatmaps. More uncertainty was found in samples that were incorrectly categorized, according to the uncertainty analysis. Applying DL techniques' explainability to additional modalities, such as laparoscopy and endoscopy, is very possible [68]. A model for hypoxemia, or the prediction of lower blood oxygen tension in surgery, was explained in explainable manner utilizing SHAP attribution. The purpose of the research was to look at both in-surgery data and preoperative factors. Tidal volume, inspired oxygen, physical state (ASA), BMI, and other recognized characteristics were all fulfilled by the attributions that were produced [69].

Attribution-based approaches, from basic CAMs to sophisticated techniques like SHAP, have evolved to give improved representations of neural networks. They illustrate that models frequently acquire good features, albeit misleading ones are discovered and handled by alterations in training approaches. Smaller, task-specific models and tailored versions of attribution techniques may further boost the identification of key variables [56].

8.3.2 Non-Attribution Based

In this section, researchers designed tactics specific to their issues rather than relying on pre-existing attribution-based methodologies. They employed strategies such as attention mapping, concept vectors, returning similar photos, expert knowledge, text justifications, generative modeling, and combining with additional machine learning techniques. These solutions, mostly post-model, generally demand particular alterations to the model structure or the incorporation of domain knowledge.

8.3.2.1 Attention-Based

Attention mechanisms, inspired by human cognition, play vital function in DL [70]. In medical picture analysis, attention-based techniques produce interpretable findings [71]. MDNet, for instance, enables a direct connection between medical photos and diagnostic reports by employing attention processes to discover discriminative patterns. SAUNet, an interpretable variant of U-Net, adds attention modules to highlight crucial shape-based characteristics with texture data, enhancing the model's interpretability [72, 73]. These techniques offer a huge advance, enabling researchers to get critical insights into decision-making process of DL techniques in medical picture applications, thereby developing trust and understanding among practitioners and stakeholders [74].

8.3.2.2 Concept Vectors

Novel approach named as TCAV was introduced for transmit characteristics obtained via successive layers for domain experts who lacked DL skills with regard to human-understandable concepts. It took network's directed derivative in idea space, similar to saliency maps' input feature space. It served as an explanation for DR level forecasts, and it effectively identified microaneurysms and aneurysms in retina [75]. This gave explanations for why particular concepts or physical elements were present in the image or absent from it that medical professionals could easily understand. However, numerous clinical concepts, such as textures or structural geometry, cannot be effectively stated with regard to existence or non existence and need continuous scale of assessment.

To identify continuous concepts, a form of TCAV was used that utilized the existence or absence of ideas by applying regression concept vectors into layer's activation space [76]. The network's purpose was to identify cancers in breast lymph node samples. The majority of the critical features, such as area and contrast, were found in early phases of model. New measure, known as uniform unit ball surface sampling, was added to TCAV as an improvement to offer layer-agnostic explanations for continuous and high-dimensional features [77]. It may explain high-dimensional radiomics ideas spanning several layers, as seen by mammographic images. The model created oscillations among core ideas, which were demonstrated to be minimized throughout SqueezeNet levels when evaluated to baseline CNN with three dense layers, explaining SqueezeNet's higher efficiency [78].

8.3.2.3 *Expert Knowledge*

The enormous majority of studies included throughout this review used a variety of approaches to try to establish a connection between model characteristics and expert knowledge. Using domain-specific information to create explanation and prediction rules was another strategy. In [79], brain midline shift estimate utilizing U-Net based architecture and key points was shown as example of utilizing task-specific information to advance results as well as explanations. It was reduced to the problem of applying the model to the domain-limited detection of midline. Displacement from the predicted midline was calculated after original midline was derived using endpoints. For end-user's benefit, the model further included confidence intervals for the predictions [83]. An further investigation used guidelines for segmenting lung nodules based on rules and then performed perturbation evaluation to measure significance of each characteristic in individual region. Explanations provided, which demonstrated bias in the data used to construct the model, were thought to be more understandable by the users and related to the previously identified regions utilizing rules. After that, this method was used to provide explanations for the whole dataset that provided a summary of the relevant qualities on a global scale [80].

8.3.2.4 *Textual Justification*

A model may directly interact with both expert and common users if it can express its conclusion in terms of word or phrase, which explain the rationale. Diagnostic phrase and visual heatmaps for breast mass classification were created using justification model, which used inputs from visual properties of classifier and embeddings of predictions. The justification generator was trained using visual word constraint loss to generate justifications when there were only restricted number of clinical reports available. Because these multi-modal explanations resemble the regular workflow and learning process, they may be used to gain higher trust from users [81].

8.4 Conclusion

In conclusion, the development of technology for medical imaging has resulted in notable progress in diagnostic capacities, especially when DL and AI are combined. But these developments also bring with them difficulties with the interpretability and explainability of AI-driven judgements, which are critical to guaranteeing the reliability and adoption of these technologies in clinical settings.

In order to address these issues, XAI has become vital field of study, offering comprehensible and transparent justifications for AI-driven medical imaging forecasts. XAI provides interpretability and insights into model predictions using backpropagation-based methodologies, attribution-based approaches, perturbation-based explanations, and innovative approaches. Although XAI approaches have shown promise in enhancing AI model comprehension, there are still issues and constraints that must be resolved. These obstacles may be addressed and the effectiveness and quality of model explanations can be further improved with the use of creative thinking and the incorporation of domain knowledge.

Overall, the implementation of XAI approaches in medical imaging offers considerable promise to increase diagnostic accuracy, streamline clinical decision-making, and ultimately enhance patient care outcomes. Continued improvements in XAI techniques will be vital in unlocking the full potential of AI-driven technology in healthcare.

References

1. Wang, J., Zhu, H., Wang, S.H., Zhang, Y.D., A review of deep learning on medical image analysis. *Mobile Netw. Appl.*, 26, 1, 351–80, 2021 Feb.
2. Chen, H., Qi, X., Yu, L., Dou, Q., Qin, J., Heng, P.A., DCAN: Deep contour-aware networks for object instance segmentation from histology images. *Med. Image Anal.*, 36, 135–46, 2017 Feb 1.
3. Razzak, M.I., Naz, S., Zaib, A., Deep learning for medical image processing: Overview, challenges and the future, in: *Classification in BioApps: Automation of decision making*, pp. 323–50, 2018.
4. Haugeland, J., *Artificial intelligence: The very idea*, MIT press, Cambridge, Massachusetts, USA, 1989 Jan 6.
5. Litjens, G., Kooi, T., Bejnordi, B.E., Setio, A.A., Ciompi, F., Ghafoorian, M., Van Der Laak, J.A., Van Ginneken, B., Sánchez, C.I., A survey on deep learning in medical image analysis. *Med. Image Anal.*, 42, 60–88, 2017 Dec 1.
6. Fukushima, K., Neocognitron: A self-organizing neural network model for a mechanism of pattern recognition unaffected by shift in position. *Biol. Cybern.*, 36, 4, 193–202, 1980 Apr.
7. Lo, S.C., Lou, S.L., Lin, J.S., Freedman, M.T., Chien, M.V., Mun, S.K., Artificial convolution neural network techniques and applications for lung nodule detection. *IEEE Trans. Med. Imaging*, 14, 4, 711–8, 1995 Dec.

8. McCarthy, J., Minsky, M.L., Rochester, N., Shannon, C.E., A proposal for the dartmouth summer research project on artificial intelligence, august 31, 1955. *AI Mag.*, 27, 4, 12–, 2006 Dec 15.
9. LeCun, Y., Bengio, Y., Hinton, G., Deep learning. *Nature*, 521, 7553, 436–44, 2015 May 28.
10. LeCun, Y., Boser, B., Denker, J.S., Henderson, D., Howard, R.E., Hubbard, W., Jackel, L.D., Backpropagation applied to handwritten zip code recognition. *Neural Comput.*, 1, 4, 541–51, 1989 Dec.
11. Hubel, D.H. and Wiesel, T.N., Receptive fields, binocular interaction and functional architecture in the cat's visual cortex. *J. Physiol.*, 160, 1, 106, 1962 Jan.
12. Shen, D., Wu, G., Suk, H.I., Deep learning in medical image analysis. *Annu. Rev. Biomed. Eng.*, 19, 221–48, 2017 Jun 21.
13. Al-Haija, Q.A., Smadi, M., Al-Bataineh, O.M., Early stage diabetes risk prediction via machine learning, in: *International Conference on Soft Computing and Pattern Recognition*, 2021 Dec 15, Springer International Publishing, Cham, pp. 451–461.
14. Singh, R.K., Pandey, R., Babu, R.N., COVIDScreen: explainable deep learning framework for differential diagnosis of COVID-19 using chest X-rays. *Neural Comput. Appl.*, 33, 8871–92, 2021 Jul.
15. Lucas, B., Vahedi, B., Karimzadeh, M., A spatiotemporal machine learning approach to forecasting COVID-19 incidence at the county level in the USA. *Int. J. Data. Sci. Anal.*, 15, 3, 247–66, 2023 Apr.
16. Wang, L., Lin, Z.Q., Wong, A., Covid-net: A tailored deep convolutional neural network design for detection of covid-19 cases from chest x-ray images. *Sci. Rep.*, 10, 1, 19549, 2020 Nov 11.
17. Younisse, R., Ahmad, A., Abu Al-Haija, Q., Explaining intrusion detection-based convolutional neural networks using shapley additive explanations (shap). *Big Data Cognit. Comput.*, 6, 4, 126, 2022 Oct 25.
18. Dong, S., Yang, Q., Fu, Y., Tian, M., Zhuo, C., RCoNet: Deformable mutual information maximization and high-order uncertainty-aware learning for robust COVID-19 detection. *IEEE Trans. Neural Netw. Learn. Syst.*, 32, 8, 3401–11, 2021 Jun 18.
19. Motamed, S., Rogalla, P., Khalvati, F., RANDGAN: randomized generative adversarial network for detection of COVID-19 in chest X-ray. *Sci. Rep.*, 11, 1, 8602, 2021 Apr 21.
20. Alnabhan, M., Habboush, A.K., Abu Al-Haija, Q., Mohanty, A.K., Pattnaik, S., Pattanayak, B.K., Hyper-tuned CNN using EVO technique for efficient biomedical image classification. *Mobile Inf. Syst.*, 2022, 1–12, 2022 Jun 22.
21. Moccia, S., Wirkert, S.J., Kenngott, H., Vemuri, A.S., Apitz, M., Mayer, B., De Momi, E., Mattos, L.S., Maier-Hein, L., Uncertainty-aware organ classification for surgical data science applications in laparoscopy. *IEEE Trans. Biomed. Eng.*, 65, 11, 2649–59, 2018 Mar 9.

22. Holzinger, A., Biemann, C., Pattichis, C.S., Kell, D.B., What do we need to build explainable AI systems for the medical domain?, arXiv preprint arXiv:1712.09923, 2017 Dec 28.
23. Singh, A., Sengupta, S., Lakshminarayanan, V., Explainable deep learning models in medical image analysis. *J. Imaging*, 6, 6, 52, 2020 Jun 20.
24. Van der Velden, B.H., Kuijf, H.J., Gilhuijs, K.G., Viergever, M.A., Explainable artificial intelligence (XAI) in deep learning-based medical image analysis. *Med. Image Anal.*, 79, 102470, 2022 Jul 1.
25. Ancona, M., Ceolini, E., Öztireli, C., Gross, M., Towards better understanding of gradient-based attribution methods for deep neural networks, arXiv preprint arXiv:1711.06104, 2017 Nov 16.
26. Montavon, G., Lapuschkin, S., Binder, A., Samek, W., Müller, K.R., Explaining nonlinear classification decisions with deep taylor decomposition. *Pattern Recognit.*, 65, 211–22, 2017 May 1.
27. Alber, M., Lapuschkin, S., Seegerer, P., Hägele, M., Schütt, K.T., Montavon, G., Samek, W., Müller, K.R., Dähne, S., Kindermans, P.J., iNNvestigate neural networks! *J. Mach. Learn. Res.*, 20, 93, 1–8, 2019.
28. Zeiler, M.D. and Fergus, R., Visualizing and understanding convolutional networks, in: *Computer Vision–ECCV 2014: 13th European Conference, Zurich, Switzerland, September 6-12, 2014, Proceedings, Part I 13*, pp. 818–833, Springer International Publishing, New York, USA, 2014.
29. Tang, Z., Chuang, K.V., DeCarli, C., Jin, L.W., Beckett, L., Keiser, M.J., Dugger, B.N., Interpretable classification of Alzheimer's disease pathologies with a convolutional neural network pipeline. *Nat. Commun.*, 10, 1, 2173, 2019 May 15.
30. Kakogeorgiou, I. and Karantzalos, K., Evaluating explainable artificial intelligence methods for multi-label deep learning classification tasks in remote sensing. *Int. J. Appl. Earth Obs. Geoinf.*, 103, 102520, 2021 Dec 1.
31. Ribeiro, M.T., Singh, S., Guestrin, C., "Why should i trust you?" Explaining the predictions of any classifier, in: *Proceedings of the 22nd ACM SIGKDD international conference on knowledge discovery and data mining*, pp. 1135–1144, 2016 Aug 13.
32. Magesh, P.R., Myloth, R.D., Tom, R.J., An explainable machine learning model for early detection of Parkinson's disease using LIME on DaTSCAN imagery. *Comput. Biol. Med.*, 126, 104041, 2020 Nov 1.
33. Uzunova, H., Ehrhardt, J., Kepp, T., Handels, H., Interpretable explanations of black box classifiers applied on medical images by meaningful perturbations using variational autoencoders, in: *Medical Imaging 2019: Image Processing*, vol. 10949, SPIE, pp. 264–271, 2019 Mar 15.
34. Dabkowski, P. and Gal, Y., Real time image saliency for black box classifiers. *Advances in neural information processing systems*, vol. 30, 2017.
35. Fong, R.C. and Vedaldi, A., Interpretable explanations of black boxes by meaningful perturbation, in: *Proceedings of the IEEE international conference on computer vision*, pp. 3429–3437, 2017.

36. Fong, R., Patrick, M., Vedaldi, A., Understanding deep networks via extremal perturbations and smooth masks, in: *Proceedings of the IEEE/CVF international conference on computer vision*, pp. 2950–2958, 2019.
37. Lundberg, S.M. and Lee, S.I., A unified approach to interpreting model predictions. *Advances in neural information processing systems*, vol. 30, 2017.
38. Petsiuk, V., Das, A., Saenko, K., Rise: Randomized input sampling for explanation of black-box models, arXiv preprint arXiv:1806.07421, 2018 Jun 19.
39. Cooper, J., Arandjelović, O., Harrison, D.J., Believe the HiPe: Hierarchical perturbation for fast, robust, and model-agnostic saliency mapping. *Pattern Recognit.*, 129, 108743, 2022 Sep 1.
40. Springenberg, J.T., Dosovitskiy, A., Brox, T., Riedmiller, M., Striving for simplicity: The all convolutional net, arXiv preprint arXiv:1412.6806, 2014 Dec 21.
41. Simonyan, K., Vedaldi, A., Zisserman, A., Deep inside convolutional networks: Visualising image classification models and saliency maps, arXiv preprint arXiv:1312.6034, 2013 Dec 20.
42. Shrikumar, A., Greenside, P., Kundaje, A., Learning important features through propagating activation differences, in: *International conference on machine learning*, PMLR, pp. 3145–3153, 2017 Jul 17.
43. Molnar, C., *Interpretable machine learning*, Lulu.com, Morrisville, North Carolina, United States, 2020.
44. De Vos, B.D., Wolterink, J.M., Leiner, T., De Jong, P.A., Lessmann, N., Išgum, I., Direct automatic coronary calcium scoring in cardiac and chest CT. *IEEE Trans. Med. Imaging*, 38, 9, 2127–38, 2019 Feb 17.
45. Mostafa, S., Mondal, D., Beck, M.A., Bidinosti, C.P., Henry, C.J., Stavness, I., Leveraging guided backpropagation to select convolutional neural networks for plant classification. *Front. Artif. Intell.*, 5, 871162, 2022 May 11.
46. Adebayo, J., Gilmer, J., Muelly, M., Goodfellow, I., Hardt, M., Kim, B., Sanity checks for saliency maps. *Advances in neural information processing systems*, vol. 31, 2018.
47. Dubost, F., Yilmaz, P., Adams, H., Bortsova, G., Ikram, M.A., Niessen, W., Vernooij, M., de Bruijne, M., Enlarged perivascular spaces in brain MRI: automated quantification in four regions. *Neuroimage*, 185, 534–44, 2019 Jan 15.
48. Bach, S., Binder, A., Montavon, G., Klauschen, F., Müller, K.R., Samek, W., On pixel-wise explanations for non-linear classifier decisions by layer-wise relevance propagation. *PLoS One*, 10, 7, e0130140, 2015 Jul 10.
49. Böhle, M., Eitel, F., Weygandt, M., Ritter, K., Layer-wise relevance propagation for explaining deep neural network decisions in MRI-based Alzheimer's disease classification. *Front. Aging Neurosci.*, 11, 194, 2019 Jul 31.
50. Singh, A., Sengupta, S., Lakshminarayanan, V., Glaucoma diagnosis using transfer learning methods, in: *Applications of machine learning*, vol. 11139, SPIE, pp. 223–232, 2019 Sep 6.
51. Yosinski, J., Clune, J., Bengio, Y., Lipson, H., How transferable are features in deep neural networks? *Advances in neural information processing systems*, vol. 27, 2014.

52. Deng, J., Dong, W., Socher, R., Li, L.J., Li, K., Fei-Fei, L., Imagenet: A large-scale hierarchical image database, in: *2009 IEEE conference on computer vision and pattern recognition*, IEEE, pp. 248–255, 2009 Jun 20.
53. Eitel, F., Ritter, K., Alzheimer's Disease Neuroimaging Initiative (ADNI), Testing the robustness of attribution methods for convolutional neural networks in MRI-based Alzheimer's disease classification, in: *Interpretability of Machine Intelligence in Medical Image Computing and Multimodal Learning for Clinical Decision Support: Second International Workshop, iMIMIC 2019, and 9th International Workshop, ML-CDS 2019, Held in Conjunction with MICCAI 2019, Shenzhen, China, October 17, 2019, Proceedings 9*, pp. 3–11, Springer International Publishing, Salmon Tower Building, New York City, 2019.
54. Pereira, S., Meier, R., Alves, V., Reyes, M., Silva, C.A., Automatic brain tumor grading from MRI data using convolutional neural networks and quality assessment, in: *Understanding and Interpreting Machine Learning in Medical Image Computing Applications: First International Workshops, MLCN 2018, DLF 2018, and iMIMIC 2018, Held in Conjunction with MICCAI 2018, Granada, Spain, September 16-20, 2018, Proceedings 1*, pp. 106–114, Springer International Publishing, Salmon Tower Building, New York City, 2018.
55. Sayres, R., Taly, A., Rahimy, E., Blumer, K., Coz, D., Hammel, N., Krause, J., Narayanaswamy, A., Rastegar, Z., Wu, D., Xu, S., Using a deep learning algorithm and integrated gradients explanation to assist grading for diabetic retinopathy. *Ophthalmology*, 126, 4, 552–64, 2019 Apr 1.
56. Yang, H.L., Kim, J.J., Kim, J.H., Kang, Y.K., Park, D.H., Park, H.S., Kim, H.K., Kim, M.S., Weakly supervised lesion localization for age-related macular degeneration detection using optical coherence tomography images. *PLoS One*, 14, 4, e0215076, 2019 Apr 5.
57. Singh, A., Mohammed, A.R., Zelek, J., Lakshminarayanan, V., Interpretation of deep learning using attributions: application to ophthalmic diagnosis, in: *Applications of machine learning 2020*, 2020 Aug 20, vol. 11511, SPIE, pp. 39–49.
58. Papanastasopoulos, Z., Samala, R.K., Chan, H.P., Hadjiiski, L., Paramagul, C., Helvie, M.A., Neal, C.H., Explainable AI for medical imaging: deep-learning CNN ensemble for classification of estrogen receptor status from breast MRI, in: *Medical imaging 2020: Computer-aided diagnosis*, 2020 Mar 16, vol. 11314, SPIE, pp. 228–235.
59. Szegedy, C., Liu, W., Jia, Y., Sermanet, P., Reed, S., Anguelov, D., Erhan, D., Vanhoucke, V., Rabinovich, A., Going deeper with convolutions, in: *Proceedings of the IEEE conference on computer vision and pattern recognition*, pp. 1–9, 2015.
60. Krizhevsky, A., Sutskever, I., Hinton, G.E., Imagenet classification with deep convolutional neural networks. *Advances in neural information processing systems*, vol. 25, 2012.

61. Lévy, D. and Jain, A., Breast mass classification from mammograms using deep convolutional neural networks, arXiv preprint arXiv:1612.00542, 2016 Dec 2.
62. Mordvintsev, A., Olah, C., Tyka, M., Inceptionism: Going deeper into neural networks. Google research blog, vol. 20(14), p. 5, 2015 Jun 17.
63. Couteaux, V., Nempont, O., Pizaine, G., Bloch, I., Towards interpretability of segmentation networks by analyzing deepdreams, in: *Interpretability of Machine Intelligence in Medical Image Computing and Multimodal Learning for Clinical Decision Support: Second International Workshop, iMIMIC 2019, and 9th International Workshop, ML-CDS 2019, Held in Conjunction with MICCAI 2019, Shenzhen, China, October 17, 2019, Proceedings 9*, pp. 56–63, Springer International Publishing, Salmon Tower Building, New York City, 2019.
64. Lin, Z.Q., Shafiee, M.J., Bochkarev, S., Jules, M.S., Wang, X.Y., Wong, A., Do explanations reflect decisions? A machine-centric strategy to quantify the performance of explainability algorithms, arXiv preprint arXiv:1910.07387, 2019 Oct 16.
65. Young, K., Booth, G., Simpson, B., Dutton, R., Shrapnel, S., Deep neural network or dermatologist?, in: *Interpretability of Machine Intelligence in Medical Image Computing and Multimodal Learning for Clinical Decision Support: Second International Workshop, iMIMIC 2019, and 9th International Workshop, ML-CDS 2019, Held in Conjunction with MICCAI 2019, Shenzhen, China, October 17, 2019, Proceedings 9*, pp. 48–55, Springer International Publishing, New York, USA, 2019.
66. Van Molle, P., De Strooper, M., Verbelen, T., Vankeirsbilck, B., Simoens, P., Dhoedt, B., Visualizing convolutional neural networks to improve decision support for skin lesion classification, in: *Understanding and Interpreting Machine Learning in Medical Image Computing Applications: First International Workshops, MLCN 2018, DLF 2018, and iMIMIC 2018, Held in Conjunction with MICCAI 2018, Granada, Spain, September 16-20, 2018, Proceedings 1*, pp. 115–123, Springer International Publishing, New York, USA, 2018.
67. Wickstrøm, K., Kampffmeyer, M., Jenssen, R., Uncertainty and interpretability in convolutional neural networks for semantic segmentation of colorectal polyps. *Med. Image Anal.*, 60, 101619, 2020 Feb 1.
68. Moccia, S., De Momi, E., Guarnaschelli, M., Savazzi, M., Laborai, A., Guastini, L., Peretti, G., Mattos, L.S., Confident texture-based laryngeal tissue classification for early stage diagnosis support. *J. Med. Imaging*, 4, 3, 034502–, 2017 Jul 1.
69. Lundberg, S.M., Nair, B., Vavilala, M.S., Horibe, M., Eisses, M.J., Adams, T., Liston, D.E., Low, D.K., Newman, S.F., Kim, J., Lee, S.I., Explainable machine-learning predictions for the prevention of hypoxaemia during surgery. *Nat. Biomed. Eng.*, 2, 10, 749–60, 2018 Oct.
70. Vaswani, A., Shazeer, N., Parmar, N., Uszkoreit, J., Jones, L., Gomez, A.N., Kaiser, Ł., Polosukhin, I., Attention is all you need. *Advances in neural information processing systems*, vol. 30, 2017.

71. Bamba, U., Pandey, D., Lakshminarayanan, V., Classification of brain lesions from MRI images using a novel neural network, in: *Multimodal Biomedical Imaging XV*, vol. 11232, SPIE, pp. 23–31, 2020 Feb 17.
72. Zhang, Z., Xie, Y., Xing, F., McGough, M., Yang, L., Mdnet: A semantically and visually interpretable medical image diagnosis network, in: *Proceedings of the IEEE conference on computer vision and pattern recognition*, pp. 6428–6436, 2017.
73. Ronneberger, O., Fischer, P., Brox, T., U-net: Convolutional networks for biomedical image segmentation, in: *Medical image computing and computer-assisted intervention–MICCAI 2015: 18th international conference, Munich, Germany, October 5-9, 2015, proceedings, part III 18*, pp. 234–241, Springer International Publishing, New York, USA, 2015.
74. Sun, J., Darbehani, F., Zaidi, M., Wang, B., Saunet: Shape attentive u-net for interpretable medical image segmentation, in: *Medical Image Computing and Computer Assisted Intervention–MICCAI 2020: 23rd International Conference, Lima, Peru, October 4–8, 2020, Proceedings, Part IV 23*, pp. 797–806, Springer International Publishing, New York, USA, 2020.
75. Kim, B., Wattenberg, M., Gilmer, J., Cai, C., Wexler, J., Viegas, F., Interpretability beyond feature attribution: Quantitative testing with concept activation vectors (tcav), in: *International conference on machine learning*, PMLR, pp. 2668–2677, 2018 Jul 3.
76. Graziani, M., Andrearczyk, V., Müller, H., Regression concept vectors for bidirectional explanations in histopathology, in: *Understanding and Interpreting Machine Learning in Medical Image Computing Applications: First International Workshops, MLCN 2018, DLF 2018, and iMIMIC 2018, Held in Conjunction with MICCAI 2018, Granada, Spain, September 16-20, 2018, Proceedings 1*, pp. 124–132, Springer International Publishing, New York, USA, 2018.
77. Yeche, H., Harrison, J., Berthier, T., UBS: A dimension-agnostic metric for concept vector interpretability applied to radiomics, in: *Interpretability of Machine Intelligence in Medical Image Computing and Multimodal Learning for Clinical Decision Support: Second International Workshop, iMIMIC 2019, and 9th International Workshop, ML-CDS 2019, Held in Conjunction with MICCAI 2019, Shenzhen, China, October 17, 2019, Proceedings 9*, pp. 12–20, Springer International Publishing, New York, USA, 2019.
78. Iandola, F.N., Han, S., Moskewicz, M.W., Ashraf, K., Dally, W.J., Keutzer, K., SqueezeNet: AlexNet-level accuracy with 50x fewer parameters and< 0.5 MB model size, arXiv preprint arXiv:1602.07360, 2016 Feb 24.
79. Pisov, M., Goncharov, M., Kurochkina, N., Morozov, S., Gombolevskiy, V., Chernina, V., Vladzymyrskyy, A., Zamyatina, K., Chesnokova, A., Pronin, I., Shifrin, M., Incorporating task-specific structural knowledge into CNNs for brain midline shift detection, in: *Interpretability of Machine Intelligence in Medical Image Computing and Multimodal Learning for Clinical Decision Support: Second International Workshop, iMIMIC 2019, and 9th International*

Workshop, ML-CDS 2019, Held in Conjunction with MICCAI 2019, Shenzhen, China, October 17, 2019, Proceedings 9, pp. 30–38, Springer International Publishing, New York, USA, 2019.

80. Zhu, P. and Ogino, M., Guideline-based additive explanation for computer-aided diagnosis of lung nodules, in: *Interpretability of Machine Intelligence in Medical Image Computing and Multimodal Learning for Clinical Decision Support: Second International Workshop, iMIMIC 2019, and 9th International Workshop, ML-CDS 2019, Held in Conjunction with MICCAI 2019, Shenzhen, China, October 17, 2019, Proceedings 9*, pp. 39–47, Springer International Publishing, New York, USA, 2019.
81. Lee, H., Kim, S.T., Ro, Y.M., Generation of multimodal justification using visual word constraint model for explainable computer-aided diagnosis, in: *Interpretability of Machine Intelligence in Medical Image Computing and Multimodal Learning for Clinical Decision Support: Second International Workshop, iMIMIC 2019, and 9th International Workshop, ML-CDS 2019, Held in Conjunction with MICCAI 2019, Shenzhen, China, October 17, 2019, Proceedings 9*, pp. 21–29, Springer International Publishing, New York, USA, 2019.

9

XAI-Enabled Telehealth

Pankaj Kumar Sharma* **and Neha Krishnarth**

Raj Kumar Goel Institute of Technology (Pharmacy), 5th KM Stone Delhi Meerut Road, Ghaziabad, Uttar Pradesh, India

Abstract

Telehealth, driven by headways in computerized innovations, has arisen as a groundbreaking power in medical services, offering far-off understanding observing, virtual conferences, and further developed admittance to clinical benefits. The reconciliation of explainable artificial intelligence (XAI) into telehealth frameworks addresses a change in outlook, tending to the basic requirement for straightforwardness, interpretability, and confidence in the dynamic cycles of simulated intelligence calculations. This theory investigates the collaborations between XAI and telehealth, accentuating the expected advantages and difficulties related to this mix. Straightforward computer-based intelligence models engage medical services experts to approve and grasp the reasoning behind simulated intelligence-driven proposals, upgrading the general trust in telehealth applications. This theory likewise digs into the assorted uses of XAI in telehealth, including symptomatic help, customized treatment proposals, and far-off understanding checking. By making computer-based intelligence-produced suggestions more open and interpretable, XAI encourages a cooperative and informed dynamic interaction between simulated intelligence frameworks and medical services suppliers. While the reception of XAI in telehealth holds gigantic commitment, difficulties like information protection, security, and the potential for predisposition in artificial intelligence models should be tended to. These theoretical features progressing research endeavors and best practices pointed toward relieving these difficulties, guaranteeing the capable and moral sending of XAI in telehealth.

Keywords**:** Explainable artificial intelligence (XAI), telehealth, transparency, interpretability, healthcare decision-making

**Corresponding author*: pankajsharma4145@gmail.com

Rishabha Malviya and Sonali Sundram (eds.) Explainable and Responsible Artificial Intelligence in Healthcare, (217–250) © 2025 Scrivener Publishing LLC

List of Abbreviations

XAI	Explainable Artificial Intelligence
TH	Telehealth
TAI	Telehealth Artificial Intelligence
T-XAI	Telehealth Explainable AI
SVM	Support Vector Machines
XTH	XAI in Telehealth
XMD	XAI Mediated Decision-making
CNNs	Convolutional Brain Organizations
RNNs	Repetitive Brain Organizations
SHAP	Shapely Added substance explanations
LRP	Layer-wise Significance Expansion
PDP	Partial Dependence Plots
THD	Telehealth Decision-making
TET	Telehealth Explainability Toolkit
TAIH	Telehealth AI Transparency and Interpretability in Healthcare
EHT	Explainable Healthcare Technology
XTDM	XAI Telehealth Decision Models
THX	Telehealth with Explainability
IHX	Interpretable Healthcare XAI
TXM	Telehealth Explainable Models

9.1 Introduction

The incorporation of computational intelligence [artificial intelligence (AI)] models to parse clinical data, find patterns, and improve patient outcomes is more known as the integration of AI in medicine. AI is rapidly evolving into modern healthcare due to recent developments in informatics and computer science. Workers in the healthcare sector are benefiting from AI algorithms and applications in medical clinics along with continuing research. Because of ongoing headways in software engineering and informatics, AI is quickly turning into a necessary part of current medical care. Man-made intelligence calculations and different applications fueled by computer-based intelligence are helping medical services experts in clinical settings and progressing research [1].

The difficulties that the coronavirus pandemic made for the vast majority of wellbeing frameworks likewise drove numerous medical care associations all over the planet to begin field-testing new AI advancements, for example, calculations intended to assist with observing patients and simulated intelligence-fueled instruments to screen coronavirus patients.

The examination and consequences of these tests are as yet being accumulated, and the general guidelines for the utilization of AI in medication are as yet being characterized. However, as amazing open doors for simulated intelligence to help clinicians, analysts, and the patients, they serve are consistently expanding. Right now, there is little uncertainty that simulated intelligence will turn into a center piece of the computerized wellbeing frameworks that shape and backing current medication.

The expression "artificial intelligence reasoning" stood initially created during a Dartmouth College conference proposal in 1955. Nevertheless, AI applications did not make their way into the healthcare sector until the mid-1970s, when research led with MYCIN expansion. The multiplication of AI research proceeded, and, in 1979, the American Relationship for AI consciousness was shaped (at present the Relationship for the Headway of Computerized Reasoning, AAAI).

9.2 Significance of Telemedicine

World Wellbeing Association utilizing data with correspondence innovations to give medical care administrations when distance is a basic factor for characterizing telemedicine [2]. The definition includes a few viewpoints, like diagnosing, treating, and forestalling illnesses and wounds, directing exploration, and proceeding with training to medical care suppliers, with the last point of advancing the soundness of people and networks. Telemedicine is a medical services technique and not a device; it very well may be brought out through various modalities, like live video meetings or store and forward informing frameworks. In spite of the fact that terms, for example, telemedicine and telehealth are much of the time utilized interchangeably [3], they convey separate specialized and administrative definitions and different terms, and, for example, computerized security and portable wellbeing are utilized to give a more extensive and more thorough perspective on individuals' medical care in the advanced age.

Telemedicine alludes explicitly arrangement of medical care administrations and meetings through far-off innovations, which envelops a more extensive scope of medical care administrations conveyed through innovation. While telemedicine centres around virtual conferences and findings, telehealth incorporates all parts of medical care that can be conveyed through innovation, like patient observation, sickness the board, and medicine adherence.

9.3 Reasonable AI Consciousness (XAI)

This concept pertains to coherent explanations of its outcomes manner understandable to humans. The necessity for clarity becomes particularly evident in intricate AI systems, such as deep neural networks, where the decision-making process can appear opaque or inscrutable to human observers [1].

The following are a couple of key perspectives and motivations behind why XAI is significant.

9.3.1 Transparency

XAI empowers clients to comprehend the reason why an AI framework went with a particular choice. This straightforwardness is essential, particularly in basic applications like medical services or money, where choices have huge results.

9.3.2 Trust

Understanding how a simulated intelligence framework arrives at its decisions constructs trust among clients, partners, and controllers. In the event that clients cannot comprehend or trust AI produced choices, they are more averse to take on or depend on simulated intelligence frameworks.

9.3.3 Accountability and Predisposition Alleviation

XAI distinguishes inclinations in the preparation information or calculations, considering acclimations to relieve these predispositions. It empowers designers to evaluate whether the model's choices line up with moral or legitimate norms.

9.3.4 User Strengthening

Giving clarifications engages clients to make informed decisions about AI created yields. For example, in clinical determination frameworks, clarifications can assist specialists with checking the computer-based intelligence's analysis and settle on better-informed treatment choices.

9.3.5 Education and Learning

XAI can likewise fill an instructive need by assisting clients with figuring out basic examples or connections in the information. This can work with learning and information move, particularly in instructive or preparing applications.

A few methods are utilized to accomplish logic in simulated intelligence frameworks [4]:

- Include Significance: Recognizing which elements or sources of info contributed most to the model's choice.
- Nearby Clarifications: Giving clarifications to individual expectations, like featuring important highlights for a particular occurrence.
- Rearrangements: Making less difficult models or decision-based frameworks that imitate the way of behaving of mind boggling AI models.
- Representations: Introducing information or model designs in visual arrangements that are more straightforward for people to decipher.
- Regular Language Clarifications: Producing clarifications in comprehensible language to portray the dynamic cycle.

XAI is a functioning area of innovative work, driven by the rising reception of simulated intelligence in different spaces and the developing acknowledgment of the significance of straightforwardness and responsibility in computer-based intelligence frameworks. As AI proceeds to advance and coordinate into additional basic applications, the interest for reasonable computer-based intelligence will probably keep on developing.

Definition and Standards of Reasonable AI consciousness [5]:

Reasonable AI consciousness (XAI) alludes to the advancement of computer-based intelligence frameworks that can be perceived and deciphered by people. The objective is to make simulated intelligence frameworks straightforward, giving clarifications to their choices and activities, especially in basic applications where trust, responsibility, and wellbeing are foremost. Here are a few standards basic XAI:

1. Transparency: XAI frameworks ought to be straightforward, meaning their inside components and dynamic cycles are

justifiable to people. This includes giving clarifications that clients can grasp without particular specialized information.
2. Interpretability: AI models ought to be interpretable, permitting people to comprehend how data sources are changed into yields. This can include methods, for example, highlight significance examination, which recognizes the most powerful factors driving a model's choices.
3. Traceability: XAI frameworks ought to empower the following of choices back to their sources. This includes keeping a record of the information, calculations, and boundaries utilized in the dynamic cycle, considering responsibility and auditability.
4. Fairness: XAI frameworks ought to be intended to stay away from predisposition and separation. This requires cautious thought of the information used to prepare the AI models, as well as the calculations and elements utilized. Straightforwardness in these cycles can help distinguish and moderate predispositions.
5. Human-driven plan: XAI frameworks ought to be planned considering human clients. This includes integrating client criticism and inclinations into the plan cycle, as well as giving clarifications and input in a configuration that is effectively reasonable and noteworthy.
6. Context-mindfulness: XAI frameworks ought to be delicate to the setting wherein they are conveyed. This incorporates thinking about the social, social, and moral standards of the clients and partners, as well as adjusting clarifications to the particular necessities and inclinations of various client gatherings.

By sticking to these standards, XAI means to construct trust in simulated intelligence frameworks, improve their ease of use, and guarantee that they are sent dependably and morally in different spaces.

9.4 Simulated Intelligence in Telemedicine

Simulated intelligence can possibly upgrade the abilities of medical services experts and work on the effectiveness and security of telemedicine. AI is expected to handle the issue of avoidable clinical blunders and improve work process efficiencies, which are as of now at a high rate in medical services provision [5]. In any case, its joining into ordinary practice has been restricted because of different elements including wellbeing, administrative, and monetary challenges [6].

Incorporating AI into telemedicine can possibly change medical care, yet it likewise represents a few difficulties and restrictions. One of the essential worries is wellbeing, as AI calculations may not generally be precise and can make blunders that could hurt patients. One more significant test is administrative consistence, as computer-based intelligence-fueled telemedicine stages should comply with severe guidelines to guarantee patient protection and information security.

Besides, the monetary element is likewise a main issue as coordinating AI in telemedicine requires a critical interest in framework and innovation, which may not be doable for little or asset-compelled medical services suppliers. Furthermore, there is a necessity to confront the ethical concerns surrounding the use of AI in healthcare, including issues of bias and transparency.

To tackle these challenges, it is imperative to establish explicit regulations and standards governing the utilization of AI in telemedicine. Healthcare institutions should also prioritize investment in training and developing their workforce to ensure competency in leveraging AI technologies.

Four arising patterns in which computer-based intelligence is affecting telemedicine [7] are as per the following: 1) observing patients, 2) involving data innovation in medical services, 3) utilization of shrewd help and determination, and 4) cooperative data examination. In spite of these impacts, the reception of AI in medical services requires persuading proof regarding its advantages for both the clinical local area and patients [8].

9.5 Challenges in Executing XAI in Medical Services

The arising jobs of computerized reasoning procedures in medical care arrangement and clinical exploration are progressively clear. Studies have featured the adequacy and capability of computer-based intelligence fueled wellbeing applications [9, 10]. These mechanical headways are additionally upheld by significant interests in man-made intelligence application inside medical services by legislatures and innovation firms, with dynamic joint effort from the US Food and Medication Organization in the presentation of AI-empowered clinical gadgets to the market [11, 12]. In our view, four key regions where AI-empowered medical care conveyance is ready to have the most effect incorporate medical service organizations, clinical choice help, patient checking, and medical care mediations [13].

The association of clinical benefits has become progressively complicated, with medical services framework in numerous nations extended to its ability because of regulatory tensions and asset imperatives [14, 15]. Data innovation apparatuses have been displayed to mitigate this weight on medical care administrations, with man-made reasoning and information mining procedures recognized as among the most encouraging ways to deal with help medical service organizations. These strategies expect to upgrade clinical consideration while lessening managerial requests on medical care suppliers [16].

9.6 Clinical Choice Help

Clinical choice emotionally supportive networks are PC; the integration of clinical information to help choices went with by medical care professionals [17]. Clinical decision genuinely steady organizations can help with reducing clinical mix-ups and increase clinical benefits consistency and capability and tries to get clinical decision sincerely encouraging groups of people into normal practice are progressing, with man-made consciousness strategies applied broadly in research on clinical choice emotionally supportive networks since the mid-1970s, including master frameworks [18]. Computer-based intelligence calculations are right now utilized to foresee the movement of septic shock, help in the therapy of persistent obstructive pneumonic illness patients, and work with different other master choices [19].

9.7 Patient Observing

The broad coordination of electronic wellbeing records, joined with the far and wide utilization of cell phones and wellness trackers, has allowed unmatched admittance to advanced information and opened up roads for applying computerized reasoning strategies in understanding reconnaissance [18]. Consequently, we now possess comprehensive insights into patients' sleep cycles, cardiovascular activity, blood pressure, and a range of other metrics that were once inaccessible. Furthermore, progress has been achieved across different environments; for instance, waveform pattern recognition has improved the monitoring and interpretation of electrocardiograms, electroencephalograms, electromyograms, and Doppler ultrasounds within hospital settings [10].

9.8 Medical Services Intercessions

The advancement of AI has facilitated the customization of healthcare interventions for individuals or specific subgroups within populations [18]. AI systems integrated into electronic health records have the ability to analyze biometric and medical supplementary data of individual patients, providing management recommendations aligned with recent medical protocols. Furthermore, AI systems linked to hospital servers can analyze stored patient data and respond to patient inquiries, thereby reducing wait times in bustling emergency departments [20]. AI systems utilizing fuzzy logic and multi-valued logic applied management medication. Fuzzy controllers are utilized to postoperative patients regulate vasodilators [10, 21].

9.9 The Requirement for Mindful Simulated Intelligence in Medical Care

Worries over simulated intelligence's absence of logic intently stream from the dinky responsibility structures that encompass it. Simulated intelligence is perceived for its capacity to distinguish and anticipate designs in information that unassisted people probably would not have the option to. Outlandish results are detectable for explicit simulated intelligence. It is feasible to follow sensible conviction why an AI went with a specific choice, what elements impacted it, and where responsibility should be put on account of a setback, be it one-sided results or improper guess. Notwithstanding, complex simulated intelligence needs straightforwardness in regards to its choice pathways. This likewise implies that any responsibility system cannot pinpoint the specific component of the algorithmic interaction that wavered to make an unfriendly result. Without a trace of a responsibility system, obligation, when required to have been laid out, is perceived as a variety of emotional elements, like the capability of mischief, the chance of predisposition, and the chance of remedy or compensation [21].

While the requirement for reasonableness through "straightforwardness" has been verbalized by global gatherings like the Association for Financial Co-activity and Advancement [22–24] (OECD) and G20, the unambiguous right to look for significant data about the presence, rationale, and extended outcomes of mechanized dynamic frameworks is as yet not laid out, provoking discussion around the need of logic and its cutoff points.

9.10 Moral Contemplations in Artificial Intelligence Sending

Potential risks or consequences unreliable AI in healthcare includes the following [25]:

9.10.1 Misdiagnosis and Treatment Mistakes

On the off chance that simulated intelligence calculations are not as expected prepared or approved, they might give erroneous conclusions or suggest improper medicines, prompting patient damage or deferred recuperation.

9.10.2 Data Inclination and Separation

AI frameworks prepared on one-sided or deficient information might propagate existing medical services aberrations, prompting inconsistent therapy or conclusion in view of elements like race, orientation, or financial status.

9.10.3 Privacy and Security Concerns

Medical services simulated intelligence frameworks expect admittance to delicate patient information, raising worries about protection breaks and unapproved access. On the off chance that these frameworks are not enough gotten, patient classification might be compromised.

9.10.4 Loss of Human Oversight

Overreliance on simulated intelligence in medical services navigation could prompt a lessened job for medical care experts, possibly diminishing the nature of care and sabotaging patient trust.

9.10.5 Regulatory and Legitimate Dangers

Conveying AI in medical services without suitable guidelines or rules can bring about lawful liabilities for medical care suppliers and engineers in instances of unfavorable results or administrative rebelliousness.

9.10.6 Ethical Quandaries

Simulated intelligence calculations might confront moral problems while pursuing choices that include compromises between various results or when defied with circumstances where there is no unmistakable "right" reply. Settling these problems requires cautious thought of cultural qualities and moral standards.

9.10.7 Algorithmic Straightforwardness and Responsibility

Absence of straightforwardness in AI calculations can pursue it challenging to comprehend how choices are made, prompting doubt among patients and medical services suppliers. Additionally, without components for responsibility, tending to mistakes or predispositions in computer-based intelligence systems might be a challenge.

9.10.8 Financial Double-Dealing

Medical services simulated intelligence advancements, while possibly not suitably directed, might be utilized to focus on benefit over persistent prosperity, prompting overdiagnosis, overtreatment, or pointless clinical mediations.

Tending to these dangers requires a multidisciplinary approach implying medical care experts, policymakers, technologists, and ethicists create and execute vigorous administrative systems, guarantee information protection and security, advance algorithmic straightforwardness and responsibility, and focus on persistent wellbeing and prosperity.

9.11 AI (ML) in Artificial Intelligence

AI (ML) in AI focuses on creating calculations and factual models that empower PCs to learn and work on their exhibition of unambiguous undertakings without direct programming. Below is an exploration of different aspects of AI encompassed by ML:

9.11.1 Types of AI

- Managed Learning: The calculation prepared a baptized dataset, meaning it gains input from yield matches. It sums up designs from known input-yield matches to pursue forecasts or choices on inconspicuous information.
- Solo Learning: Unaided learning manages unlabeled information. The calculation gains examples and designs from input information without unequivocal criticism. Grouping and dimensionality decrease are normal undertakings of this sort.

- Semi-Directed Realizing: This learning approach falls between supervised and unsupervised learning, where the model is trained using a small amount of labeled data alongside a large quantity of unlabeled data.
- Support Learning: Support learning includes a specialist cooperating with a climate to get familiar with a strategy that boosts some thought of combined reward. It learns through experimentation, getting criticism as remunerations or punishments.

9.11.2 Algorithms

- Straight Relapse: A basic type of directed learning utilized for relapse undertakings, where the objective is to foresee a persistent worth.
- Choice Trees: A tree-like model of choices utilized for grouping and relapse.
- Irregular Backwoods: A strategy for gathering discovering that includes making different choice trees during the preparation cycle and conglomerating the class results (for characterization) or normal expectations (for relapse) from these singular trees.
- Support Vector Machines: Managed learning model that examines information for grouping and relapse examination.

9.11.3 Deep Learning

- Brain Organizations: Profound gaining designs draw motivation from the unpredictable association and functional standards of the human mind. These models contain layered organizations of hubs (likened to neurons) that dissect input flags and refine their boundaries utilizing a system named backpropagation.
- Convolutional Brain Organizations (CNNs): CNNs are a kind of brain network especially powerful for picture acknowledgement and grouping errands. They use convolutional layers to consequently and adaptively gain spatial orders of highlights from input pictures.
- Repetitive Brain Organizations (RNNs): RNNs are intended to perceive designs in successions of information, making them reasonable for undertakings like normal language handling and time series expectation.

9.11.4 Model Assessment and Improvement

- Cross-Approval: A strategy used to evaluate the exhibition and generalizability of a model.
- Hyperparameter Tuning: Changing the settings of a model (hyperparameters) to streamline its exhibition.
- Overfitting and Underfitting: Overfitting happens when a model learns the preparation information excessively well, including commotion, and performs inadequately on concealed information. Underfitting happens when a model is excessively easy to catch the fundamental construction of the information.

9.11.5 Applications

- Picture Acknowledgment: Recognizing objects, individuals, places, and different components inside pictures.
- Regular Language Handling (NLP): Handling and examining human language, including undertakings like feeling investigation, machine interpretation, and text age.
- Medical Services: Prescient examination, infection identification, customized therapy plans, and medication disclosure.
- Finance: Misrepresentation identification, algorithmic exchanging, risk evaluation, and credit scoring.
- Independent Vehicles: AI is fundamental for self-driving vehicles to see their environmental elements and simply decide.

AI in simulated intelligence is a tremendous field with consistent progressions and applications across different spaces, driving development and robotization in various enterprises as discussed in Table 9.1.

Table 9.1 Frequent terminology, definitions, and real-world illustrations employed in the realm of artificial intelligence [22, 31, 62].

Frequent terminology	Prevalent descriptions in medicine	Illustrative instances in anesthesiology, critical care, and pain management
Artificial intelligence	Methods enabling computers to emulate human cognitive functions.	Enhancement of resource management; support in non-specialist training; enhancement of peri-operative assessment.

(Continued)

Table 9.1 Frequent terminology, definitions, and real-world illustrations employed in the realm of artificial intelligence [22, 31, 62]. (*Continued*)

Frequent terminology	Prevalent descriptions in medicine	Illustrative instances in anesthesiology, critical care, and pain management
Machine learning	A domain of computer science focused on instructing computers to perform tasks by discerning patterns in data, devoid of explicit programming.	Forecasting intra-operative complications; optimizing post-operative pain management; managing resources in operating rooms and intensive care units; forecasting response to therapy; identifying anatomical structures to aid procedures.
Deep learning	Machine learning autonomously learns represents data as a hierarchy of concepts, defining each concept relative to simpler ones.	Monitoring anaesthesia depth. Identifying ultrasound-based anatomical structures.
Artificial neural networks	A network of interconnected nodes or "neurons" performing computational operations to accomplish specific tasks by tuning weighted connections.	Identification of US anatomical structures; prediction of difficult intubation and airway evaluation.
Telemedicine	Delivering healthcare services using communication technology to diagnose and treat illnesses, as well as providing ongoing education to healthcare providers in locations where distance presents a challenge.	Remote assessment prior to surgery, continuous monitoring of patients post-operation, and healthcare services tailored to specific geographical regions.
Big Data	A vast volume of electronic health data is challenging to handle using conventional software.	A fundamental resource for developing novel artificial intelligence algorithms.
Clinical decision support system	A diverse array of computerized utilities and interventions crucial for optimizing the advantages of electronic health records and computerized physician order entry.	A tool facilitating decision-making systems and ensuring accurate drug prescriptions (including considerations for allergies, dosage, interactions, and contraindications).

(*Continued*)

Table 9.1 Frequent terminology, definitions, and real-world illustrations employed in the realm of artificial intelligence [22, 31, 62]. (*Continued*)

Frequent terminology	Prevalent descriptions in medicine	Illustrative instances in anesthesiology, critical care, and pain management
Block chain technology	Cutting-edge technology employed to pioneer innovative solutions; its network integrates within the healthcare system to safeguard and exchange patient data across hospitals, diagnostic labs, pharmacies, and medical practitioners.	The storage and linkage of encrypted records, enabling the secure sharing and authorization of information.
Wearable device(s)	Smart wearable devices are designed to aid individuals.	Internal hospital monitoring of patient movements and resource allocation; remote surveillance of patient conditions.

9.12 Strategies for Interpretable AI Models

The procedures are Shapely Added substance explanations (SHAP), Close by Interpretable Model-freethinker Explanations (LIME), Tendency weighted Class Activation Arranging (GradCAM) [26], Layer-wise Significance Expansion (LRP), Soft Classifier [27, 28], and Partial Dependence Plots (PDP) [29].

Feathery Classifier: Originating from fluffy rationale, which mirrors human direction by taking into account different conceivable outcomes among "yes" and "no" [30], it contains four parts: the information base, fuzzifier, fluffy induction motor, and de-fuzzifier.

Dataset: This part stores the contingent "if then" rules given by human specialists.

Fuzzifier: Information is changed over into fluffy sets (e.g., little, medium negative, huge negative, medium positive, and generally certain) by the fuzzifier.

Fluffy Deduction Motor: This part matches the fluffy information sets created by the fuzzifier to the standards in the dataset to deliver fluffy result sets.

De-Fuzzifier: At long last, fresh qualities are produced utilizing the result sets from the fluffy induction motor [28].

A fluffy classifier is perhaps of the least complex strategy in logical man-made brainpower (XAI) [31].

Slope-weighted Class Enactment Planning (Graduate CAM): Graduate CAM is an improved adaptation of Class Actuation Planning intended to recognize the vital elements important for model expectation, especially material in clinical imaging strategies and offices. It is pertinent just to CNN (convolutional brain organization) models without completely associated layers, especially powerful at the last convolutional layer. While keeping up with the intricacy of Graduate CAM, it expects to save the interpretability of CNN models and produce heatmaps [28].

Graduate CAM is utilized to give a visual clarification of CNN models, using class-explicit slope data (in light of the angle-based strategy) streaming to the last convolution layer to create a limitation map in the picture of a huge locale for characterization models, improving interpretability. To make a high-goal class-discriminative portrayal, the makers of Graduate CAM likewise showed the way that the strategy can be coordinated with existing pixel-space perceptions, known as Coordinated Graduate CAM. Impediments of Graduate CAM and CAM: Because of its halfway subordinate suppositions, it cannot confine objects showing up in that frame of mind in a picture. Likewise, due to the ceaseless all-over examining processes, it cannot precisely deal with class-locale inclusion in a picture and the expected misfortune in signal [32].

Grad-CAM++ is an upgrade of Graduate CAM procedures giving a decent visual clarification of CNN models. It is more dependable in multi-mark characterization errands, as the shifting loads allocated to every pixel empower the slope highlight guide to catch the meaning of every pixel exclusively [32].

Graduate CAM is a post-hoc clarification, engendering values from the result layer toward the last convolutional layer [33].

9.13 Layer-Wise Relevance Propagation

Like Grad-CAM, it additionally creates heatmaps in view of the basic locales. LRP crosses in reverse from the model's classifier layer, at first registering the pertinence score for a particular result, which is likewise a last layer. It then, at that point, continues in reverse until it arrives at the info picture, processing the significance score of individual neurons in each layer. Consequently, it produces a heatmap in view of the importance score to feature the critical districts significant for expectation. LRP works with three standards: "fundamental standards," "epsilon rules," and "gamma rules," which can be applied to the upper layer, center layer, and lower layer of the model, separately. Notwithstanding, it shows less straightforwardness contrasted with Graduate CAM [28].

LRP does not rely upon slope data; all things considered, it characterizes the significance score for the neuron's result. To distribute an importance score to each component, it uses redistribution rules for the model's expectation [34].

9.14 Local Interpretable Model-Agnostic Explanations

LIME is utilized to produce limited clarifications of the model and distinguish huge highlights applicable for expectation. Like SHAP, it does not depend on the game hypothesis. All things being equal, it takes on an immediate methodology by irritating the info information of models and noticing the progressions made by the model's forecast. Clarifications given by LIME depend on individual cases as opposed to a whole dataset [28].

An illustration of an intermediary model is LIME, which is used to foresee the black box model. It locally prepares the model and decides the singular expectation of the model. The essential disadvantages of LIME are its non-deterministic nature because of arbitrary irritation of focuses and the absence of solidness. To resolve these issues, Muhammad Rehman Zafar proposes DLIME, or Deterministic Nearby Interpretable Model-freethinker Clarifications, pointed toward producing a steady clarification for a test occurrence [35].

To upgrade the solidness of LIME, rather than utilizing irregular irritation, it utilizes progressive bunching to bunch the preparation information and, then, at that point, chooses the most significant group for the examples [36].

One of the most normally used interpretable methodologies for black box models is the LIME strategy [32]. Two CNN models were furnished clarifications utilizing the LIME approach with the Fix Camelyon dataset. LIME offers an answer for the proxy model [37]. LIME gives a neighborhood clarification just; in this manner, it has been improved into two varieties as follows [34].

9.14.1 Subset-Based LIME (sp-LIME)

Subset-based choices are utilized to give the worldwide clarification of the model, utilizing subset-based determinations to recognize the sub-particular occasions of the forecast model. SP-LIME fills in as a worldwide intermediary, model-rationalist, and post-hoc approach, which upgrades the LIME procedures.

9.14.2 k-LIME

This technique is used for the black-box model, where bunching calculations are utilized to recognize the k-gatherings.

9.15 Partial Dependence Plots (PDPs)

One of the most normally utilized post-hoc strategies, PDP plots the impacts of element subsets on the model's forecasts to comprehend the black-box model. A device for showing the connection between the reaction and indicator factors in a restricted element space is the halfway reliance plot returned by the capability [38].

9.15.1 SHAP (Shapley Additive Explanations)

SHAP works much the same way as an "added substance attribution structure." It works likened to a game hypothesis strategy, upgrading the interpretability of every individual expectation by computing the significance values for each element. SHAP values keep three critical properties: precision, consistency, and missingness, at a joined degree of component importance. SHAP is simpler to carry out and all the more broadly acknowledged with regard to interpretability. It is utilized to produce both neighborhood and worldwide clarifications, is model-rationalist, and is more solid with information.

Shapley values are used to assign awards for players by registering the commitment of every player, fulfilling four maxims for computing the commitment of every player: effectiveness, equilibrium, joke, and additivity. SHAP was presented by Shapley in 1951 and is used to depict the particular result in view of the commitment of each contribution to a forecast. It very well may be applied to substitute models. Proposed SHAP clarifications are separated into two unmistakable variants as follows [34].

9.15.2 Partial SHAP

Coordinating Shapley values and LIME into a model-freethinker system for result understanding, Fractional SHAP looks like Nearby Interpretable Model-rationalist Clarifications (LIME) in that it is additionally used to prepare the neighborhood intermediary model. In any case, the restricted model is to direct partisan relapses, and the preparation is likewise led to scheduled altered datasets. Besides, fractional SHAP centers around the instances of interest. Shapley values used to give the chosen clarification consequently mirror each element's commitment to the result. Fractional SHAP has a restriction and is not a reasonable model of worldwide clarification [36].

9.15.3 Deep SHAP

A model-explicit methodology used to translate the results of DL models by coordinating the Shapley values with DeepLIFT. Profound SHAP uses the idea of DeepLIFT, yet the thing that matters is that, as opposed to relegating a worth to the information highlight, it draws motivation from the game hypothesis by considering each information included as a player and their commitment in a game utilizing the Shapley esteem [36].

SHAP can yield predictable outcomes; however, the disadvantage is the high calculation speed. The proposed Tree-Explainer resolves the issue for tree-based man-made intelligence calculations like Irregular Woodlands, Choice Trees, and slope-supported trees. SHAP and Tree Explainer are comparable concerning their usefulness. In Tree Explainer, expectations can be made in view of the benchmark of simulated intelligence and used to examine worldwide information [40]. Shap clarifications can be registered in polynomial time by the calculation [39]. Contrasted with LIME scores, SHAP values exhibited altogether more noteworthy intra-consistency values [41, 42]. Many classified SHAP into a gathering of irregular SHAPs, an outfit of irregular weighted SHAPs, troupe of irregular SHAPs produced by the arbitrary woods.

Logical AI (XAI) is essential and arising, particularly in the field of clinical examination, which will increment trust in simulated intelligence. Straightforwardness prompts producing experiences during the time spent demonstrating and decides the outcomes, prompting better comprehension of the issue explanation. In this way, it is gainful to work on the model and give a superior application space. XAI clarifies the response to the inquiry "why," which can be given in the customary model, subsequently imparting trust in AI utilizing XAI to lessen the effect of model predisposition [43].

Scientific AI will help facilitate the interaction between AI experts and external parties and will support the improvement of the model when it is not yet reliable enough to be deployed [44]. AI-powered image analysis employs sophisticated algorithms to extract complex patterns and features from images, offering unparalleled accuracy and efficiency in tasks like object detection and classification. In contrast, traditional techniques often rely on manual intervention and predefined rules, limiting their adaptability and scalability in handling diverse image data. AI's ability to learn and adapt from data enables it to uncover intricate insights and trends, revolutionizing image analysis across various domains as illustrated in Figure 9.1.

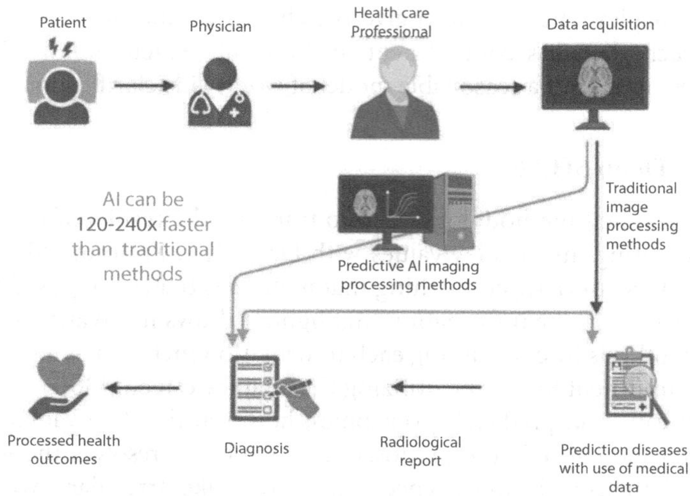

Figure 9.1 Image analysis (AI vs. traditional techniques).

9.16 Straight Forwardness in Artificial Intelligence Calculations

Calculations are just basically as great as the information used to prepare them. In situations where preparing information are fractional or fragmented or just mirror a subset of a given populace, the subsequent model might be pertinent to the number of inhabitants in individuals addressed in the dataset [45]. This brings up the issue about information provenance [46, 47] and addresses a bunch of issues connected with the predispositions that are incorporated into calculations used to illuminate independent direction. One high-profile model was the recruiting predisposition displayed when calculations were utilized to pursue employing choices at Amazon, bringing about just men being progressed to ensuing phases of recruiting [48]. This is eminent to some degree in light of the fact that the calculation performed all around founded on the accessible information, basically expanding the predisposition that generally existed in recruiting rehearses at the organization. When applied to medical care general well-being, information provenance and potential predisposition in preparing information address significant issues that are probably going to be of central issue for the partners associated with the execution of a ML drive.

A further test with the idea of the information on which calculations are prepared connects with idea float, a peculiarity where information on which a calculation is prepared changes after some time (or becomes obsolete), which changes the exhibition of the calculation as new information are obtained [49].

9.17 Difficulties of Reasonable Artificial Intelligence Logical

Artificial intelligence consciousness thought features interconnected research issues.

9.17.1 General Straightforwardness Versus Logic

Given that the guideline of simulated intelligence through an iterative course of clinical assessment and execution observing is not economical, guaranteeing patient wellbeing while not overregulating is basic. As expressed in 20 programming clinical gadget guidelines, the level of guideline required is evaluated against the gadget's gamble classification, which is an element of the meaning of the data it gives on the medical care condition and the medical services condition itself. A computer-based intelligence programming that illuminates store network the executives for inoculation, in this manner, need not be dependent upon the very level of examination as a gadget that analyzes pathology affirming the presence of a dangerous cancer [50].

9.17.2 Logic Precision Compromise Profound

Learning is at the front of AI for medical care arrangements. Its exactness permits it to perform better compared to conventional AI strategies and makes it particularly valuable [51] in clinically high-stakes settings. This was found on account of Mount Sinai's "Profound Patient" in 2015. Applying unaided profound component figuring out how to EHRs of around 700,000 patients, considerably further developed the expectation execution for serious diabetes, schizophrenia, and different types of diseases [52]:

- instructions to make models that are more straightforward to make sense of;
- instructions to foster clarification interfaces; and
- the most effective method to fathom the mental circumstances important for enticing clarifications [53].

9.18 Consolidating Computer-Based Intelligence in Medical Services Conveyance

9.18.1 Clinical Considerations

The logical positions of modernized thinking procedures in clinical consideration movement and clinical assessment are ending up being continuously apparent. Studies have included the feasibility and capacity of PC-based insight engaged prosperity applications. These mechanical movements are right now being enhanced by immense premium in the utilization of automated thinking in clinical consideration by states and development associations, and the US Food and Medicine Association is successfully connected with the introduction of man-made brainpower-engaged clinical contraptions into the market. In our perspective, four locales where computerized reasoning enabled clinical consideration transport is likely going to have the most impact are clinical benefits association, clinical decision help, patient checking, and clinical benefits intercessions.

9.18.2 Healthcare Administration

The administration of medical services conveyance has become progressively perplexing, with medical care frameworks in numerous nations confronting development past their ability because of authoritative tensions and asset requirements. Data innovation instruments have been exhibited to lighten this weight on medical care administrations, with computerized reasoning and information mining strategies distinguished as among the most encouraging ways to deal with help medical service organizations by improving clinical consideration and diminishing regulatory requests on clinicians [56]. Via mechanizing redundant errands, for example, patient information section and computerized survey of lab information and imaging results, man-made brainpower can save time for clinicians to give direct consideration to patients [57]. Coordinating computer-based intelligence calculations with electronic wellbeing records can help clinicians and managers in recovering exact and setting important patient data [58]. By utilizing simulated intelligence and idea-based data recovery frameworks, search precision and recovery speed can be improved.

9.18.3 Clinical Decision Support

Clinical choice emotionally supportive networks are PC programs that influence clinical information and data to help choices made by medical care experts [59]. These frameworks can assist with decreasing clinical mistakes and increment medical services consistency and productivity, and endeavors to integrate clinical choice emotionally supportive networks into routine practice are expanding [58]. Man-made intelligence procedures have been utilized in clinical choice emotionally supportive network research since the mid-1970s, as found in master frameworks. AI calculations are currently being utilized to anticipate the advancement of septic shock and aid the conclusion and therapy of patients with persistent obstructive aspiratory sickness and different other expert choices [59]. They additionally can possibly customize treatment choices for patients by drawing for enormous scope information about previous cases that would some way or another have been hard to use in clinical direction.

9.18.4 Patient Monitoring

Clinical choice emotionally supportive networks are PC programs that influence clinical information and data to help choices made by medical care experts [59]. These frameworks can assist with diminishing clinical mistakes and increment medical services consistency and effectiveness, and endeavors to integrate clinical choice emotionally supportive networks into routine practice are expanding [58]. AI strategies have been utilized in clinical choice emotionally supportive network research since the mid-1970s, as found in master frameworks. Artificial intelligence calculations are presently being utilized to foresee the improvement of septic shock and aid the determination and therapy of patients with persistent obstructive aspiratory sickness and different other expert choices [59]. They likewise can possibly customize treatment choices for patients by drawing for huge scope information about previous cases that would some way or another have been hard to use in clinical direction [60].

9.18.5 Healthcare Interventions

The advancement of AI reasoning has empowered medical care mediations to be customized for people or subgroups of populaces [62]. AI programs coordinated with electronic wellbeing records can break down biometric and other clinical information of individual patients and suggest treatment plans in light of current clinical rules [54, 55]. AI programs connected to clinic servers and equipped for examining recorded patient information and introducing patient questions can diminish holding up times in packed crisis offices [61]. AI programs in view of fluffy rationale, a type of multi-esteemed rationale, can be utilized to control drug. For instance, fluffy regulators have been utilized to direct vasodilators for postoperative patients [63].

Figure 9.2 demonstrates various networks of AI, each tailored to specific tasks. Convolutional neural networks (CNNs) to recurrent neural networks (RNNs) for image processing for sequential data analysis: These diverse structural designs showcase AI's versatility in solving complex problems across different domains. Each network's unique design and functionality contribute to the advancement of AI-driven solutions depicted in the illustration below.

9.19 Functional Ramifications of XAI in Medical Services Reasonable [62]

Artificial intelligence consciousness (XAI) has acquired expanding consideration in the medical services space because of its capability to work on persistent results and improve clinical navigation. In this segment, we talk about the down to earth ramifications of utilizing XAI strategies in

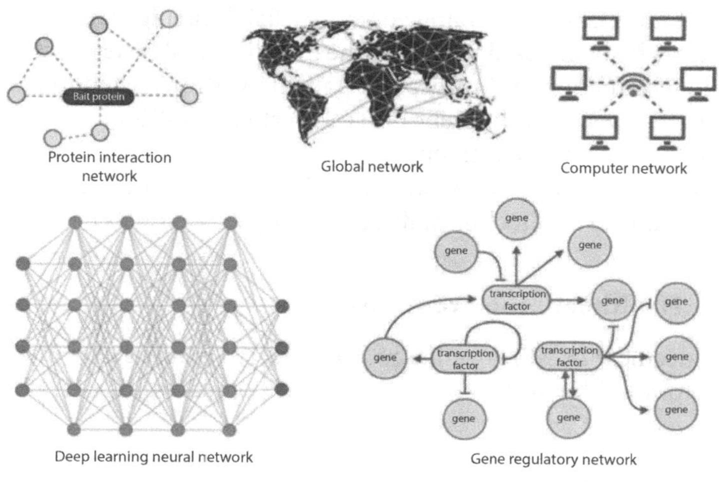

Figure 9.2 Different network of artificial intelligence.

medical services settings, featuring what its execution has decidedly meant for clinical practices, quotes for work flow furthermore, specialized difficulties looked by suppliers and patients as depicted in Table 19.2.

Table 9.2 The main topics, supporting themes, and illustrative quotes that best capture the technological challenges and process complexities faced by patients and healthcare professionals [65–67].

Domains	Illustrative quote
Integration of auxiliary staff (interpreters, nutritionists, communal worker, etc.) was challenging	"The social specialist visits the center on more than one occasion per week and works from home on different days. In a perfect world, I favor the social specialist to be available in the center because of the broad requirements of our patients. It is quite difficult while attempting to get to them during telehealth arrangements."
Challenges for patients with restricted admittance to wide band and phone administrations	"We actually do sound just visits since that has been broadened. So there are a few patients who regardless of the amount we attempt they are simply not going to have the option to do the video, they do not have the web. Band width is an immense issue for patients. They do not have information or advanced mobile phones at times."
Telehealth undermined group based care and correspondence between colleagues	"There is no linkage of the group to the real cooperation. We have no colleagues on the call or cannot get to colleagues. The development from the calls is not quite as great as it very well may be. What we need to do in follow up is send notes to our practices and aides, or request that our patients themselves call the training, to set up whatever should be finished and follow up. It is not as coordinated in to our training as genuine visits have been."
Technological challenges consumed more time	"We likewise do not have cameras in that frame of mind in the workplace. For me, it is an additional move toward have someone arrangement a camera."

9.19.1 Worked on Quiet Results and Informed Navigation

One of the critical common-sense ramifications of XAI in medical care is its capacity to work on persistent results by giving straightforward bits of knowledge into the dynamic course of simulated intelligence models. XAI methods, like LIME, SHAP, and Graduate CAM, have empowered medical services experts to acquire a more profound comprehension of the elements adding to display forecasts. This interpretability enables clinicians to go with additional educated and sure choices, prompting precise determinations, advanced treatment plans, and better understanding consideration [63].

9.19.2 Predisposition Discovery and Moderation

One more useful ramifications of XAI in medical services is its part in recognizing possible predispositions in AI models. By uncovering predispositions in the information and model results, XAI permits medical care frameworks to resolve issues connected with decency and value. This guarantees that AI fueled medical services intercessions are more comprehensive and give impartial therapy to every patient gathering. Customized Medication and Custom-made Treatment Plans: XAI has worked with the reception of customized medication in medical services. Concluding the straightforward and interpretable flora of AI replicas, XAI empowers medical care experts to fit therapy plans to individual patients in view of their extraordinary clinical history and attributes [63].

9.19.3 Decreased Clinical Blunders and Early Infection Location

Reported cases and observational proof from different medical care establishments demonstrate execution of XAI has added to diminishing clinical mistakes and recognition sicknesses. The interpretability of computer-based intelligence permits medical care suppliers to get possible mistakes and distinguish peculiarities in clinical information, prompting convenient mediations and better understanding results [52].

9.19.4 Contextual Analyses and Experimental Proof

An abundance of contextual investigations and observational proof exists, exhibiting the viable effect of XAI in medical care. These recorded cases grandstand occurrences where the execution of XAI has fundamentally further developed clinical direction, analytic precision, and patient consideration [52]. The sensible repercussions of XAI in clinical consideration are broad huge potential for changing clinical practices. Straightforwardness and interpretability of man-made consciousness models given by techniques have chipped away at figuring out results of XAI, worked with weak drugs, and diminished clinical botches [64].

9.20 Available XAI Besides the Costs of Logic

While the advantages of making computer-based intelligence calculations reasonable remember higher trust for and responsibility of the innovation item, logic itself is not innate to the plan of computer-based intelligence based innovation. The need to produce a clarification for a result will in general increment with the outcome of the result, making what is known as a sliding size of reasonableness, addressing its compromise with the exactness of the calculation. However, it very well may be contended that regardless of the transient costs forced on trend-setters, XAI has long haul legitimate advantages that may be judicious for medical care pioneers to put resources into [67, 68].

Costs like plan costs (unequivocally planning a clarification capability in the calculation, which takes care of the relevant requirement for clarification and cannot be normalized) and the production of review logs (putting away algorithmic choices for a predetermined period after they are made to give nearby clarifications on choices made) could straightforwardly dissuade pioneers from putting resources into reasonableness. Besides, opportunity costs as lower exactness and infringement of proprietary innovations make reasonableness a less open choice for trend-setters. Uncovering exclusive calculations and their internal functions to shoppers and controllers can prompt a deficiency of the upper hand trailblazers have invested impressive energy and assets to accomplish. This could accomplish little in light of the fact that unadulterated reasonableness of the internal activities of simulated intelligence does not guarantee understandability by the normal patient. In such a situation, reasonableness just attempts to raise dependability (in medical service offices and experts) and straightforwardness (for certificate and watchfulness organizations) [65].

9.21 Conversation

Going over enigmatic black box models is a significant challenge, and controlling model complexity can play a critical role in achieving greater precision in estimations in the field of computerized reasoning. This offers a fundamental scenario that might have profound effects on the viability of the framework, even if it may not have truly tended to. Being clear-cut is essential to building the model's legitimacy, especially when applying it to fundamental domains like security, money, or medical care. Profound learning is gaining attention because of its exceptional accuracy, which is attributed to its preparation with enormous datasets.

Whatever the case, the lack of transparency about the model's output or the dynamic cycle makes it a "black box" model.

A transition toward "reasonable man-made consciousness" (XAI) is occurring in an effort to better understand the model's cycles and outcomes.

The review's findings reveal that XAI's impact varies depending on the application. Additionally, we have included a diagram based on applications that illustrate various systems utilized for analysis and methods for creating the XAI characterization. These systems cover concepts related to value, methodology, the foundation of XAI, logical simulated intelligence standards, informative features, and obstacles. To acquire model understandings across changing outcome designs, many methodologies have been used (numerical, rule-based, text-based, visual, and blended). Processes have been chosen based on the statement of the problem, and the concept of the explanation may change depending on how far the model is extended. Logical phases help structure how both post-hoc and hoc strategies are developed and applied, with post-hoc strategies focusing on retrospective analysis and hoc strategies dealing with immediate, often unplanned actions. These phases ensure that each approach is methodical and thorough, whether it's looking back at past events or responding to current challenges. The significance values for each component are meticulously analyzed and clearly presented to highlight how each individual aspect contributes to and impacts the overall expectation. This thorough processing ensures that the influence of each component on the expected outcome is well understood, enabling more informed decisions and interpretations. Rationalist neighborhood interpretable model explanations provide amazing insights. In addition to being less complicated, inclination weighted class initiation planning generates a visual explanation. Layer-wise pertinence proliferation describes the significance score and generates a heatmap. A fluffy classifier is used when standards are met. Fractional reliance plots perfectly demonstrate the correlation between an ingredient and a purpose.

9.22 Conclusion

With the help of large funding from the public and private sectors, AI research is taking shape. This points to a future in which AI will be extensively incorporated into healthcare services, offering huge cost reductions and quality improvements. However, there are still questions about the course and mode of action of this shift. It becomes essential to address "soft" concerns including equitable and transparent data access, managing medico-legal duties, and ensuring fair benefit sharing in addition to guaranteeing rigorous engineering procedures and evidential requirements prior to implementation. Governmental investments in AI research and use in the healthcare industry need to be balanced with cautious caution and careful planning in order to maximise potential benefits.

The demand for transparency in new technologies like AI, particularly in healthcare, can be approached in two ways: demonstrating that its accuracy is equal to or better than that of a clinician (focusing on AI's result accuracy) or showing that its bias stems from biased input rather than its process itself (thus focusing on how it can be rectified). Transparent AI, or AI that is sufficiently transparent to be able to explain its outcomes, is one approach to addressing the need for transparency but poses complex challenges for those seeking to create conditions for its success.

References

1. Saranya, A. and Subhashini, R., A systematic review of Explainable Artificial Intelligence models and applications: Recent developments and future trends. *Decis. Anal. J.*, 100230, 2023 Apr 17.
2. WHO A, Health telematics policy in support of WHO's Health-For-All strategy for global health development. Report of the WHO group consultation on health telematics, pp. 11–6, 1997 Dec 11.
3. Bitar, H. and Alismail, S., The role of eHealth, telehealth, and telemedicine for chronic disease patients during COVID-19 pandemic: A rapid systematic review. *Digit. Health*, 7, 20552076211009396, 2021 Apr.
4. Roy, K., Khandelwal, V., Goswami, R., Dolbir, N., Malekar, J., Sheth, A., Demo alleviate: Demonstrating artificial intelligence enabled virtual assistance for telehealth: The mental health case, in: *Proceedings of the AAAI Conference on Artificial Intelligence*, vol. 37, no. 13, pp. 16479–16481, 2023 Sep 6,.
5. Topol, E.J., High-performance medicine: the convergence of human and artificial intelligence. *Nat. Med.*, 25, 1, 44–56, 2019 Jan.

6. Faes, L., Liu, X., Wagner, S.K., Fu, D.J., Balaskas, K., Sim, D.A., Bachmann, L.M., Keane, P.A., Denniston, A.K., A clinician's guide to artificial intelligence: how to critically appraise machine learning studies. *Transl. Vision Sci. Technol.*, 9, 2, 7–7, 2020 Jan 28.
7. Pacis, D.M., Subido, E.D., Bugtai, N.T., Trends in telemedicine utilizing artificial intelligence. *AIP Conf. Proc.*, 1933, 1, 2018 Feb 13.
8. Kazancigil, M.A., Big medical data, cloud computing, and artificial intelligence for improving diagnosis in healthcare, in: *Big Data Analytics for Healthcare*, pp. 139–150, Academic Press, Cambridge, Massachusetts, 2022 Jan 1.
9. Reddy, S., Fox, J., Purohit, M.P., Artificial intelligence-enabled healthcare delivery. *J. R. Soc. Med.*, 112, 1, 22–8, 2019 Jan.
10. Holmes, J., Sacchi, L., Bellazzi, R., Artificial intelligence in medicine. *Ann. R. Coll. Surg. Engl.*, 86, 334–8, 2004, DOI: 10.1016/j.artmed.2017.06.011.
11. Kiser, C.R. and Harrison, E.B., Bridging the American Health Care and Digital Divide: Broadband Deployment, Artificial Intelligence, and Telehealth Services, 2018.
12. Pisipati, S.C. and Midelf, S.L., Managing Responsibility & AI in Healthcare, 2022.
13. Tirrell, M., FDA moves to encourage AI in medicine, drug development, CNBC News, 2018.
14. Rapport, F., Francis-Auton, E., Cartmill, J., Ryder, T., Braithwaite, J., Clay-Williams, R., A mobile methods pilot study of surgical spaces:'f it for purpose? Organisational productivity and workforce wellbeing in work spaces in hospital'(FLOURISH). *BMC Health Serv. Res.*, 20, 1–5, 2020 Dec.
15. Wells, J., Canadian Health System, like UK,"Stretched To Max Capacity", American Council on Science and Health, 2017.
16. Snyder, C.F., Wu, A.W., Miller, R.S., Jensen, R.E., Bantug, E.T., Wolff, A.C., The role of informatics in promoting patient-centered care. *Cancer J.*, 17, 4, 211–8, 2011 Jul 1.
17. Salunkhe, S.S., Jacob, V., Tandon, A., Jeevitha, S., Arora, R.K., Laddha, S., Portable healthcare computing and clinical decision support system enabled by artificial intelligence. *Int. J. Eng. Syst. Modell. Simul.*, 13, 3, 228–33, 2022.
18. Leung, R., Using AI–ML to augment the capabilities of social media for telehealth and remote patient monitoring. *Healthcare*, 11, 12, 1704, MDPI, 2023 Jun 10.
19. Anakal, S. and Sandhya, P., Clinical decision support system for chronic obstructive pulmonary disease using machine learning techniques, in: *2017 International Conference on Electrical, Electronics, Communication, Computer, and Optimization Techniques (ICEECCOT)*, IEEE, pp. 1–5, 2017 Dec 15.
20. Yousefi, M., Yousefi, M., Ferreira, R.P., Kim, J.H., Fogliatto, F.S., Chaotic genetic algorithm and Adaboost ensemble metamodeling approach for

optimum resource planning in emergency departments. *Artif. Intell. Med.*, 84, 23–33, 2018 Jan 1.
21. Doshi-Velez, F., Kortz, M., Budish, R., Bavitz, C., Gershman, S., O'Brien, D., Scott, K., Schieber, S., Waldo, J., Weinberger, D., Weller, A., Accountability of AI under the law: The role of explanation, arXiv preprint arXiv:1711.01134, 2017 Nov 3.
22. OECD, Recommendation of the council on artificial intelligence, OECD Legal Instruments, 2019.
23. Sharma, Y., Verma, A., Rao, K., Eluri, V., 'reasonable explainsability' for regulating ai in health. ORF Issue Brief, vol. 401, pp. 1–6, 2020 Sep 21.
24. Sharma, S., Rawal, R., Shah, D., Addressing the challenges of AI-based telemedicine: Best practices and lessons learned. *J. Educ. Health Promot.*, 1, 1, 338, 2023 Sep.
25. Ting, D.S., Deshmukh, R., Ting, D.S., Ang, M., Big data in corneal diseases and cataract: Current applications and future directions. *Front. Big Data*, 6, 1017420, 2023 Feb 1.
26. Han, M. and Kim, J., Joint banknote recognition and counterfeit detection using explainable artificial intelligence. *Sensors*, 19, 16, 3607, 2019 Aug 19.
27. Nor, A.K., Pedapati, S.R., Muhammad, M., Leiva, V., Overview of explainable artificial intelligence for prognostic and health management of industrial assets based on preferred reporting items for systematic reviews and meta-analyses. *Sensors*, 21, 23, 8020, 2021 Dec 1.
28. Loh, H.W., Ooi, C.P., Seoni, S., Barua, P.D., Molinari, F., Acharya, U.R., Application of explainable artificial intelligence for healthcare: A systematic review of the last decade (2011–2022). *Comput. Methods Programs Biomed.*, 226, 107161, 2022 Nov 1.
29. Zhang, Y., Weng, Y., Lund, J., Applications of explainable artificial intelligence in diagnosis and surgery. *Diagnostics*, 12, 2, 237, 2022 Jan 19.
30. Keneni, B.M., Kaur, D., Al Bataineh, A., Devabhaktuni, V.K., Javaid, A.Y., Zaientz, J.D., Marinier, R.P., Evolving rule-based explainable artificial intelligence for unmanned aerial vehicles. *IEEE Access*, 7, 17001–16, 2019 Jan 15.
31. Bahani, K., Moujabbir, M., Ramdani, M., An accurate fuzzy rule-based classification systems for heart disease diagnosis. *Sci. Afr.*, 14, e01019, 2021 Nov 1.
32. Linardatos, P., Papastefanopoulos, V., Kotsiantis, S., Explainable ai: A review of machine learning interpretability methods. *Entropy*, 23, 1, 18, 2020 Dec 25.
33. Ayyar, M.P., Benois-Pineau, J., Zemmari, A., Review of white box methods for explanations of convolutional neural networks in image classification tasks. *J. Electron. Imaging*, 30, 5, 050901, 2021 Sep 1.
34. Burkart, N. and Huber, M.F., A survey on the explainability of supervised machine learning. *J. Artif. Intell. Res.*, 70, 245–317, 2021 Jan 19.
35. Zafar, M.R. and Khan, N.M., DLIME: A deterministic local interpretable model-agnostic explanations approach for computer-aided diagnosis systems, arXiv preprint arXiv:1906.10263, 2019 Jun 24.

36. Sahakyan, M., Aung, Z., Rahwan, T., Explainable artificial intelligence for tabular data: A survey. *IEEE Access*, 9, 135392–422, 2021 Sep 29.
37. Nazar, M., Alam, M.M., Yafi, E., Su'ud, M.M., A systematic review of human–computer interaction and explainable artificial intelligence in healthcare with artificial intelligence techniques. *IEEE Access*, 9, 153316–48, 2021 Nov 12.
38. Guidotti, R., Monreale, A., Ruggieri, S., Turini, F., Giannotti, F., Pedreschi, D., A survey of methods for explaining black box models. *ACM Comput. Surv. (CSUR)*, 51, 5, 1–42, 2018 Aug 22.
39. Van den Broeck, G., Lykov, A., Schleich, M., Suciu, D., On the tractability of SHAP explanations. *J. Artif. Intell. Res.*, 74, 851–86, 2022 Jun 23.
40. Ponn, T., Kröger, T., Diermeyer, F., Identification and explanation of challenging conditions for camera-based object detection of automated vehicles. *Sensors*, 20, 13, 3699, 2020 Jul 1.
41. Lombardi, A., Diacono, D., Amoroso, N., Monaco, A., Tavares, J.M., Bellotti, R., Tangaro, S., Explainable deep learning for personalized age prediction with brain morphology. *Front. Neurosci.*, 15, 674055, 2021 May 28.
42. Utkin, L. and Konstantinov, A., Ensembles of random SHAPs. *Algorithms*, 15, 11, 431, 2022 Nov 17.
43. Lombardi, A., Diacono, D., Amoroso, N., Biecek, P., Monaco, A., Bellantuono, L., Pantaleo, E., Logroscino, G., De Blasi, R., Tangaro, S., Bellotti, R., A robust framework to investigate the reliability and stability of explainable artificial intelligence markers of Mild Cognitive Impairment and Alzheimer's Disease. *Brain Inf.*, 9, 1, 17, 2022 Dec.
44. Rony, M.K., Parvin, M.R., Ferdousi, S., Advancing nursing practice with artificial intelligence: Enhancing preparedness for the future. *Nurs. Open*, 11, 1–9, 1, 2024 Jan.
45. Mittelstadt, B.D., Allo, P., Taddeo, M., Wachter, S., Floridi, L., The ethics of algorithms: Mapping the debate. *Big Data Soc.*, 3, 2, 2053951716679679, 2016 Nov.
46. Vayena, E., Blasimme, A., Cohen, I.G., Machine learning in medicine: addressing ethical challenges. *PLoS Med.*, 15, 11, e1002689, 2018 Nov 6.
47. Yu, K.H. and Kohane, I.S., Framing the challenges of artificial intelligence in medicine. *BMJ Qual. Saf.*, 28, 3, 238–41, 2019 Mar 1.
48. Higginbottom, K., The pros and cons of algorithms in recruitment. Forbes, October, vol. 10, 2018.
49. Tsymbal, A., The problem of concept drift: definitions and related work, vol. 106(2), Computer Science Department, Trinity College Dublin, p. 58, 2004 Apr 29.
50. Beaudouin, V., Bloch, I., Bounie, D., Clémençon, S., d'Alché-Buc, F., Eagan, J., Maxwell, W., Mozharovskyi, P., Parekh, J., Flexible and context-specific AI explainability: a multidisciplinary approach, arXiv preprint arXiv:2003.07703, 2020 Mar 13.

51. O'Mahony, N., Campbell, S., Carvalho, A., Harapanahalli, S., Hernandez, G.V., Krpalkova, L., Riordan, D., Walsh, J., Deep learning vs. traditional computer vision, in: *Advances in Computer Vision: Proceedings of the 2019 Computer Vision Conference (CVC)*, vol. 11, pp. 128–144, Springer International Publishing, Midtown Manhattan, New York City, 2020.
52. Miotto, R., Li, L., Kidd, B.A., Dudley, J.T., Deep patient: an unsupervised representation to predict the future of patients from the electronic health records. *Sci. Rep.*, 6, 1, 1–0, 2016 May 17.
53. Gunning, D. and Aha, D., DARPA's explainable artificial intelligence (XAI) program. *AI Mag.*, 40, 2, 44–58, 2019 Jun 24.
54. Fosch-Villaronga, E. and Drukarch, H., *AI for healthcare robotics*, CRC Press, Boca Raton, Florida, 2022 Jun 7.
55. Ramesh, A.N., Kambhampati, C., Monson, J.R.T., Drew, P.J., Artificial intelligence in medicine. *Ann. R. Coll. Surg. Engl.*, 86, 334–338, 2004.
56. Seroussi, B. and Zablit, I., Implementation of Digital Health Ethics: A First Step with the Adoption of 16 European Ethical Principles for Digital Health, in: *MEDINFO 2023—The Future Is Accessible*, pp. 1588–1592, IOS Press, Amsterdam, 2024.
57. Derrington, D., Artificial intelligence for health and health care, Available from: https://www.healthit.gov/sites/default/files/jsr-17-task-002_aiforhealthandhealthcare12122017.pdf, [Accessed 8 November 2018].
58. Saria, S., A $3 trillion challenge to computational scientists: Transforming healthcare delivery. *IEEE Intell. Syst.*, 29, 4, 82–7, 2014 Sep 24.
59. Musen, M.A., *Biomedical Informatics*, pp. 698–736, Springer, New York, 2006, Available from: http://link.springer.com/10.1007/0-387-36278-9, [Accessed 8 November 2018].
60. Silva, S.N. and Karunaratne, M.D., Patient Satisfaction on Telehealth Services Used in Urban Sri Lankan Settings, During the COVID-19 Pandemic. *Stud. Health Technol. Inf.*, 310, 1586–7, 2024 Mar 1.
61. Skevas, C., de Olaguer, N.P., Lleó, A., Thiwa, D., Schroeter, U., Lopes, I.V., Mautone, L., Linke, S.J., Spitzer, M.S., Yap, D., Xiao, D., Implementing and evaluating a fully functional AI-enabled model for chronic eye disease screening in a real clinical environment. *BMC Ophthalmol.*, 24, 1, 51, 2024 Feb 1.
62. Verri, F.M., Dallmeier, D., Kumlehn, B., Swoboda, W., Denkinger, M., The need for a multidimensional assessment in frail patients. *Dtsch. Med. Wochenschr. (1946)*, 149, 1-02, 23–9, 2023 Dec 29.
63. Wang, C., Ba, Y., Ni, J., Huang, R., Du, X., Role of Telemedicine Intervention in the Treatment of Patients with Chronic Heart Failure: A Systematic Review and Meta-analysis. *Anatol. J. Cardiol.*, 1–14, 2024 Mar 1.
64. Ali, S., Akhlaq, F., Imran, A.S., Kastrati, Z., Daudpota, S.M., Moosa, M., The enlightening role of explainable artificial intelligence in medical & healthcare domains: A systematic literature review. *Comput. Biol. Med.*, 4, 107555, 2023 Oct.

65. Maggio, M.G., Baglio, F., Arcuri, F., Borgnis, F., Contrada, M., Diaz, M.D., Leochico, C.F., Neira, N.J., Laratta, S., Tonin, P., Calabrò, R.S., Cognitive telerehabilitation: an expert consensus paper on current evidence and future perspective. *Front. Neurol.*, 15, 1338873, 1–10, 2024 Feb 15, DOI: 10.3389/fneur.2024.1338873.
66. Yakubu, A.O., Nwachukwu, C., Morakinyo, O., Amuta, A.C., Olajide, T.N., Yakubu, W., Fagbemi, A., Ogunjimi, L., Yakubu, A., OLAJIDE, T.N., Survey of Teleneurology Use by Neurologists in a Low-Middle Income Country. *Cureus*, 16, 2, 2024 Feb 1.
67. Reilly, K. and Ebersole, A., Confidentiality and privacy considerations for adolescents receiving contraceptive health services via telemedicine: A narrative review. *Women's Health*, 20, 1–11, 17455057241233126, 2024 Mar., DOI: 10.1177/17455057241233126.
68. Olowoyo, K.S., Esan, D.T., Adeyanju, B.T., Olawade, D.B., Oyinloye, B.E., Olowoyo, P., Telemedicine as a tool to prevent multi-drug resistant tuberculosis in poor resource settings: Lessons from Nigeria. *J. Clin. Tuberc. Other Mycobact. Dis.*, 35, 100423, 2024 Feb 24, DOI:10.1016/j.jctube.2024.100423.

10

Intelligent Algorithm for Seizure Alignment Using EEG Clustering with Special Reference to Discrete Wavelet Transform Theory

Pankaj Kalita[1*], Arup Sarmah[2], Chayanika Devi[3], Partha Pratim Kalita[4] and Arnabjyoti Deva Sarma[5]

[1]*Department of Zoology, Eastern Karbi Anglong College, Sarihajan, Karbi Anglong, Assam, India*

[2]*Department of Computer Science, Pub Kamrup College, Baihata Chariali, Kamrup, Assam, India*

[3]*Department of Zoology, Pub Kamrup College, Baihata Chariali, Kamrup, Assam, India*

[4]*Program of Biotechnology, Faculty of Science, Assam Down Town University, Panikhaiti, Guwahati, Assam, India*

[5]*Program of Radiology, Faculty of Paramedical Sciences, Assam Down Town University, Panikhaiti, Guwahati, Assam, India*

Abstract

Seizure is a neurological disorder that is diagnosed by observing the electroencephalogram (EEG) signal of a patient. Electroencephalogram signifies the brain–computer interface of the neuroscience study. Abnormality in EEG indicates the abnormal brain activity. Conventionally, EEG classification was done by visual analysis in analog dataset. Advanced computational and machine learning approach reflects the EEG data in digital form, resulting in accurate diagnosis and pathophysiology of EEG patterns. Discrete wavelet transform (DWT) is a widely implemented approach among different wavelet family for EEG clustering and its feature extraction approach for its efficient and effective pathophysiological study of EEG. In the present article, different wavelet transform algorithm has been documented, which are useful for clustering of EEG signal for classification of seizure

**Corresponding author*: kalita.pankaj9@gmail.com; ORCID: 0000-0003-2681-9594

Rishabha Malviya and Sonali Sundram (eds.) Explainable and Responsible Artificial Intelligence in Healthcare, (251–276) © 2025 Scrivener Publishing LLC

in different types. The authors also forward a reliable and automated system using DWT algorithm for fast and accurate diagnosis of seizures through quantitative analysis of EEG signals as a model for seizure classification. The proposed model involves pre-processing of EEG data, which eliminates noise followed by feature extraction using DWT and classification employing an artificial neural network tool box in MATLAB R2008a version. Kaiser window–based low-pass filter was used for reducing noise in the EEG signals. A two-fold cross-validation technique was employed for performance of the assessment of the classification system, yielding an accuracy of 98.33% on the testing dataset. The present approach explores the potentiality in enhancing seizure prediction and diagnosis through effective analysis of EEG data.

***Keywords*:** Seizure pathophysiology, electroencephalogram, wavelet transform algorithm, neural network toolbox, MATLAB

10.1 Introduction

Seizure is characterized by the abnormality in the brain activity. The effect of seizure can vary from tonic-clonic seizure to absence seizure. Repeated seizure caused by electrical firing of different brain cells collectively resulting epilepsy [1]. Seizure is characterized by different behavioral and cognitive changes like myoclonic seizure, forebrain seizures, grand mal seizure, and barrel rotations [2]. Electroencephalogram (EEG) is an important technique to monitor the epileptic patients' brain activity and hence to diagnose epilepsy. Analyzing EEG recordings manually to detect epileptic activity is a time-consuming and tiresome job. But a timely and precise diagnosis of epilepsy is crucialfor antiepileptic drug therapy initiation [2]. Quantitative analysis (QA) of EEG provides reliableinformation to the healthcare professionals for fast, accurate, and easy diagnosisof neural diseases [3]. QA evaluates the pattern mediated signals to its finer details encouraging the large scale data analysis in diagnosis research in contrary to manual inferences (MIs) of signals that require visual expertise of trained personnel, resulting in an extremely burdensome effort and also subjective to errors [4]. Thus, QA provides a more viable and effective automatic supportive system over MI and thus, becoming a viable [5].

Structurally, brain is divided into cerebrum (the largest part), cerebellum (second largest part), and brainstem (connecting the spinal cord and the cerebrum). EEG provides functional reflection of electrical scenario of the brain. Thus, EEG is an extensively used technique for studying the brain functions and, therefore, helps in diagnosing different the neurological disorders including epilepsy. Some other problems like abnormalities, behavioral disturbances, attention disorders, and learning problems can also be suggested for treatment. This is a revolutionary idea of Hans Barger in 1929, helped to create a new branch of medical science.

Different QA approaches that define different feature extraction strategies from EEG data have been reported recently, and the results motivate the quest of better algorithms. A time-frequency–based method for detecting seizures was created by Hassanpour *et al.* [6]. Singular value decomposition is used to characterize seizure and normal patterns of EEG using artificial neural network (ANN). The author of another study [7] created a flexible method based on DWT (discrete wavelet transform) in which compact patterns and feature space extracted from DWT space are fed to support vector machines (SVMs) for analysis of the pathological EEG. A linear programming boosting (LPBoost) approach has been employed by Hassan *et al.* [8]. Initially, the EEG is broken down and categorized using ensembled empirical mode of decomposition followed by spectral moment calculation. The authors also report various QA methods, bootstrap collecting in tunable-Q factor wavelet transform [9]. Orhan *et al.* introduced a multilayer perceptron neural network using DWT sub-band coefficients for epilepsy diagnosis [10]. Here, coefficients are clustered using K-means algorithm and then computed probability distributions for pattern classification. Canonical correlation analysis and neural network were used together by Soomro *et al.* [11] to predict epileptic seizures. Power spectral density of DWT was employed by Kiymik *et al.* [12] as an ANN input that produces the distinct alert, drowsy, and sleep output. As stated previously, this technique works well, but it has certain drawbacks. As suggested, physical intervention is typically necessary while employing the DWT function for the first time [13]. Different workers have proposed different models of EEG clustering in different phase of time [23–31]. DWT decomposes different EEG patterns into different bands or scales depending on its frequency.

10.2 Different Intelligent/Computational Approaches for Seizure Classification

Seizure classification is an essential task within epilepsy diagnosis and management, playing a crucial role in determining the treatment course and eventual patient outcome. Categorized correctly, seizures help to understand underlying neurological backgrounds and help clinicians formulate pertinent therapeutic interventions. In the last several years, the fusion of intelligent and computational methodologies has become a key aspect of seizure classification, transcending traditional diagnostic principles. Advances in intelligent and, particularly, computational approaches have introduced a new era in seizure classification, helping to develop novel methods that work beyond traditional diagnostic paradigms. In a recent systematic review, the authors borrowed advanced concepts in machine learning (ML), signal processing, and artificial intelligence to measure and prepare pertinent data associated with EEG and seizure data [32–35].

Medical research technology has ushered in a bold new age of precision medicine, sparking new strides in automation, efficiency, and classification precision. The seizure classification creates a dynamic front that shifts sharply from the classical to the avant-garde due to breakthroughs and interdisciplinary coordination. The research contributes to the quest by exploring the outrageous types of intelligent and computational methods that have been deployed in classification in the past, explaining their processes, applications, and shortcomings, as well as the future path. By dissecting these procedures, we hope to uncover the nuanced interplay between technology and neuroscience, which holds the promise of establishing game-changing protocols for epilepsy. Many computational techniques, such as ensemble methods, transfer learning, ML algorithms, CNNs, RNNs, and hybrid approaches, can be used to categorize seizures. Here, we go over a few of the several creative and sophisticated methods for classifying seizures [36–38].

10.2.1 Machine Learning Techniques

This chapter explained how ML has advanced seizure classification, proving to be a fast and accurate method of epilepsy diagnosis and management. Based on the presented information, this paper provided several ML algorithms, feature extraction methods, and challenges of utilizing ML in seizure categorization. Seizure-type variety billing ML-based seizure classification is beneficial, as it allows one to learn patterns from labeled EEG data with extracted excellent features. By using ML-based seizure categorization, it is possible to scale the system according to data, adapt to new circumstances, and analyze data in real time [34].

10.2.1.1 Support Vector Machines (SVM)

SVM is a popular ML method for seizure classification. The popular supervised method finds the hyperplane that separates the optimal margin between the data points, placing them into two different classes. SVM has been applied to EEG data with a high degree of accuracy, imitating results by using suitable feature sets [37].

10.2.1.2 Random Forests

Random forests have been useful in all areas of ML. Specifically, ensemble learning techniques train multiple distinct decisions and combine them to increase prediction accuracy. In seizure classification, random forests outperform other methods by performing best on multi-dimensional data and finding connections between EEG features and seizure types [42].

10.2.1.3 Neural Networks

RNNs and CNNs have revolutionized this field by exposing the wide generality of deep learning models. While RNNs identify temporal relationships and CNNs extract spatial characteristics from EEG data, together they allow for a reliable and accurate classification of seizures [35].

10.2.2 Feature Extraction Methods

The study of EEG signals is mostly dependent on feature extraction techniques, which enable the extraction of relevant data for brain–computer interfaces (BCIs) and clinical diagnoses. These techniques offer important insights into the dynamics and operation of the brain by describing the temporal, spectral, and nonlinear characteristics of EEG data. Developing reliable and effective EEG-based analysis and classification algorithms requires addressing issues such as feature selection, artifact removal, and inter-subject variability [39]. Numerous analysis methods are employed in order to extract discriminative features, including the following.

10.2.2.1 Statistical Features

When describing EEG signals, statistical metrics including mean, variance, skewness, and kurtosis are frequently employed [39].

10.2.2.2 Frequency-Based Features

Information about the frequency distribution of EEG signals can be gleaned from power spectral density, spectral entropy, and peak frequencies [39].

10.2.2.3 Wavelet Distortion

Wavelet coefficients are useful features for classifying seizures because they record both frequency and temporal information [39].

10.2.2.4 Nonlinear Features

Metrics like approximation entropy, fractal dimension, and Lyapunov exponent can be used to quantify the nonlinear dynamics of EEG data [39].

10.2.3 Convolutional Neural Networks (CNNs)

CNNs have emerged as powerful tools for EEG signal analysis, offering automatic feature learning, improved accuracy, and real-time capabilities. Overcoming challenges such as interpretability and data scarcity will pave the way for further advancements, unlocking the full potential of CNNs in neuroscience research and clinical applications [35].

The fundamental architecture of CNN comprises convolutional layers, pooling layers, and fully connected layers. In the context of EEG analysis, let us delve into how CNNs are structured and applied to EEG data, highlighting their significance, challenges, and applications.

10.3 The Architecture of EEG-Specific CNNs

10.3.1 Input Layer

EEG signals are represented as multi-dimensional arrays, with time as one dimension and electrode channels as others. The input layer accepts these multi-channel time-series data.

10.3.2 Convolutional Layers

These layers perform convolutions, where filters (also called kernels) slide across the input data, extracting local patterns. In EEG CNNs, these filters capture spatial-temporal features from EEG electrodes over time, such as frequency changes associated with different brain states.

10.3.3 Pooling Layers

After convolution, pooling layers down samples the feature maps, reducing computational complexity and capturing the most salient features. A common type of pooling is known as max pooling, which maintains the maximum value in each sub region, protecting vital information.

10.3.4 Fully Connected Layers

The flattened output from pooling layers is fed into fully connected layers, which perform classification tasks. These layers combine extracted features from the preceding layers to make predictions about the input data, such as whether a seizure is present or not [35].

10.4 Training EEG-Specific CNNs

Training CNNs for EEG analysis involves several steps.

10.4.1 Data Preprocessing

EEG data often undergo preprocessing steps like filtering (e.g., band-pass filtering to isolate frequency bands of interest), artifact removal, and normalization to enhance signal quality and consistency.

10.4.2 Data Augmentation

Given the limited availability of EEG datasets, data augmentation techniques such as time warping, adding noise, or applying random shifts can increase the diversity of training samples, improving the model's generalization ability.

10.4.3 Model Training

CNNs are trained using backpropagation and optimization algorithms like stochastic gradient descent or its variants. To better categorize EEG data, the model learns to minimize a predetermined loss function during training by changing its parameters.

10.4.4 Validation and Hyperparameter Tuning

Validation datasets are used to evaluate the performance of the model and the tuned parameters like learning rate, kernel size, and network depth to optimize performance and prevent overfitting [35].

10.5 Significance of EEG CNNs

10.5.1 Automatic Feature Learning

CNNs eliminate the need for human feature extraction, which can be time-consuming and biased. They pick up hierarchal features from raw EEG data by themselves.

10.5.2 Improved Accuracy

The inherent complex spatial-temporal properties of EEG signals can be captured by CNNs. This high-level abstraction aids in more accurate seizure detection, seizure-type classification, and BCI.

10.5.3 Generalization

Trained CNN-based EEG classifier models generalize well to new unseen data, which is required for out of lab or real-world usage over multiple subjects.

10.5.4 Real-Time Applications

Advances in optimizations and CNN design make it possible for these classifiers to be implemented in real-time, allowing for clinical purposes and wearable gadgets and assistive technology.

10.6 Challenges and Future Directions

10.6.1 Interpretability

Despite high classification accuracy, CNNs are regarded as unwieldy due to their interpretability drawbacks—from poorly described input features to minimal visibility into what features contribute to classification judgments.

This problem is particularly pressing in the medical sector where high interpretability is required.

10.6.2 Data Scarcity

Inaccessibility of large, labeled EEG datasets for training CNNs is primarily attributed to privacy concerns, the complexity of performing experiments, and the variability between subjects. Collaboration and data-sharing can help address this issue.

10.6.3 Personalized Models

Large disparities in the underlying EEG signal between individuals depending on factors such as age, sex, and comorbidities make it challenging for a single CNN to classify the signals accurately. Personalized approaches can be used to help meet the criteria.

10.6.4 Multimodal Integration

Multimodal integration refers to combining EEG data with additional modalities such as functional MRI or electrocorticography. This method could provide CNNs with a far richer data set, allowing them to perform more evaluation of the brain state.

10.7 Recurrent Neural Networks

Neural networks that are well-suited to sequence data are typically referred to as recurrent neural networks. These types of data are encoded in an example known as electroencephalography. RNNs have been designed to manage these varieties of data by recollecting knowledge from previous time steps known as the inner state or memory.

The following points describe how RNNs operate when applied to EEG data.

10.7.1 Sequential Processing

Fundamentally, this refers to the fact that the majority of EEG data is a gathering of one sort that measures voltage obtained from scalp electrodes over time. As a result, the activity of the brain gets encapsulated by each data point measured at a specific moment in time in the time series.

This kind of data may be fed into an RNN, which has the property of taking in one-time step input at a moment and preserving an internal state that retains information from the previous time steps.

10.7.2 Recurrent Connections

RNNs also have recurrent connections, allowing information to persist across time, unlike standard feed-forward neural networks. At each time step, the input and internal state from the prior time step are combined and then passed through a non-linear function to generate the output from that time step. This helps the network to find correlations in the temporal data.

10.7.3 Long Short-Term Memory and Gated Recurrent Unit

While primary RNNs can recognize short-term dependencies, they are unable to identify long-term–dependent relationships in the sequential data. To overcome this obstacle, more complicated RNN variants like long short-term memory and gated recurrent units have been developed. These versions are more effective when they pertain to activities that have longer temporal dependencies, such as analyzing EEG data lapses, because they have systems for selectively recalling or forgetting information over extensive sequences.

10.8 Applications in EEG Analysis

RNNs can be applied to various tasks involving EEG data, including but not limited to the following.

10.8.1 Brain–Computer Interface (BCI)

RNNs can be used to decode EEG signals for controlling external devices or interfaces based on brain activity.

10.8.2 Seizure Prediction and Detection

RNNs can analyze EEG signals to predict or detect epileptic seizures based on patterns in brain activity.

10.8.3 Cognitive State Classification

RNNs can classify EEG signals into different cognitive states (e.g., attention and drowsiness) based on patterns in brain activity.

10.8.4 Brain Signal Denoising

RNNs can be trained to denoise EEG signals by learning to distinguish between signal and noise components in the data [40].

10.9 Ensemble Methods

Discussing ensemble approaches to EEG (electroencephalography) refers to strategies that combine several models or classifiers to increase the precision and resilience of tasks involving EEG-based analysis. Electrodes are usually implanted on the scalp to capture electrical activity in the brain using the EEG technique. Ensemble approaches use a variety of models to get over the constraints of individual models and improve performance overall [41].

10.9.1 Application of Ensemble Methods to EEG Analysis

10.9.1.1 Bagging (Bootstrap Aggregating)

Using a random sample with replacement, bagging entails training multiple EEG classifiers on different sets of EEG data. For regression tasks, the absolute prediction is often determined by averaging the predictions of all classifiers, whereas for classification tasks, a majority vote is taken. Each classifier is trained independently. Bagging helps reduce variance and can improve generalization by mitigating overfitting.

10.9.1.2 Boosting

Boosting is another ensemble technique where models are trained sequentially, with each subsequent model focusing on the instances that previous models struggled with. In the context of EEG analysis, boosting algorithms like AdaBoost or gradient boosting can be used to iteratively improve classification accuracy by assigning higher weights to misclassified EEG samples.

10.9.1.3 *Random Forests*

Decision trees and bagging are combined in Random Forests. Several decision trees are trained using arbitrary subsets of the EEG data, and the predictions of each tree are combined to get the final prediction. Random forests are less prone to overfitting in comparison to individual decision trees and can handle high-dimensional EEG data.

10.9.1.4 *Stacking*

Stacking involves training multiple diverse EEG classifiers and then combining their predictions using a meta-classifier, which learns how to best weigh or combine the outputs of the base classifiers. Stacking can capture the complementary strengths of different EEG classifiers and often leads to improved performance.

10.9.1.5 *Voting Classifiers*

In this approach, multiple EEG classifiers are trained independently, and the final prediction is made based on a majority vote or weighted combination of their predictions. Voting classifiers can be used with various base classifiers, such as SVMs, neural networks, or k-nearest neighbors [41].

10.10 Transfer Learning

Transfer learning in EEG analysis can significantly reduce the need for large, labeled datasets, improve model generalization, and accelerate the development of EEG-based applications such as BCIs, cognitive state monitoring, and clinical diagnosis of neurological disorders [9]. By leveraging knowledge from related tasks or domains, transfer learning enables more efficient and effective utilization of EEG data for various applications. Various transfer learning applications can be applied to EEG analysis:

10.10.1 Pre-Trained Models

Pre-trained models, which have been trained on an extensive set of data for a related task, such as image classification using natural photos, are frequently the first step in the transfer learning process. These pre-trained models can be applied to EEG data because they have previously picked up helpful features from the data.

10.10.2 Feature Extraction

EEG data typically consists of high-dimensional time-series data recorded from electrodes. Using trained models to extract pertinent information from the unprocessed EEG signals is one method of transfer learning. From EEG electrode setups, methods such as convolutional neural networks (CNNs) pre-trained on image data can be adjusted to extract spatial characteristics.

10.10.3 Fine-Tuning

Fine-tuning entails training of pre-trained models on a smaller labeled EEG dataset, following its use in feature extraction. Through this approach, the model can retain the valuable features it learnt from the pre-trained model and adjust its parameters to better fit the EEG data and the task requirements.

10.10.4 Domain Adaptation

EEG data often comes from different sources or experimental setups, leading to domain shifts that can degrade model performance. Domain adaptation techniques aim to mitigate this issue by aligning the distributions of the source (pre-trained model) and target (EEG) domains. This can involve methods like adversarial training or domain-adversarial neural networks.

10.10.5 Multi-Task Learning

It is in different scenarios where multiple tasks to be solved together allowing the models to jointly perform the tasks available in multiple models. In EEG clustering, various cognitive parameters can be predicted simultaneously.

10.10.6 Data Augmentation

Data augmentation technique is an enhanced effort in improving the transfer learning model in EEG clustering involving different modifications like temporal wrapping, noise addition, positional shifting of the electrode [43].

10.10.7 Hybrid Approaches

It refers to the hybridization of different models or techniques in addressing the complexities and challenges in EEG clustering. This approach screens the advantages of different models and work together to enhance the performance interpretability and gives better insights in EEG clustering [44]. There are different types of hybrid approaches like feature fusion, model fusion, multimodal integration, feedback integration, deep learning with traditional methods and adaptive approaches.

Epilepsy diagnosis and management and, hence, EEG clustering for seizure classification is a crucial requirement that influences the effective antiepileptic therapeutics. In recent years, merging of different intelligent computational approaches like artificial intelligence, ML, signal processing of EEG data has revolutionized the seizure classification approach yielding remarkable advancements enhancing accuracy, efficiency, and automation in the classification process. Thus, based on the EEG features, the approaches like SVM, random forests, and neural networks effectively can classify different forms of seizure, thus helping in accurate diagnosis and personalized treatment strategies. These feature extraction techniques help in revealing the non-linear, spectral, and temporal characteristics of EEG data interpreting in seizure categorization.

10.11 Seizure EEG Clustering Using Discrete Wavelet Transform Algorithm

An EEG, a non-invasive medical imaging technique, can be used to monitor the electrical activity of the brain [17, 18]. Electrodes are positioned along the scalp in the manner depicted in the image to retrieve the electrical impulses from the brain. It captures aberrant voltage fluctuations in the brain caused by ionic current flow during signal transmission in the brain's nerve cells. Therefore, in a therapeutic setting, electroencephalography (EEG) serves as a means of recording spontaneous electrical activity in the brain at specific times, as sensed from the scalp. The spectral content of an EEG signal, which is a form of cerebral oscillations known as "brain waves," is taken into consideration in a diagnostic setting. Four categories are used to categorize brain waves: (i) beta (>13 Hz), (ii) alpha (8–13 Hz), (iii) theta (4–8 Hz), and (iv) delta (0.5–4 Hz).

Each signal consist of n = 4,079 sample at sampling rate 173 Hz. The frequency range falls 0 Hz to 85 Hz. The low-pass filter was set at 40 Hz. However, for analysis, only n = 2,000 samples were considered from each pre-defined subject groups. The block diagram for the suggested method in this study is displayed in Figure 10.1.

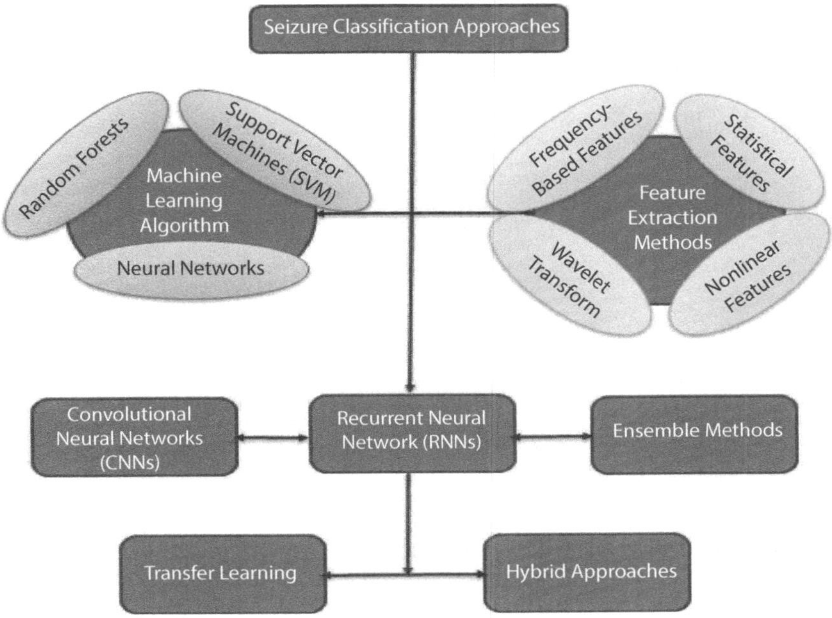

Figure 10.1 Flowchart shows various seizure classifications [45].

10.11.1 Pre-Processing of the EEG Data

Removing noise and the causes of it from signals is one of the primary requirements in biological signal processing. In biomedical signal analysis, the signal-to-noise ratio (SNR) must be maximized. The artifactual bioelectric activity (muscle contractions, eye movements, etc.) or ambient electrical activity (monitors, etc.) or neural EEG properties other than those required for control can be sources of noise in EEG signals [14]. In the current study, we processed the signals and reduced the noise level using a Kaiser window–based low-pass filter of order 20, with a cutoff frequency of 0.5 kHz and a sampling frequency of 1 kHz.

10.11.2 Feature Extraction and Fusion

The initial EEG signal has a distributed energy distribution and is a time domain signal. The noise obscures the signal characteristics. To extract the characteristics, the EEG signal is analyzed to describe the signal energy as a function of time and/or frequency. According to earlier research, characteristics obtained from the frequency domain are among the best for

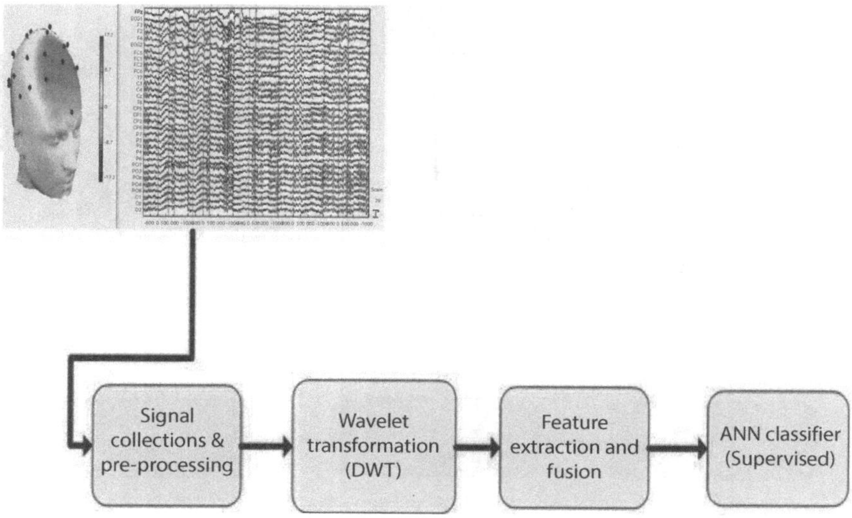

Figure 10.2 Block diagram of the proposed approach.

using EEG data to identify mental tasks [15]. To extract feature vectors for the current investigation, wavelet transformation (WT) was applied to the original features space. The signal is broken down by the WT into detail coefficients (Dn) and coarse approximation (An). The original signal is filtered using low-pass and high-pass filters. The WT characteristics were obtained by using approximation coefficients (Figure 10.2).

10.11.3 Classification

Artificial neural network (ANN) implementation is divided into three stages: design, training, and execution. During the design phase, the architecture of the network is specified, including the quantity of inputs, outputs, layers, and activation functions of the neurons. In the training phase, the weights of the network's links are established using a learning technique such as back propagation. In the end, the execution phase of the network is carried out using its fixed parameters, which were acquired during the learning phase [16, 19].

To determine the distinctions among the different points in the feature, we utilized an ANN to determine the most effective bounds for different EEG signal classes in the features space [20–22]. The MATLAB R2008a version's neural network toolbox was utilized for our work. Throughout our study, we encountered the limits by using the back propagation algorithm.

10.12 Present Findings

An EEG recording is a characteristic of a seizure in clinical biology. EEG is a non-invasive method of diagnosing seizures in which brain waves are recorded using electrodes applied to the brain's surface. These electrodes record the physiological activity of the brain as waves, which are then further represented in the output as graphs. The sole method used to analyze these analog outputs is manual visual observation. It is proposed that it would be more accurate to diagnose and categorize particular types of epilepsy and seizures if the output data could be stored in a digital data format, with each digit representing a particular class of EEG pattern of seizure. A result of this type of EEG clustering technique has been shown in the following section.

10.12.1 Seizure Prediction Using Computational Biology Approach

The observed one-dimensional (1D) time course X(n) is rescaled using the formula Y(n) = X(n)/c + b, where c is a user-defined constant that can have any value in the range 0 < c <– max(|x(n)|), due to the high level of amplitude in mV (Figure 10.3). Given that, the frequency of the EEG signal is in

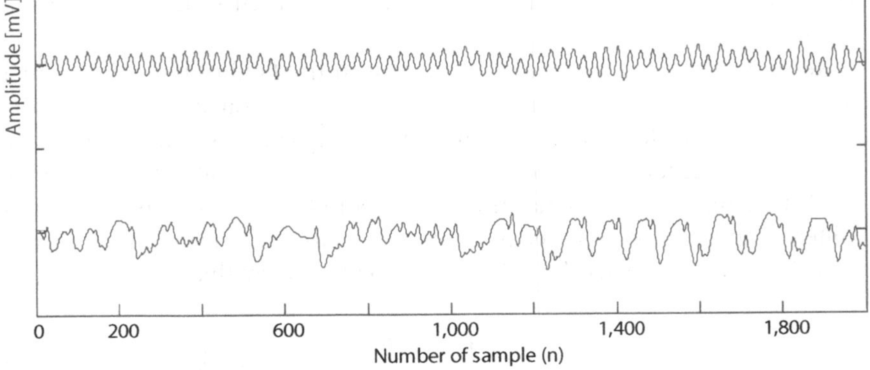

Figure 10.3 EEG signals extracted from three different subjects.

the lower frequency range. We designed a Kaiser window–based low-pass filter of order n = 20 with a cutoff frequency of fc = 0.5 kHz and a sampling frequency of fs = 1 kHz to reduce the noise level in the signals.

10.12.2 Feature Extraction

A mathematical or symbolic property of an object's aspect is called a feature. A vector containing one or more attribute values of an object is called a feature vector. Feature vectors are used in ML tasks to describe the numerical or symbolic distinctiveness. Feature vectors are important in many ML applications. In the past, learning algorithms have required a mathematical representation of the objects in order to process and analyze data statistically. A signal can be described by its feature, just like any other object or event. For classification reasons, these features can be arranged in a certain way. Feature vector refers to this feature arrangement. Let us take a feature vector X, and it can be expressed as equation shown below.

$$\mathrm{X} = \begin{bmatrix} X_1 \\ X_2 \\ X_3 \\ X_4 \\ \cdot \\ \cdot \\ X_n \end{bmatrix}$$

where X_1, X_2, X_3, …, X_n are descriptors associated with the pattern of the signal.

Recently, there has been a lot of interest in the field of biological signal processing and analysis regarding WT, wave packet transformation, short-time Fourier transformation, and time-frequency analysis of non-stationary signals. It makes it possible to localize signals' spectra—that is, the frequency bands that appear at particular times—temporally. It may also be utilized as a filter, in addition. WT is used in this work to extract the feature vector from the original feature space. The WT transition looks like this:

$$w(b,s) = \sum_{n \in Z} Y_j(n) \frac{\mathbf{1}}{\sqrt{s}} \psi^{\Upsilon}\left(\frac{n-b}{s}\right) \qquad j = 1,2,..p \tag{10.1}$$

where s > 0 is dilation or scale factor and b is spatial position conjugate mother wavelet [Daubechies (db) is used here].

The signal is broken down by the WT into detail coefficients (Dn) and coarse approximation (An). Following high-pass and low-pass filtering of the original signal, the following first-level output is produced:

$$y_{low} = \sum_{n} Y_j[n]\kappa(2k-n) \qquad \eta(n) \qquad \kappa(n) \tag{10.2}$$

$$y_{high} = \sum_{n} Y_j[n]\eta(2k-n) \tag{10.3}$$

The WT features are extracted using approximation coefficients A (n). The three-level decomposition using db3 is shown below (Figure 10.4). This way also reduces the high frequency noise levels in signals. Figure 10.5 describes the feed forward back propagation neural network.

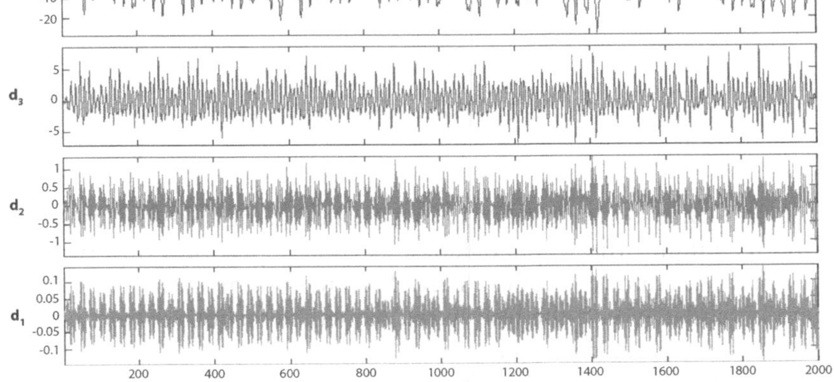

Figure 10.4 DWT decomposition using db3 level-3.

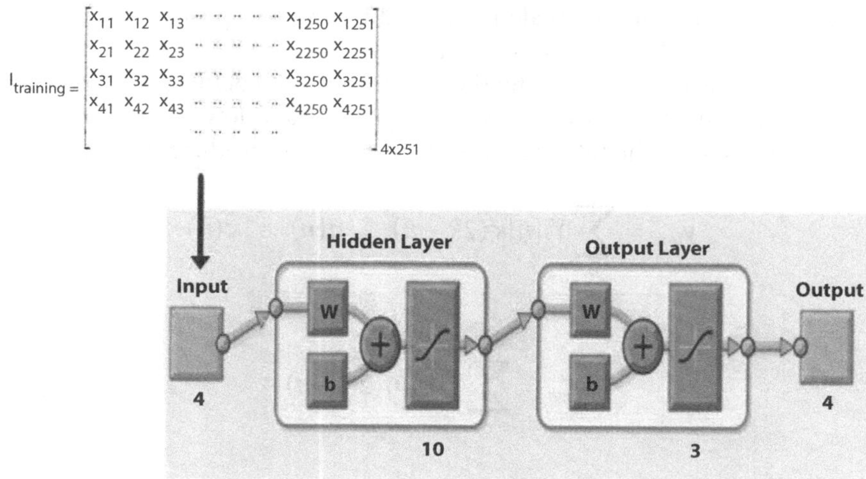

Figure 10.5 Processing block diagram with feed-forward back propagation neural network (number of layer, 2; number of neuron, 10; performance function, mean square error (MSE).

10.12.3 Quality Assessment Parameters

$$\text{Accuracy} = \frac{TP_{Q1} + TP_{Q2} + TP_{Q3} + TP_{Q4}}{C_T} \tag{10.4}$$

$$\text{Sensitivity} = \frac{TP}{TP + FN} \tag{10.5}$$

$$\text{Specificity} = \frac{TN}{TN + FP} \tag{10.6}$$

The performance of classifier is investigated using two-fold cross validation technique. The whole database is equally partition into two sets, *viz.*, training set and testing set. After obtaining optimal level of MSE, the system is validated with the testing set. Nonetheless, both dataset contain different data extracted subjects.

The accuracy of the classifier in testing dataset is 98.33%. The sensitivities are 93.55% (Q2), 100% (Q3), and 93.55% (Q4), and the specificity is 100% (Q1).

Table 10.1 A confusion matrix of sensitivity and specificity of various subjects.

	Predicted by ANN				
Actual		Q1	Q2	Q3	Q4
	Q1	T_{P1}	F_{12}	F_{13}	F_{14}
	Q2	F_{21}	T_{P2}	F_{23}	F_{24}
	Q3	F_{31}	F_{32}	T_{P3}	F_{34}
	Q4	F_{41}	F_{42}	F_{43}	T_{P4}

Here: **Q1**, normal; **Q2**, focal epileptic EEG; **Q3**, generalized epileptic EEG; and **Q4**, absence epileptic EEG.

Table 10.1 shows the confusion matrix through which the result is investigated in terms of sensitivity and specificity of various subjects. The proposed work describes a computational biology approach for seizure prediction utilizing EEG data. The study's researchers focused on pre-processing the EEG signals to lower noise and to increase SNR. EEG signals may include artefacts like muscular or ocular movements, as well as noise from surrounding electrical activity. The researchers used a Kaiser window–based low-pass filter with precise parameters, including an order of 20, a 0.5-kHz cutoff frequency, and a 1-kHz sampling frequency, to reduce noise.

The results of this investigation comply with the seizure prediction approach where it was examined using a confusion matrix and quality assessment criteria. The system achieved an accuracy of 98.33% on the testing dataset which had high sensitivity (93.55% to 100%) and specificity (100%) for different classes of EEG signals. As a whole, this computational biology approach shows potential for improving seizure prediction using effective processing of EEG data. Artificial neural network classification, wavelet-transformed feature extraction, and preprocessing techniques combine to reliably detect and categorize patterns linked to seizures in EEG data. These findings might help in the diagnosis and classification of specific types of epilepsy and seizures.

10.13 Conclusion

EEG signal is one of the reliable data source for different diseases of the nervous system. The computational biology–based approach using DWT has a great potentiality in enhancing the diagnosis and treatment strategies for seizure patients. Further research is expected to focus on expanding the dataset, exploring various feature extraction techniques, incorporating deep learning methods, developing real-time implementation, exploring multimodal data fusion, and optimizing signal processing techniques. These advancements can further enhance the accuracy and applicability of seizure prediction systems, ultimately improving the management and treatment of epilepsy and related conditions

References

1. Kalita, P. and Barthakur, M., Microanatomical deformation after PTZ induced seizure in mice brain. *Int. J. Pharm.*, 3, 3, 618–620, 2013.
2. Veliskova, J. and Velisek, L., Behavioral Characterization and Scoring of Seizures in Rodents, in: *Models of Seizures and Epilepsy*, http://dx.doi.org/10.1016/B978-0-12-804066-9.00009-2.
3. Zhou, M., Tian, C., Cao, R., Wang, B., Niu, Y., Hu, T., Guo, H., Xiang, J., Epileptic Seizure Detection Based on EEG Signals and CNN. *Front. Neuroinf.*, 12, 95, 2018.
4. Hazarika, A., Sarmah, A., Borah, R., Boro, M., Dutta, L., Kalita, P., Choudhury, B.K.D., Discriminant feature level fusion based learning for automatic staging of EEG signals. *Healthcare Technol. Lett.*, 5, 6, 226–230, 2018.
5. Sarmah, A., Hazarika, A., Kalita, P., Choudhury, B.K.D., A subspace projection based feature fusion: An application to EEG clustering. *Proceedings of International Conference on Signal Processing and Communication (ICSPC)*, pp. 472–476, IEEE, 2017.
6. Hazarika, A., Sarmah, A., Boro, M., Kalita, P., Choudhury, B.D., Discriminant Correlation-Based Information Fusion for Real-Time Biomedical Signal Clustering, in: *Advances in Communication, Devices and Networking*, p. 465, 2018.
7. Hassanpour, H., Mesbah, M., Boashash, B., Time-frequency feature extraction of newborn EEG seizure using SVD-based techniques'. *EURASIP J. Appl. Signal Process.*, 16, 2544–2554, 2004.
8. Subasi, A. and Gursoy, M.I., EEG signal classification using PCA, ICA, LDA and support vector machines'. *Expert Syst. Appl.*, 37, 8659–8666, 2010.
9. Hassan, A.R. and Subasi, A., Automatic identification of epileptic seizures from EEG signals using linear programming boosting'. *Comput. Methods Programs Biomed.*, 136, 65–77, 2016.
10. Hassan, A.R. and Haque, M.A., Computer-aided obstructive sleep apnea screening from single-lead electrocardiogram using statistical and spectral features and bootstrap aggregating'. *Biocybern. Biomed.*, 36, 256–266, 2016.
11. Orhan, U., Hekim, M., Ozer, M., EEG signals classification using the K-means clustering and a multilayer perceptron neural network model. *Expert Syst. Appl.*, 38, 13475–13481, 2011.

12. Soomro, M.H., Musavi, S.H.A., Pandey, B., Canonical correlation analysis and neural network (CCA-NN) based method to detect epileptic seizures from EEG signals. *Int. J. Bio-Sci. Bio-Tech.*, 8, 11–20, 2016.
13. Kiymik, M.K., Akin, M., Subasi, A., Automatic recognition of alertness level by using wavelet transform and artificial neural network. *J. Neurosci. Methods*, 139, 231–240, 2004.
14. Naik, G., Selvan, S., Nguyen, H., Single-channel EMG classification with ensemble-empirical-mode-decomposition-based ICA for diagnosing neuromuscular disorders. *IEEE Trans. Neural Syst. Rehabil. Eng.*, 24, 734–743, 2016.
15. Limaye, T., Kumaran, K., Joglekar, C., Bhat, D., Kulkarni, R., Nanivadekar, A., Yajnik, C., Efficacy of a virtual assistance-based lifestyle intervention in reducing risk factors for Type 2 diabetes in young employees in the information technology industry in India: LIMIT, a randomized controlled trial. *Diabet. Med.*, 34, 4, 563–568, 2017.
16. Zhang, J. and Zhang, D., A novel ensemble construction method for multi-view data using random cross-view correlation between within-class examples. *Pattern Recognit.*, 44, 1162–1171, 2011.
17. Hassanpour, H., Mesbah, M., Boashash, B., Time-frequency feature extraction of newborn EEG seizure using SVD-based techniques. *EURASIP J. Appl. Signal Process.*, 2004, 2544–2554, 2004.
18. Bhadra, S. and Kumar, C.J., An insight into diagnosis of depression using machine learning techniques: a systematic review. *Curr. Med. Res. Opin.*, *38*, 5, 749–771, 2022.
19. Bhadra, S. and Kumar, C.J., Enhancing the efficacy of depression detection system using optimal feature selection from EHR. *Comput. Methods Biomech. Biomed. Eng.*, 27, 2, 222–236, 2023, doi: 10.1080/10255842.2023.2181660.
20. Sharma, M., Kumar, C.J., Deka, A., Early diagnosis of rice plant disease using machine learning techniques. *Arch. Phytopathol. Plant Prot.*, *55*, 3, 259–283, 2022.
21. Sharma, M., Nath, K., Sharma, R.K., Kumar, C.J., Chaudhary, A., Ensemble averaging of transfer learning models for identification of nutritional deficiency in rice plant. *Electronics*, *11*, 1, 148, 2022.
22. Kumar, C.J. and Das, P.R., The diagnosis of ASD using multiple machine learning techniques. *Int. J. Dev. Disabil.*, *68*, 6, 973–983, 2022.
23. Sharma, M. and Kumar, C.J., Improving Rice Disease Diagnosis Using Ensemble Transfer Learning Techniques. *Int. J. Artif. Intell. Tools*, *31*, 08, 2250040, 2022.
24. Quirago, R.Q. and Schurmann, M., Functions and sources of event-related EEG alpha Oscillations studied with the wavelet transform. *Clin. Neurophysiol.*, 110, 4, 643–654, 1999.
25. Poh, N. and Kittler, J., Multimodal Information Fusion, pp. 153–169, CVSSP, University of Surrey, Guildford, GU2 7XH, Surrey, UK, 2010.

26. Kisku, D.R., Rattan, A., Gupta, P., Sing, J.K., Biometric Sensor Image Fusion for Identity Verification: A Case Study with Wavelet-based Fusion Rules and Graph Matching, in: *Proc. of 3rd IEEE International Conference on Technologies for Homeland Security (HST'09)*, MA-Greater Boston, USA, IEEE Press, pp. 433–439, 2009.
27. Vishi, K. and Yayilgan, S.Y., Multimodal Biometric Authentication using Fingerprint and Iris Recognition in Identity Management. *Ninth International Conference on Intelligent Information Hiding and Multimedia Signal Processing*, 2013.
28. Gajic, D., Djurovic, Z., Gligorijevic, J., Di Gennaro, S. and Savic-Gajic, I., Detection of epileptic form activity in EEG signals based on time frequency and non-linear analysis. *Front. Comput. Neurosci.*, 9, 38, 2015, doi: 10.3389/fncom.2015.00038
29. Ioannides, A.A., Poghosyan, V., Dammers, J., Streit, M., Real-time neural activity and connectivity in healthy indiviuals and schizophrenia patients. *Neuroimage*, 23, 2, 1–2, 2004.
30. Aris, S., Taib, N., Lias, S., N., Feature Extraction of EEG Signals and Classification Using FCM, in: *The Proceeding of the UKSim 13th International Conference on Modelling and Simulation*, pp. 54–58, 2011.
31. Guler, I. and Ubeyli, E.D., Multiclass Support Vector Machines for EEG-Signals Classification. *IEEE Trans. Inf. Technol. Biomed.*, 11, 2, 117–127, 2007.
32. Lee, H. and Choi, S., PCA+HMM+SVM for EEG Pattern Classification. *Signal Processing and Its Applications*, pp. 541–544, 2003.
33. Andrzejak, R.G., Lehnertz, K., Rieke, C., Mormann, F., David, P., Elger, C.E., Indications of nonlinear deterministic and finite-dimensional structures in time series of brain electrical activity: Dependence on recording region and brain state. *Phys. Rev. E*, 64, 6, 061907, 2001.
34. Acharya, U.R., Sree, S.V., Swapna, G., Martis, R.J., Suri, J.S., Automated EEG analysis of epilepsy: A review. *Knowl.-Based Syst.*, 37, 354–370, 2012.
35. Schirrmeister, R.T., Springenberg, J.T., Fiederer, L.D.J., Glasstetter, M., Eggensperger, K., Tangermann, M., Ball, T., Deep learning with convolutional neural networks for EEG decoding and visualization. *Hum. Brain Mapp.*, 38, 11, 5391–5420, 2017.
36. Roy, Y., Banville, H., Albuquerque, I., Gramfort, A., Falk, T.H., Deep learning-based electroencephalography analysis: a systematic review. *J. Neural Eng.*, 16, 5, 051001, 2019.
37. Subasi, A., EEG signal classification using wavelet feature extraction and a mixture of expert models. *Expert Syst. Appl.*, 32, 4, 1084–1093, 2007.
38. Shoeb, A., Application of machine learning to epileptic seizure onset detection and treatment, MIT, 2009.
39. Minaee, S., Wang, Y., Wang, L., Deep learning in bioinformatics. *IEEE Trans. Neural Netw. Learn. Syst.*, 31, 11, 3773–3787, 2020.

40. Ma, T., King, I., Lyu, M.R., I know the relationships: Zero-shot action recognition via two-stream graph convolutional networks and knowledge graphs, in: *Proceedings of the IEEE International Conference on Computer Vision*, pp. 4355–4364, 2017.
41. Banville, H., Chehab, O., Falk, T.H., How many EEG electrodes are needed in a brain-computer interface? *IEEE Trans. Neural Syst. Rehabil. Eng.*, 27, 8, 1680–1687, 2019.
42. Liu, Z., Zhang, M., Tang, J., Han, J., Yang, Y., Hierarchical attention networks for document classification, in: *Proceedings of the 2018 World Wide Web Conference*, pp. 1865–1874, 2018.
43. Halder, S., Varkuti, B., Bogdan, M., Kübler, A., Rosenstiel, W., Sitaram, R., Birbaumer, N., Convolutional Neural Networks and Transfer Learning for the Continuous Classification of EEG Signals, 2019, arXiv preprint arXiv:1904.02225.
44. Li, Y., Cao, S., Liu, J., Li, X., A Hybrid Method for Epileptic Seizure Prediction Using Long Short-Term Memory Network and Convolutional Neural Network. *Front. Neuroinf.*, 12, 89, 2018, doi: 10.3389/fninf.2018.00089.
45. Rajasree, R., Brintha Rajakumari, S. Ensemble-of-classifiers-based approach for early Alzheimer's Disease detection. *Multimed. Tools Appl.* 83, 16067–16095, 2024, doi: 10.1007/s11042-023-16023-3.

11

Analysis of Biomedical Data with Explainable (XAI) and Responsive AI (RAI)

Arjun K.R., Girish Kanavi K., Varshitha B.R., Mythreyi R., Sridhar Muthusami, Nandini G. and Kanthesh M. Basalingappa*

Division of Molecular Biology, School of Life Sciences, JSS Academy of Higher Education & Research, Mysuru, Karnataka, India

Abstract

Artificial intelligence (AI) is essential to healthcare because it helps with patient diagnosis, medication discovery and development, better patient-physician communication, and medical record transcription. The two key pillars of healthcare are explainable and responsive AI (XAI and RAI), which enable morally and transparently sound decision-making. They may alter the way healthcare is provided by increasing the quantity and scalability of healthcare workers. AI algorithms are frequently more cost-effective and accurate than human physicians when it comes to analyzing medical imaging data to find early signs of illnesses like cancer. XAI techniques clarify complex model predictions and highlight important features of biological datasets. The ethical use of AI is simultaneously guided by RAI principles, which ensure equity, rectify biases, and encourage openness throughout the model life cycle. The responsible interpretation of patient outcomes made possible by the combination of XAI and RAI promotes accountability and trust. In order to facilitate responsible AI deployment in biomedical contexts, regulatory frameworks must be adjusted and model complexity and interpretability must

**Corresponding author*: kantheshmb@jssuni.edu.in;
ORCID: https://orcid.org/0000-0002-6970-4546
Arjun K.R.: ORCID: https://orcid.org/0009-0002-2600-9655
Girish Kanavi K.: https://orcid.org/0009-0002-8100-040X
Varshitha B.R.: ORCID: https://orcid.org/0009-0007-7910-8856
Mythreyi R.: ORCID: https://orcid.org/0000-0002-1018-1859
Sridhar Muthusami: ORCID: https://orcid.org/0000-0002-3595-9081
Nandini G.: ORCID: https://orcid.org/0009-0002-6668-6730

Rishabha Malviya and Sonali Sundram (eds.) Explainable and Responsible Artificial Intelligence in Healthcare, (277–296) © 2025 Scrivener Publishing LLC

be balanced, among other issues addressed in this analysis of present issues and potential future developments. Apart from that, the overall performance and reliability of AI models in biological applications and healthcare analysis are covered in this chapter, along with ongoing research to improve the explainability and accountability of deep learning models. This chapter also covers the techniques used in XAI and RAI and its applications to data analytics, biomedical image processing, and classification.

***Keywords*:** Artificial intelligence, explainable artificial intelligence, responsible intelligence, healthcare, diagnosis, XAI, RAI, AI

Abbreviations

XAI	Explainable Artificial Intelligence
RAI	Responsive Artificial Intelligence
AI	Artificial Intelligence
CDSS	Clinical Decision Support Systems
ML	Machine Learning
DL	Deep learning
GPU	Graphics Processing Units
DSS	Decision Support Systems
XAICFS-BDA	Explainable Artificial Intelligence Correlation-Based Feature Selection Biomedical Data Analysis
FKNN	Fuzzy K-Nearest Neighbor
KNN	K-nearest neighbor
CSV	comma-separated values
BWO	Black Widow Optimization
CNN	Convolutional Neural Network
CT	Computed Tomography
CXR	Chest X-Ray
TB	Tuberculosis
Grad	CAM- Gradient-weighted Class Activated Mapping
SHAP	Shapley Additive Explanation
LIME	Local Comprehensible Model-Agnostic Explanation
ReLU	Rectified Linear Unit
HCI	Human-Computer Interaction
HM	Hospital Mortality
BSI	bloodstream infections
AKI	acute kidney damage
LRP	Layer-wise Relevance Propagation
CAM	Class Activation Map

DNF	disjunctive normal form
GDM	Generative Discriminative Machines
NLP	Natural language processing
F-SVD	frame singular value decomposition
IoT	Internet of Things
EHRs	Electronic Health Records
DNN	deep neural network
MLP	Multilayer Perceptron
WF	Wiener filtering
ResNet152	Residual Network
DenseNeT	Densely Connected Network

11.1 Introduction

A new field of study called biomedical research examines how various biological disorders and processes lead to illness and how those processes must be understood in order to develop successful medical interventions. AI techniques assist in resolving difficult problems and achieving a high degree of accuracy by becoming adept at handling challenging computational tasks. In order to enhance the machine learning (ML) model's capabilities, XAI is introduced to boost the efficacy of AI. It produces explanations for the operation of machine models for learning, neural network, and advanced learning specifically and enhances these models' predictive accuracy. It increases ML models' accuracy in predictions and provides an understanding of their workings, particularly deep learning (DL) and neural network models. Artificial intelligence (AI) is widely used in the medical field through clinical decision support systems (also known as CDSS), which help doctors identify and treat patients. AI-based CDSS uses an AI model built on patient data that meets the use case at hand, as opposed to traditional CDSS, which compares a patient's characteristics to an existing knowledge base. However, even with its apparent promise, AI is not a comprehensive fix [1].

History has shown that technological advancement frequently results in new questions and significant issues. The ML approach has been significantly altered by the relatively new DL technique. Deep learning (DL) is not a method in and of itself; rather, it is a collection of techniques utilizing deep layers in neural networks. Because of its immense size, this neural network could only be operated on computer node clusters. To train them efficiently, modern computing techniques like graphics processing units are needed. The DL approach is efficient for handling large amounts of data, and, even though a task is challenging (due to unstructured data, for example), it is not more difficult to design the functionality [2].

It is believed that incorporating AI into the current healthcare system can assist keep our aging population healthy, aid in clinical decision-making, lower healthcare costs, and lessen the burden of chronic sickness. To handle the substantial changes in the healthcare industry brought about by the rise in "Internet hospitals," electronic health records, and new technologies for data gathering and assessment, a workforce with a strong technological foundation will be required, and empowered by technology healthcare consumers. Robust model preparation is aided by explainable ML techniques that handle parameter explanation. A clinician typically gathers data from patient symptoms and confirmed diagnosis. As a result, a doctor's ability to diagnose patients greatly depends on their knowledge. As a result of the ease with which vast amounts of information can now

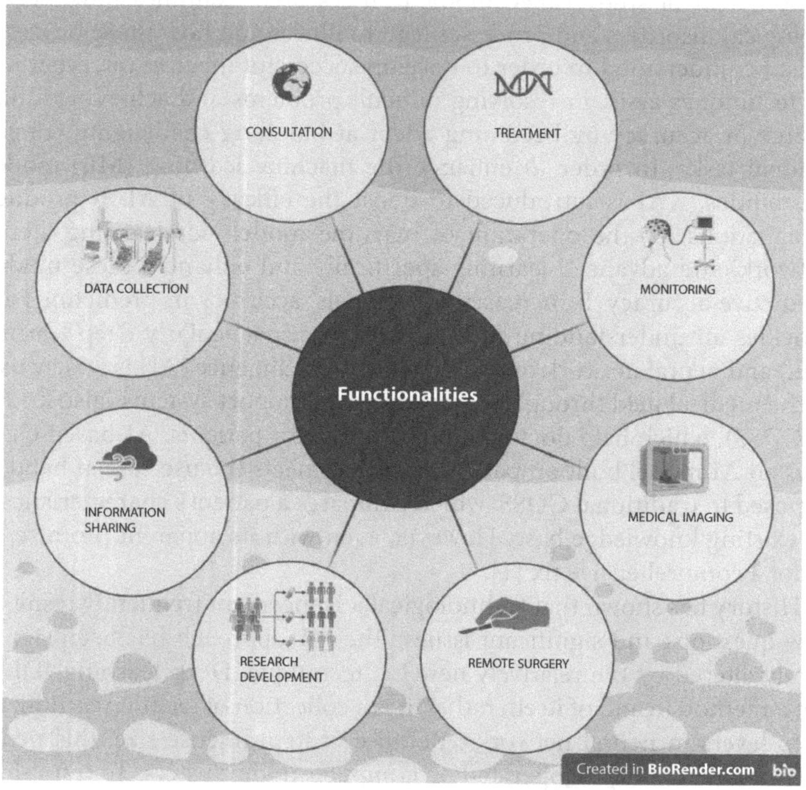

Figure 11.1 Basic functionalities of XAI and RAI in biomedical data analysis [2].

be stored and obtained digitally, computational medical decision support systems (DSS) are emerging as a viable tool to help doctors diagnose patients accurately and quickly. This approach is categorized as a classification task, with the goal being to anticipate (i.e., diagnose) new instances based on feature and record availability. It is possible to view this categorization problem as the most challenging in the field of medical informatics as represented in the Figure 11.1. Despite the fact that several statistical models are used in the classification of medical data, their main drawback is that their successful use is predicated on certain assumptions. Soft computing–based methods, on the other hand, rely less on that information. This study looked at and forecasted a number of soft computing–based classifications for precisely classifying healthcare data. Even though the majority of healthcare datasets have a vast amount of characteristics, it might be difficult and important to efficiently extract potential risk factors using Fahr's syndrome (FS) approaches [3].

11.2 Explainable Artificial Intelligence Modeling for Biomedical Data Analysis Using a Correlation-Based Feature Selection Method

This work has established an efficient XAICFS-BDA approach for data analysis and biological decision-making. The four stages of the XAICFS-BDA technique include preprocessing, BWO-based parameter optimization, FKNN-based classification, and chronic fatigue syndrome (CFS)-based feature selection. Three processes comprise the pre-processing of data in a main phase: class labeling, data normalization and format conversion. Currently, clinical data has been converted to a suitable arff format from any format (including CSV). The min-max approach was then used after the data normalization process. At this stage, the number is effectively normalized and both the upper and lower values beneath the data are reached. The objective is to distribute a different value within the intended range after normalizing the input numbers to fall between zero and one. Finally, using data samples from the dataset that have been allocated to suitable class labels, such as zero and one, the class labeling procedure was carried out.

The CFS strategy eliminates the less significant component of the FS method. Prior to searching the feature asset's intersection gaps for the optimal feature set, the CFS calculates the category-to-feature and class-to-feature interactions. One statistical similarity metric for assessing the links between two elements is correlation [4].

The correlation coefficient values between the two parameters are 0 when they are unrelated. In addition, the correlation coefficient between linked features typically ranges from −1 to +1. The coefficients are frequently used to calculate the correlations between two variables or random characteristics. A data theory coefficient is being used in one and a linear correlation coefficient in the other. To classify the medical data, the chosen feature subsets are extracted from the classification model and put into the FKNN model. The distance was considerably weighted by the fuzzy strength parameter (m) while calculating the membership value of all neighbors' participants. It is customary to use the Euclidean distance as the distance metric, which is the separation between x and their neighboring neighbor, x j. Furthermore, the value of ui j indicates the degree to which x's k-adjacent neighbors in the customized set of class I belong to the pattern x j. Throughout this research, the constraint fuzzy association technique has been utilized, leading to the specification of the KNN of each customized design (xk, for instance) [5].

The BWO method may be used to change the FKNN model's parameter tuning. The BWO is a cutting-edge, fascinating meta-heuristic method for handling challenging numerically optimized problems [6]. The BWO has accepted that aspect of evolutionary approaches due to its purposes. Darwin's natural selection, which is described as extraction with modification, the emergence of new ones, and the notion of developing specimens over a period of time, served as the paradigm for the BWO approach. The BWO is the best technique for addressing a range of optimized problems with many local optimalities while preserving the equilibrium between the periods of exploration and exploitation because it offers quicker convergence and stays away from the local optimum.

In the initial stage, the populace is the number of widows of size N. To represent the answer to the issue, each window is shown as an array of 1 × Nvar. widow = {x1, x2,..., xNvar}, where Nvar is the dimensions of the optimized problem, is the formula used to determine this array. In addition to Nvar, this indicates how many threshold values there are needed to be reached by the method, and xi represents the Beginning with a population of spiders that has been randomly initialized from the size matrix with possible answers. The method that is being provided replaces f with FF Otsu. Npop×Nvar, the optimal technique, is carried out. The procreate phase and mating process are then carried out by the parents in an arbitrary manner, but the black male widow is swallowed by the female either during or after.

An array called alpha α is created in the procreate phase if the widow array includes arbitrary values that include. Three types of cannibalism have been identified: sibling, sexual in nature, and cannibalism (often observed when a young spider consumes its mother). Afterward, all through the cannibalism execution process, a new population was determined and preserved from variable pop2. The capricious selection of a Mutepop number of people among the altered population finished the mutation process. Every solution that is chosen joins two array items arbitrarily [7].

Following the executing mutation, a new population—specifically, pop3—was calculated and preserved from the novel population. Finally, a new population was reached by the migration of pop2 and pop3, which is set up to return an ideal widow of threshold values in the Nvar dimensional space.

The four stages of the XAICFS-BDA technique include preprocessing, BWO-based parameter optimization, FKNN-based classification, and CFS-based feature selection. In order to maximize the XAICFS-BDA technique's decision-making performance, improved DL models with hyperparameter tuning procedures will be used in the future.

11.3 Biomedical Data Analysis of Various Diseases: The Functions of XAI and RAI

11.3.1 Diagnosis and Analysis of Cardiovascular Diseases

To increase the effectiveness of AI and enhance the capabilities of the ML model, XAI is presented. It produces explanations for the operation of ML models, especially DL as well as neural network models, and increases the prediction accuracy of those models. Chest X-rays are being utilized to diagnose and assess adolescent pneumonia using CNN-based models [8].

Models based on DL are useful for chest X-ray image analysis and CT scans, prognosis for heart disease [9], and the trustworthy identification of lung conditions from medical pictures. They can also look into how RhoB predicts outcomes in rectal cancer patients [10].

The research is the target audience in XAI, and explainability comprises arguments and specifics. An ML model simplifies and clarifies how it operates [11].

"Explainable AI, a collection of ML algorithms, will let individual people understand, adequately trust, and interact with the future generation of intelligent artificial intelligence partners." An understandable model with a description portal is included in the training materials when a new ML process is introduced in XAI. The explainable model is able to comprehend and control the input assignment. The output of the ML models—primarily the black-box ML models—is reliable and accurately characterized. The black-box AI model follows the comprehensible methods of the model, which consist of (a) visualization approaches, (b) model clarification, (c) picking features, (d) feature significance, (e) model reduction in complexity, (f) model description by illustration, and (g) text clarifications.

The ML model and XAI model are combined to primarily address the three questions of why, when, and how. These keywords primarily highlight the ML model's predictions, the importance of believing these forecasts, and how mistakes in the model can be fixed. Integration of XAI with ML is crucial, particularly when the outcomes of the ML model have an influence on people's lives or society. These fields include medical, healthcare, education, finance, and weather forecasting, among others. The XAI model is required to forecast a patient's illness derived from the ML model in order to determine whether to accept the ML model.

11.3.2 Diagnosis and Analysis of Respiratory Diseases

High accuracy in CXR picture categorization has been attained by DL-based techniques [12].

More resources are needed for model development and verification because DL-based methods that use pre-trained models have more parameters. The less weight, scratch-trained DL models are not capable of interpreting results. The current DL algorithms for classifying CXR images give priority to accuracy above helped interpret the model's results. When medical practitioners use such a paradigm, there is always a risk to their health [13].

A DL architecture based on XAI to identify and categorize using CXR for COVID-19, pneumonia, and TB pictures in order to overcome these shortcomings can be suggested. Our suggested model can be implemented on computer systems with limited resources as it is lightweight and has fewer parameters (in millions). In order to identify the affected area of the CXR picture, the suggested model is then explained using three popular XAI algorithms: gradient-weighted class-activated mapping (Grad-CAM), SHapley Additive exPlanation (SHAP), and local comprehensible model-agnostic explanation (LIME). In addition, the viewpoint of the medical expert was validated alongside the model explanations.

Several researches about medical analysis of images have found that ML and DL models enhance CT and CXR image-based computer-aided medical diagnostics illness identification, including COVID-19, pneumonia, and tuberculosis. CXR images of different resolutions are used in real-world applications, and characteristics derived from the deep visual words (BoDVW) single-scale bag are not sufficient to capture the complex semantic information of the lung infected regions. They use three alternative kernels (1 × 1, 2 × 2, and 3 × 3) to execute the max pooling technique combined with convolution across the multiple scales bags with deep visible word–based features' fourth pooling layer. The suggested characteristics were assessed using the support vector machine (SVM) classification algorithm, and, for four public CXR datasets, their technique yielded remarkable classification accuracy of 84.37%, 88.88%, 90.29%, and 83.65% [14].

Three disease classifications (COVID-19, TB, and pneumonia) were binary classified using six distinct datasets obtained from publically accessible CXR pictures, using a DL model that was trained from scratch. The accuracy ratings that the model produced on COVID-19 were 99.76% on TB, 98.89% on COVID-19 versus pneumonia, 98.99% on COVID-19 versus TB, and 100% on pneumonia versus TB were the results for pneumonia. Six datasets were used to assess the model independently, each containing two classes, even though it was very accurate in categorizing the sickness classes. Their model is even more mysterious because no XAI was employed in the study.

This study builds a lightweight CNN model for CXR classification utilizing thick layers, dropout, max-pooling, 2D convolution, and flattening. It consists of five convolution layers, each of which is followed by a max-pooling and dropout layer, with the exception of the convolution layer next to the input layer. The flatten layer transforms 2D data into 1D features, which are subsequently fed into the dropout and dense layers. Lastly, classification is done using soft-max activation. As an activation function, the rectified linear unit (ReLU) is added to each convolution layer. Explicit parameters for CNN are provided, including for max-pooling layers, poolsize; for dropout layers, dropout value; and for the convolutions levels, kernels size, gracefully, and filtering. The 3 × 3 kernel size was used because a smaller kernel size might better capture the damaged region on the CXR image [15].

11.4 A Comparative Study Between Manual Analysis and Analysis with XAI and RAI

The need for DL-based techniques to be explainable is becoming more and more pressing, especially in fields where important choices must be made quickly, like medical image analysis. An introduction of the analysis of medical images using deeper learning and explainable AI (XAI) is provided in this survey. To categorize medical image analysis techniques based on DL, a set of XAI criteria is presented. Next, a survey and anatomical location classification are applied to papers on XAI approaches in medical picture analysis [16]. Approaches to comprehend the black box better have been called for. These methodologies are usually denoted as XAI or interpretable DL [17, 18]. Lately, artificial intelligence (XAI) has taken center stage in research efforts aimed at enhancing working model transparency with users. The development of AI has a limited history that includes ML, data science, computer vision, statistical analysis, and natural language processing. Even with these advancements, human intellect could not be surpassed; neural networks, reinforcement learning, and DL eventually made this possible. These developments in AI applications were discovered to be crucial for the improvement of the medical field as well as useful for self-driving cars, weather forecasting analysis, and the game AlphaGo, which can match human skill levels [19, 20]. Research on human-computer interaction is also advancing to offer solutions and automate several applications [21]. However, recent advancements in life expectancy via the application of cutting-edge technology will continue to be helpful in addressing issues encountered in several medical sector categories. Thus, advancements in the medical field are examined, with a particular emphasis on the prediction of hospital mortality, bloodstream infections, acute kidney damage, and pneumonia status [22].

11.5 Differentiation of AI and XAI/RAI Methods

11.5.1 Interpretation or Analysis

Given the high degree of responsibility and openness in the medical industry, the algorithm must be more interpretable. Interpretability should be handled carefully even if it is addressed similarly in all hospitals; medical procedures should be the primary emphasis for analytical development, and technology applications that require data based on mathematical understanding are encouraged. Both perceptual and mathematical structures are among the several interpretability types that are mentioned here. Most of the perceptual interpretability comes from visual evidence that may be examined with saliency maps like layer-wise relevance propagation, class activation map, and LIME [23]. Signal approaches, like feature mapping and activation maximization, are used to identify the stimulation or collection of neurons. The comprehensible for human reasoning assertions based on predicates and connectives, that is, disjunctive normal form and NLP are what constitute verbal interpretability. Although predefined models—like logistic regression, generative discriminative machines, and reinforcement learning—represent relationships between input and output variables, ML and neural network algorithms frequently rely on the interpretability of mathematical structures. Finally, features from the provided source are retrieved using clustering, frame singular value decomposition, graph presentation, etc. [24].

11.5.2 Transparency

Openness in the process of the system: The system's usability and transparency have been restricted by the use of traditional black-box-based AI algorithms. Thus, clear systems that provide the details of the model building, gathering of data, and thorough execution, and conclusion are what make XAI approaches well-known. The user may later change, enhance, version, and audit the system because of transparency, which gives them access to the whole design [24].

11.6 Analyzing Data Using Traditional Methods Versus Using AI can Differ Significantly in Several Aspects

Compared to conventional analysis techniques, AI has a number of benefits, including automation, scalability, efficiency, and speed. On the other hand, interpretability and early expenses can present problems.

11.7 Advantages of AI

More individuals are becoming aware of the various features of AI in the field of healthcare, such as image analysis, genomics, and bioinformatics, where it is used to evaluate massive volumes of complex data and produce findings without the need for human intervention. Even if this technology might be useful for diagnosing and treating conditions, there might still be risks and challenges related to various safety concerns. This article's goal is to examine AI in healthcare and talk about how it can affect patient safety. This study shows that the main strategies for leveraging AI to develop safer technology are safe fail, safety reserves, safe design, and protective measures in place. Every potential technology system should undergo a cost-risk-uncertainty analysis. To develop and apply it is also suggested that specific rules and procedures be created and distributed to all relevant parties in order to promote safer AI technology in the healthcare industry as mentioned in Table 11.1 [25].

Table 11.1 Advantages of XAI and RAI [25].

1. Speed and Efficiency	Compared to labor- and time-intensive traditional approaches, AI can evaluate massive datasets considerably more quickly. Complex data structures and patterns that may be difficult for conventional techniques to handle may also be handled by AI.
2. Accuracy	Particularly with complicated datasets, artificial intelligence (AI) may frequently produce more accurate answers because it can spot minute patterns and linkages that human analysis or conventional statistical approaches can overlook.
3. Scalability	AI models can scale to analyze large datasets with ease, whereas traditional methods may struggle with scalability, requiring more resources and time.
4. Automation	Workflows may become more streamlined and effective by eliminating the need for manual involvement by automating the analytical process with AI.
5. Interpretability	Conventional techniques frequently yield results that are easier to interpret, which helps people comprehend and have more faith in the study. Deep learning models in particular can occasionally be viewed as "black boxes," making it difficult to understand the judgments they make.
6. Flexibility	Because AI can be educated on a variety of datasets and adapt to various problem domains, it can be more versatile in handling various data kinds and analytical jobs.
7. Cost	The initial cost of using AI for analysis may be higher because it requires specific knowledge and infrastructure. However, because of its speed and efficiency, AI may eventually prove to be more economical.

Particularly in the healthcare sector, AI technologies—such as ML, the Internet of Things, algorithms, and robots—are used to monitor, diagnose, treat, and quantify risks and benefits. The CFS methodology eliminates one of the FS method's less significant aspects. In order to identify the best feature set, the CFS first calculates the correlations between features and between features and classes. It then searches the correlated space of the characteristic subset. Correlation is one statistical similarity measure that may be used to evaluate the connections between two items. Data integration, privacy concerns, legal obstacles, and patient safety are a few of the difficulties. Based on this systematic study, some of the AI approaches that are most commonly employed in the health industry consist of the fields of data science, augmented reality, vision in computers, mining data, processing images, neural networks, and specialist systems. AI has several uses in the medical industry, including information sharing, data collection, remote surgery, diagnosis, treatment, security, and consulting. This review paper gives information on recent advances in AI and how they might be applied practically in healthcare [26].

11.8 Comparison of AI's Pros and Cons

Artificial intelligence (AI) has become a hot topic of discussion and is being used to improve and simplify operations in almost every sector. Even while AI has many advantages, it also has drawbacks. For this reason, we will look at both the positive and negative aspects of AI in real life.

Pros:

Minimizing Errors: Because activities might be monotonous or complex, humans are prone to making mistakes when performing them. AI-powered devices are unique in this sense. Reason: Their capacity to reduce mistake risk by basing judgments on complex algorithms and historical data.

Better Risk-taking Abilities: By combining robotic engineering with AI, we may overcome human limits. Actually, AI solutions might make it possible to accomplish previously unthinkable tasks, including sending a robot to different planets, exploring deeper space, carrying out intricate surgical procedures, and obtaining energy from renewable sources. Furthermore, both natural and man-made calamities may be addressed by these cutting-edge AI technologies as diagrammatically represented in Figure 11.2.

Dealing With Repetitive Jobs Smartly: While robots do not require breaks to recover from fatigue and increase production, humans do. AI-driven

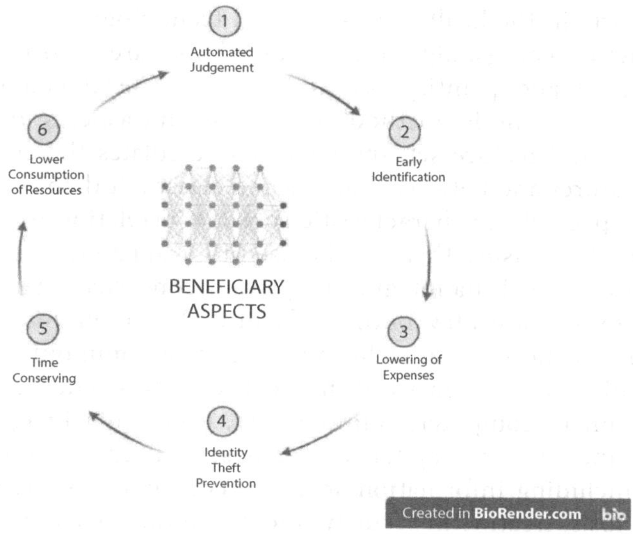

Figure 11.2 Beneficiary aspects of XAI and RAI in healthcare [26].

systems are able to complete monotonous tasks for extended periods of time without experiencing any slowdown.

At Your Disposal at All Times: Human constraints, including sleep schedules or time constraints, do not inhibit AI. AI and ML may run continuously and uninterrupted on the cloud, carrying out their designated tasks without stopping.

Scientific Research and Development: Large-scale data analysis helps expedite research and development. AI has aided in measuring the human genome and in the prediction of novel medications.

Cons:

Lack Creativity: Artificial intelligence is unable to display originality from the beginning; instead, it learns from pre-fed facts and prior experiences.

Demands Huge Funding: Artificial intelligence solutions are extremely expensive because they require the purchase of expensive hardware and software in order to stay up to date with the newest requirements.

Ethics and Morality: Integrating ethics and morality two important human qualities into the field of AI is a substantial problem as represented in Figure 11.3.

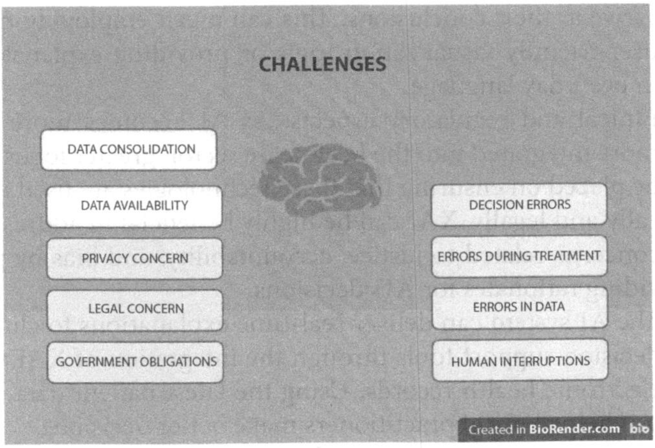

Figure 11.3 Challenges faced in the usage of AI and RAI [27].

11.9 Future Aspects

Explainable AI (XAI) holds immense promise for the future of healthcare. Artificial intelligence–driven algorithms are beginning to significantly affect the medical field. But the lack of transparency in models like deep neural networks (DNNs) raises concerns about consumer trust. Explainable artificial intelligence (XAI) aims to develop intelligent systems that help humans understand the predictions and decisions made by the AI, improving the transparency and dependability of the systems.

1. Increased trust and adoption patients and medical professionals will be better equipped to comprehend AI-driven decisions as XAI techniques develop. This increased transparency may increase trust in AI systems and promote their wider application in healthcare settings.
2. Enhanced clinical decision support, or XAI, helps doctors understand the reasoning behind AI-generated recommendations so they can make better decisions. This may lead to more customized treatment plans and improved patient results.
3. Interpretability and explainability: Future XAI models are likely to focus on this area to enhance interpretability and make it easier for laypeople to understand how AI systems

arrive at their conclusions. This can mean employing more user-friendly visualization tools or providing explanations in everyday language.

4. Ethical and regulatory aspects: As AI becomes more and more integrated into the healthcare sector, greater focus will be placed on ensuring that these technologies are used ethically and legally. XAI can be highly beneficial in addressing concerns related to justice, accountability, and bias by providing rationales for AI's decisions.
5. The AI system can deliver real-time explanations to clinical decision support tools through the integration of XAI with electronic health records. Using the latest patient data, this can help medical practitioners make better decisions.
6. Patient empowerment and education: XAI can help patients take a more active role in their healthcare decisions by providing context for AI-generated recommendations. This could lead to improved patient involvement and adherence to the treatment strategy.
7. Research and development: XAI has the potential to greatly swiftly advance the biomedical studies and developments sector by providing insights into complex biological processes and illness causes. This could lead to the creation of novel remedies and cures [27].

Future Perspective of RAI in Healthcare

Ensuring the ethical, transparent, and conscientious application of AI technology requires the implementation of RAI (responsible AI) in the healthcare sector.

1. Ethical guidelines and norms: As RAI develops, more comprehensive ethical standards and regulations specific to the healthcare sector will undoubtedly be created in the future. These frameworks will help ensure that AI systems used in healthcare are developed and applied ethically, taking safety, equality, and patient privacy into account.
2. Transparency and explainability: RAI will focus on enhancing the transparency and explainability of AI systems used in the medical sector. To do this, methods for educating patients and medical professionals about the reasoning behind AI-driven decisions would need to be developed in order to increase their level of trust in these systems.

3. Bias and fairness: Ensuring justice and combating bias in AI systems will be key components of RAI in healthcare. Future technologies will attempt to identify and lessen bias in AI systems to stop them from unfairly harming particular groups or generating disproportionately unfavorable outcomes.
4. Accountability and oversight: Another top goal for RAI is to set up protocols for the oversight and responsibility of AI systems in the medical field. To do this, protocols for auditing AI systems and algorithms must be established, keeping users and developers responsible for their decisions and actions.
5. Security and privacy of data: RAI will always place a high priority on preserving the security and privacy of patient data. The focus of future developments will be on implementing robust data security procedures and ensuring AI systems comply with relevant legal and regulatory requirements.
6. Working together and being involved: More cooperation and interaction with stakeholders, including as patients, industrial partners, regulators, and healthcare providers, will be required for RAI in the healthcare sector. This will make it easier to make sure AI technologies are in line with society values and satisfy the requirements and expectations of all stakeholders [27].

11.10 Conclusion

The amount of healthcare data has increased dramatically in recent years, making biomedical data analysis a difficult task. The burgeoning field of XAI and RAI has tools that may be used to analyze and classify biological data in an efficient manner. Furthermore, in order to lower the complexity level, the large dimensionality of the medical data necessitates careful feature selection. An AI approach for biomedical data analysis using correlation-based feature selection (XAICFS-BDA) is presented. The XAICFS-BDA method is used for classification of data for biomedical decision-making after selecting the best characteristics. Furthermore, the interaction-based feature selection method is used by the XAICFS-BDA methodology to pick features optimally. It is thought that the developing field of XAI in the healthcare area is crucial. In the meantime, in order to comprehend specific choices, outcomes, and the state of the patient's problems at that moment, it is imperative that the medical domain incorporate explanations about legal and ethical AI. Explainable artificial intelligence (XAI) is becoming a popular area of study for applications in healthcare and biology. Healthcare is one area where the XAI idea finds use due to its benefits in processing large and complex data sets. The advancements in XAI and ML have the potential to significantly raise the caliber of healthcare services. In order to predict and classify mental disorders, this paper develops an ideal boosting label weighting extreme learning machine optimal boosting label weighting extreme learning machine for mental disorder prediction and classification (OBWELM-MDC) approach. Determining the various DAS levels is the aim of the OBWELM-MDC approach. Parkinson's disease is a chronic, progressive movement disorder that affects a large global population. As Parkinson's disease worsens, the afflicted individual typically loses the ability to control their activities. People with Parkinson's disease exhibit symptoms such as tremor episodes and impaired gait during different phases of the illness. Medical diagnosis is a crucial yet challenging task that needs to be completed accurately and consistently. Automation would be highly beneficial in this regard. The DNN is used to classify medical data, and the Nadam optimizer–based hyperparameter tuning method may be used to increase the DNN's performance even more. A unique benchmark medical dataset is used to assess the XAIMFS-BMC technique's performance validation, and the findings are examined from a number of angles. The XAI/RAI technique can be expanded in the future to include feature selection and feature reduction methodology design. In order to eliminate the noise present in the test CXR picture, the suggested MMFBDL model uses Wiener filtering–based preprocessing. Next, three DL models—Densely Connected Network (DenseNet), Inception v4, and Residual Network (ResNet152)—are presented. Furthermore, to improve the classification performance, a multimodal fusion procedure combining all three models is performed. Ultimately, the input pictures are detected and classified into discrete class labels using a multilayer perceptron.

References

1. Payrovnaziri, S.N., Chen, Z., Rengifo-Moreno, P., Miller, T., Bian, J., Chen, J.H., Liu, X., He, Z., Explainable artificial intelligence models using real-world electronic health record data: a systematic scoping review. *J. Am. Med. Inf. Assoc.*, 27, 7, 1173–85, 2020 Jul.
2. Markus, A.F., Kors, J.A., Rijnbeek, P.R., The role of explainability in creating trustworthy artificial intelligence for health care: a comprehensive survey of

the terminology, design choices, and evaluation strategies. *J. Biomed. Inf.*, 113, 103655, 2021 Jan 1.

3. Azar, A.T. and El-Said, S.A., Performance analysis of support vector machines classifiers in breast cancer mammography recognition. *Neural Comput. Appl.*, 24, 1163–77, 2014 Apr.
4. Gumaei, A., Sammouda, R., Al-Rakhami, M., AlSalman, H., El-Zaart, A., Feature selection with ensemble learning for prostate cancer diagnosis from microarray gene expression. *Health Inf. J.*, 27, 1, 1460458221989402, 2021 Feb.
5. Cai, Z., Gu, J., Wen, C., Zhao, D., Huang, C., Huang, H., Tong, C., Li, J., Chen, H., An intelligent Parkinson's disease diagnostic system based on a chaotic bacterial foraging optimization enhanced fuzzy KNN approach. *Comput. Math. Methods Med.*, 2018, 1, 2396952, 2018 Jun 21.
6. Hayyolalam, V. and Kazem, A.A., Black widow optimization algorithm: a novel meta-heuristic approach for solving engineering optimization problems. *Eng. Appl. Artif. Intell.*, 87, 103249, 2020 Jan 1.
7. Houssein, E.H., Helmy, B.E., Oliva, D., Elngar, A.A., Shaban, H., A novel black widow optimization algorithm for multilevel thresholding image segmentation. *Expert Syst. Appl.*, 167, 114159, 2021 Apr 1.
8. Ravi, V., Narasimhan, H., Pham, T.D., A cost-sensitive deep learning-based meta-classifier for pediatric pneumonia classification using chest X-rays. *Expert Syst.*, 39, 7, e12966, 2022 Aug.
9. Sharma, S. and Parmar, M., Heart diseases prediction using deep learning neural network model. *Int. J. Innov. Technol. Explor. Eng. (IJITEE)*, 9, 3, 2244–8, 2020 Jan.
10. Pham, T., Ravi, V., Liu, N., Luo, B., Fan, C.W., Sun, X.F., Tensor decomposition of largest convolutional eigenvalues reveals pathological predictive power of RhoB in rectal cancer biopsy.
11. Gunning, D., Stefik, M., Choi, J., Miller, T., Stumpf, S., Yang, G.Z., XAI—Explainable artificial intelligence. *Sci. Rob.*, 4, 37, eaay7120, 2019 Dec 18.
12. Mahbub, M.K., Biswas, M., Gaur, L., Alenezi, F., Santosh, K.C., Deep features to detect pulmonary abnormalities in chest X-rays due to infectious diseaseX: Covid-19, pneumonia, and tuberculosis. *Inf. Sci.*, 592, 389–401, 2022 May 1.
13. Antoniadi, A.M., Du, Y., Guendouz, Y., Wei, L., Mazo, C., Becker, B.A., Mooney, C., Current challenges and future opportunities for XAI in machine learning-based clinical decision support systems: a systematic review. *Appl. Sci.*, 11, 11, 5088, 2021 May 31.
14. Sitaula, C., Shahi, T.B., Aryal, S., Marzbanrad, F., Fusion of multi-scale bag of deep visual words features of chest X-ray images to detect COVID-19 infection. *Sci. Rep.*, 11, 1, 23914, 2021 Dec 13.
15. Sitaula, C. and Hossain, M.B., Attention-based VGG-16 model for COVID-19 chest X-ray image classification. *Appl. Intell.*, 51, 5, 2850–63, 2021 May.

16. Van der Velden, B.H., Kuijf, H.J., Gilhuijs, K.G., Viergever, M.A., Explainable artificial intelligence (XAI) in deep learning-based medical image analysis. *Med. Image Anal.*, 79, 102470, 2022 Jul 1.
17. Murdoch, W.J., Singh, C., Kumbier, K., Abbasi-Asl, R., Yu, B., Interpretable machine learning: definitions, methods, and applications, arXiv preprint arXiv:1901.04592, 2019 Jan 14.
18. Adadi, A. and Berrada, M., Peeking inside the black-box: a survey on explainable artificial intelligence (XAI). *IEEE Access*, 6, 52138–60, 2018 Sep 16.
19. Esmaeilzadeh, P., Use of AI-based tools for healthcare purposes: a survey study from consumers' perspectives. *BMC Med. Inf. Decis. Making*, 20, 1–9, 2020 Dec.
20. Houben, S., Abrecht, S., Akila, M., Bär, A., Brockherde, F., Feifel, P., Fingscheidt, T., Gannamaneni, S.S., Ghobadi, S.E., Hammam, A., Haselhoff, A., Inspect, understand, overcome: A survey of practical methods for ai safety, in: *Deep Neural Networks and Data for Automated Driving: Robustness, Uncertainty Quantification, and Insights Towards Safety*, pp. 3–78, Springer International Publishing, Cham, 2022 Jun 18.
21. Ferreira, J.J. and Monteiro, M.S., What are people doing about XAI user experience? A survey on AI explainability research and practice, in: *Design, User Experience, and Usability. Design for Contemporary Interactive Environments: 9th International Conference, DUXU 2020, Held as Part of the 22nd HCI International Conference, HCII 2020, Copenhagen, Denmark, July 19–24, 2020, Proceedings, Part II 22*, pp. 56–73, Springer International Publishing, 2020.
22. Xie, S., Yu, Z., Lv, Z., Multi-disease prediction based on deep learning: a survey. *Comput. Model. Eng. Sci.*, 128, 2, 489–522, 2021 Aug 10.
23. Tjoa, E. and Guan, C., A survey on explainable artificial intelligence (xai): Toward medical xai. *IEEE Trans. Neural Netw. Learn. Syst.*, 32, 11, 4793–813, 2020 Oct 20.
24. Yang, G., Ye, Q., Xia, J., Unbox the black-box for the medical explainable AI via multi-modal and multi-centre data fusion: A mini-review, two showcases and beyond. *Inf. Fusion*, 77, 29–52, 2022 Jan 1.
25. Ellahham, S., Ellahham, N., Simsekler, M.C., Application of artificial intelligence in the health care safety context: opportunities and challenges. *Am. J. Med. Qual.*, 35, 4, 341–8, 2020 Jul.
26. Ali, O., Abdelbaki, W., Shrestha, A., Elbasi, E., Alryalat, M.A., Dwivedi, Y.K., A systematic literature review of artificial intelligence in the healthcare sector: Benefits, challenges, methodologies, and functionalities. *J. Innov. Knowl.*, 8, 1, 100333, 2023 Jan 1.
27. Lipton, Z.C., The mythos of model interpretability: In machine learning, the concept of interpretability is both important and slippery. *Queue*, 16, 3, 31–57, 2018 Jun 1.

12

Classify Chronic Wounds: The Need of Explainable AI and Responsible AI

Saurav Sarkar[1], Soma Das[2*], Ananya Chanda[2] and Sayan Biswas[2]

[1]*Division of Pharmaceutics, Department of Pharmaceutical Technology, University of North Bengal, Raja Rammohunpur, Dist. Darjeeling, West Bengal, India*
[2]*Department of Pharmaceutical Technology, School of Health and Medical Sciences, Adamas University, Barasat, West Bengal, India*

Abstract

Chronic wounds offer a substantial healthcare burden, requiring accurate categorization for efficient treatment. Artificial intelligence (AI) has shown potential in automating wound categorization operations in recent years. As we explore using AI for this goal, two important factors become apparent: the necessity of explainable AI (XAI) and the importance of responsible AI deployment.

Because most machine learning models, especially deep neural networks, are black boxes, XAI has emerged in importance. When it comes to identifying chronic wounds, doctors should trust and apply AI-derived insights into their decisions, setting up alternatives that come from AI. This way, although it cannot perform any better than current traditional black-box models, in which issues rooted deep within the field of medicine itself are transparent and accurate at making forecasts for the future, it may be problematic. Therefore, it is essential to employ XAI methods to explain how decisions are made, so that medics can understand and verify the AI-generated classifications received. What is more, for healthcare to be fairer and for the built-in biases to be removed in arenas such as medicine, successful implementation of AI is a priority. For marginalized groups, algorithm design and data collection may exacerbate the inequality in healthcare access. Inaccurate labeling by prejudiced AI models when it comes to determining wound types or demographics could result in diagnostics and chronic wound patients all receiving unfair treatment. To guarantee justice and fairness in wound categorization, it is necessary to adopt responsible AI methods, such as collection of representative

**Corresponding author*: somapharma@gmail.com

Rishabha Malviya and Sonali Sundram (eds.) Explainable and Responsible Artificial Intelligence in Healthcare, (297–322)

and diverse datasets, measures to identify as well as remove bias, and continual evaluation on how effectively these systems are operating.

This underlines the importance of incorporating techniques of deployable AI and XAI into the characterization of chronic wounds. Clinicians can understand model predictions better by governing their decisions with openness and accountability in AI. It promotes collaboration and trust between AI systems and healthcare providers. This post argues that responsible AI and XAI are not only desirable; they are essential for ethical use in the categorization of chronic wounds. These principles enable healthcare professionals and improve patient outcomes, laying the foundation for a future when AI will support moral medical wound care practitioners rather than replacing them. By making judgment less mysterious, reducing bias, and fostering trust, these principles of responsible AI thus allow the development of a service that must be maintained morally.

Keywords: Chronic wounds, explainable AI, responsible AI, healthcare, interpretability

List of Abbreviation

AI	Artificial Intelligence
XAI	Explainable Artificial Intelligence
NLP	Natural language processing
EHRs	Electronic health records
LIME	Local interpretable model-agnostic explanations
SHAP	Shapley Additive Explanations
CNN	Convolutional neural network
LNN	Logical neural network
AUC	Area under the curve
CMGE	Counterfactually supports fact extraction
EMRs	Electronic medical records
App	Application
MDS	Minimum dataset

12.1 Introduction

The categorization of chronic wounds is vital in contemporary healthcare to guide treatment choices and enhance results for patients. However, the difficulty of determining chronic wounds and the rapid pace of medical inventions underscore the need for advanced, responsible, and ethically accurate solutions. In this context, this introductory essay argues the importance of classification of chronic wounds to responsible AI frameworks and XAI. This essay will demonstrate through discussing the limitations of traditional classification methods, the potential of AI-driven approaches, and the brief overview of two articles on how responsible AI protects against medical biases and enables ethical use and how XAI enables clear AI-driven conclusions. Understanding the symbiotic to what accord the "infectious" accurate categorization could be with principled AI approaches essential in a possible motivational response to achieving this building distinguished opportunity in disadvantaged sufferings.

12.1.1 Background on Chronic Wounds

The chronic wounds heal for longer than expected; they are close to the most challenging sock of global health deterrence. They are more likely to ensue among characters who acquire diabetes, vascular illness, and pressure ulcers. Although they are not comparatively confining, they are tough to handle efficaciously and need extensive relevant reaches and specialized work. Suitable solutions are practicable because complications are catastrophic, and numerous issues have disastrous implications and yield amputations [1].

Responsible AI and XAI are necessary for eradicating the problems with chronic wound treatments. XAI ensures that the used AI system's decision-making processes are fathomable and open. Transparency is a critical issue for AI advice that clinicians can trust and base their decision-making on. There are many reasons; a scope as critical as wounds is no exception. A patient and a healthcare giver have much more confidence if the model recommends a healing policy they can follow [2].

Furthermore, responsible AI frameworks underscore responsibility where AI developers and systems are accountable for their actions and consequences. In the case of chronic wound management, liability restricts the damage that may be caused to patients and promotes the ethical use of AI as a supportive tool in the healthcare sector. Continuous monitoring and assessment are encouraged to ensure safety and efficacy [3].

Bias mitigation is another major problem addressed utilizing XAI. By identifying and removing biases from AI models, healthcare providers can make reasonable treatment suggestions across different patient populations. In chronic wound management, this cannot be overstated; patients need equal access to good treatments for favourable outcomes [4].

Trust in patients goes a long way in healthcare. XAI makes a patient understand why an AI makes the recommendations and by doing so, enables trust. This paves the way for the patient to fully accept and follow the line of treatment, adherence to medication, and other recommendations. Thus, in cases where the patient knows why a machine recommended something over another, they are more likely to actively participate in their healthcare [5]. The repeated nature of XAI leads to improved AI models. By giving the insight of how the model behaves and its performance, a doctor and a developer may fine-tune these models to improve accuracy, safety, and efficiency with time. This process ensures that AI personalized medicines for chronic wounds as per the needs of patients and health systems [6].

12.1.2 Importance of Accurate Classification

Efficient treatment and management also depend on the proper categorization of the chronicity of wounds. In this way, accurate processing and categorization ensure that the patient is provided with the most appropriate care, as different types of chronic wounds require different treatment procedures. This is where the role of XAI and responsible AI in general is valuable [7].

With proper processing, the correct categorization ensures that all patients receive personalized treatment and show better and faster healing results and cost the healthcare system less. Improper categorization could lead to interdisciplinary treatment applied longer and higher risk of adverse effects. Thus, AI systems need to be able to categorize accurately available persistent wound groups to correctly support clinicians with therapy choice [8].

The classification of chronic wounds by AI models necessitates XAI. To completely rely on their recommendations, clinicians must be able to fully comprehend the processes that these AI algorithms use to arrive at their decision-making realities. Explainable AI makes it possible for healthcare providers to justify and verify output classification judgments. Greater transparency increases a physician's or nurse's confidence in AI-driven classifications, which may help them make more informed decisions, which may benefit patients in the long run [9].

Responsible AI guaranteed the ethics and responsibility of the creation and subsequent application of classification algorithms. Miscalculations or misclassifications in final outputs could result from biases in the training data and algorithmic architecture. Responsible AI frameworks must be validated and tested extensively to expose and address biases that lead to chronic wounds being classified differently among diverse patient populations. Moreover, responsible AI promotes transparency, responsibility, and patient safety in every stage of development and deployment [10].

Responsible AI emphasizes the importance of ongoing monitoring and assessment to ensure that the classification model remains accurate and reliable for various populations. Therefore, feedback loops empower clinicians to provide perioperative data to improve their performance in real-world practices [11].

12.1.3 Role of AI in Wound Classification

The role of AI is becoming increasingly critical to the importance of AI technologies for chronic wound classification. AI provides innovative and advanced solutions to the difficult challenge of effective identification and categorization of such diseases. However, utilizing AI in this context necessitates a framework for XAI and responsible AI principles. Thus, from photo, patient backgrounds, and clinical notes, AI technologies such as machine learning and deep learning models have shown impressive abilities in analyzing large amounts of wound-related information [12]. These technologies can detect tiny patterns or characteristics that human observers might miss, leading to more accurate and consistent wound classification. Using AI, medical specialists can speed healing determination, individualize their care strategies, and ascertain wound change with greater accuracy and efficacy [13].

Nevertheless, the non-transparency of AI decision-making may present important issues, especially in sensitive sectors like medicine and critical wound classification. Explainable AI resolves this challenge by offering an explanation about the reasoning in arriving at their decisions. In the chronic wounds environment, XAI explains the reasoning behind classification decisions, thus assisting physicians in understanding and trusting AI's recommendations. This transparency not only promotes the explanation of AI outputs but also allows health personnel to verify the accuracy and reliability of AI-driven classifications; in the long run, they promote patient well-being [14].

Responsible AI principles are vital to reduce biases and assure the fair and ethical application of AI in wound classification. Biases within the training data or algorithm design can result in errors or inconsistencies in the classification outputs, undermining the acceptability of clinical decision-making. Responsible AI practices include thorough validation, continuous monitoring, and mitigation approaches to ensure fairness, accountability, and patient safety. Compliance with responsible AI principles allows healthcare providers to minimize the dangers linked to the application of AI, enhance trust among patients and providers, and insulate themselves from unforeseen repercussions [15].

12.2 Understanding Chronic Wounds

One way of doing this is by ensuring that there is understanding around chronic wounds. The third is the use of XAI, which enables transparency and accountants. XAI ensures that stored data is reliable for the accurate predictions to identify persistent wounds. Fourthly, responsible AI ensures justice and availability by reflecting accountability. Persistent wound management cannot function without XAI and responsible AI [16].

12.2.1 Definition and Types of Chronic Wounds

Chronic wounds are injuries that do not heal within a reasonable period, and they could persist for weeks, months, or even years. They are often arising from other health conditions, such as diabetes, vascular disease, or injuries pressure ulcers, among others. Common wound types include diabetic foot ulcers, venous leg ulcers, arterial ulcers, and pressure ulcers [17]. XAI in chronic wound healing is essential for enhancing classification and therapy decision-making procedures and boosting transparency and understanding. XAI allows healthcare providers to understand how AI algorithms arrive at their outcomes, and it encourages transparency of reasoning used for classification and therapy recommendations. This improves trust and assurance to physicians who will depend on the system to make proper decisions and personalize therapies to individual needs [18].

Responsible AI concepts are just as important in chronic wound therapy for ensuring fairness, accountability, and an ethical AI application. Bias in the data or the design of the algorithm can result in bias in the classification result, which may harm the patient. Responsible AI frameworks need thorough validation and constant control to detect and minimize bias, allowing for fair recommendations across populations. Furthermore, responsible AI focuses on patient safety and privacy, protecting sensitive medical data and following ethical standards at all AI life development stages [19].

12.2.2 Causes and Complications

Chronic wounds result from various health disorders and causes, which cause prolonged healing time and higher risks of severe consequences. The following are the etiologies of persistent wounds. Firstly, persistent wounds result from causes of persistent wounds:

a. **Diabetes:** Diabetic nerve damage and poor circulation to the lower limbs result in slow healing and high infection-risk diabetic foot ulcers [20].
b. **Vascular disease:** Disorders such as peripheral artery disease limit blood flow to tissues, which exacerbates the healing of wounds and raises the risk of long-term injuries such arterial ulcers [21].

c. **Pressure ulcers:** Peripheral artery disease and blood supply blockage to the tissues effectuate diminished wound healing and predisposed persistent arterial ulcers [22].
d. **Traumatic injuries:** Notable injuries, burns, or surgery wounds can progress into persistent wounds. This is true if the injury penetrates the skin into the underlying tissues and gets infected [23].

Chronic wound complications can be detrimental to patients' overall health and quality of life. These include the following:

i. **Infection:** Chronic wounds are vulnerable to bacterial infection, which can impede their recovery, induce necrosis of tissues, and cause systemic infection [24].
ii. **Delayed healing:** Inflammation, impaired circulation, and comorbidities can prolong healing, resulting in the development of a chronic wound [25].
iii. **Pain and discomfort:** Chronic wounds cause constant pain and discomfort in the patients, limiting their mobility and affecting their quality of life [26].
iv. **Amputation:** The worst-case scenario, persistent wounds unhealing with therapy may require surgery, even amputation, to prevent systemic infection and other complications [27].

The cure to the issues brought forth by chronic wounds as well as their ramifications can primarily be solved through XAI and responsible AI. XAI ensures that providers can understand and trust AI generated wound care recommendations, ensuring openness and comprehension into the AI decision-making procedure. It is critical to have this information in order to customize treatment for each patient and to achieve the best outcome [28].

12.2.3 Current Methods of Wound Classification

Methods of chronic wound classification rely mostly on the clinical judgment of medical professionals, albeit reinforced with photography and ultrasound-based imaging. First and foremost, this approach is inherently subjective and doctors often disagree on how to distinguish one type of wound from another, leading to substantial diagnostic and medical plan errors. Furthermore, chronic wounds multifactorial nature makes them barely susceptible to conventional treatments [29].

Explainable AI is an ideal solution to these difficulties as it enhances AI integration by providing transparency and interpretability when categorizing the wound. XAI algorithms shine a light on the decision-making of AI models and allow healthcare clinicians to understand the reasoning behind the classification recommendations. Clarity on how AI makes its recommendations encourages doctors to trust AI-integrated systems and make well-informed decisions in wound treatments. Transparency is especially impactful in chronic wound categorization because proper diagnosis and the provision of a targeted treatment technique are critical in improving patient outcomes [30].

Similarly, responsible AI concepts are essential for chronic wound classification both to ensure fairness, accountability, and the ethical deployment of AI technology. Categorization outcomes could vary due to biases in the training data or algorithmic design. Manifold outcomes may result in a greater level of health inequality. In particular, they may need transparent and responsible frameworks for validation, monitoring, and mitigation to detect and eliminate biases, ensuring equitable treatment recommendations across diverse patients. In the example above, responsible AI also places emphasis on safety, privacy, consent fairness, accountability, and ethical deployment of AI safeguarding against unintended consequences, establishing ethical principles throughout the AI lifecycle [31].

Ambitious incorporation of XAI and responsible AI principles into wound classification may play a vital role in improving the management of chronic wounds by enhancing the accuracy, consistency, and fairness of diagnostic and care decisions. Adopting these constructs will enable physicians to take advantage of the potential of AI for greater patient care while maintaining the highest standards of moral and just healthcare delivery. Additionally, the steady improvement and ongoing optimization achievable through XAI and responsible AI principles indicate that AI-driven categorization systems would evolve to satisfy the changing needs of patients and care delivery alike, leading to superior outcomes for those suffering from chronic wounds [32].

12.3 The Rise of AI in Wound Classification

The development of AI in chronic wound classification is promising, but it is also fraught with difficulties. To maintain transparency, including allowing the doctor to understand the algorithm of how AI makes a decision, one of the key concepts is XAI. This concept also applies to the development of AI solutions and discusses the main algorithm of responsible AI. Justice, accountability, and the correct relationship development between man and machine are key concepts to consider. XAI and responsible AI are vital in the complex genre of chronic wound classification to ensure accurate diagnosis, personalized therapy, and improved patient outcomes through the adherence to ethical standards and trust in AI-powered healthcare solutions [33].

12.3.1 Overview of AI Technologies

The use of AI technology in chronic wounds management is a bright future. This technology stretches from various AI-based approaches such as machine learning algorithms to deep learning models, computer vision, and natural language processing. However, the incorporation of such a potential framework that guarantees transparency, accountability, and moral integrity is essential to the use of AI in the seminal AI structure [34].

Machine learning algorithms accomplish a significant role in chronic wound care by assessing massive datasets of patient data to notice patterns and estimate results. These algorithms can support doctors in perceiving chronic wounds, forecasting healing trajectories, and improving treatment methods based on precise patient features. However, the lack of transparency of machine learning models results of issues in grasping how they attain at their findings, emphasizing the need for XAI [35].

Deep learning methods, a subsection of machine learning, have proven its potential in image-based wound classification. By assessing wound photos, these models can categorize wounds according to its kind, severity, and healing possibility. Although deep learning algorithms may attain great levels of exactness, their black-box nature frequently limits their interpretability. Explainable AI techniques are essential for enlightening the decision-making process for these models, empowering clinicians to comprehend and belief in their decisions [36].

Computer vision procedures provide automatic analysis of wound images, thus enabling rapid and neutral assessment of wound features such as size, depth, and tissue composition. By mixing computer vision algorithms, healthcare personnel can expedite wound documentation, monitor healing progress, and detect early indicators of problems. However, promising the reliability and accuracy of computer vision systems has been crucial, requiring complete validation and obedience to responsible AI standards [37].

Natural language processing (NLP) technologies are vital in mining insights from clinical notes, electronic health records (EHRs), and medical literature connected to chronic wounds. These technologies can support doctors in producing huge capacities of textual data, perceiving relevant information, and allowing evidence-based decision-making. Nonetheless, the possibility for bias in NLP algorithms underscores the need of responsible AI practices in data curation, algorithm development, and authentication [38].

12.3.2 Applications in Healthcare and Wound Management

In healthcare for treatment of chronic wounds, the realm of AI holds enormous potential for enhancing patient amenability, enlightening clinical decision-making, and expanding resource allocation. However, in spite of these benefits, there is a urgent need for XAI and responsible AI techniques to endorse transparency, accountability, and ethical integrity in healthcare systems driven by AI [39].

One significant use of AI in healthcare is in the detection and categorization of chronic wounds. AI techniques, namely, machine learning as well as deep learning models, can evaluate patient data, consisting of wound photos, clinical notes, and medical histories, to precisely classify wounds according to kind, severity, and healing possibility. By employing AI for wound classification, healthcare personnel may accelerate diagnosis, personalize treatment strategies, and healing progress with better precision and efficiency. However, the opacity of AI decision-making processes offers issues in understanding how these models arrive at their findings, necessitating the incorporation of XAI techniques to explicate their thinking and ensure the credibility of AI-generated recommendations [40].

One of the major useful application of AI in management of wound is concerned with monitoring of wound and its surveillance. AI-driven systems, using computer vision techniques, may analyze wound photos to assess healing progress, detect indicators of infection or problems, and give early intervention when necessary. By automating wound documentation and analysis, AI solutions optimize clinical workflows, minimize manual workload for healthcare personnel, and increase the timeliness and accuracy of wound assessment. Nevertheless, appropriate AI methods are needed to avoid potential biases in algorithmic design or training data to ensure equal and unbiased healthcare delivery [41].

Moreover, AI has major implications for individualized treatment planning and decision support in chronic wound management. By analyzing patient data and clinical guidelines, AI systems can create individualized therapy suggestions based on specific patient features, comorbidities, and preferences. These AI-driven decision support technologies help healthcare clinicians to make evidence-based treatment decisions, optimize resource allocation, and enhance patient outcomes. However, transparent and responsible AI systems are vital to ensure that treatment suggestions correspond with ethical norms and patient-centered care principles, hence encouraging confidence and acceptance among healthcare professionals and patients [42].

12.3.3 Benefits and Challenges

Chronic wounds present both considerable obstacles and possible benefits in healthcare. The wounds, remaining beyond distinctive healing periods, can affect from many underlying disorders such as diabetes, vascular disease, or pressure ulcers.

As wounds of chronic nature have a potential of major financial burden for patients in healthcare system, when combined together, XAI and responsible AI principles can help in addressing these problems and development of useful solutions for their management [43]. One of the major advantages of incorporating AI in management of chronic wound is the chance of increasing the accuracy if diagnosis and precise treatment approaches. Different AI algorithms, namely, machine learning and deep learning can easily scan large number of complicated datasets encompassing patient histories, clinical notes, and photos of the wound for accurately identifying wounds and forecasting healing trajectories. By combining AI, healthcare providers can use personalized treatment plans for specific patient needs, optimize the allocation of resources, and improve patient outcomes [44]. In order to gain such benefits, various obstacles present in chronic wound treatment must be addressed. One of these obstacles is the complexity and variable nature of chronic wounds. This can make correct diagnosis and treatment approaches difficult. Several underlying reasons are involved in the development of chronic wounds, which requires a full evaluation of the health condition and nature of wound of the patient. The subjective nature of wound evaluation and the option of variety across healthcare practitioners might further complicate decision-making of chronic wound management [45]. Explainable AI (XAI) is important in determining these difficulties by offering transparency and interpretation of AI-driven decision-making processes. XAI methods highlight how AI algorithms attain at their results, serving healthcare providers understand the rationale behind cataloguing and therapy approvals. This transparency endorses clinician's trust in AI-driven systems, nurtures collaboration between AI and human specialists, and ultimately advances the correctness and effectiveness of chronic wound management [46].

Furthermore, responsible AI concepts are vital in minimizing potential biases and guaranteeing the ethical distribution of AI in chronic wound management. Biases in training data or algorithmic design can cause inequalities in categorization outcomes, thus affecting the truthfulness of healthcare choices. Responsible AI frameworks necessitate extensive validation, monitoring, and mitigation techniques to promote equity, transparency, and patient safety throughout the AI lifespan [47].

12.4 Explainable AI: Unravelling the Black Box

The non-intuitive and opaque structure of machine learning models hinders the widespread adoption of AI, despite the enormous benefits it offers across multiple industries [48]. Understanding the intricate internal workings of an AI model necessitates a solid mathematical foundation. This may provide a serious obstacle to entrance. An AI model can be explained using one of two methods: (i) the interpretable model or (ii) the intelligible model. Post-hoc explainability approaches are used to explain coherent models. Regression models and decision trees, two examples of traditional machine learning techniques, are interpretable models because they exhibit greater transparency than convolutional networks [49]. The machine learning model is treated as a black box with inputs and certain outputs by generalized XAI techniques. Local interpretable model-agnostic explanations (LIME) is one of these techniques. By training local surrogate models on perturbed inputs rather than globally, LIME discovers the statistical relationship between the input and the model prediction [50]. It offers a visualization along with an interpretable representation that explains an instance. This work presents the explainability and transparency of the classification of chronic wounds through the use of Keras and XAI algorithms for transfer learning implementation.

Such models use input data to make predictions; however, the logic and decision-making process underlying the projections are hidden from the user. This lack of transparency makes it difficult for users to understand the model's behavior, spot any biases or errors, or hold the model accountable for its decisions.

In XAI, "black-box" models are sometimes contrasted with "white box" or "transparent" models, where the internal mechanisms and reasoning behind the predictions are easily accessible and understandable. It helps users completely understand and trust the decisions that these algorithms make [51].

12.4.1 Importance of Explainability in Healthcare AI

Very context-sensitive AI predictions and data-driven are being utilized to guide decisions regarding delirium, a highly relative syndrome in older individuals. Using machine learning algorithms to assess EHRs and identify patients at risk of delirium is one example of this. These algorithms can estimate a patient's risk of delirium based on a variety of patient-specific data, such as demographics, drug use, and findings from laboratory tests [52].

An expert-level laser surgery option selection model using a multiclass XGBoost model. The suggested approach was validated by the authors using patients who underwent refractive surgery at the B&VIIT Eye Centre, and it produced results with an accuracy of 78.9% on an external validation dataset. It also provides a clinical understanding of the SHapley Additive exPlanations (SHAP)–based machine learning methodology. Mirchi *et al.* presented a surgical training paradigm with automated instructional visual feedback. The authors trained and evaluated a support vector machine model with simulated medical and surgical data, obtaining 100% sensitivity, 82% specificity, and 92% accuracy [53]. A convolutional neural network (CNN)–based model for categorizing chronic wounds was developed, and its explanation was given using the XAI technique LIME. By applying the transfer learning technique, the proposed CNN-based model achieved an average precision of 95%, an average recall of 94%, and an average F1-score of 94%. The model could give clinicians visual signals by utilizing LIME. To diagnose fenestral otosclerosis, Tan *et al.* presented an otosclerosislogical neural network (LNN) on temporal high-resolution computed tomography bone slices. The external test dataset yielded an area under the curve (AUC) of 99.5% for the suggested approach. They also used the XAI technique to visualize the LNN model's learned deep representations [54].

A multi-granularity graph that counterfactually supports fact extraction (CMGE) in the diagnosis of lymphedema. A graph-based neural network called CMGE is capable of extracting data from electronic medical records (EMRs). It might also establish a cause-and-effect link between the traits. The suggested model was tested using real Chinese EMRs, and, by offering counterfactual data, it proved to be a precise and understandable method. A computer-aided diagnosis system for lung cancer that includes explanation phrases. The suggested solution is divided into two sections: the first uses LIME to create a local post-hoc XAI model, and the second converts the relevant properties that have been chosen into plain language [55]. An ensemble clustering-based XAI model for traumatic brain injury prognostic and diagnostic analysis was published by Yeboah *et al.* [56]. A CNN-based model for COVID-19 case detection with chest X-ray images called COVID-Net. Additionally, the authors contrasted COVID-Net with ResNet-50 and VGG-19. On the COVIDx test dataset, COVID-Net obtained a 93.3% accuracy and a 91% sensitivity [57].

12.4.2 Techniques for Making AI Models Interpretable

In the present investigation, methods such as SHAP and LIME are used to implement the explainability of the AI model to comprehend the explainability of the black box model [58]. A systematic technique for assessing the relative importance of characteristics in various models has the acronym SHAP. The Shapley values, which give the average fractional contributions of the specific feature value possible feature combinations, are related to the explanations. As a result, the Shap estimated values match the Shapley values of the dependent probability function in the model [59].

12.4.2.1 SHapley Additive exPlanations

A method for attributing the additive characteristics primarily conveyed by Shapley value explanations is called SHAP, and it is related to lime. A method called SHAP is used to give a summary of each forecast as it occurs within theoretically optimal Shapley values in game theory. Because they are beneficial approaches with favorable qualities, the Shapley values have become very popular in collaborative game theory [60].

12.4.2.2 Local Interpretable Model-Agnostic Explanations

The machine learning model's capability and the understanding of its predictions will be enhanced by the application of the LIME technique for explainability. As a result, the method is suitable for assessing a local model and clarifies the classifier for a single instance. Different perceptions can be obtained from every categorization model with just one anticipated value. The synthetic randomly chosen facts are created close to the input instance from which the forecast is derived for every event and the prediction that goes along with it. The likelihood of each such occurrence is computed and weighted according to how similar the generated instance is to the supplied situation [61]. The LIME's basic function is to verify the model's local transparency and understandability regardless of the technology or techniques used throughout the design phase. To assess the model's local transparency, the features used during the prediction phase are crucial. Although the local explainability sharpens the prediction process, it might not always fit the model exactly on a global scale. Let h: $\mathbf{Rx'} \lhd \mathbf{R}, \mathbf{h} \in \mathbf{H}$ be the representation of the explainable model, where the variable **H** stands for the XAI model, such as a rule-based classifier or decision tree. Given a model $\mathbf{h} \in \mathbf{H}$, which denotes the model through a variety of textual and visual aids, it is established that each **h ϵ H** model may be fully explained. Therefore, the quantity **Ωh** denotes the interpretability's complexity concerning the soft and hard restrictions [62].

12.5 Responsible AI in Wound Classification

The conceptual framework of responsible AI is predicated on safeguarding stakeholder interests and societal values. In addition to ensuring transparency, the system becomes truly intelligent when ethical considerations are given significant weight in the decisions made by these AI algorithms. This is because inherited duty is part of the algorithm. The following elements should be considered to guide the creation of responsible AI:

a) The public's perception of the acceptability of responsible AI in society will be influenced by the acceptance of responsibility. Governments and the general public must work together to address the reliability concerns around AI [63].
b) AI models that use self-justification will be able to reason and create an ethical code based on human ideals. According to a recent study, there is an insufficient connection between decisions and the ethical situation [64].
c) The application of AI in daily life to create rules for responsible AI is a part of the participation process. Here, education is vital in making people aware of the fact that their opinions matter much in determining how responsible AI becomes in society [65].

12.5.1 Ethical Considerations in AI Development

There are ethical concerns with using private data and information in AI algorithms. In addition to the data that it uses for testing and training, AI can access whatever data you share. Improper treatment or protection of personal data may lead to a major breach of privacy. Laws and safeguards protecting data privacy are necessary to guarantee ethical AI development. This is particularly true in cases when the data contains sensitive personal information that could be subject to legal action, such as biometric data or a person's financial history. Additionally, there needs to be a lot of accountability and oversight for AI systems.

These technologies can reveal any possible issues and lessen their effects, allowing for further advancements in AI innovation [66].

AI "fits within existing legal categories or whether a new category with its special features and implications should be developed" is a matter that is subject to ongoing debate. Healthcare could be greatly improved by utilizing AI in clinical settings, but there are still ethical issues that need to be resolved. For AI in healthcare to realise its full potential, four primary ethical issues must be addressed: Key factors to take into account are as follows:

(1) informed consent for data use;
(2) safety and transparency;
(3) algorithmic fairness and biases; and
(4) data privacy.

The question of whether AI systems may be regarded as lawful is both legally and politically sensitive (European Parliament Resolution, 16 February 2017) [67].

12.5.2 Addressing Bias and Fairness

The information demonstrates AI models' large-scale deployment and embedding of social and human biases. But the real culprit here should be the underlying data rather than the algorithm. Data reflecting human decision-making or the second-order repercussions of historical or societal injustices can be used to train models. In addition, bias can be introduced by the methods used to gather and process data, as well as by user-generated data operating as a feedback loop [68]. Although there are not any established standards or procedures for reporting and comparing these models to our knowledge, future work in this area should be done to help physicians and researchers.

AI is becoming a necessary component of contemporary digital systems, going beyond being a "nice-to-have." As the amount of time we spend using AI to make judgments increases, we need to ensure sure these choices are fair, impartial, and morally sound. We believe that responsible AI systems ought to be transparent, accountable, and explicable. The application of AI is expanding and has the potential to sometimes outperform human competence in improving surgical outcomes and patient experiences.

It may be sparse, coexist with, or replace present systems. Artificial intelligence is bringing about a new era in healthcare, and not utilizing it may be unethical and unscientific [69].

12.5.3 Regulatory Frameworks and Guidelines

The policy department for "Citizens' Rights and Constitutional Affairs" was asked by the European Parliament's Committee on Legal Affairs to commission, supervise, and publish the study that formed the basis of the resolution. The study emphasizes how critical it is to adopt a resolution calling for the quick creation of a legal framework governing robotics and AI that can foresee and adapt to any medium-term technological advancements [70].

12.6 Case Studies and Applications

12.6.1 Real-World Example of AI in Wound Classification

Using deep learning on mobile devices, Ramachandram *et al.* [71] presented a fully automated wound tissue segmentation technique. During the COVID-19 pandemic, Barakat-Johnson *et al.* [72] assessed an AI app for wound assessment and care.

12.6.2 Success Stories and Challenges Faced

A CNN, or deep learning network, was created and assessed by Ramachandram *et al.* [71] for completely automated wound tissue segmentation utilizing a mobile device. Mobile device-captured digital photos of wounds are the main source of input data for AI algorithms. For healthcare providers, the system is more convenient and accessible because the photographs are probably taken utilizing smartphones or other similar mobile devices. The deep learning models' outputs would include the segmentation of the injured tissue in the original pictures. The models would provide masks at the pixel level that distinguish between several forms of wound tissue, including granulation tissue, necrotic tissue, and healthy tissue. These segmentation masks facilitate precise wound assessment and treatment planning by giving clinicians comprehensive information about the extent and spatial distribution of various wound components. A collection of 58 anonymized wound photos of different kinds of chronic wounds from Swift Medical's Wound Database was used in the study. Using a browser-based picture annotation tool, five wound doctors labeled four different tissue types (epithelial, granulation, slough, and eschar) within the wound bed at one-week intervals. Two deep CNN architectures were created and applied sequentially in the procedure for tissue and wound segmentation.

A total of 465,187 and 17,000 image-label pairs were used to train these models. The system helped clinicians accurately document wounds by providing objective wound tissue identification and measurement. One of the study's benefits is the creation of a portable, affordable, and easily navigable method for segmenting wound tissue, which may enhance wound evaluation and treatment. The study also showed that deep learning algorithms for medical picture analysis on mobile devices are feasible and effective. The authors recognized that distinguishing between epithelialization and epithelial tissue would be difficult and that this would result in the model performing relatively poorly for epithelial tissue. There are more potential restrictions. Initially, the lack of information regarding the study's cohort size and participant demographics made it difficult to evaluate how representative the sample was. A larger and more varied sample would have improved the external validity of the research and the applicability of the results. Secondly, it is conceivable that not all potential wound kinds, sizes, and locations were fully represented in the dataset that was used to train the deep learning model. This might make it more difficult for the model to segment wound tissues correctly in situations that are not included in the training dataset. A consequence of the above is that the automatic segmentation tool's performance for other types of wounds, other than the ones considered in the study, may differ. The fourth limitation is it would be difficult to present and measure the advantages and disadvantages of the proposed strategy relative to the current techniques without developing a framework for comparison with other methods or a benchmark for wound tissue segmentation. More specifically, although the study demonstrated the deep learning approach's possibility and efficiency when implemented in the mobile environment, there was no comparison with other similar algorithms. Little information on biases presents in the dataset and employed counter measures was reported. It is possible that the deep learning model's performance and generalizability are significantly impacted by biases in the dataset utilized for training. It is imperative to tackle and disclose data biases to guarantee the dependability and relevance of the automated segmentation technique. Lastly, the algorithm's effect on the results of wound healing was not assessed in this study; this is something that has to be looked into in other studies. Given these drawbacks, greater investigation and verification using bigger and more varied datasets are required to validate the efficacy and stability of the suggested automated wound tissue segmentation technique.

During the COVID-19 epidemic, Barakat-Johnson *et al.* [72] investigated the usability and efficacy of an AI application for objective wound assessment and care. Providing virtual treatment has shown to be quite advantageous, particularly in light of the COVID-19 epidemic. It has allowed for remote patient monitoring, improved patient adherence, better efficiency, shortened patient travel times, shared plans amongst clinicians, and optimal wound care. Retrospective data from wound patients assessed with the AI mobile application (app) was included in the study in comparison to patients assessed with conventional methods. Digital photos of wounds collected by patients or medical professionals using cell phones or other devices would be the AI app's inputs. The wounds' assessment and treatment suggestions have been included in AI app's outputs. Combination of computer vision techniques with machine learning algorithm is being used to examine the submitted photographs using algorithms of AI to spot the various wound characteristics, such as wound type, depth, color, size, and presence of necrotic or granulation tissue. The app would suggest suitable wound care techniques, such as topical drug delivery, wound dressing, or professional referral, based on this research. These results are intended to help healthcare professionals make well-informed treatment decisions by increasing the precision and effectiveness of wound assessment. During the COVID-19 epidemic, the study extended important proof of the efficacy and acceptance of AI software for enhancing wound assessment and management. Certain benefits to the study have been noted. First, it exhibited that, when compared to conventional approaches, the AI app enhanced the consistency and accuracy of wound assessment and care. Second, the study illustrated that using the AI app decreased the demands for in-person consultations, which is advantageous during the COVID-19 pandemic when it is recommended to have remote consultations. Third, the study demonstrated that patients and medical professionals found the AI app to be user-friendly and admissible. This research has certain drawbacks. Initially, the research was carried out just at one location, perhaps restricting the applicability of the results in different contexts. Secondly, the research included retrospective data, which could potentially introduce bias and confounding. Thirdly, the long-term effects of utilizing the AI app, like patient satisfaction and wound healing rates, were not assessed in the study.

12.7 Conclusion

The literature study indicates that there are numerous chances to automate sophisticated wound assessment and wound-healing prediction through the use of AI. These are relatively unexplored fields of study, and, to perform translational medicine for bettering human health and cutting hospital costs, researchers studying wounds and AI should work together more closely. The reasoning is that improved clinical practice and increased performance-based compensation could result from accurate wound healing prediction.

12.7.1 Recap of Key Points

- Applications of XAI in AI have great promise to increase explainability and transparency in high-risk sectors like healthcare, where trust is essential.
- Limitations in the classification task extend to the model's explanation section.
- The location of the wound greatly reduces the number of potential wound types.
- Explainer employs a qualitative technique to elucidate decisions, albeit in varying ways for each class.
- Given the difficulties in comprehending quantitative methods, qualitative methods can help to enhance human reasoning.
- XAI can significantly increase model performance by evaluating the significance and impact of attributes.

12.7.2 Future Prospects and Areas of Further Research

Even though AI in healthcare and medicine has grown significantly and is now one of the most significant uses of AI, its potential for automated wound assessment and healing prediction is still mostly unexplored. One primary factor impeding the AI research community's inquiries is the dearth of publicly available wound data. Some recent attempts have been made to support the development of algorithms for forecasting wound healing rates and standardized procedures for precise wound measuring. For the aforementioned reasons, it has been suggested that a national minimum dataset (MDS) be established and used throughout England for general wound evaluation and tracking the advancement of wound healing to satisfy the requirements of standardization and variable assessment [73]. Similar to the MDS, the "WoundCareLog APP" is a recording and communication tool that has been launched to help physicians in China who treat wounds [74]. This technique makes it possible to register digital images of chronic refractory wounds to obtain the morphological parameters necessary for wound management and recovery prediction, in situations where the information offered by standard medical history records is insufficient for the intended purpose. "ComplexWoundDB," a new image database designed to classify complex wounds at the pixel level into five categories—granulation, fibrinoid tissue, dry necrosis, hematoma, and non-wound region—is now available to the general public [75]. The collection, which comprises of 27 photos that were taken at the patients' residences and annotated by four medical specialists, is little, though. Additionally, created AI algorithms for wound evaluation can be modified to assess additional digital wound photos and documentation on EMR systems, or they can be expanded to automate the measurement of additional wound aspects. It would be beneficial to look at the integration of machine learning and other computational techniques for additional feature extraction from deep learning features at different CNN levels in order to enhance prediction AI models for wound healing. The development of AI-based systems for evidence-based wound care decision-making could be advantageous to the growth of state-of-the-art wound research. It would be essential to thoroughly validate AI-based performance in helping physicians obtain accurate wound assessments to guide clinical management.

References

1. Sarp, S., Kuzlu, M., Wilson, E., Cali, U., Guler, O., The enlightening role of explainable artificial intelligence in chronic wound classification. *Electronics*, 10, 12, 1406, 2021.
2. Sarp, S., Kuzlu, M., Wilson, E., Cali, U., Guler, O., A highly transparent and explainable artificial intelligence tool for chronic wound classification: XAI-CWC, 2021.
3. Zhang, Y., Weng, Y., Lund, J., Applications of explainable artificial intelligence in diagnosis and surgery. *Diagnostics*, 12, 2, 237, 2022.
4. Nguyen, H., Agu, E., Tulu, B., Strong, D., Mombini, H., Pedersen, P., Lindsay, C., Dunn, R., Loretz, L., Machine learning models for synthesizing actionable care decisions on lower extremity wounds. *Smart Health*, 18, 100139, 2020.
5. Anisuzzaman, D., Wang, C., Rostami, B., Gopalakrishnan, S., Niezgoda, J., Yu, Z., Image-based artificial intelligence in wound assessment: A systematic review. *Adv. Wound Care*, 11, 12, 687–709, 2022.
6. Srinivasu, P.N., Sandhya, N., Jhaveri, R.H., Raut, R., From blackbox to explainable AI in healthcare: existing tools and case studies. *Mobile Inf. Syst.*, 2022, 1–20, 2022.
7. Adadi, A., Berrada, M., Peeking inside the black-box: a survey on explainable artificial intelligence (XAI). *IEEE access*, 9, 16, 6, 52138–60, 2018.
8. Encarnação, R., Manuel, T., Palheira, H., Neves-Amado, J., Alves, P., Artificial Intelligence in Wound Care Education: Protocol for a Scoping Review. *Nurs. Rep.*, 14, 1, 627–640, 2024.

9. Madanu, R., Abbod, M.F., Hsiao, F.-J., Chen, W.-T., Shieh, J.-S., Explainable ai (xai) applied in machine learning for pain modeling: A review. *Technologies*, 10, 3, 74, 2022.
10. Chemello, G., Salvatori, B., Morettini, M., Tura, A., Artificial intelligence methodologies applied to technologies for screening, diagnosis and care of the diabetic foot: a narrative review. *Biosensors*, 12, 11, 985, 2022.
11. Sheu, R.-K. and Pardeshi, M.S., A survey on medical explainable AI (XAI): Recent progress, explainability approach, human interaction and scoring system. *Sensors*, 22, 20, 8068, 2022.
12. Khanna, N.N., Maindarkar, M.A., Viswanathan, V., Puvvula, A., Paul, S., Bhagawati, M., Ahluwalia, P., Ruzsa, Z., Sharma, A., Kolluri, R., Cardiovascular/stroke risk stratification in diabetic foot infection patients using deep learning-based artificial intelligence: an investigative study. *J. Clin. Med.*, 11, 22, 6844, 2022.
13. Subramanian, M., Wojtusciszyn, A., Favre, L., Boughorbel, S., Shan, J., Letaief, K.B., Pitteloud, N., Chouchane, L., Precision medicine in the era of artificial intelligence: implications in chronic disease management. *J. Transl. Med.*, 18, 1–12, 2020.
14. Gomolin, A., Netchiporouk, E., Gniadecki, R., Litvinov, I.V., Artificial intelligence applications in dermatology: where do we stand? *Front. Med.*, 7, 100, 2020.
15. Amini, M., Bagheri, A., Delen, D., Discovering injury severity risk factors in automobile crashes: A hybrid explainable AI framework for decision support. *Reliab. Eng. Syst. Saf.*, 226, 108720, 2022.
16. Zhang, Z., Beck, M.W., Winkler, D.A., Huang, B., Sibanda, W., Goyal, H., Opening the black box of neural networks: methods for interpreting neural network models in clinical applications. *Ann. Transl. Med.*, 6, 11, 2018.
17. Cheng, C.S., Behzadan, A.H., Noshadravan, A., Uncertainty-aware convolutional neural network for explainable artificial intelligence-assisted disaster damage assessment. *Struct. Control Health Monit.*, 29, 10, e3019, 2022.
18. Nagahisarchoghaei, M., Nur, N., Cummins, L., Nur, N., Karimi, M.M., Nandanwar, S., Bhattacharyya, S., Rahimi, S., An empirical survey on explainable ai technologies: Recent trends, use-cases, and categories from technical and application perspectives. *Electronics*, 12, 5, 1092, 2023.
19. Sahoh, B. and Choksuriwong, A., The role of explainable Artificial Intelligence in high-stakes decision-making systems: a systematic review. *J. Ambient Intell. Hum. Comput.*, 14, 6, 7827–7843, 2023.
20. Saraswat, D., Bhattacharya, P., Verma, A., Prasad, V.K., Tanwar, S., Sharma, G., Bokoro, P.N., Sharma, R., Explainable AI for healthcare 5.0: opportunities and challenges. *IEEE Access*, 10, 84486–84517, 2022.
21. Hossain, M.M., Ali, M.S., Ahmed, M.M., Rakib, M.R.H., Kona, M.A., Afrin, S., Islam, M.K., Ahsan, M.M., Raj, S.M.R.H., Rahman, M.H., Cardiovascular disease identification using a hybrid CNN-LSTM model with explainable AI. *Inf. Med. Unlocked*, 42, 101370, 2023.

22. Ng, Z.Q.P., Ling, L.Y.J., Chew, H.S.J., Lau, Y., The role of artificial intelligence in enhancing clinical nursing care: A scoping review. *J. Nurs. Manage.*, 30, 8, 3654–3674, 2022.
23. Ehsan, U. and Riedl, M.O., Human-centered explainable ai: Towards a reflective sociotechnical approach, in: *HCI International 2020-Late Breaking Papers: Multimodality and Intelligence: 22nd HCI International Conference, HCII 2020, Copenhagen, Denmark, July 19–24, 2020, Proceedings 22*, pp. 449–466, Springer, 2020.
24. Cavallaro, M., Moran, E., Collyer, B., McCarthy, N.D., Green, C., Keeling, M.J., Informing antimicrobial stewardship with explainable AI. *PLOS Digital Health*, 2, 1, e0000162, 2023.
25. Kibria, H.B., Nahiduzzaman, M., Goni, M.O.F., Ahsan, M., Haider, J., An ensemble approach for the prediction of diabetes mellitus using a soft voting classifier with an explainable AI. *Sensors*, 22, 19, 7268, 2022.
26. Ghassemi, M., Oakden-Rayner, L., Beam, A.L., The false hope of current approaches to explainable artificial intelligence in health care. *Lancet Digit. Health*, 3, 11, e745–e750, 2021.
27. Pflanzer, M., Traylor, Z., Lyons, J.B., Dubljević, V., Nam, C.S., Ethics in human–AI teaming: principles and perspectives. *AI Ethics*, 3, 3, 917–935, 2023.
28. Zhang, J. and Zhang, Z.-M., Ethics and governance of trustworthy medical artificial intelligence. *BMC Med. Inf. Decis. Making*, 23, 1, 7, 2023.
29. Kuzlu, M., Cali, U., Sharma, V., Güler, Ö., Gaining insight into solar photovoltaic power generation forecasting utilizing explainable artificial intelligence tools. *IEEE Access*, 8, 187814–187823, 2020.
30. Kanda, E., Epureanu, B.I., Adachi, T., Tsuruta, Y., Kikuchi, K., Kashihara, N., Abe, M., Masakane, I., Nitta, K., Application of explainable ensemble artificial intelligence model to categorization of hemodialysis-patient and treatment using nationwide-real-world data in Japan. *PLoS One*, 15, 5, e0233491, 2020.
31. Ihalapathirana, A., Explainable Artificial Intelligence to predict clinical outcomes for adults with Type 1 diabetes, 2022.
32. O'Sullivan, S., Nevejans, N., Allen, C., Blyth, A., Leonard, S., Pagallo, U., Holzinger, K., Holzinger, A., Sajid, M.I., Ashrafian, H., Legal, regulatory, and ethical frameworks for development of standards in artificial intelligence (AI) and autonomous robotic surgery. *Int. J. Med. Robot. Comput. Assist. Surg.*, 15, 1, e1968, 2019.
33. Rahman, A., Hossain, M.S., Muhammad, G., Kundu, D., Debnath, T., Rahman, M., Khan, M.S.I., Tiwari, P., Band, S.S., Federated learning-based AI approaches in smart healthcare: concepts, taxonomies, challenges and open issues. *Cluster Comput.*, 26, 4, 2271–2311, 2023.
34. Kelly, C.J., Karthikesalingam, A., Suleyman, M., Corrado, G., King, D., Key challenges for delivering clinical impact with artificial intelligence. *BMC Med.*, 17, 1–9, 2019.

35. Dana, J., Venkatasamy, A., Saviano, A., Lupberger, J., Hoshida, Y., Vilgrain, V., Nahon, P., Reinhold, C., Gallix, B., Baumert, T.F., Conventional and artificial intelligence-based imaging for biomarker discovery in chronic liver disease. *Hepatol. Int.*, 16, 3, 509–522, 2022.
36. Sun, J., Dong, Q.-X., Wang, S.-W., Zheng, Y.-B., Liu, X.-X., Lu, T.-S., Yuan, K., Shi, J., Hu, B., Lu, L., Artificial intelligence in psychiatry research, diagnosis, and therapy. *Asian J. Psychiatry*, 87, 103705, 2023.
37. Chan, B., Applying a common enterprise theory of liability to clinical AI systems. *Am. J. Law Med.*, 47, 4, 351–385, 2021.
38. Woo, K., Song, J., Adams, V., Block, L.J., Currie, L.M., Shang, J., Topaz, M., Exploring prevalence of wound infections and related patient characteristics in homecare using natural language processing. *Int. Wound J.*, 19, 1, 211–221, 2022.
39. Esmaeilzadeh, P., Mirzaei, T., Dharanikota, S., Patients' perceptions toward human–artificial intelligence interaction in health care: experimental study. *J. Med. Internet Res.*, 23, 11, e25856, 2021.
40. Baker, S. and Xiang, W., Artificial intelligence of things for smarter healthcare: a survey of advancements, challenges, and opportunities. *IEEE Commun. Surv. Tutor.*, 25, 2, 1261–1293, 2023.
41. Raeesi Vanani, I. and Amirhosseini, M., IoT-based diseases prediction and diagnosis system for healthcare, in: *Internet of Things for Healthcare Technologies*, pp. 21–48, 2021.
42. Roy, S., Meena, T., Lim, S.-J., Demystifying supervised learning in healthcare 4.0: A new reality of transforming diagnostic medicine. *Diagnostics*, 12, 10, 2549, 2022.
43. Khanna, N.N., Maindarkar, M.A., Viswanathan, V., Fernandes, J.F.E., Paul, S., Bhagawati, M., Ahluwalia, P., Ruzsa, Z., Sharma, A., Kolluri, R., Economics of artificial intelligence in healthcare: diagnosis vs. treatment. *Healthcare*, 10, 12, 2493, MDPI, 2022.
44. Al Kuwaiti, A., Nazer, K., Al-Reedy, A., Al-Shehri, S., Al-Muhanna, A., Subbarayalu, A.V., Al Muhanna, D., Al-Muhanna, F.A., A review of the role of artificial intelligence in healthcare. *J. Pers. Med.*, 13, 6, 951, 2023.
45. Catania, Louis J. Foundations of Artificial Intelligence in Healthcare and Bioscience: A User Friendly Guide for IT Professionals, Healthcare Providers, Researchers, and Clinicians. Academic Press, 2020.
46. Wang, D., Wang, L., Zhang, Z., Wang, D., Zhu, H., Gao, Y., Fan, X., Tian, F., "Brilliant AI doctor" in rural clinics: challenges in AI-powered clinical decision support system deployment. *Proceedings of the 2021 CHI conference on human factors in computing systems*, pp. 1–18, 2021.
47. Chen, K., Stotter, C., Klestil, T., Nehrer, S., Artificial intelligence in orthopedic radiography analysis: a narrative review. *Diagnostics*, 12, 9, 2235, 2022.
48. Krizhevsky, A., Sutskever, I., Hinton, G.E., Imagenet classification with deep convolutional neural networks, in: *Advances in Neural Information Processing Systems, 25*, 2012.

49. Silver, D., Huang, A., Maddison, C.J., Guez, A., Sifre, L., van den Driessche, G., Schrittwieser, J., Antonoglou, I., Panneershelvam, V., Lanctot, M., Dieleman, S., Grewe, D., Nham, J., Kalchbrenner, N., Sutskever, I., Lillicrap, T., Leach, M., Kavukcuoglu, K., Graepel, T., Hassabis, D., Mastering the game of Go with deep neural networks and tree search. *Nature*, 529, 7587, 4, 2016.
50. Hassija, V., Chamola, V., Mahapatra, A., Singal, A., Goel, D., Huang, K., Scardapane, S., Spinelli, I., Mahmud, M., Hussain, A., Interpreting black-box models: a review on explainable artificial intelligence. *Cognit. Comput.*, 16, 1, 45–74, 2024 Jan.
51. Mohseni, S., Zarei, N., Ragan, E.D., A multidisciplinary survey and framework for design and evaluation of explainable ai systems. *ACM Trans. Interact. Intell. Syst.*, 11, 3, 4, 1–45, 2021.
52. Mittu, R., Sofge, D., Wagner, A., Lawless, W., *Robust intelligence and trust in autonomous systems*, 1, 12, 270, 2016.
53. Angelov, P., Soares, E., Jiang, R., Arnold, N., Atkinson, P., Explainable artificial intelligence: An analytical review. *Wiley Interdiscip. Rev.: Data Min. Knowl. Discov.*, 11, 5, 1424, 2021.
54. Li, B., Tan, Y., Wu, A., Duan, G., A distributionally robust optimization based method for stochastic model predictive control. *IEEE Trans. Autom. Control*, 67, 11, 5762–76, 2021.
55. Guo, G., Wang, H., Bell, D., Bi, Y., Knn model-based approach in classification, 2004.
56. Chemello, G., Salvatori, B., Morettini, M., Tura, A., Artificial intelligence methodologies applied to technologies for screening, diagnosis and care of the diabetic foot: a narrative review. *Biosensors*, 12, 11, 985, 2022 Nov.
57. Biswas, S.K., Chakraborty, M., Purkayastha, B., Roy, P., Thounaojam, D.M., Rule extraction from training data using neural network. *Int. J. Artif. Intell. Tools*, 26, 3, 1750006, 2017.
58. Zhou, Z.H., Jiang, Y., Chen, S.F., Extracting symbolic rules from trained neural network ensembles. *AI Commun.*, 16, 1, 3–15, 2003.
59. Fayek, A., Fuzzy logic and fuzzy hybrid techniques for construction engineering and management. *J. Constr. Eng. Manag.*, 146, 04020064, 2020.
60. Wachter, S., Mittelstadt, B., Russell, C., Counterfactual explanations without opening the black box: Automated decisions and the gdpr. *Harv. J. Law Technol.*, 31, 841–87, 2018.
61. Tjoa, E. and Guan, C., A survey on explainable artificial intelligence (xai): Toward medical xai. *IEEE Trans. Neural Netw. Learn. Sys.*, 32, 11, 4793–4813, 2020.
62. Rohmetra, H., Raghunath, N., Narang, P., Chamola, V., Guizani, M., Lakkaniga, N.R., Ai-enabled remote monitoring of vital signs for covid19: Methods, prospects and challenges. *Computing*, 105, 783–809, 2023.
63. Becker, S., Ackermann, M., Lapuschkin, S., Müller, K., Samek, W., Interpreting and explaining deep neural networks for classification of audio signals. CoRR, 2018, abs/1807.03418.

64. Zhao, K., Jia, Z., Jia, F., Shao, H., Multi-scale integrated deep selfattention network for predicting remaining useful life of aeroengine. *Eng. Appl. Artif. Intell.*, 120, 10586, 2023.
65. Schwalbe, G. and Finzel, B., A comprehensive taxonomy for explainable artificial intelligence: a systematic survey of surveys on methods and concepts. *Data Min. Knowl. Discov.*, 1–59, 2023.
66. Shin, D., User perceptions of algorithmic decisions in the personalized ai system: perceptual evaluation of fairness, accountability, transparency, and explainability. *J. Broadcast. Electron. Media*, 64, 4, 541–65, 2020.
67. Gabbay, F., Bar-lev, S., Montano, O., Hadad, N., A lime-based explainable machine learning model for predicting the severity level of covid-19 diagnosed patients. *Appl. Sci.*, 11, 10417, 2021.
68. Tan, S., Caruana, R., Hooker, G., Lou, Y., Distill-and-compare, in: *Proceedings of the 2018 AAAI/ACM Conference on AI, Ethics, and Society*, 2018.
69. Kaur, S., Singla, J., Nkenyereye, L., Jha, S., Prashar, D., Joshi, G.P., El-Sappagh, S., Islam, M.S., Islam, S.M.R., Medical diagnostic systems using artificial intelligence (AI) algorithms: principles and perspectives. *IEEE Access*, 8, 228049–69, 2020.
70. Bunt, A., Lount, M., Lauzon, C., Are explanations always important? A study of deployed, low-cost intelligent interactive systems, in: *Proceedings of the 2012 ACM International Conference on Intelligent User Interfaces, ser. IUI '12*, Association for Computing Machinery, pp. 169–78, New York, NY, USA, 2012.
71. Ramachandram, D., Ramirez-GarciaLuna, J.L., Fraser, R.D.J., Martínez-Jiménez, M.A., Arriaga-Caballero, J.E., Allport, J., Fully automated wound tissue segmentation using deep learning on mobile devices: cohort study. *JMIR Mhealth Uhealth*, 10, e36977, 2022.
72. Barakat-Johnson, M., Jones, A., Burger, M., Leong, T., Frotjold, A., Randall, S. *et al.*, Reshaping wound care: evaluation of an artificial intelligence app to improve wound assessment and management amid the COVID-19 pandemic. *Int. Wound J.*, 19, 1561–77, 2022.
73. Coleman, S., Nelson, E.A., Vowden, P., Vowden, K., Adderley, U., Sunderland, L. *et al.*, Development of a generic wound care assessment minimum data set. *J. Tissue Viability*, 26, 226–40, 2017.
74. Dong, W., Nie, L.J., Wu, M.J., Xie, T., Liu, Y.K., Tang, J.J. *et al.*, WoundCareLog APP–a new application to record wound diagnosis and healing. *Chin. J. Traumatol.*, 22, 296–9, 2019.
75. Pereira, T.A., Popim, R.C., Passos, L.A., Pereira, D.R., Pereira, C.R., Papa, J.P., ComplexWoundDB: a database for automatic complex wound tissue categorization, in: *IWSSIP 2022: Proceeding of the 29th International Conference on Systems, Signals and Image Processing*, Sofia, Bulgaria, IEEE, Piscataway, pp. 1–4, 2022 Jun 1–3.

13

Bone Metastases: Explainable AI and Responsible AI

Avipsa Hazra, Gowrav Baradwaj, Sushma R., Sudipta Choudhury, Mythreyi R. and Kanthesh B.M.*

Division of Molecular Biology, School of Life Sciences, JSS Academy of Higher Education and Research, Mysuru, Karnataka, India

Abstract

Artificial intelligence (AI) is anticipated to become the go-to-care facility in the near future. It is owing to the fact that AI has enhanced speed, accuracy, effectiveness, and rates of true detection in healthcare diagnostics as well as treatment. This has caused both governmental bodies and tech corporations to increase their attention and financial support for AI medical applications. Bone metastasis that commonly appears in the advanced stages of cancers leads to a great reduction in the life expectancy of the patients, which might be around 6 months in case of bone metastases. A greater overall survival time and enhanced quality of life for patients can be achieved by selecting a treatment plan that takes into account early diagnosis of bone metastases. Because of its benefits for whole-body detection and high sensitivity, bone scintigraphy is one of the most often used diagnostic procedures to identify bone metastases in cancer patients. However, due to the low resolution of Bone scintigraphy (BS) pictures, interpretation is a labor-intensive process that requires skill and has drawbacks such as subjectivity, distinct inaccuracy, and insufficient efficiency. To get over this problem, a variety of AI algorithms have lately been applied in conjunction with conventional diagnostic methods to boost imaging efficiency and resolution. One such technique used in the detection of bone metastases is deep neural networks (DNN). Deep neural networks are one of the computational techniques that enable an algorithm to program itself. This eliminates the need for explicit rule specification by allowing the algorithm to learn from a huge collection of instances that exhibit the desired behavior. This is more efficient compared to the traditional methods because it can extract image features automatically, which rules out the possibilities of false results. TNM staging system

**Corresponding author*: kantheshmb@jssuni.edu.in

Rishabha Malviya and Sonali Sundram (eds.) Explainable and Responsible Artificial Intelligence in Healthcare, (323–348) © 2025 Scrivener Publishing LLC

is another tool that is being widely used to detect the bone metastases in case of NSCLC, and it has more efficiency when paired up with AI-coded algorithms. It has successfully detected the bone metastases and has provided diagnosis images with better resolution compared to computed tomography (CT) and magnetic resonance imaging (MRI) scans. Another AI-assisted technique for detection of bone metastases includes the use of deep learning algorithms. These deep learning algorithms along with the traditional imaging techniques have proven to be highly efficient and sensitive in providing high-resolution images of osseous metastases. They have also successfully predicted the metastases onset with the omics data much prior to the medical imaging. While these AI-driven activities might not be flawless, they usually yield good enough results for fast visual interpretations, which is particularly useful in situations when local knowledge is scarce. It is also envisaged that, with a qualified healthcare practitioner supervising the process, AI-assisted picture interpretation for bone metastases will achieve the same degree of effectiveness. There are numerous benefits to employing AI to detect bone metastases. Large volumes of data may be processed rapidly and precisely by AI algorithms, leading to quicker and more accurate diagnoses.

Keywords: Artificial intelligence, neuroscience, neurological disorders, cognition, neuroinformatics

Abbreviations

AI	Artificial Intelligence
TNM	Tumor, Node, Metastasis
DNN	Deep Neural Networks
NSCLC	Non Small Cell Lung Cancer
CT	Computed Tomography
MRI	Magnetic Resonance Imaging
QOL	Quality of Life
ADLs	Activities of Daily Living
DTCs	Disseminated Tumor cells
SREs	Skeletal Related Events
99mTC	Metastable Technetium 99
SPE CT	Single Photon Emission CT
PET	Poistron Emission Tomography
SBRT	Steriotactic Body Radiation Therapy
RT	Radiation Therapy

BTA	Bladder Tumour Antigen
BPs	Bisphosphonates
BTM	Bone Turnover Markers
PIs	Proteasome Inhibitors
BMD	Bone Mineral Density
OBMC	Origin Bone Metastatic Cancer
HE	Hematoxylin Eosin
CNN	Convolutional Neural Network
GLUE	Global Local Unified Emphasis

13.1 Introduction to Bone Metastases

The bone is a dynamic structure that stores minerals and energy in addition to being essential for mobility and structural support. The primary location of postnatal hematopoiesis, the bone marrow, is also found in these bone fragments [1]. It is the third most common site of metastasis among solid tumors, accounting for lung, colorectal, thyroid, prostate, breast, gynecologic, and melanoma; in fact, 70% of patients with metastatic breast and prostate cancer also had bone metastases. Table 13.1 bears evidence to the statistical data of incidence of bone metastases in case of each type of cancer [2]. After a cancer diagnosis, the most important thing to do is determine the extent of the disease's metastasis. Metastatic illness is a terrible and often incurable sickness that can affect any organ; nevertheless, among the various organs that may experience it, the biology of bone metastasis may be distinct [3]. In the improbable event that cancer spreads to the bone, there are several morbidities linked to it, such as discomfort, an elevated risk of rupture, and hypercalcemia. Because of this, specialists in the domains of cancer biology and bone biology have turned their attention to the study of the bone, discovering that both have a lot to teach one another [1]. The survival rate of patients with advanced-stage tumors has increased because of recent advancements in cancer therapy, including the discovery of immune checkpoint inhibitors and molecule-targeted medicines [5]. Bone metastases significantly worsen the morbidity of patients with advanced-stage cancerous disorders. A patient's prognosis is impacted by morbidities that impair their quality of life (QOL) and ability for performing activities of daily living, such as neurological immobility and congenital fractures. This occurs when a patient's principal disease therapy is discontinued and their general health deteriorates [4].

Table 13.1 Different types of cancer and their incidence rate of bone metastases.

Type of cancer	Prevalence (in thousands)	Incidence rate of bone metastases (%)	Median survival from diagnosis (in months)
Prostate	1555	65-75	12-53
Breast	3860	65-75	19-25
Lung	1394	30-40	6
Bladder	1000	40	6-9
Renal	480	40-25	12
Thyroid	475	60	48

Of all the carcinogenic mechanisms, the biological process of bone metastasis is one of the most intricate and fascinating, even though it is a morbid process. The multiphase processes of osteogenesis, hematopoiesis, and osteolysis are collaboratively regulated in a spatially restricted setting inside the intricately organized bone microenvironment [3]. Seldom were serious consequences including discomfort, compression of the spinal cord, and pathological fractures, found before bone metastases were discovered. Recent research has demonstrated that, in order to successfully prevent major problems from bone metastases, bone management regimes must be started concurrently with cancer therapy [4]. Because of their special capacity to alter these organic elements of the bone stroma, disseminated tumor cells (DTCs) can produce pathological osteolytic or osteoblastic lesions. Many common malignancies, such as those of the kidney, lung, breast, myeloma, and prostate, can give rise to these DTCs. Dormancy, outgrowth, and seeding are the three primary stages of colonization. The latent and early expansion phases are where the highest therapeutic potential is observed [3]. In order to ensure timely identification and appropriate integration of systemic and local treatment, a skilled multidisciplinary team is required to handle bone metastases. Figure 13.1 shows us the overlapping of the different niches that leads to metastasis, which also can be understood using model system study thus making identification of it easier [6]. Patients with bone metastases may experience skeletal problems, commonly referred to as skeletal-related events (SREs). Pathological fractures, hypercalcemia, injury to the spinal cord, and unbearably high pain

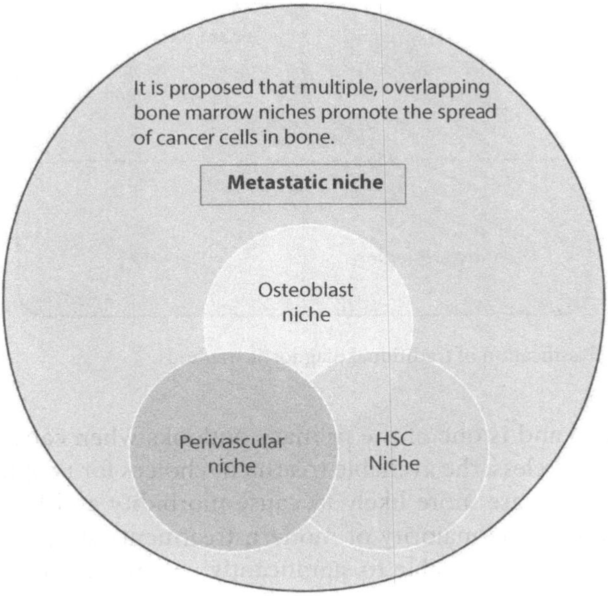

Figure 13.1 Certain niches in the bone marrow are colonized by tumor cells. Model systems provide evidence that tumor cells first invade highly vascularized regions of trabecular bone. An illustration of the idea that, in model systems, many overlapping bone marrow niches may be implicated in bone metastases. (HSCs, hematopoietic stem cells [6]).

requiring radiation treatment or bone surgery are some of these outcomes. The primary goals of treatment for BM are symptom relief and preventing SRE, whereas targeted anti-cancer medications are administered in tandem to lessen the tumor load at the extra-skeletal and skeletal locations. Systemic and locoregional methods are used in bone-targeting therapies. The former is often used to manage bone pain and avoid pathological fractures and is mostly represented by orthopedic surgery and radiation therapy (RT). These latter comprise anabolic steroids, radiopharmaceuticals, and inhibitors of bone resorption, whose actions are intended to restore the natural turnover of bone, which is severely compromised in patients with bone metastases [7].

13.2 Traditional Diagnostic and Therapeutic Method for Bone Metastasis

The bone and its marrow are the most common sites where cancer spreads. It usually occurs due to detail in the prognosis of the cancer in

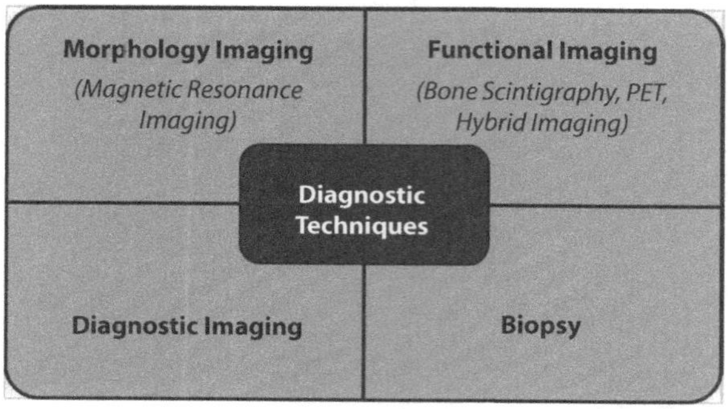

Figure 13.2 Classification of traditional diagnostic methods.

the individual and is one of the primary outlooks when cancer has to be treated. Nevertheless, the available treatment choices for people with bone metastatic illness are more likely to cause morbidity and have little efficacy. As a result, the majority of modern treatments are primarily palliative. However, they are able to significantly enhance patients' quality of existence and reduce the course of the disease, along with new, well-tolerated medicines that target the molecular mechanisms underlying the bone metastasis process that are being developed [8].

Early on, before symptoms appear, a primary tumor may metastatically spread. Cells that have spread widely may remain latent for years before showing symptoms. According to certain research, early in the tumor's progression, disseminated cancer cells are able to effectively implant themselves in the bone marrow throughout the metastatic process of tumors. It is difficult for doctors to detect bone metastasis early during staging and monitoring in terms of accurately determining subsetting and prognosis. More functional and diagnostic imaging is being done in the direction of this objective. Modern morphologic and functional examinations have made it possible to identify early bone metastases thanks to innovative technology. Imaging is thought to be essential for both diagnosis and for locating lesions of interest in local therapies [9]. Figure 13.2 describes the different classification developed in diagnostic techniques.

13.2.1 Morphologic Imaging

Morphologic examinations rely on variations in bone density, such as CT or radiography. Imaging patterns of metastases (lytic, sclerotic, or mixed) can vary depending on the behavior of the metastasis. Bone metastases must have a density loss of 25%–50% and a minimum size of one centimetre in order to be seen on CT scans. Breast cancer bone metastases are often lytic; however, they can develop peripherally osteosclerotic following treatment as a result of an osteoblastic reaction. Soft-tissue invasion outside of bone is also able to be deciphered using CT. Furthermore, morphologic examinations are essential for identifying important bone metastases sites that are susceptible to SRE.

13.2.1.1 Magnetic Resonance Imaging

Traditional MRI has a recorded sensitivity of 100% and specificity of 90%, has sequences with T1, T2, and DWI investigations that can identify bone metastases of cancer. As a result, they are utilized when unsure and are extremely helpful for early determination. Low T1-signal, DWI signal inhibitions, and T2 hyperintensity are typically determined by the signaling of MRI behavior of bone metastases. By using MRI, lesions can be seen with extreme precision. It is also helpful for researching the spinal cord's integrity and, eventually, the state of its compression. An MRI without contrast is used to analyse bones; however, contrast is necessary to research the spinal cord or adjacent soft tissue. While whole-body magnetic resonance imaging is recently established for studying the complete bone compartment, its clinical practice utility is still being studied, particularly with regard to early bone metastasis identification. In any event, its use for oligometastatic patient early detection may be intriguing. WB-MRI has been demonstrated in the literature to have superior sensitivity and specificity over skeletal scintigraphy. Its results also provide an estimate indicator for treatment response in bone metastases [10, 11].

13.2.2 Functional Imaging

13.2.2.1 Bone Scintigraphy

Functional imaging plays a part in breast cancer phasing, staging, and follow-ups in bone metastases detection. For bone scintigraphy, metastable technetium 99 (99mTc)–labeled diphosphonates are the osteotropic compounds utilized for bone imaging. Since the 1970s, 99mTc-radiolabeled diphosphonates have been used extensively for first-level staging due to their affordability and effectiveness. Specificity and sensitivity are reported to be 48% and 78%, respectively. Because bone turnover is typically detected by bone scintigraphy, disorder with a common lytic behavior is often regarded as a false negative. A change in 5%–10% of bone, which is not always connected to cancer, might result in an increase of molecules on bone imagings; however, it can be a concerning issue when it comes to benign pathologies like degenerative disease.

Because of this, in cases that are in the gray area, a second-level exam may be necessary. A further drawback of the bone scan is its low spatial definition (<1 cm) and lack of volumetric assessment. Single photon emission CT (SPECT/CT) is an example of how a bone scan is implemented. During the acquisition of further axial slices, the identical radioisotope used in traditional skeletal scintigraphy is introduced, with the potential for volumetric estimation [9].

13.2.2.2 Positron Emission Tomography (PET)

In regard to spatial resolution and tomographic image capture, PET is better than bone scans. It also offers details on the prognosis and response to treatment. For skeletal investigations, 18F NaF and 18F fluorodeoxyglucose (FDG) are the most commonly used radiopharmaceutical agents. In the remodeling skeletal areas, fluoride ions clustering make 18F-NaF PET very sensitive to osteoblastic activity. The patient population for which 18F-NaF PET may be helpful has not yet been determined, but it is more effective than 18F FDG in detecting bone metastases, with a high sensitivity (100%) and specificity (97%). When it comes to tumor, bone tropism, including lobular or luminal cancer, may be taken into account for particular 18F-NaF PET methods. Furthermore, the subtypes that exhibit slower cellular development and hence reduced glucose uptake have poor 18-FDG PET/CT sensitivity, making it possible to overlook their spread. Alternatively, 18-FDG PET/CT is thought to be helpful for staging, assessing prognosis, and assessing therapy response in cases of locally severe or metastatic illness. Its agent accumulation occurs in high turnover locations. Even though it can vary depending on the subtype, 18F-FDG PET has 98% sensitivity and 56% specificity for the determination of bone metastases. The indication for follow-up use is still debatable [9].

13.2.2.3 Hybrid Images

Molecular and hybrid imaging are becoming more and more important for early bone metastasis detection and early response monitoring. Functional imaging modalities like emission computed tomography (SPECT/CT), positron emission tomography/CT (PET/CT), or PET/MRI may be helpful in identifying early individuals who do not respond to systemic therapies, thereby increasing the efficiency of disease control and the efficiency of healthcare systems. In this way, these patients may be moved to a subsequent line of treatment. This benefit stems from the integration of morphologic, physiologic, and metabolic aspects in the assessment of the skeleton. When reviewing the data in the literature, PET/MRI still has limited benefits, and most research focuses on identifying the optimal patient setting [10].

13.2.3 Imaging in Treatment Planning of Radiotherapy

Morphologic imaging can be used to detect bone lesions and soft tissue injuries. CT scan simulation enables radiologists to contour surrounding soft tissue while providing palliative RT for big metastases. Sometimes, co-registration with a contrast-enhanced diagnostic CT scan can help distinguish between healthy soft tissue and tissue that is implicated in the spread of the condition beyond bone metastases. Radiation therapies benefit from the higher precision that MRI provides in terms of gross tumor volume and spinal cord contouring. Greater local control is usually correlated with reduced side effects along with higher precision. An MRI is required before beginning stereotactic body RT, focused on damage with an mm perimeter and a high dosage. Functional imaging is utilized lesser to shape bone metastases in cancer, but it can help with lesion detection during co-registration [9].

13.2.4 Biopsy of Bone Metastasis

Metastatic presentation generally requires a biopsy to assess prognostic factors, especially when systemic drugs are required to establish the kind of malignancy and set the conditions for a relapse. Pathologic investigation is usually performed on soft-tissue or early tumors among individuals with de novo metastatic cancer. If there is a relapse, a tumor biopsy may be required, especially if there is an isolated bone presentation. There are more situations in which a biopsy might be necessary, such as when differential diagnosis is needed. A few possible differential diagnoses for bone metastases include multiple myeloma, chondrosarcoma, post-radiation sarcoma, primary malignant lymphoma of the bone, and osteomyelitis. It is important to distinguish between metastatic injuries and significant osteoporotic fractures using radiographic imaging. While it is typically damaged in following disorders, the cortical bone may be preserved in osteoporosis. The inability of routine MRI scans to reliably distinguish tumors from metastatic lesions raises the possibility of sarcoidosis as a further differential diagnosis. Increased 18F-FDG absorption can resemble metastatic disease when sarcoidosis and a cancer that may metastasis to the bone are present in the same patient, lowering the specificity of 18F-FDG PET/CT. Nevertheless, granulomatous bone marrow infiltration can be detected with high sensitivity using 18F-FDG PET/CT [9].

13.2.5 Therapeutic Approaches to BM

13.2.5.1 Locoregional Treatments

Two locoregional therapies for breast cancer (BM) that target SREs, such as spinal cord compression and pathological fractures, in addition to pain relief are RT and orthopedic surgery. Regarding RT, lytic BM ossification usually onsets 3–6 weeks after therapy initiation and peaks in 6 months. During the initial 2 weeks of treatment, almost half of those treated had almost complete pain relief. Patient characteristics and preferences can impact RT dosages, techniques, and regimens alongside primary cancer morphology and medical assessment. In the United States, extended fractionated regimens are the norm; in Europe and Canada, short-course therapies are more commonly delivered.

Both fractionated and single-fraction treatments were shown to be equally effective in controlling pain across many randomized studies testing various fractionation regimens. The same anatomical region may be re-irradiated if the first therapeutic efficacy is insufficient to prevent pain recurrence. Because single-fraction RT takes less time, patients and caregivers tend to favor it more; on the other hand, retreatment rates are higher. Conversely, acute toxicities tend to complicate long-term regimens more often than short-term ones.

The prognosis of the patient and the precise location of metastases will determine the best course of treatment. In particular, metastatic spinal trauma may culminate in substantial instability, which can cause unbearable pain and an increased risk of spinal cord damage. Orthopedic surgery is usually employed to maintain high-risk lesions as well as treat pathological fractures.

In addition to conventional surgery, less invasive methods like kyphoplasty and percutaneous vertebroplasty might be investigated for some patients. These methods aim to level out vulnerable spinal BM and reestablish its natural height while preventing neurological effects by introducing bone cement within the vertebral body. Stereotactic radiosurgery is commonly used to treat spinal lesions and avoid open surgery and standard RT, which can destroy bone marrow. However, the results of randomized clinical studies need to be collected before determining its safety and efficacy in relation to traditional irradiation. Cryoablation and radiofrequency ablation are two other locoregional treatment approaches that reduce the tumor strain in bone by heating or freezing tissue, accordingly [11].

13.2.5.2 *Systemic Treatments (Classification has been Depicted via Figure 13.3)*

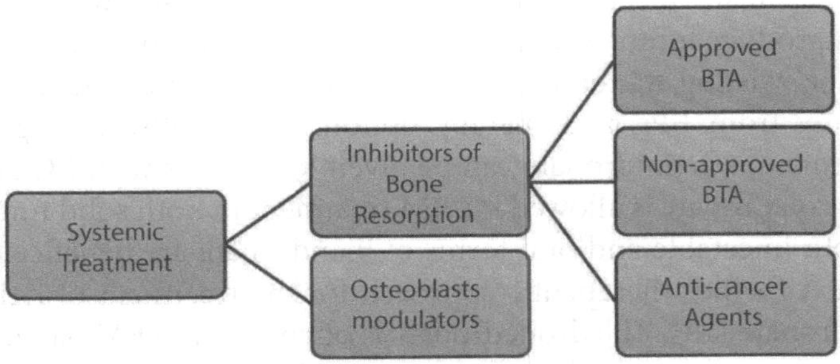

Figure 13.3 Classification of traditional systemic treatments.

13.2.5.2.1 Inhibitors of Bone Resorption

Systemic approaches to BM include BTA, where anti-resorptive medications are the cornerstone of BM treatment, and specific anti-cancerous therapies that are necessary to control the disease's course at bone locations. This class of agents includes both licensed (denosumab and bisphosphonates) and unlicensed (cathepsin-K inhibitors and c-Src inhibitors) medications. Numerous drugs (including androgen modulators, proteasome inhibitors, and mTOR inhibitors) have been shown to mediate osteoclastogenesis among systemic anti-cancer therapy. Examples of a few drug classes are BPs, which are able to reduce mevalonate allowing activity and survival of osteoclasts [12]. Denosumab class of drugs allows osteoclast differentiation, thus enhancing their activities, and thus can treat bone metastases in case of certain solid tumors [13].

13.2.5.2.1.1 APPROVED BTA

Bisphosphonates (BPs): Pyrophosphate analogs, or BPs, have a variable R' chain and a P-C-P core region that binds to the bone matrix. Depending on whether a nitrogen atom is present in R', bisphosphonates are categorized as "nitrogen-containing" (N-BPs: zoledronate, ibandronate, etc.) or "non-nitrogen-containing" (non-N-BPs: clodronate, etidronate, etc.). By blocking farnesyl pyrophosphate synthase, the former prevent osteoclasts from activating or surviving, whereas the latter are metabolized to create cytotoxic analogs of adenosine triphosphate that kill osteoclasts. Numerous cell types have been shown to be targets of bone morphogenetic proteins (BPs), including immune cells, osteoblasts, and endothelial cells. *In vitro* and *in vivo* studies have also reported a direct anti-tumor action for N-BPs. By upregulating γδT-cells, BPs promote the innate immune response against cancer. Furthermore, in mouse models of BC, zoledronate can produce tumor-suppressive bone marrow stromal cells (BMSCs). As per the existing standards, individuals with bone metastases can benefit greatly from BPs as a therapy option. Specifically, among intravenous medicines, pamidronate can be given to patients with BC and MM, whereas zoledronate is allowed for BM treatment in both solid tumors and MM. Both injectable and oral forms of ibandronate are beneficial for BC patients. A further therapeutic approach for the treatment of lytic BM is oral clodronate [13]. Zoledronedronate is often given to BM patients every 3.4 weeks; however, a number of recent trials have demonstrated that a less rigorous frequency (every 12 weeks) is equally effective, at least for BC, PC, and MM patients. These findings imply that, while not altering the course of therapy, a 3-monthly plan might be taken into account to lower the likelihood of adverse events [13].

Denosumab: This substance is a completely human anti-RANK-L IgG2 antibody, which lowers osteoclast development and activity by blocking the connection between RANK-L and RANK. Less rigorous denosumab treatment regimens are not supported by evidence at this time; unlike BPs, the antibodies do not build up in bone, and its cessation, even for a short period of time, may reduce the effectiveness of treatment. In fact, after stopping denosumab, osteoporotic patients saw a rebound increase in vertebral fractures as well as bone resorption [13].

13.2.5.2.1.2 Non-Approved Agents

Cathepsin-K inhibitors: Osteoclasts produce the lysosomal proteinase known as cathepsin-K, which is involved in collagen cleavage and the breakdown of bone matrix. A number of cathepsin-K antagonists, such as reversible and permanent inhibitors of its enzymatic site, have been created. The latter (such as odanacatib, dutacatib, and balicatib) have been the subject of preclinical and clinical studies for the treatment of osteoporosis, osteoarthritis, and BC-related BM. In particular, it has been shown that odanacatib reduces the bone-breakdown process in post-menopausal osteoporotic women and lowers bone turnover markers in those with BM from BC. Sadly, the administration of odanacatib was linked to the development of atrial fibrillation and stroke, which resulted in the suspension of medication development and the withdrawal of clinical trials [13].

Inhibitors of c-Src: The non-receptor tyrosine kinase (TK) encoded by the c-Src proto-oncogene is implicated in cancer cell movement, invasiveness, and RANK-L–induced osteoclastogenesis. Because osteopetrosis and impaired dentition are associated with c-Src mutant mice, pharmaceutical inhibition of this kinase may be able to prevent bone resorption in lytic bone marrow. In mouse models of BC, pre-clinical research using c-Src inhibitors has shown its effectiveness in reducing visceral and bone metastases, with a positive effect on survival. In combination with anti-myeloma drugs, dasatinib, a dual Src/Abl inhibitor, decreased tumor growth in mouse models of multiple myeloma [13].

13.2.5.2.1.3 Anti-Cancer Agents Modulating Bone Resorption

mTOR Inhibitors: In osteoclasts, mTOR has pro-differentiative and anti-apoptotic effects. In preclinical research, rapamycin analogs that inhibited mTOR caused lytic BM to decrease while bone mass increased in tumor-bearing animals. Many research studies in bone-metastatic cancers were initiated as a result of these observations [13].

Clinical trials demonstrated everolimus' safety and effectiveness when used with BPs in kidney cancer, PC, and bone-metastatic lung cancer. In patients with multiple myeloma, phase I trials established the anti-myeloma activity of everolimus alone or in combination with lenalidomide [13].

Proteasome Inhibitors (PIs): By inhibiting NF-kB, these drugs decrease RANK-L–mediated osteoclastogenesis. By stimulating osteoblast proliferation and increasing the synthesis of type I collagen and BMP, they demonstrate anabolic effects on bone. Bortezomib was the first PI to be licensed for the treatment of multiple myeloma due to its combined anti-myeloma and anti-osteoclast action, which boosted PFS, OS, and response rate. However, bortezomib resistance mechanisms in multiple myopathies (MM) have been reported, involving drug extrusion from tumor cells and upregulation of proteasomes. Additionally, second-generation restrictors have been created to get around the drawbacks of bortezomib [13].

Androgen Modulators: PC represents an androgen-dependent disease that responds well to androgen-deprivation therapy in its early stages. Even in the CR context, the cornerstone of PC therapy is androgen signaling mediation. Introducing new drugs (such as abiraterone acetate and enzalutamide) into clinical practice has significantly improved OS and PFS in patients undergoing both chemotherapy and docetaxel. Enzalutamide specifically inhibits the androgen receptor, whereas biraterone acetate, an irreversible cytochrome P17 inhibitor, prevents the manufacture of androgens. Both of these drugs have been shown to lessen bone pain and delay the onset of SREs, even if the precise mechanisms underlying these advantages unique to bones are yet unknown. Non-cytotoxic dosages of abiraterone promoted *in vitro* osteoblast proliferation and bone matrix buildup, but they significantly inhibited osteoclast formation and activity (Iulani *et al.*). However, rather than altering bone turnover, enzalutamide's effects on bone appear to be related to its anti-cancer properties [13].

13.2.5.2.2 Osteoblast Modulators

Liquid bone mass (BM) is a result of impaired bone formation, whereas sclerotic BM is caused by excessive osteogenesis. Thus, in order to manage BM, researchers have looked into the formation of osteoblast modulators. As of right now, neither of the agents in this group have a license to prohibit SREs. This section will cover TK inhibitors (TKIs), an anti-cancer medication that has demonstrated efficacy in bone-related outcomes and may help restore normal osteogenesis. One such instance is the medication cabotinib, which treats metastatic renal cell cancer in its third phase [14].

Parathyroid hormone (PTH): By upregulating Wnt pathway genes and diminishing sclerostin and DKK-1 in osteoblasts, PTH can have anabolic effects on bone. It is interesting to note that PTH decreased tumor cell migration toward bone and increased osteoblast development in mouse models of MM and BC, improving bone mineral density. Furthermore, it has been demonstrated that teriparatide, a PTH analog that is authorized for the treatment of osteoporosis, can cause osteosarcoma in mice, raising questions regarding the safety of administering PTH to patients with cancer [14].

Anti-Sclerostin Antibodies: Sclerostin, an inhibitor of Wnt, effectively inhibits osteoblast differentiation, which is attributed to the generation of osteoblasts by MPC, BC cells, and osteocytes [14].

DKK-1 Inhibitors: MM, PC, and BC are among the tumors that manufacture DKK-1, another Wnt inhibitor. DKK-1 decreases β-catenin levels in addition to sclerostin, which impairs osteoblastogenesis [14].

Activin-A: A cytokine secreted by osteoblasts, osteoclasts, and BMSCs. In addition to promoting osteoclastogenesis in conjunction with RANK-L, it also suppresses osteoblast differentiation by activating SMAD-2 [14].

TKIs: The relationship among vascular endothelial growth factor and its receptor VEGFR also promotes osteoblast hyperactivation in PC. Furthermore, the formation of pre-metastatic niches has been linked to the VEGFR production by bone marrow progenitors of endothelial and hematopoietic cells. TKIs have so tried to target VEGFR, albeit early research with sunitinib and sorafenib produced disappointing results [14]. Several clinical trials were triggered by the discovery that the more selective TKI cabotantinib, which selectively binds VEGFR2 as well as the hepatocyte GF receptor, inhibited BM in PC animal models [14]. Interestingly, in the randomized open-label phase III METEOR study involving 658 patients with advanced renal cell carcinoma, cabozantinib was found to improve both OS and PFS compared with everolimus [14].

13.3 AI Involvement in Diagnosis and Therapy of Bone Metastasis

Unexpected progress in image identification tasks such as classifying and characterizing various malignancies has been made possible by the quick development of artificial intelligence (AI) algorithms (certain examples are described in Table 13.2) [15].

Table 13.2 Examples of AI tools available for bone metastasis.

Artificial intelligence method	Objectives	Performance
Machine-learning classifier (LogitBoost)	Classification of long bone atypical cartilaginous tumours and higher-grade chondrosarcoma	AUC 0.78, Accuracy 0.750
Deep convolutional neural network via VGG19 architecture	Categorizing benign and cancerous bone lesions	Specificity: 0.85; Sensitivity: 0.90; Accuracy: 0.88
Radiomics using PET/CT machine learning techniques	Make the distinction between benign and malignant spinal lesions	Accuracy: 0.750 (Decision Tree), 0.875 (LR), and 0.834 (SVM)
Radiomics using MRI machine learning techniques	Determine which cartilaginous lesions are high-grade versus low-grade	Accuracy: 0.750 (test), 0.857 (training); AUC: 0.850 (test), 0.78 (training)
Super label guided convolutional neural network	Separate benign from malignant bone tumours and categorise the matrix of bone malignancies	Accuracy: 0.740

Clinical practice is increasingly utilizing AI systems that are based on machine learning methods. Traditional machine learning methods serve as the foundation for the creation of most models, such as support decision trees, random forests, vector machines, and Bayesian networks. XGBoost, or rigid gradient boosting, a usual boosting technique, aims to be extremely effective, adaptable, and portable. Using an ensemble approach called "boost," new models can correct faults made by older models. These benefits ensure XGBoost's strong performance, which has been effectively applied to various studies and domains and yields good results in machine learning competitions [16]. Multivariable logistic regression analysis was used in the study to estimate the risk variables for breast cancer bone metastases. Meanwhile, prognostic variables for breast cancer with bone metastasis (BCBM) were determined using Cox proportional hazards regression analyses.

Race, treatment, age, grade, and sex are among the variables that have been used in the development of numerous prediction models for BCBM in recent years. But there is definitely space for these models to be more accurate and practical. Model development: Because machine learning is accurate, creative, and practical, medical professionals are using it more and more; nomogram is the recent most often used prediction system. Machine learning predictive models were constructed with Python software. Among the most notable Python machine learning libraries is the scikit-learn 0.24.1 package, which includes the four primary machine learning algorithms: clustering, reduced dimension, regression, and classification. Three modules are also included in it: model evaluation, data processing, and feature extraction. A generalized model of linear regression analysis is the logistic regression model. The main application of logistic regression in epidemiology is to investigate disease risk factors and forecast the likelihood of a disease developing based on those factors.

A decision tree in machine learning is a predictive model that shows the link of feature mapping to tag mapping. Each node of the tree signifies an item, and every fork path shows an attribute's probable value. Ultimately, the value of the object signified by the path from the root node to the leaf node corresponds to each leaf node. The name of the technique, random forest, implies that a forest is formed randomly. The forest is full of decision trees, and each in the random forest each decision tree is uncorrelated with the others [17].

Surgery, radionuclide therapy, drug therapy, and local radiotherapy are available as treatments for cancer with metastases to the bone. The primary site determines the precise treatment. These days, bone metastatic cancer (OBMC) origin may be inferred using different methodologies, namely, biopsy immunohistochemistry testing, whole-body imaging, and primary tumor biomarkers. The scientists created a deep learning–based algorithm for OBMC prediction that could extract crucial data on bone metastasis cancer using hematoxylin-eosin (HE) staining slides of biopsy tissues. Pathologists' segmentation of the tumor region on HE slices served as the input for their prediction model. The researchers transformed small patches in each location into structured feature vectors by adjusting a number of cutting-edge deep learning feature extractors. They then accomplished region-level prediction by fusing the feature vectors using an attention method to maintain highly representative and useful information flow to the tumor region [18].

While bone metastases can frequently be detected with bone scans, more research may be necessary due to their limited specificity. Although they need programming and medical knowledge, deep learning models have the potential to increase diagnostic accuracy. A doctor specializing in nuclear medicine used ChatGPT 3.5 (OpenAI) to create a deep learning model. ResNet50, a kind of deep learning neural network model with strong performance, was used in the first deep learning model [19].

The discipline of radiomics is constantly changing, and, in the detection and characterization of bone impairments, the use of radiomics is a relatively new development. In addition to detecting the source tumor, separating metastases from other bone impairments, and predicting mutation stats, radiomics can also predict the presence of bone metastases and distinguish skeletal regions free of lesions from those with metastases [20].

Osteoclastic and osteoblastic activities are kept in a condition of dynamic equilibrium inside the bone. Reactive changes in osteoblastic and osteoclastic scenarios happen instantaneously with the growth of metastatic foci within the marrow. Based on the primary method in which the metastases interfere with normal bone remodeling steps and alter radiotracer uptake, traditional classifications categorize radiographic presentations of bone metastases into three types: mixed, osteolytic, and osteoblastic.

Promising outcomes have been observed in the detection of osseous metastases on multiple imaging modalities by recent breakthroughs in AI. Even while these AI-driven activities might not be flawless, they usually yield answers that are precise enough for speedy image interpretations, which is particularly useful in situations when local expertise is limited. With a qualified healthcare practitioner in charge, AI-assisted image interpretation for bone metastases will also be as successful. In order to diagnose bone metastases in individuals with prostate cancer on whole-body bone scintigraphy (WBS), a strong convolutional neural network (CNN)–based model was developed. Their model was built using raw WBS data to address a straightforward, two-way categorization issue. Because there are no color components in these RGB photos, they merely display as gray-scale. Each color channel was subjected to a 2D CNN application by the authors, who then combined the inputs into the network's final dense layer. The most effective RGB-CNN model outperformed other systems with classification accuracies ranging from 89.78% to 93.06%, having a classification precision of 91.42% ± 1.64% [21].

13.4 Case Studies of Current AI Success in Bone Metastasis

The most popular method for detecting cancer metastases to the bone is WBS with 99 mTc-MDP because of its excellent specificity and ability to examine the entire body. With a reasonable specificity (79%–86%) and selectivity (81%–88%), WBS is a viable method for identifying metastases in a variety of cancer, including prostate, breast, as well as lung cancer. This is because radioactive tracers typically concentrate in areas of enhanced osteoblastic activity [22].

An AI model constructed using a deep neural system was created by Zhao *et al.* to help nuclear medicine doctors assess WBS for bone metastases. The study contained 12,222 instances of bone scintigraphy photos from patients who had received a final diagnosis; 1,223 cases were the test set, 1,223 cases were the validation category, and 9,776 cases were part of the training cohort. The dataset more closely resembled a true index compared to the data from the prior studies, even after omitting possibly deceiving cases, such as individuals who had big bladders, sternotomies, or fractures. When compared to seasoned nuclear medicine doctors, the AI model saved 99.88% of the time on the identical 400-case workload. Apart from its speed, the AI model demonstrated superior diagnostic performance with comparable specificity (93.50% vs. 94.50%), higher accuracy (93.5% vs. 89.00%), and superior sensitivity (93.5% vs. 85.00%). The study found that the main causes of false-positive results were postoperative alterations, inflammation, degeneration, and size/number of lesions, whereas the main causes of false-negative results were fractures and neighboring dispersed signals. Clinicians have been able to redetermine their incorrect diagnosis and identify false-negative injuries that were either excessively tiny or had inadequate radioactive absorption by checking the AI data. For the preliminary time, lung cancer was examined as a separate subgroup, and the model for this disease achieved a 93.36% diagnostic accuracy. The use of a multi-input deep CNN system, as opposed to more conventional techniques, improved the AI model's ability to follow natural distributions, lessen doctors' subjective judgment, improve generalization effectiveness, and provide an assumption that was closer to the typical clinical setting [22].

As in the previous study, Papandrianos *et al.* created a robust CNN-based model to identify bone metastasis in prostate cancer patients using whole blood specimens (WBS). This study focused solely on the AI's ability to assist nuclear medicine physicians in identifying bone metastasis [23].

This system was built for addressing a basic two-way categorization issue using raw WBS without any processing. The original photos are in RGB format with three channels of color information, obtained from the WBS scanning instrument. The lack of color components in these RGB photos causes them to only display as grayscale. For every color channel, the authors used a 2D CNN, aggregating the inputs to form the network's final dense layer. The most efficient RGB-CNN model has a general classification success rate of 91.42% ± 1.64%, which is higher than other models with classification rates ranging from 89.78% to 93.06%. RGB mode outperformed, or, at least, held par with, other cutting-edge CNN models seen in texts, such as ResNet50, VGG16, Inception V3, and Xception. Moreover, the simpler RGB-CNN model has the advantage of being able to train on a smaller dataset than CNN, which is generally accepted to require a large dataset. Similarly, a CNN model was developed by Papandrianos *et al.* identify bone metastases in WBS in individuals with breast cancer, which was trained on 408 samples [23].

The RGB picture classification accuracy was 92.50%, higher than that of the grayscale mode. This is better than some other popular CNN constructions, such as ResNet50, VGG16, MobileNet, and DenseNet. If an enormous amount of training data is available, then 2D-CNN modeling works well for planar nuclear medical scans such as WBS because it has less trainable parameters than labeled data. However, deep neural networks DNNs are often not as useful on WBS due to the laborious work needed to generate precise labels for large datasets. In an effort to get around this restriction, For the WBS of patients with prostate cancer, Han *et al.* created a 2D CNN classifier-tandem architecture that incorporates both local patches and the complete body. The term "global–local unified emphasis" (GLUE) refers to this architecture [24].

Even though the training, validation, and test sets were limited to 10%, 40%, and 50% of the total number of WBS, 9,113, the GLUE model models had significantly higher AUCs (0.894–0.908 vs. 0.870–0.877) and overall accuracies (GLUE, 0.900; WB, 0.889) than the WB model. The authors showed how, by creating local regions to add the quantity of sampled data and combining them with sliding regions and conventional whole-body input, 2D CNN might perform better in a scenario with less data while lowering the risk of overfitting [25, 26].

The bare minimum amount of free parameters and differences in multiscale extraction of features improve the network's capacity to generalise, even for a tiny training set. Their LB-FCN light model was applied to the three-class problem of categorization (malignant bone metastases, degenerative changes, and normal) using BS images from prostate cancer patients. The classification accuracy of 97.41% beat all state-of-the-art networks (InceptionV3, 88.96%; ResNet50, 90.74%; and Xception, 91.54%) when tested on the same set of data. Because LB-FCN lite required at least 10 times less CPU power than other CNN networks in terms of the number of flexible free parameters and FLOPs, it could be used on embedded and mobile devices [27].

Like all other types of deep learning systems, the LB-FCN lite model makes no sense and leaves no explanation behind its decisions; nevertheless, lesion-based analysis can provide insight into the algorithms that an AI model uses to make decisions. Liu *et al.* performed an injury number-based per-group assessment in WBS using a 2D CNN model [27].

On 99 mTc-MDP WBS pictures, about 14,972 identifiable bone injuries from 3,352 individuals were manually defined and classified as benign or malign. Based on the number of lesions per WBS image, the cases were divided into three groups: few lesions group (1–3), medium lesions group (4–6), and severe lesions group (>6). Based on the subgroup analysis, their CNN model demonstrated significantly better accuracy (82.79%) in the extensive-lesion group as compared to the models used in the few-lesion group (81.78%) and medium-lesion group (78.03%). This result suggests that the inference mechanism of the CNN model roughly mimics the mental procedure that nuclear medicine doctors use to recognize metastases. A solitary lesion, for example, may be difficult for a doctor to assess, but when several lesions appear close together, the chance of malignancy rises. Even while the CNN's internal workings are yet unknown, the patterns it can identify may justify its use as a diagnostic tool in medical situations. Liao *et al.* went above and beyond simply resolving a classification problem by developing a feature detection algorithm that precisely locates metastatic tumors on WBS images, thereby minimizing false negatives and minimizing the amount of work that physicians must perform when annotating images [28].

For training, an entirety of 870 pictures was used, out of which 450 had verified bone metastases. Their model was constructed using R50-FPN (ResNet50-backed feature pyramid network) and Faster R-CNN (faster area–based convolutional neural system with local proposal system) as the foundation. For testing, a collection of 50 pictures (20 having bone metastases) was used. In order to recognize objects, the Dice similarity coefficient (DSC) is employed to compare two bounding boxes. Its values range from 0 to 1, with 1 denoting the best overlap and 0 the worst. Their object detection model's maximum DSC was 0.6640. With a tiny differential of only 0.04 compared to the physicians' greatest DSC of 0.7040, the model's performance may very well be able to mimic that of a qualified physician. While the annotation was done blindly with no reference to virtually any other clinical data, the DSC between clinicians can be not appreciated; the outcome showed that fully computerized object detection methods can securely assist in identifying bone metastases, offering a fail-safe against negligent omission.

13.5 Recent Advancements and Future Perspectives

It is crucial in the field of computer vision to compare several approaches using the same benchmark. The popular LUNA2016 dataset, which comprises CT image sequences from 888 individuals, has been used as a standard for comparing various approaches to the identification of metastases from bone scans and for classification studies [29]. Ladder networks have also recently been utilized to train neural network backbones to detect bone lesions, and it has been demonstrated that this approach is more effective in detecting lesions than using untrained NN backbones or conventional diagnosis techniques. The trained NN provided information to more precisely locate lesions, and the sensitivity of the detection was also higher than that of conventional approaches [30]. The gathering and exchange of data has advanced significantly in recent years. Numerous publicly available datasets for cancer have been published, including TCGA, CCC-EMN, and 55 TCGA Research Network. Several techniques that used these datasets had good results. Sadly, the majority of publicly accessible databases lack information on bone cancers, which makes deep learning in this area difficult. However, because learning new tasks will require a considerably lower amount of data and effort, transfer learning, which entails training the system on different publicly available medical scans before applying against target images, might become one of the viable strategies [31, 32]. Negative mining and deep learning methods are being used lately in individuals with prostate cancer to diagnose lesion-dependent bone metastases, and it has been providing promising results in the spotting bone metastases with high precision and sensitivity. Negative mining has also been effective in evading false-positive results [33].

AI has been used along with conventional diagnosis methods to yield better results. Recently, artificial neural networks are being used along with bone scintigraphy, which has been efficient in detecting bone metastases and reducing the risks of false-positive results. A modified and revised version of this software has been created by Japanese called as BONENAVI, which has provided results with high accuracy in detection [34]. Recently, CNN has been utilized to identify thoracic bone pictures from SPECT nuclear imaging based on the image's feature level, and the experimental findings have demonstrated a superior SPECT image classification [35]. AI enables machines to perform tasks that are typically performed by humans, including perception, learning, reasoning, and decision-making. AI may examine many imaging techniques, including WBS, CT, MRI, and PET/CT, in relation to bone metastases. It can distinguish between different lesions, identify subtle differences in the texture of bone tissue, and extract quantitative information from images to act as biomarkers. But applying AI to the diagnosis of bone metastases is not without its difficulties and restrictions. Deep learning techniques in particular demand large and diverse datasets for both training and validation. Several approaches, including augmentation of data, translation of cross-modal pictures, multi-center cooperation, and the development of self or semi supervised models, can be used to address these problems [21].

Machine learning applications are a new field of study. Several analyses, including diagnosis, tumor type differentiation, therapy suggestion, and other prognoses aimed at improving QOL and extending life, can be performed using it when the cancer has spread to a metastatic stage. Because the majority of curated data are image-based, hence creating resource-efficient algorithms should be the main goal of future research. This might be accomplished by using architectures that make predictions with less information taken from tumor images. Another tactic is to construct a hybrid model that fuses the cost effective throughput of machine learning alongside the precise, detail-oriented mining of characteristics of deep learning [36]. Another major concept in AI is the use of explainable AI, which is a fast-growing concept which will gain a lot of importance in future in the field of tumor research. It should become apparent over time how important it is to comprehend, analyze, and evaluate machine learning outcomes. By using approaches such as grad-CAM technique, the use of XAI can make the detection of the bone metastases easier and efficient [37]. Future research on cancer metastases will also concentrate on federated learning, transfer learning, quantum computing, and using a varied population for training data—all of which are critical for identifying bone metastases [38].

13.6 Conclusion

Bone is a dynamic structure that stores minerals and is very important for structural support and mobility. In cases of prostrate and breast cancer, there has been an increase in bone metastases, and it has become very essential for the development of diagnosis methods to effectively diagnose and treat these malignancies. Various traditional methods are being used for the diagnosis of bone metastases in various cancers, which include CT, MRI, PET, BS, and biopsy. While these methods are effective in yielding results on the metastases stage, they are time-consuming, require continuous supervision by physicians, and sometimes can lead to false-positive results. Therefore, development of methods that are more effective while also being less time-consuming are necessary. This led to the introduction of AI into the medical field, with more and more algorithms developed every day that are proven to be better than conventional diagnosis techniques. Various AI models are being used for the diagnosis of bone metastases, which include DNNs that stored data on images of bone scintigraphy from various patients that were used as references for doctors to detect bone metastases. This AI model has been effective in providing results with better accuracy and less time-consuming. This model has also helped the doctors to avoid false-positive test results by checking the AI data. Other than that CNN can also be employed to diagnose bone metastases in individuals suffering from prostate cancer, which has provided highly accurate data, which is being used for analysis of bone metastases in patients diagnosed with breast and prostate cancer. All things considered, the application of AI in medicine has resulted in revolutionary advancements in the fields of diagnosis and treatment. As a result of ongoing research, AI will increasingly be used in the future to diagnose and treat a variety of cancers.

References

1. Fornetti, J., Welm, A.L., Stewart, S.A., Understanding the bone in cancer metastasis. *J. Bone Miner. Res.*, 33, 12, 2099–113, 2018 Dec 1.
2. Hernandez, R.K., Wade, S.W., Reich, A., Pirolli, M., Liede, A., Lyman, G.H., Incidence of bone metastases in patients with solid tumors: analysis of oncology electronic medical records in the United States. *BMC Cancer*, 18, 1–1, 2018 Dec.
3. Esposito, M., Guise, T., Kang, Y., The biology of bone metastasis. *Cold Spring Harbor Perspect. Med.*, 8, 6, 323, 324, 2018 Jun.

4. Kimura, T., Multidisciplinary approach for bone metastasis: a review. *Cancers*, 10, 6, 156, 2018 May 24.
5. Bandini, M., Pompe, R.S., Marchioni, M., Zaffuto, E., Gandaglia, G., Fossati, N., Cindolo, L., Montorsi, F., Briganti, A., Saad, F., Karakiewicz, P.I., Improved cancer-specific free survival and overall free survival in contemporary metastatic prostate cancer patients: a population-based study. *Int. Urol. Nephrol.*, 50, 71–8, 2018 Jan.
6. Coleman, R.E., Brown, J., Holen, I., Bone metastases. *Abeloff's Clin. Oncol.*, 1, 809–30, 2020 Jan.
7. D'Oronzo, S., Coleman, R., Brown, J., Silvestris, F., Metastatic bone disease: Pathogenesis and therapeutic options: Up-date on bone metastasis management. *J. Bone Oncol.*, 15, 100205, 2019 Apr 1.
8. Ban, J., Fock, V., Aryee, D.N.T., Kovar, H., Mechanisms, Diagnosis and Treatment of Bone Metastases. *Cells*, 10, 11, 2944, 2021.
9. Marazzi, F., Orlandi, A., Manfrida, S., Masiello, V., Di Leone, A., Massaccesi, M., Moschella, F., Franceschini, G., Bria, E., Gambacorta, M.A. *et al.*, Diagnosis and Treatment of Bone Metastases in Breast Cancer: Radiotherapy, Local Approach and Systemic Therapy in a Guide for Clinicians. *Cancers*, 12, 9, 2390, 2020.
10. Cook, G. and Goh, V., Molecular imaging of bone metastases and their response to therapy. *J. Nucl. Med.*, 61, 799–806, 2020.
11. Stecco, A., Trisoglio, A., Soligo, E., Berardo, S., Sukhovei, L., Carriero, A., Whole-Body MRI with Diffusion-Weighted Imaging in Bone Metastases: A Narrative Review. *Diagnostics*, 8, 45, 2018.
12. Sousa, S. and Clézardin, P., Bone-targeted therapies in cancer-induced bone disease. *Calcif. Tissue Int.*, 102, 227–250, 2018, 10.1007/s00223-017-0353-5.
13. Raje, N., Terpos, E., Willenbacher, W., Shimizu, K., Garcia-Sanz, R., Durie, B. *et al.*, Denosumab versus zoledronic acid in bone disease treatment of newly diagnosed multiple myeloma: an international, double-blind, double-dummy, randomised, controlled, phase 3 study. *Lancet Oncol.*, 19, 3, 370–381, 2018, 10.1016/S1470-2045(18)30072-X.
14. Escudier, B., Powles, T., Motzer, R.J., Olencki, T., Arén Frontera, O., Oudard, S. *et al.*, Cabozantinib, a new standard of care for patients with advanced renal cell carcinoma and bone metastases? Subgroup analysis of the METEOR trial. *J. Clin. Oncol.*, 36, 8, 765–772, 2018, 10.1200/JCO.2017.74.7352.
15. Ong, W., Zhu, L., Tan, Y.L., Teo, E.C., Tan, J.H., Kumar, N., Vellayappan, B.A., Ooi, B.C., Quek, S.T., Makmur, A., Hallinan, J.T., Application of machine learning for differentiating bone malignancy on imaging: a systematic review. *Cancers*, 15, 6, 1837, 2023 Mar 18.
16. Huang, Z., Hu, C., Chi, C., Jiang, Z., Tong, Y., Zhao, C., An artificial intelligence model for predicting 1-year survival of bone metastases in non-small-cell lung cancer patients based on XGBoost algorithm. *Biomed Res. Int.*, 2020, 335, 2020 Jun 28.

17. Zhong, X., Lin, Y., Zhang, W., Bi, Q., Predicting diagnosis and survival of bone metastasis in breast cancer using machine learning. *Sci. Rep.*, 13, 1, 18301, 2023 Oct 25.
18. Fang, M., Wang, Z., Tian, J., Dong, D., Predicting origin for bone metastatic cancer using deep learning-based pathology. *Ebiomedicine*, 88, 336, 2023 Feb 1.
19. Son, H.J., Kim, S.J., Pak, S., Lee, S.H., ChatGPT-assisted deep learning for diagnosing bone metastasis in bone scans: Bridging the AI Gap for Clinicians. *Heliyon*, 9, 12, 337, 2023 Dec 1.
20. Faiella, E., Santucci, D., Calabrese, A., Russo, F., Vadalà, G., Zobel, B.B., Soda, P., Iannello, G., de Felice, C., Denaro, V., Artificial intelligence in bone metastases: an MRI and CT imaging review. *Int. J. Environ. Res. Public Health*, 19, 3, 1880, 2022 Feb 8.
21. Dong, X., Chen, G., Zhu, Y., Ma, B., Ban, X., Wu, N., Ming, Y., Artificial intelligence in skeletal metastasis imaging. *Comput. Struct. Biotechnol. J.*, 337, 342, 2023 Nov 4.
22. Dong, X., Chen, G., Zhu, Y., Ma, B., Ban, X., Wu, N., Ming, Y., Artificial intelligence in skeletal metastasis imaging. *Comput. Struct. Biotechnol. J.*, 23, 157–164, 2024, ISSN 2001-0370.
23. Papandrianos, N., Papageorgiou, E.I., Anagnostis, A., Development of convolutional neural networks to identify bone metastasis for prostate cancer patients in bone scintigraphy. *Ann. Nucl. Med.*, 34, 338, 339, 2020, 10.1007/s12149-020-01510-6.
24. Han, S., Oh, J.S., Lee, J.J., Diagnostic performance of deep learning models for detecting bone metastasis on whole-body bone scan in prostate cancer. *Eur. J. Nucl. Med. Mol. Imaging*, 49, 339, 2022, 10.1007/s00259-021-05481-2.
25. Ntakolia, *et al.*, developed a new WBS-based architecture with a notably smaller amount of floating-point operations (FLOPs) as well as optional parameters in an effort to reduce the computational load of traditional CNN.
26. Ntakolia, C., Diamantis, D.E., Papandrianos, N., Moustakidis, S., Papageorgiou, E.I., A lightweight convolutional neural network architecture applied for bone metastasis classification in nuclear medicine: a case study on prostate cancer patients. *Healthc.*, 8, 339, 2020, 10.3390/healthcare8040493.
27. Liu, Y., Yang, P., Yong, P., Jiang, L., Zhong, X., Cheng, J. *et al.*, Automatic identification of suspicious bone metastatic lesions in bone scintigraphy using convolutional neural network. *BMC Med. Imaging*, 21, 1–9, 2021, 10.1186/s12880-021-00662-9.
28. Liao, C.W., Hsieh, T.C., Lai, Y.C., Hsu, Y.J., Hsu, Z.K., Chan, P.K. *et al.*, Artificial intelligence of object detection in skeletal scintigraphy for automatic detection and annotation of bone metastases. *Diagnostics*, 13, 340, 2023, 10.3390/diagnostics13040685.
29. Shorten, C. and Khoshgoftaar, T.M., A survey on image data augmentation for deep learning. *J. Big Data*, 6, 1, 1–48, 2019 Dec.
30. Apiparakoon, T., Rakratchatakul, N., Chantadisai, M., Vutrapongwatana, U., Kingpetch, K., Sirisalipoch, S., Rakvongthai, Y., Chaiwatanarat, T.,

Chuangsuwanich, E., MaligNet: semisupervised learning for bone lesion instance segmentation using bone scintigraphy. *IEEE Access*, 8, 27047–66, 2020 Feb 3.

31. Tomczak, K., Czerwinska, P., Wiznerowicz, M., The Cancer Genome Atlas (TCGA): an immeasurable source of knowledge. *Wspolczesna Onkol.*, 19, 1A, A68–A77, 2015.
32. Abeshouse, A., Adebamowo, C., Adebamowo, S.N., Akbani, R., Akeredolu, T., Ally, A., Anderson, M.L., Anur, P., Appelbaum, E.L., Armenia, J., Auman, J.T., Comprehensive and integrated genomic characterization of adult soft tissue sarcomas. *Cell*, 171, 4, 950–65, 2017 Nov 2.
33. Cheng, D.C., Hsieh, T.C., Yen, K.Y., Kao, C.H., Lesion-based bone metastasis detection in chest bone scintigraphy images of prostate cancer patients using pre-train, negative mining, and deep learning. *Diagnostics*, 11, 3, 518, 2021 Mar 15.
34. Koizumi, M., Motegi, K., Koyama, M., Terauchi, T., Yuasa, T., Yonese, J., Diagnostic performance of a computer-assisted diagnosis system for bone scintigraphy of newly developed skeletal metastasis in prostate cancer patients: search for low-sensitivity subgroups. *Ann. Nucl. Med.*, 31, 521–8, 2017 Aug.
35. Lin, Q., Li, T., Cao, C., Cao, Y., Man, Z., Wang, H., Deep learning based automated diagnosis of bone metastases with SPECT thoracic bone images. *Sci. Rep.*, 11, 1, 4223, 2021 Feb 19.
36. Petinrin, O.O., Saeed, F., Toseef, M., Liu, Z., Basurra, S., Muyide, I.O., Li, X., Lin, Q., Wong, K.C., Machine learning in metastatic cancer research: Potentials, possibilities, and prospects. *Comput. Struct. Biotechnol. J.*, 342, 2023 Mar 29.
37. Selvaraju, R.R., Cogswell, M., Das, A., Vedantam, R., Parikh, D., Batra, D., Grad-cam: Visual explanations from deep networks via gradient-based localization, in: *Proceedings of the IEEE international conference on computer vision*, pp. 618–626, 2017.
38. Ogier du Terrail, J., Leopold, A., Joly, C., Béguier, C., Andreux, M., Maussion, C., Schmauch, B., Tramel, E.W., Bendjebbar, E., Zaslavskiy, M., Wainrib, G., Federated learning for predicting histological response to neoadjuvant chemotherapy in triple-negative breast cancer. *Nat. Med.*, 29, 1, 135–46, 2023 Jan.

Index

Printed in the USA/Agawam, MA
September 18, 2026

910661.115